Conversation and Community

CSLI Lecture Notes Number 94

Conversation and Community
Chat in a Virtual World

Lynn Cherny

CSLI
PUBLICATIONS
Center for the Study of
Language and Information
Stanford, California

Copyright © 1999
CSLI Publications
Center for the Study of Language and Information
Leland Stanford Junior University
Printed in the United States
03 02 01 00 99   5 4 3 2 1

Library of Congress Cataloging-in-Publication Data

Cherny, Lynn.
Conversation and community : chat in a virtual world / Lynn Cherny.
    p.   cm. – (CSLI lecture notes ; no. 94)
Includes bibliographical references.

ISBN 1-57586-155-0 (cloth : alk. paper).
ISBN 1-57586-154-2 (pbk. : alk. paper)

1. Community–Computer network resources Case studies. 2. Social
interaction–Computer network resources Case studies. 3. Multi-user
dungeons Case studies. 4. ElseMOO. 5. Internet (Computer network)–Social
aspects. I. Title. II. Series.
HM756.C48   1999
302.23—dc21   99-19792
CIP

∞ The acid-free paper used in this book meets the minimum requirements of
the American National Standard for Information Sciences—Permanence of
Paper for Printed Library Materials, ANSI Z39.48-1984.

CSLI was founded early in 1983 by researchers from Stanford University, SRI
International, and Xerox PARC to further research and development of integrated
theories of language, information, and computation. CSLI headquarters and CSLI
Publications are located on the campus of Stanford University.

CSLI Publications reports new developments in the study of language, information,
and computation. In addition to lecture notes, our publications include
monographs, working papers, revised dissertations, and conference proceedings.
Our aim is to make new results, ideas, and approaches available as quickly as
possible. Please visit our web site at
http://csli-www.stanford.edu/publications/
for comments on this and other titles, as well as for changes and corrections by the
author and publisher.

Contents

Acknowledgments

I owe a great debt to many friends and colleagues who encouraged me in the past three years, particularly Nancy Baym (who had wonderful suggestions for improvements), Susan Herring, Julia Hirschberg, Erik Ostrom, Lori Kendall, Vernon Lee, Beth Kolko, Simeon Yates, Ken Fox, Dave Kormann, and Michael Kearns. Special thanks to Charlotte Linde, who supported me in my pursuit of a strange and different research topic. If it weren't for the care of my very patient editor, Shoshanna Green, this book wouldn't be here at all.

But I owe the largest debt to all the regulars on ElseMOO, who were funny and provocative, kept me company on lonely work nights, and became my friends—especially Tom, Ray, Shelley, George, lidda, Sadness, Penfold, ls, Conner, Bonny, foliage, della, Damon, Ellen, and Kurt. Thanks to Mouse, Mike, Ted, Karen, Sleep, Fred, and especially Egypt, who gave me useful comments and feedback on work in progress. Thanks also to lew, from the MUD next door, whose generosity with his memories of MUD history made this story so much richer. And to TomTraceback—what can I say?

1

Introduction to MUDs

Chat systems abound on the Internet today. They are almost as ubiquitous as the rhetoric about virtual communities is in the business and popular press. In the business press, "chat" is usually used to refer to any real-time conversation application.[1] Chat supposedly keeps Web sites busy and rewards and encourages repeat visitors. The word is considered almost synonymous with "virtual community." In order to have a virtual community you must provide chat at your site, and if you provide chat, you host a virtual community.[2] "On the net, community usually boils down to finding ways to let users talk to each other in real-time chat rooms, as well as on bulletin boards" (Ryan 1997).

Despite this interest in chat in the business press, it is clear that chat also has a reputation as a time-wasting kids' activity, a haven for child pornographers, a pickup scene, a site for harassment. Arnaut 1998 says, "Over the years, online chat has earned a reputation as the seamy underbelly of cyberspace—a magnet for misfits who live out their role-playing fantasies under the cloak of Internet anonymity." Why would anyone want to talk to strangers, unless he or she were up to no good? Moderated chat sites like Talk City, which attempt to provide harassment-free conversation, are one response to chat's seedier reputation; strictly-for-business applications of chat are another.[3]

Those of us who have spent significant amounts of time chatting online in different forums are bemused by the perceptions of chat in the business press. Just as conversation face-to-face can be time-wasting,

---

[1] Usually, in a chat application, the conversation is visible as it happens, unlike in some instantaneous "message" applications, in which messages may be sent back and forth in real time but require individual access, like email messages. "Messages" are also saved for the user until she reads them, while chat is usually not saved and is only visible to the users connected to the server or application as it happens.

[2] See Hof, Browder, and Elstrom 1997; Hirschman 1997; Reichard 1997.

[3] See Flynn 1997 and Bransten 1997.

1

X-rated, or harassing, conversation online can be these things; but conversation online can also provide all of the good things that we expect from conversations face-to-face. And certainly the contexts for conversations of all kinds have impact on conversational content and uses, as the Talk City case illustrates.

Although the Internet industry interest in chat is obvious, and chat applications are springing up everywhere, there is a relative dearth of research on chat use and chat application design. People seem to want to chat online, and people seem to be using existing applications, so why should industry invest in potentially time-consuming research about chat usage and system design? Eventually, competitive forces will come into play once there are enough applications with profit potential competing for users' time and attention, and it will be important for developers to understand

- what facilities and features users look for in chat,
- what attracts them initially and holds their interest long-term,
- what successful virtual communities look like,
- how communities evolve without self-destructing or fragmenting,
- how the social and technical forces interact in multi-user systems,
- how communication and culture evolve and support the virtual community.

Many of these issues are interesting from an academic research perspective as well. However, it is clear that research on virtual communities and on computer-mediated communication (CMC) has occurred on the fringes of many disciplinary traditions, often making it difficult to find previous work on the topic. There is a pressing need for consensus on—or at least discussion about—what the research questions are, what study methods are appropriate, what case studies exist already, what the research coverage is for different kinds of computer-mediated communication, and where the good comparative studies are that build on existing work.[4]

My academic background is in linguistics, the study of language use and structure. Although linguists have for the most part been wary of data gathered in virtual (non-face-to-face) settings, there are a growing number of linguistic and communication-focused studies of naturalistic online discourse, including the collection of essays in Herring 1996a and several issues of the online Journal of Computer-Mediated

---

[4]There have been a number of good academic contributions to research on virtual community in the past few years, including Smith 1992; Kollock and Smith 1996; Baym 1993, 1995; Jones 1995, 1997; Reid 1994a, 1994b; and others. I'll discuss these and others in more detail later.

Communication.[5] This book starts from a linguistic perspective, and attempts to define and address a small set of pressing research questions raised by my own study of a particular chat community. At the time of my study (1993–1995), there weren't many linguistic sources to draw on for CMC research, and my work was exploratory, drawing inspiration from conversation analysis and from sociolinguistic discussions of speech communities, of special speech registers, of genre; I used ethnographic methods and did rudimentary statistical analysis of my data. I have since read more widely in the sociology and anthropology of community, and that literature has also influenced the shape of this book.

1.1   MUDs

Fundamentally, this work is an ethnographic study of a particular community. Throughout 1994, I participated in an online community that chat was a significant component of. Connected to the Internet from a Unix machine in the basement of the linguistics department at Stanford University, I split my attention between online chat and class work. Most of the people I was talking to online were also students somewhere or were multi-tasking on the job. Conversation scrolled across my screen at any hour of the day, and I joined in eagerly.

Although conversation was the primary method of interaction, the context for that conversation, the application that we were all connected to, had important attributes that supported both chatting and the more abstract processes of community formation and reinforcement. Unlike many chat systems on the Internet (for example, Internet Relay Chat and industrial chat systems built on top of it, like Talk City), our system allowed conversations to occur in a virtual world with objects that players could look at, discuss, and interact with. Players, or users, are represented in the chat space as characters, with descriptions that other users may read and discuss, as in the example below. The description we discussed was attached to the new character flora, and included the sentence, "She is friendly and attractive and you can see the shape of her body beneath her t-shirt."[6] (My character is lynn, a full participant in the interaction.)

```
Ronald [to anna]: do you think a description like
    flora's means that she's intending to get hit
    on, or just that she wants people to think
    that she's friendly and attractive?  (And I do
    think there's a difference.)
```

---

[5] See http://209.130.1.169/jcmc/index.html.
[6] This is a paraphrase; for privacy reasons I won't give the actual description here.

Ronald says, "whether her description is convincing
and effective is another story, but."
lynn [to Ronald]: i think there is some difference
too, btw. Did I ever say there wasn't?
lynn says, "friendly and attractive can still be aimed
at men, too."
Ronald says, "No. but you seemed to think she was
definitely in the former category."
anna says, "i think the latter...that she wants people
to perceive her as friendly."
lynn says, "no, when did I say that? I said that she
wants to meet men."
Tim thinks she's intending to get hit on.
lynn says, "friendly and attractive is usually aimed
at men."
Tim says, "it's meant to attract the attention of men,
i think"
lynn nods.
Ronald says, "but suppose she already has a boyfriend,
and just wants to meet people to talk to?"
Tim says, "i'm not saying she's looking for
netsex..just that she seems to be looking for
men to flirt with"
Tim says, "it's still aimed at men though, i think"
lynn agrees with Tim.
anna would say that it's aimed at men, though, yeah...
the "shape beneath" bit is a little more than
"please think i'm friendly"...

All of this text was produced during ordinary social interaction, using basic communication commands in the chat system. Although this is a conversation about "picking up" men online, it should be obvious that for us, the participants, it's a fairly serious conversation about a substantive topic. At stake here is a community norm: this is not a pickup joint, and users who choose suggestive descriptions for their characters will not fit in. But also at stake are different perceptions of intent behind the texts that make up the substance of this world. The fact that there are persistent texts (and persistent objects) for us to argue about contributes to the impression we all have that this is a real place with real issues to argue about. We are caught within webs of significance (Geertz 1973), even—or *especially*—webs made of words.

The type of chat system we were using is called a MUD. MUDs, or Multi-User Dungeons (or Dimensions), are programs that multiple people can connect to simultaneously over a network; they allow people to communicate with each other in real time, and interact with each other and with objects in a virtual geography. MUDs are also known as "text-based virtual realities." A database of connected "rooms" makes up the MUD "world"; the world's rooms may be laid out and described to suggest a house, a medieval town, a space station, an undersea kingdom. The overarching world design metaphor is known as the **theme** on most MUDs. As noted above, the users of MUDs manipulate "characters" in the MUD world, through which they speak and interact with the world and other users.

Many MUDs are user-extensible, which means that users can add to the geography or program "objects" to interact with in the MUD.[7] Often users can even add their own communication commands, as I will discuss in later chapters.

MUDs come in a variety of types, e.g., MUCKs, MUSHes, Unter-MUDs, LP MUDs, and MOOs,[8] named for the variety of server software supporting the MUD. The term "MUD" is often used to refer generically to all types of MUDs.[9] The names of MUDs are often formed by affixing the server type to another word, like "ElseMOO."[10] MUD types differ according to differences in the server code that implements the MUD environment that users experience, and often make different commands available to users. MUD servers may also be put to different uses, hosting online gaming, purely social chat, virtual classrooms, or work groups.

The original MUDs were games, however. The first MUD, called MUD1, was designed by Roy Trubshaw in 1978 (with assistance from Richard Bartle in 1979) at the University of Essex. It was inspired by single-user text-based fantasy games like ADVENT (Reid 1994b), in which players solved puzzles and searched for treasures using short commands like "get chalice" and "look at mirror." MUD1 was also based on the fantasy genre, and players earned points for achieving goals or killing monsters or other players during their quests. Many of the orig-

---

[7]Objects are programmatic constructs that usually relate metaphorically to real-world objects, such as a "car" that transports characters around the virtual geography with commands like "drive to the park."

[8]For some good online documents about MUD history and MUD evolution, see Keegan 1997; Cowan 1997; Burka 1993, 1995.

[9]Some MUDders use the term "MU*," rather than "MUD," to refer to the superset of MUDs. Distinctions between "MUDs and MOOs" found in Bennahum 1994, for example, are specious according to this classification scheme.

[10]"ElseMOO" is a phrase meaning "on another MOO," according to my speech community.

inal MUD players went on to design their own MUD servers, like Alan
Cox's AberMUD; Bartle himself sold a MUD called "British Legends"
to CompuServe.

The game-based MUD tradition has continued strong and may account for the majority of MUDs on the Internet (Ito 1994, 1997). In
these MUDs, players combat automated monsters and sometimes other
players to develop their characters' skills and experience, which are usually numerical scores that increase based on the number and quality
of these battles. Players may also pursue quests, performing tasks like
hunting for treasure or killing dragons (or whatever the local theme's
mythological variant is). The administrative players on the MUD, often
called "wizards" or "gods," are responsible for designing quests, building monsters, and maintaining the integrity of the game. As players'
characters advance in skill or experience levels, they become more powerful and may take on an administrative role in the game, even helping
design part of it. In most adventure MUDs, players may not modify
the environment at all until they achieve a certain level, determined by
the internal scoring system. (This contrasts with the situation in many
social MUDs descended from TinyMUD, which I discuss next.) This hierarchical aspect of play, in which characters who have committed time
and effort are paid off with increasing responsibility and power, is a
common attribute across most MUD types (Bruckman 1992), although
in combat MUDs it is reified most explicitly in the software.[11]

There are a variety of non-game-focused MUD types on the Internet,
which include social MUDs purely intended for chat within a virtual
world setting, social role-playing MUDs, educational MUDs, and work-
supporting MUDs. Social MUDs, of which LambdaMOO is probably the
most famous, are generally run on servers descended from TinyMUD, a
server type created by Jim Aspnes in 1989.[12] LambdaMOO runs on the
MOO server, developed by Stephen White and Pavel Curtis in 1990 as
an object-oriented TinyMUD.[13]

Social MUDs tend to be hangouts for chat and often for building

---

[11]For interesting discussions of combat MUDs, see Ito 1997; Ackerman and Muramatsu 1998; Reid 1996; Masterson 1996.

[12]"Talker" MUDs evolved independently in England, apparently originating in 1990
as descendants of LP MUDs. See

   http://ulibnet.mtsu.edu/~msimms/lists/talkers/ew/about_ew/

for more information and some history of talkers.

[13]The server is the program that manages connections; the database of world objects,
including users' characters, is called the "core" of a MOO. LambdaMOO is a specific
place on the Internet, using a particular core, the Lambda core, running on a MOO
server. Other MOOs may also have started from the Lambda core, although they
will not have the same world of objects accreted over time in LambdaMOO.

virtual MUD scenery and interactive objects. Such MUDs may have a particular community of focus, like schoolchildren or a particular professional group, and they may be distinguished by the particular theme of the geography: science-fictional post-apocalyptic landscape, the canals of Venice, a Gothic castle, a college campus, a house and surrounding neighborhood in Silicon Valley. Social MUDs are usually not obviously goal-oriented, the way game MUDs are, but they may still be intended to support particular communities or activities, and they may be more or less "private" or "invitation-only."[14] And of course, game playing may exist on a social MUD (LambdaMOO hosts a role-playing game as well as being more generally a place for hanging out, exploring, or adding to the MOO geography, as many social MUDs are). Social MUDs, like other MUD types, are often founded by MUDders who have a lot of experience MUDding and have the energy, ideas, and access to a platform machine they need to start MUDs of their own. Because LambdaMOO was the first MOO with a significant user population, many of the early social MOOs were founded by users of LambdaMOO as alternative hangouts for them and their friends, particularly when LambdaMOO's server became slow and the MOO was perceived as crowded (because its database had grown so large). ElseMOO, which was the site for my research, is one such spin-off of LambdaMOO.

Social MUDs based on fictional universes with a focus on role-playing are an important genre of social MUDs. Sometimes called "social role playing" MUDs, these MUDs might be modeled after the Star Trek universe (e.g., TrekMUSE, discussed in Bruckman 1992), or the Pern novels by Anne McCaffrey (e.g., PernMUSH, discussed in Curtis 1992); players are expected to role-play characters who fit into the fictional universe. On these MUDs, rich and intricate interactive storytelling occurs, featuring collaborative plots and counter-plots and improvisational responses to individual and group actions. Individuals may be more or less central to key story developments, depending on their character's centrality, the amount of time they can contribute to the role-playing, and their history on the MUD. As I understand it, role-playing in these environments is more akin to improvisational acting in an ensemble than individual identity exploration of the sort discussed in Turkle 1996 (although of course therapeutic aspects may still exist).[15] Such MUDs are the least studied and among the most interesting on the Internet.

---

[14]One method of controlling access is to prevent the address of the machine the MUD runs on from appearing in lists of public MUDs that appear on Usenet or Web pages.

[15]If you are "out of character" (OOC) you have lapsed in your role-playing, usually by acting or speaking as yourself, rather than your character. There are often particular rooms or channels for OOC conversation. Schwartz 1994 is an excellent article

Educational MUDs are another important presence on the Internet, although they may be more prominent in the research literature than on the Internet itself. Educational MUDs range from MUDs designed as educational play spaces for children to MUDs for college students in which structured classroom activities occur. MicroMUSE, also known as "Cyberion City," is an educational play space founded by Stan Lim in 1990 and further developed by Barry Kort. As of January 1997 it had 800 members, of which half were children (Bruckman 1997). Rheingold 1993a says that Kort's inspiration was psychologist Jean Piaget's interest in play as a form of learning. A similar interest in educational play inspires Bruckman's work on MOOSE Crossing, a MOO inspired by work in constructionism. Constructionism is a theoretical extension of Piagetian ideas about the value of "knowledge built by the learner," especially when the learner is building an external artifact.[16]

MariMUSE was begun by researchers Billie Hughes and Jim Walters from Phoenix College in 1993 for elementary school children in a mixed ethnic area (Hughes and Walters 1995). An extension of the MariMUSE project involved researchers from Xerox PARC (the Xerox Palo Alto Research Center) and the move from MUSE to MOO software in 1995; the new MOO site is called Pueblo (O'Day, Bobrow, and Shirley 1996; O'Day, Bobrow, Hughes, et al. 1996). Other educational MUD efforts have involved older students using MUDs as extensions of classroom activities, for instance in conjunction with composition classes (Fanderclai 1996). Diversity University is another educational MUD project hosting diverse groups: "Instructors to date have 'brought' their students to DU for instruction in many areas (including History, Biology, Information Systems, English Literature, Philosophy and Psychology). Teaching methods in these courses have ranged from traditional classroom lectures (utilizing available objects for technological support) to student participation in the simulation of historical events" (Diversity University 1998). The papers in Haynes and Holmevik 1998 describe a number of other educational MUD projects.

Another application of MUDs is computer-supported cooperative work, or CSCW. CSCW applications support multiple users collaborating on work, often remotely over a network. Evard 1993 describes InfoPark, a MOO for system administrators at Northeastern University; the system administrators keep in touch and even socialize on the MOO when they are physically scattered across campus. The Jupiter

about role-playing in AmberMUSH, which tackles the difficult topic of "addiction" to MUDding with sensitivity rather than hysteria.

[16]See Bruckman 1997; Bruckman and Resnick 1995; and Papert 1991.

project at Xerox PARC (Curtis and Nichols 1993) was an effort to extend a MOO with videoconferencing and audio software. AstroVR (Van Buren et al. 1994; Curtis and Nichols 1993; Brundage 1998) is a collaborative work tool based on MOO and Jupiter that makes it possible for astronomers to share views of data as well as to collaborate over video and audio. BioMOO (Glusman 1997) and MediaMOO (Bruckman and Resnick 1995) are MOOs for biologists and media researchers to meet and brainstorm on.[17] MediaMOO also hosted a successful series of weekly discussion seminars called the Tuesday Cafe, organized by Tari Fanderclai and Greg Siering, which were of particular interest to the computers and writing research community.[18]

Most MUD servers are adaptable for multiple application types: for instance, a MUSH server could be used for building a role-playing game, a purely social MUD open to anyone with a Net connection, or an educational MUD for college students. However, certain aspects of MUD server infrastructure may influence choice of server type for a particular application type. Some MUD servers, e.g., LP MUDs, have been primarily used for adventure games, in part because of the programming infrastructure available for building games in LP MUDs.[19] Bruckman 1992 suggests that TinyMUDs are more egalitarian and "pacifist" than the combat MUDs that preceded them, partly because of the difference in software design. She quotes Aspnes, the author of the first TinyMUD, saying that his design did not incorporate any scoring system such as is found in game MUDs, because he wanted use of the MUD to be more "open-ended" and less goal-oriented. He and Bruckman speculate that TinyMUDs encouraged a more egalitarian community of users.

I hesitate to attach such descriptions to populations of MUDders, particularly when I think further study of game-playing communities is needed. However, the implication that differences in the infrastructure impact application types and perhaps user communities is important. From a simple access perspective, there are visible cultural divides between users of social MUDs and users of combat MUDs, and even between users of server types (MOO vs. DikuMUD, for instance). It is rare to find a MUDder who is fluent in the commands of many server

---

[17]The "purpose" statements for both MediaMOO and BioMOO say, "It is a place to come meet colleagues in [media/biology] studies and related fields and brainstorm, to hold colloquia and conferences, to explore the serious side of this new medium." The MediaMOO statement predates and inspired the BioMOO statement, I believe.

[18]Those meetings are now held on another MOO, Connections; see
http://web.nwe.ufl.edu/~tari/connections.

[19]The infrastructure consists of class libraries that are available for LPC, the programming language that LP MUDs are written in. The class libraries "define the atmosphere of the game" (http://www.mudconnect.com/mud_intro.html).

types and maintains an active presence on multiple types of MUD, particularly game MUDs as well as social MUDs. But researchers should beware of technologically deterministic beliefs: users of technologies are not necessarily victims of the technologies' limitations and affordances and diverse populations won't necessarily perform similarly in the same systems. Social structures have some impact on behavior quite apart from the technical infrastructure available to the communities of users.

Aside from not having a scoring system, TinyMUD and its descendants were more "open-ended" because users could build rooms and, on some systems, interactive objects. For many users of MUDs, the extensibility of the environments is what makes MUDs compelling and different from other common chat applications. MOO worlds are extensible by design, but some MOO administrators limit, via technical or policy means, who is allowed to build what on their MOOs. The basic software might support more open access to system resources, but like many multi-user applications, MUDs are social systems, with emergent politics, practices, and cultures of use. The community I studied was based on a MOO server, and there were complicated local politics around programming and extending the environment. The community was perceived as hierarchical and as having a "power elite." The constraints and affordances of the systems, but also the location of knowledge and power in the user population, are critical factors influencing the culture of use. The technology alone does not create the character of the community.

1.2   My Introduction to MUDs

I discovered MUDs around 1993. In mid-1993, a friend of mine gave me the telnet address of ElseMOO and told me it was a fun, relatively mature MUD on which he'd had some interesting conversations. I connected intermittently to ElseMOO for several months before I began spending many hours a day logged in there. I also spent some time on LambdaMOO, because I had read some of the articles about it.[20] LambdaMOO seemed like an enormous bright city, and ElseMOO, with its less populated geography and restricted theme, felt like a conservative small town. (Although I recognize the forces that have made the two distinct, the fact that ElseMOO was modeled after a Midwestern house and town and LambdaMOO after a Silicon Valley house, complete with hot tub, probably has something to do with my perception of their different atmospheres at the time. Certainly, theme alone was not responsible for their differences, but the power of metaphor on these systems should not be underestimated.)

---

[20] E.g., Quittner 1993; Germain 1993; Leslie 1993.

LambdaMOO was, at the time of my first connection, already three years old, while ElseMOO was only one year old. LambdaMOO is without doubt the most publicized MUD on the Internet. Pavel Curtis, of Xerox PARC, opened LambdaMOO on October 30, 1990. He advertised it to the public on the newsgroup rec.games.mud on February 5, 1991. It has since become famous for being a research project on virtual community evolution, the site of a famous "netrape" (Dibbell 1993), an elaborate experiment in virtual democracy, and a good place to hang out and play with virtual toys. It has been described in a chapter in Rheingold 1993a, numerous *Wired* articles (Kelly and Rheingold 1994; Quittner 1994; Turkle 1996), the much-discussed *Village Voice* article by Julian Dibbell (Dibbell 1993; see also Davis 1994), articles in *Time* (Germain 1993), *Newsday* (Quittner 1993), *Lingua Franca* (Bennahum 1994), *The Washington Post* (Schwartz 1994), *The Wall Street Journal* (Rigdon 1995), the *Atlantic* (Leslie 1993). It has been the site for research in numerous papers available on the Internet.[21]

Begun as a research project, LambdaMOO received institutional support that most MUDs do not receive, including machine resources like extra memory and processor improvements as the size and demands of the system grew. By virtue of this institutional support and the publicity the MUD has received, LambdaMOO cannot be considered typical of most MUDs on the Internet (I return to this below). One ramification of institutional support is its long life span.[22] LambdaMOO also hosts a large population, partly due to life span and publicity.[23] Many MOOs have been "founded" and settled by former LambdaMOO users who became tired of the ever-present "lag" (network and server delay in processing commands) and the social changes the MOO has seen, not all of which are viewed positively by everyone. ElseMOO is one such spin-off community. Many LambdaMOO users remained active presences on LambdaMOO as well as on another MOO or two of choice, as MOOs spread in the early 1990s. ElseMOOers also remained active to varying degrees on LambdaMOO.

The close political relationship between LambdaMOO and ElseMOO made spending time on both of them important for my research, but I also used them very differently. LambdaMOO was my place for playing

---

[21]See, e.g., Serpentelli 1993; Marvin 1995; Schiano 1997; Carlstrom 1992; Rosenburg 1992.

[22]LambdaMOO's life is exceeded by some MUDs. DragonMUD, five years old in 1994, was the oldest continuously running MUD at that time (Clodius 1994).

[23]Other MUDs I know of with large populations include DragonMUD, FurryMUCK, and AmberMUSH, which is a social role playing environment thematically based on fantasy novels by Roger Zelazny.

with world creation and designing toys, and ElseMOO was a place for conversation. The original and still central geographic theme of LambdaMOO is a large, rambling California house. I built a room of my own attached to the house, in the form of a large white paper cup lying on the roof. Since an enormous number of half-finished, forgotten programming projects cluttered the MOO, I thought it appropriate to design my room in the image of actual litter. I programmed a handful of other objects as well, including a wandering soap bubble that roamed the rooms of the MOO and changed its description in each room to show a reflection of a single object in the room with it.[24]

Because ElseMOO (EM) had a restrictive building policy and few people were given programming privileges, it wasn't the place to try building fanciful objects. Several years after my first experiences on EM, the administrators loosened their policies regarding programming, perhaps in an attempt to rejuvenate a flagging sense of playfulness that the MOOers had once felt about their community MOOing, but the general atmosphere—perfectionism of design and operation, "themeliness" of all building—probably acted as deterrents for most people there. I'll describe some of this atmosphere and the tensions around building policies in chapter 6. I myself did little programming on EM; I started building a Coke machine, consumable food being a MUD standard, but found the object-oriented design too difficult for my limited programming ability and time. And I knew that on EM, it had to really *work*, and work well, to be an acceptable addition to the virtual world, so it never made it past the drawing board.

I chose to write about the ElseMOO community because it is an example of a reasonably well-defined speech community, with members who had a significant history of MUDding for recreation on EM and on

---

[24]Because LambdaMOO is a place that allows building and has a long history, it has a large number of useful "generic" objects in its database for other programmers to make use of. Generic objects are creations (authored by other community members) that act as templates for new objects; for instance, if I create an object based on a generic object, my object will inherit features of the generic, which saves me having to program those features all over again. My soap bubble was relatively easy to make because it was based on a generic mobile object that wandered the landscape of the MOO database. I created an instance of the mobile object, called it a soap bubble, and wrote a small program on it to generate a new description every time someone looked at it (with the "**look**" command), a description including a reflection of a random object in the room with it. Some of the most interesting community challenges for MOOs involve this collaborative building process and ownership of resultant code. It's not uncommon for angry MOOers to destroy useful generic programming of theirs that many other users depend on, as a way of illustrating their own importance and contributions to the community, or as a form of revenge on the community for perceived wrongs.

other MUDs as well. A speech community is a community with shared rules of speaking and interpretations of speech performance (Hymes 1972) whose members frequently interact (Gumperz and Hymes 1964). Some of the newer MUDs (e.g., academic sites) may have communities entirely unconnected historically to the other MUDs on the Net; their cultures and speech habits will have evolved differently.[25]

1.3 Studying a MUD

Bell and Newby suggest in their 1974 book on community studies that there are six approaches to the study of community:

- the ecological approach: study of community as organism. Spatial consequences of social organization.[26]
- communities as organizations: study of community action and community power.
- communities as microcosms: communities as samples of the larger society and culture. Community representativeness must be established, or validity of generalizations must be clear.
- community study as method: the community is merely a source of data, not the object. This method concerns the study of human behavior in communities, and generally involves "massive immersion" or ethnography.
- communities as types: a typological approach, usually part of a theory of social change; study of stages of differentiation, nature and direction of social processes.
- community and networks: investigation of social groups and interactions within them ("social networks").[27]

When I began my work, I had no particular background in community studies. I pursued community study as method, targeting a group that I felt was well-bounded and self-aware enough that it probably was a "community" under certain definitions and that appeared in particular to satisfy the definition of a speech community. (I'll discuss definitions of community in chapter 6.) I approached my subjects with the assumption in the linguistic work of Milroy (1987, p. 17), that "a community might be considered as a social unit whose language patterns

[25] One way to investigate this is to look at the local netiquette (Internet etiquette) guide, which is called "help manners" on LambdaMOO after the command used to display it. If there isn't a netiquette guide in the database or on an associated web page, interviewing community members can elicit politeness norms.
[26] The Chicago School studies in the 1930s are examples. This work has broadened to take factors other than locale into consideration.
[27] The traditional notion of community is a locality-bound, close-knit network.

are amenable to study." My primary interest was in certain linguistic behaviors, though it later evolved into an interest in the socio-technical system and interface characteristics that produced the behavior and culture I participated in. I was peripherally interested in social networks, and this interest influenced some aspects of my study.

A general assumption shared by many researchers interested in virtual communities is that case studies of communities are intended as microcosms of virtual culture as a whole. This assumption leads to the question I (and many other ethnographers) have often been asked: What makes your study interesting, or relevant, or representative?

This type of question carries with it several implications: if Else-MOO isn't representative, this study is automatically less interesting, and whatever lessons are learned here are less applicable to other online communities and system design—"science" hasn't been served because generalizations from the particulars aren't possible.[28] I certainly can't say with any authority that ElseMOO is a "representative" MUD, partly because I don't know what a representative MUD would be. However, ElseMOO is at least *more* representative of a class of social MUDs than the more famous LambdaMOO (contrary to Schiano 1997), for the reasons I mentioned above (for instance, LambdaMOO's size and age). Most MUDs I am aware of have less committed institutional support than LambdaMOO: they are barely tolerated by system administrators or run by system administrators "on the side" of systems they support for other purposes.[29]

Most MUDs also do not have a complicated infrastructure that supports democracy or other participatory governments. Most MUDs that I am aware of are governed by the "wizards," who are the system administrators of the MUD's internal operation (one of whom is often a system administrator for the machine the MUD is running on). Government by a small committee,[30] usually the same people who have technical powers or knowledge on the MUD, is common; ElseMOO may therefore be rep-

---

[28]Schiano (1997), e.g., suggests that Cherny 1995 is one of several works whose generalizations are "difficult to assess" because they are based "solely on qualitative, anecdotal methods" and a tendency to use only "a small sample of participants, selected without systematic attention to factors affecting representativeness." Her own study focuses solely on a subset of the population of LambdaMOO, which she considers a "classic" social MUD, an assumption I dispute.

[29]Sometimes small Internet service providers allow customers to run small MUDs as long as they don't interfere with system security or performance. MUDs run by system administrators are the most stable and last the longest, but even they may change sites or IP addresses, moves that inevitably lose users who didn't get notified about the move and can't find them when they try to connect.

[30]I use the term "committee" loosely here; most MUDs probably don't use this term or create formal structures, unlike ElseMOO.

resentative in this manner. However, on ElseMOO there was an effort to distinguish between wizards with technical abilities and the committee that made social decisions, which was only partially successful, as I will describe in detail.

There are at least two aspects to population size that are relevant when comparing MUDs: the number of registered characters who connect regularly (for some value of "regularly"), and the average number of users who are on the MUD at the same time. Further distinctions might be made, such as regular visitors who aren't part of the core community and number of registered users overall. The number of registered users overall is rarely very interesting, at least compared to the number of active participants. Some MUDders collect characters on MUDs that might someday be interesting to them, and many of the characters are rarely if ever used. (The practice on LambdaMOO of comparing the object numbers of characters as a way of dating yourself or establishing pedigree might influence registration behavior on other MUDs: it's a status symbol to have an "old" character on a popular MUD, because it shows you were there ahead of the crowd.) On the other hand, on LambdaMOO the wizards measured the effect of publicity by the increase in number of registered characters.[31] The petitions on LambdaMOO in 1994 to limit population growth drew a connection between the number of registered characters, crowding, and the impact of new users on the overloaded system.

Two large MUDs that I know of, LambdaMOO and AmberMUSH, may have 200 users connected at a time and regularly have more than 100. They also have many thousands of registered characters. Clodius (1994, p. 12) says of her DragonMUD research site that it "consists of a stable core group of about 500 people and an ever-changing peripheral group of about 1500 people." ElseMOO usually had around 30 users connected at a time (and 30 to 40 members who constituted the very active core community, most of whom were connected daily or multiple times a week). It had 100 to 150 who connected regularly—say, once every few months at least; this might be comparable to Clodius's figure of 500, although I am not sure whether she would make a further small-group distinction for the participants who were active daily, as seems necessary in describing EM. ElseMOO is probably comparable in these population characteristics to other medium-sized MUDs in existence for more than a year.

---

[31]There were 6000 players registered on LambdaMOO in March 1994, and 8000 registered in April 1994. I heard wizards reporting the numbers on ElseMOO several times, and connecting the growth with publicity. Quittner's *Wired* article, "Johnny Manhattan Meets the Furrymuckers," was published in March 1994 (Quittner 1994).

It's easy to dismiss or miss the insight and contributions of situated, detailed studies of particular communities, practices, individuals, events, moments in time. But before a general theory of electronic community evolution is possible, an enormous number of case studies are necessary, as well as some sophisticated comparison between these studies. The good ethnographer offers grounding detail even when theory is lacking, so that future efforts can benefit from her study. I hope my ElseMOO study offers some of this detail for future comparisons, despite my particular focus on linguistic interaction. To build on ethnographic work like this isn't to dismiss the sites as "unrepresentative" but to look for the factors that make sites different from other sites. If we can understand differentiating factors, we can also begin to understand how sites are similar, and what a general "macro" theory might involve. In other words, community studies like this one can become building blocks in a theory of community types, as Bell and Newby (1974) describe.

Just as there are legitimate questions about the interpretation of field sites in contrast to other sites, there are a host of questions surrounding the interpretation of the description of the site itself. I'll discuss some of these issues in chapter 7 in my discussion of methods and ethics. But I note here that my subjective experience of this community was no doubt shaped largely by the people I became friends with in ElseMOO. Tom, also known as TomTraceback, was a key informant. My association with him and his friends has impacted my description of this site in ways that I can't quantify (cf. Rabinow 1977).

1.4   How Does One Use MUDs?

A MUD consists of a server program, running on a machine connected to the Internet that accepts connections from client programs on users' own machines. The simplest client program is telnet, but because telnet is so primitive (and doesn't separate input and output text in a user-friendly manner), MUDders generally use client programs designed specifically for MUDding.[32] Users connect to a MUD using the MUD's IP address and port number, where they then provide a password for their character[33] or connect to a guest character if one is available. Once connected, users have access to the contents of the MUD database: the objects that make up the virtual world and, in some MUDs, a programming language to modify or add to them.

A **player** is a MUD user, who manipulates a character. The terms

---

[32] Examples include TinyFugue, MUD Dweller, an Emacs client (a client that runs inside a text editor, which is what I used), and Pueblo.

[33] One user may have one or more characters on a MUD, but multiple people do not generally use a single character.

user and **player** are usually interchangeable. The **character** is the representative of the user in the database that describes the virtual world. A character has a user-selected name and description, which can be viewed with the "**look**" command. Character names may be lower-case or upper-case, and are one source of play with identity in the virtual world (see Danet, Ruedenberg, and Rosenbaum-Tamari 1998; Ruedenberg, Danet, and Rosenbaum-Tamari 1995). My character description is shown here as it appears on my screen in response to my typing the **look** command at the > prompt. The programmed **objects** my character is carrying are listed below the character description.

```
>look lynn
A short woman in a black dress who wishes she were
reading something trashy everytime she opens an
academic journal. Her shadow is in the shape of an
unfinished dissertation on MOO conversation
structure, so she may be logging conversation
around here, just so you know...
She is awake and looks alert.
Carrying:
lynn's nametag           a Generic Drinkable Liquid
a Dispenser              a tutorials
a Generic Food           a bottle
a soda machine
```

Character gender is selectable; most MUD parsers determine which pronouns to use in system messages based on what gender has been set by the user. Some MUDs allow many possible genders, such as "plural" or "neuter," as well as "female" and "male." The female gender of my character causes the MOO server to use the female pronoun for the announcement that my character has been active recently, shown above, under my description: "`She is awake and looks alert.`"

The MUD geography is generally modeled after physical geography (although some MUDs use non-Euclidean spaces). Its basic unit is the room. Even "outdoor" spaces like highways or parks are composed of rooms connected to one another by compass directions. Navigation and communication in the MUD world are accomplished by short text commands. For example, if I type "**north**" when my character occupies a MUD room with an exit called "north," my character is moved through the exit, out of the first room and into another to the north.

Rather than requiring the user to remember a sequence of compass directions to navigate, ElseMOO has commands that move characters from one point to another by name, e.g., "**walk to library**." When I navigate through ElseMOO using its automatic path-finding function, messages scroll up my screen telling me which rooms I pass through as I move. A room name appearing on a line of its own tells me I have entered that room. If there are objects in the room, I see a message telling me what they are. (In the example below, the > is my MUD client's input prompt, followed by what I typed. Lines with no > in front of them are MOO output from my command.)

```
>walk to library
You head up the stairs to the patio.
The Patio
You see a map of Ray's house and the projects
   chalkboard here.
The West Patio
You open the door and walk into the house.
Ray's Bedroom
You leave Ray's room finally.
The Downstairs Hallway
You see a flat-top trunk and a round-top
   trunk here.
You walk up the stairs.
The Upstairs Hallway
The Library
You see:
Log of Hunt          large box of blank nametags
Treasure Hunt        yellowed piece of parchment
slate dispenser      note on the builder's editor
Library's slate      New Hacker's Dictionary Gateway
sysadmin-abstract
Tom is here.
```

In the next example, I typed "west," which moved me into a new room called "E. Some Tree Street"; I saw the description of the room (the street) as soon as I entered it, including the fact that another MUD character occupied the room ("Mike is here").

```
>west
You leave the busy highway for a less noisy street to
the west.
E. Some Tree Street
A boring suburban east-west street named after some
deciduous tree. To the north is a park.  To the east
is a busy highway.  Running along the southern
sidewalk is an ivy-covered wall surrounding a
```

```
two-story white house.  A gate in the wall is closed.
Mike is here.
```

Normally a user sees only the communication that occurs within the room her character occupies. The room is a filter on input to the user: it determines the boundaries of public conversations. In some other synchronous computer-mediated communication modes, like Internet Relay Chat (IRC), the "channel" you are in determines which conversation you can hear. The label on an IRC channel may or may not accurately reflect the current conversation topic, of course; but there is a general belief that labels should be relevant to each channel's topic. MUD rooms are roughly analogous to the topic-based channels in IRC, but they persist in the database and are organized by geographical metaphor, rather than topic. IRC channels are created and destroyed constantly and are not related to one another the way rooms in MUDs are connected by paths corresponding to geographical directions.

After entering a room that contains another user's character, I can communicate by using other commands. The main communication commands on social MUDs are the "say" and "emote" (or "pose") commands. An example of a say is shown below. Here I type the say command in line 1, followed by what I want to say, and everyone in the room (myself included) sees line 2 below. My actual typing (line 1) is visible only to me; the MOO parser interprets it and renders the output shown in line 2.[34]

```
1 >say hi
2 lynn says, "hi"
```

A common alternative to the say on many MOOs is the "directed speech" command, which shows the addressee in a theatrical script style. In order to direct a comment to Tom, for instance, I type a single back quote before Tom's name followed by my intended speech:[35]

```
>'tom hi
lynn [to Tom]: hi
```

An "emote," which on some MUDs is called a "pose," allows a user to express actions or internal states of mind. The user may either type the full command name, emote, followed by the text she wishes to communicate, or use a synonymous shorthand, a colon, followed by

---

[34]Lines are not actually numbered by the MOO, of course. In this book I number lines in examples when I want to refer to specific ones, and not otherwise.

[35]As for many commands, there are synonyms for the back quote form, including typing "tom, hi" and "to tom hi."

the text. (For the say command, there is also a shortcut synonymous command, a double quote mark.)

```
>emote waves.
lynn waves.
>:was up all night.
lynn was up all night.
```

There are commands that allow private conversation, but private communication is generally limited to two characters (see Reid 1994b, appendix, who quotes discussion by Jennifer Smith of the evolution of these commands). A "**page**" commands allows two users to communicate privately between any two locations on the MUD; a "**whisper**" command allows private two-person communication within the same room. (The page command properly subsumes the whisper command in functionality, but some users prefer the whisper metaphor when they are in the same room—it feels more intimate.) Basic communication commands are summarized in Table 1.

TABLE 1 Basic MOO communication commands

Command Name	Private?	Used For Talk...
Say	No	within a room
Emote	No	within a room
Page	Yes	across room boundaries
Whisper	Yes	within a room

In addition to the programmatic messages and the commands for speech, there are specialized commands that act as shorthand for certain common utterances in MOO conversation. For example, on ElseMOO it is common to express attention, agreement, or understanding by nodding, either with an emote or by using a shorthand command—here, "**nd**"—to produce the same effect:

```
>emote nods.
lynn nods.
>nd
lynn nods.
```

Messages are system responses to user commands; examples of messages are text strings that announce a character's entrance into a room, e.g., line 1 below, which is seen by all the users with characters in the room Marie is entering. Other examples of messages are the text that announces successful interaction with an object (e.g., lines 3, 5). In response to my command to "drop" the object called "bottle" that my character is carrying, I (and the other players occupying the same MUD room my character is in) see a message saying I dropped the bottle. The other players see "lynn drops the bottle," while I see it with a second person pronoun. (Occasional examples of MUD discourse in this book will have second person pronouns rather than my character name.)

```
1 Marie arrives along the path from the north.
2 >drop bottle
3 You drop the bottle.
4 >get bottle
5 You get the bottle.
```

As must be clear by now, a complicated array of commands provides many ways of interacting with the world of the MUD database and with other users. Becoming a MUDder, and a member of a particular MUD community, means learning the general commands and the commands that are particular to the MUD community. Users illustrate their knowledge in everyday conversation. In chapter 3 I describe the enormous linguistic repertoire of ElseMOOers and discuss how this repertoire is related to other MUD repertoires and how it is unique.

1.5   Theoretical Background and Foreshadowing

1.5.1   Background

There are a number of ways of studying communities and talking about communities. Online communities today are largely constructed of textual, linguistic interactions.[36] Much earlier work on computer-mediated communication occurred within a psychology framework. A lot of that work has assumed that media characteristics predetermine the types of interactions that users experience, a view I follow Markus 1994 in calling "technological determinism"; it seeks to predict behavior based on the theory that "social outcomes derive primarily from the material characteristics of a technology, regardless of users' intentions" (Markus 1994, p. 121). Much research on the effects of limited bandwidth on communication falls into what Culnan and Markus (1987) call the "cues-filtered-out" approach; some examples include the social presence model (e.g., Short, Williams, and Christie 1976), the cuelessness model (Rutter 1984, 1987) , the lack of social context cues model (Kiesler, Siegler, and McGuire 1984; Sproull and Kiesler 1986), and media richness (Daft and Lengel 1984, 1986; Trevino, Daft, and Lengel 1990). (For useful summaries of this work, see Walther 1992; Spears and Lea 1992; Cherny 1995c.) Laboratory studies of mediated communication often conclude

---

[36]There are already important graphical chat systems, such as the Palace, but much of the interaction still occurs in textual communication.

that the reduced number of communication channels leads to less awareness of other actors, and hence more hostile and task-oriented behavior
instead of social, solidarity-oriented behavior. Mediated communication
has also been claimed to result in more "democratic" exchanges, since
fewer status cues are available to reinforce hierarchies (but see Herring
1993 and Sutton 1994).

Independent of these academic theories, there have been some compelling real-world examples of social CMC use in the past few years: from
the discussion groups of the Well (Rheingold 1993a, 1993b; Smith 1992)
to those of the New York–based ECHO (Horn 1998) to the many posting
groups on Usenet (e.g., Baym 1993), not to mention MUDs like LambdaMOO. In all such systems, linguistic interactions have been primary:
users exchange messages that cement the social bonds between them,
messages that reflect shared history and understandings (or misunderstandings) about the always evolving local norms for these interactions.

Increasing numbers of researchers are paying some attention to the
language used in CMC as a feature of emergent cultures and practices,
related at least peripherally to the notion of speech community, a concept
important to me. For example, McLaughlin, Osborne, and Smith (1995)
explore the impact of discourse processes on social structures and vice
versa in the evolution of norms of behavior on Usenet, an asynchronous
(i.e., not real-time) Internet discussion forum. They suggest that justification for the use of the term "community" in the CMC research
literature comes from approaches that justify it in terms of discourse
processes in CMC forums (the creation of speech communities) and approaches that seek evidence of social structures. Their own approach is
to assume that virtual processes and structures are analogous in function to real-life processes and structures, and furthermore, "discourse
processes generate social structures, which in turn affect discourse processes" (p. 94). Baym (1993) focuses specifically on rec.arts.tv.soaps,
one Usenet discussion group, arguing that it is a folk group with its own
"ways of speaking," genres of posts, and types of performances. In an
early discussion of synchronous Internet communication (i.e., real-time
communication, or chat), Reid (1991) examines how shared communicative conventions in IRC help produce a common culture, focusing specifically on expression of non-verbal information in a textual form (e.g.,
with emoticons or "smileys"). Curtis, in an early (1992) article about
LambdaMOO, suggests that communities on MUDs exist because "participants slowly come to consensus about a common (private) language,
about appropriate standards of behavior, and about the social roles of

various public areas (e.g., where big discussions usually happen, where certain 'crowds' can be found, etc.)" (p. 16). Gurak (1997) invokes the notion of discourse community, with a focus on the use of discourse for "purposeful social action in a public arena" (p. 11), in her discussion of online protests against the Lotus marketplace database and the Clipper chip.

If culture is composed of symbols and meanings (Schneider 1976) and rules for interpreting them (Geertz 1973), then a linguistic approach to the study of online culture is particularly apt. "Ethnography of speaking" is my approach to studying online culture. In general, the ethnography of speaking is concerned with asking what a speaker needs to know to communicate appropriately within a speech community and how she learns it. This knowledge is called **communicative competence** (Saville-Troike 1982). I characterize a speech community as a community with shared rules of speaking and interpretations of speech performance (Hymes 1972) whose members frequently interact (Gumperz and Hymes 1964). For it to be a speech community, its members must see language as playing a significant role in marking the community's boundary (Saville-Troike 1982, p. 20). Specialized language and special language use help to unify the members and exclude others.

Closely related to the concept of a speech community (even overlapping it) are notions of community of practice (Lave and Wenger 1991), interpretive community (Harris 1989), and discourse community (Swales 1990; Gurak 1997).

Lave and Wenger (1991) focus on the ways in which learning occurs in different community settings, e.g., the apprenticeship of meat cutters and of Yucatec midwives. They define "community of practice" as "a set of relations among persons, activity, and world, over time and in relation with other tangential and overlapping communities of practice. A community of practice is an intrinsic condition for the existence of knowledge, not least because it provides the interpretive support necessary for making sense of its heritage" (p. 98). They suggest that their use of the term "community" doesn't require co-presence or a well-defined group, but does require "participation in an activity system about which participants share understandings concerning what they are doing and what that means in their lives and for their communities" (p. 98). The notion of community of practice is a broader one than many other definitions of community (which I will review in chapter 6). However, Lave and Wenger make clear that we operate in multiple communities of practice, intersecting and overlapping, and they deliberately leave the notion vague and intuitive. Certainly learning linguistic practices is a part of becoming a member of a community of practice, and linguistic practices themselves may constitute a community of practice.[37]

Harris 1989, cited in Gurak 1997, suggests that an interpretive community is constituted by a "loose dispersed network of individuals who share certain habits of mind" (p. 14), or a like-minded grouping with shared values and culture. Gurak 1997 identifies "discourse community" as a theoretical reinterpretation of "interpretive community" by composition scholars.

In an interesting discussion of cross-disciplinary relationships between concepts, Swales (1990) concludes that most definitions of speech community do not make an alternate definition of discourse community redundant. He suggests that speech communities are usually composed of individuals geographically co-located, in much the way that most definitions of community assume territorial proximity (see further discussion in chapter 6). For him, discourse involves writing, and literacy allows communication across distances (although he doesn't address media like the telephone, radio, and television, which also allow non-local speech communication). He makes a further distinction between a "sociolinguistic grouping" and a "socio-rhetorical grouping." In the sociolinguistic notion of speech community, communication determinants are primarily social, such as the need for socialization or group solidarity. In contrast, he sees the socio-rhetorical discourse community as having functional, goal-oriented communication determinants. (He allows that socialization and solidarity may consequently occur.) His archetypal discourse community example is a special-interest group. The discourse community as defined by Swales (1990) may be characterized as having (1) a broadly agreed-upon set of common public goals, (2) mechanisms for communication among the community members, (3) participatory mechanisms used primarily for information and feedback, (4) one or more genres, (5) a specific vocabulary of communication, and (6) a threshold level of members with a suitable degree of relevant content and discourse experience ("survival of the community depends on a reasonable ratio between novices and experts") (pp. 24–27).

Many studies of linguistic phenomena in CMC have addressed one of the related topics of style, genre, and register. There is significant overlap in the applications of these terms. "Genre" is a term often used for literary or textual analysis; Ferguson 1994 suggests that genre refers to message types that recur regularly in a community, with identifying internal structure. Baym 1995 presents a genre analysis of Usenet news-

---

[37]See Eckert and McConnell-Ginet 1992 for one application to a linguistic domain.

group posts, and Erickson 1997 analyzes genre in the discussions on Cafe Utne, a Web discussion site.

As noted above, Swales (1990) refers to genre in his definition of discourse community. He defines genre as a class of communicative events, sharing communicative purposes recognized by expert members of the discourse community. Its purposes, or rationale, influence its structure, content, and style, and the intended audience is similar across examples of the genre. Labels for genres offered by a discourse community are useful for ethnographic research, but may need further validation (e.g., because labels may be inherited from other groups or institutionally imposed, and labels may persist despite major substantive changes in the genres).

"Style" is more often used to describe spoken language, in the context of sociolinguistics (Biber and Finegan 1994); style refers to a continuum of speech formality. In the context of research on CMC, style more generally refers to features of language, i.e., "oral" versus "written" features. Because of the interactivity of CMC, a number of researchers have wrestled with the fact that some CMC apparently has features of oral language in a textual medium. Reinman (1995) discusses the "orality" of email language, suggesting that much email style is informal, similar to spoken language; December (1993) also describes oral features in Usenet posts. Maynor (1994) speculates that there is an online style, which she calls "e-style," which is similar to speech style. Reid (1991) and Werry (1996) discuss the "orality" of language practices in IRC. Yates (1996) analyzes a large CMC corpus of different message types and shows that CMC is more like written language in its vocabulary, but more like spoken language in its use of pronouns. Other researchers have attempted to move away from the oral/literate style debate and focus more on textual characteristics. Collot and Belmore (1992) present a corpus analysis of CMC data according to the textual dimensions Biber (1988) uses, which presume that different genres of texts (where "genre" is used as a convenient term that includes transcriptions of oral language) differ along multiple dimensions according to density of different linguistic features, rather than in a purely binary oral/literate classification.[38]

---

[38] In light of the stylistic debates about CMC language, I am not sure that Swales's (1990) distinctions between speech community and discourse community are particularly helpful when considering highly interactive online groups like ElseMOO. Although technically the inhabitants of ElseMOO correspond in writing, the highly interactive, non-persistent status of their texts—combined with the high degree of sociability above and beyond any stated rationale they might have for their community's existence—makes them more plausibly a speech community than a discourse community in Swales's sense.

A register is a special variety of speech adapted for a particular recurrent situation of use. Ferguson (1994, p. 20) says of registers, "A communicative situation that recurs regularly in a society (in terms of participants, setting, communicative functions, and so forth) will tend over time to develop identifying markers of linguistic structure and language use, different from the language of other communication situations." According to this definition, members of speech communities (and discourse communities, Swales 1990) may make use of one or more registers depending on the communicative situations they find themselves in. Some examples of register studies include Ferguson 1964 on baby talk, Ferguson 1975 on foreigner talk, Ferguson 1983 on sportscaster commentary, Janda 1985 on note-taking, Straumann 1935 on newspaper headline language, and Gibbon 1985 on amateur radio speech. Registers may include the use of special vocabulary (abbreviations, special terms for common events or objects), special syntax, semantics, phonology. Often these special forms are for ease of communication in a mediated situation; but many forms are also used to mark in-group status and define the community as a speech community with shared conventions. Since all communication occurs in a social context, the speaker who uses a short form to simplify production must use a form recognized by the community, making it difficult to separate the two sources of innovation in the register. CB speech, for instance, features use of the police "10-codes" for simpler reference to recurrent events, as well as more complex jargon that doesn't save time but marks insider status (such as "negatory" for "no"). Even the "10-code" must be learned and recognized as insider language, however.

Within the tradition of systemic linguistics, variables named *field*, *tenor*, and *mode* are relevant for the description of registers. The field specifies the activity and subject of discourse, the tenor describes the status role relationships among the participants, and the mode specifies the channel or medium of communication (Halliday 1979). Swales (1990, and citations therein) suggests that, in order to untangle genre and register, we may think of genres as being realized through registers. Genres are categorizations for completed texts, in light of the importance of text structure for most understandings of genre, while registers are linguistic variations utilized by members of discourse communities to create those genres.

Communicating on a MUD, with a text interface and no possibility of overlap (or interruption) because of the one-way channel, poses unusual communication challenges. The language produced in a CMC environment is a response to the limits of the medium and a function of community norms for language use that are reinforced and displayed with each utterance. As such, it may be considered a linguistic register. Since register has already been used as an analytic category for mediated communication, I find that notion most useful for situating CMC research against other linguistic study of special communication situations. Additionally, the linguistic interactions in ElseMOO are most amenable to description in terms of register, rather than genre, since the interaction is usually highly participatory, focused on sociability rather than pre-determined goals, generally free-form rather than highly structured. In this book, I describe that register by describing the special linguistic characteristics of speech in the MOO, including the impact of the mode (or medium), and discuss the speech community and speech situations. The register is a linguistic variety used by the ElseMOO regulars, who are individuals in regular sociable communication via the mode of the MOO. These individuals constitute a speech community in virtue of having in common distinguishing rules of speech conduct and linguistic forms.

More generally, questions of concern to me in the next few chapters are common questions for the ethnography of speaking, and deal directly with the formation of community: what does language do to establish, challenge, and recreate social identities and social relationships, and to frame or situate events at the societal as well as individual level (Duranti 1988)? In order to explore these questions, it is necessary to consider linguistic interaction in context, as active rather than static discourse production. Pursuing an ethnography of speaking requires doing ethnographic work the same way other immersive studies of community often require ethnographic work. In chapter 7, I discuss in detail some of the issues facing the cyber-ethnographer regarding ethics of data collection, my own methods, and qualifications of my conclusions based on my position in the community.

1.5.2 Upcoming Chapters

ElseMOO was my research site of choice because of its strong sense of language identity and its interesting relationships with other MUD communities. In chapter 2 I outline the community's history and describe some of its characteristics. Most of the ElseMOOers are students, and most participated in other MUD communities as well. LambdaMOO was particularly relevant, since in some ways ElseMOO was a spin-off of LambdaMOO. The ambiguous category of "power elite" users on LambdaMOO, who were seen as talented programmers and friends of the wizards, included by some reckonings the founders of ElseMOO. Despite this close relationship, ElseMOO differs from LambdaMOO in impor tant ways, remaining a small (in contrast) MOO with more restrictive policies regarding programming and use of the space. The participants in ElseMOO recognize it as a community with its own culture and conventions. Much of this recognition is due to perceptions about local language. ElseMOOers use a lot of idiosyncratic language; the community even began a project to document what they described as the "jargon" used on the MOO in 1994. Their listing of items they thought important to document was very helpful to me in writing chapter 3, in which I discuss the speech patterns of the community. The speech routines (Coulmas 1981) and ritual utterances on ElseMOO were either locally established or inherited from an older MUD community on Seashore MUSH. ElseMOOers, like most MUDders, are members of multiple MUD communities, and some are also regulars or frequent visitors in the Seashore community. These multiple community memberships establish routes for the routines and rituals to spread among MUDs.

In chapter 3, I describe and discuss some specific features of the MUD register. ElseMOO speakers display syntactic and morphological alternations, such as the deletion of prepositions and various conventionalized contractions (like "onna" for "on the"). They also participate in a number of special speech activities, derived in part from technical features of the MOO environment.

The software infrastructure affects communication as well as social structures in complex ways. Programmed commands may be added that extend or change the repertoire of speech commands, tying linguistic behavior patterns explicitly to programming capabilities and indirectly to social status on the MOO. A relationship exists on ElseMOO (and on many MUDs) between programmed commands and discourse routines, which are commonly occurring linguistic interactions. Often a routine interaction will be simplified by rendering it as a command or by programming an object with commands on it; many objects and commands on ElseMOO therefore serve as records of local history and culture. However, on ElseMOO not everyone is entitled to program the environment; aside from the fact that programming ability of at least a rudimentary sort is needed, even skilled programmers don't necessarily have permission on ElseMOO to alter the MOO database by creating new objects or commands. Arguments over who should have permission to do what have been a source of considerable conflict on ElseMOO, with permission being seen as a status marker by many people because it indicates that the user has been approved by the community as a responsible and desirable programmer. Having permission to program enables a user to alter the discourse structures, since programmers may create the commands available to "speak" with. ElseMOO programmers are responsible for some command types that are used on most MOOs on the Net now, and derivatives occur on other MUD servers as well.

In the next two chapters I look both at features specific to the Else-MOO register and at ones that occur in other MUD registers as well. In chapter 4 I focus on methods for turn-taking in the one-way text medium, invoking some conversation analysis literature as background. I discuss some ways that speakers in ElseMOO handle turn-taking and repair misunderstandings. Turn length is predicted to be longer in typed exchanges than in face-to-face speech by a number of researchers, but I show that in ElseMOO turn length is in fact shorter than the average for face-to-face conversation in Örestrom's 1983 study of the London-Lund corpus. Dynamic adjustment of turn size according to the rate of conversation is part of the communicative competence of ElseMOO speakers. The text channel provides challenges for turn-taking strategies and communication of information that is usually available in visual form or as simultaneous background speech, for example the signs of understanding or agreement that are often called "back channels" (Yngve 1970). Providing frequent back channel responses using conventionalized utterances like "Tom nods" is important for establishing understanding. I suggest that these back channels also increase the sense of co-presence felt in the medium, the sense that other actors are present.

One of the peculiarities of the MUD register is the "**emote**" (or "**pose**") command. The emote command enables third person utterances like "Tom waves" or "Tom hated that movie." The use of the present tense for many descriptions of actions (with the emote command) is an interesting aspect of MUD speech in general, not just of ElseMOO's register. In chapter 5 I categorize types of emotes that occur regularly into five types: conventionalized openings/closings for interactions (like "Tom waves"), back channels that show attention or comprehension ("Tom nods"), byplay (usually prompted by conversational context, joking interactions like "Mike drops a brick on Tom's head"), narration of real-life actions while MUDding ("Tom sends mail to the user group"), and expository background information ("Tom hated that film"). All occur in the present tense, except for the last, which may occur in any tense.

I then offer some theoretical linguistic analysis and speculation about present tense emotes in MUD discourse. The emoted present tense appears to be related to the present tense in performative utterances like "I christen this ship the *Marie Claire*" and the present tense in the simultaneous sports commentary register. Cases in which the MUD emote refers to real-world simultaneous actions, like sending email, are more like sports commentary speech; the other types, which have no real-world referents, are more like performatives, evoking an imagined action with the utterance itself. In chapter 5 I discuss the semantics of the present tense in the MUD register and compare and contrast it with observations in the literature on sports commentary present tense and other uses of the present tense. I investigate the interpretation of present tense utterances in different aspectual classes, and suggest that reference to the MUD world or real world, plus aspectual category, determines whether the action described has just been completed or is ongoing. Activities, for instance, are interpreted as ongoing in the real world, but as just completed in the MUD world.

Stepping back from specifically linguistic aspects of community, in chapter 6 I discuss broader sociological and anthropological definitions of community. I group research on community into categories: tradition and practice definitions, social network studies, collective action and collective goods definitions, boundary theories, and study of utopian representations. I consider facets of ElseMOO against these definitions, to assess to what degree ElseMOO matches traditional notions of "community." To illustrate how these other research traditions may be applicable, I present several narratives of conflict over power, access, and identity on ElseMOO. Power structures are particularly apparent and contentious on ElseMOO. Technical ability is closely related to social influence; the term "power elite" is routinely used to refer to the programmers who founded the MUD, both by outsiders on other MUDs and by ElseMOOers themselves. I discuss the continued evolution and problematic denotation of this term. The social network of relationships on ElseMOO is reflected in gossip patterns on the MOO, and I show that the network reflects the existence of a power elite subgroup who are particularly closely linked. Gossip is an important indicator of a strong community, as well as a mechanism for social change.

In sum, this book represents an addition to the literature on computer-mediated communication and community. I provide an ethnographic look at a particular online community and focus on linguistic analysis of the members' speech patterns. This recreational online community, centered around a MUD, has its own power structures and culture of use. Users adapt to the medium, developing a special variety of speech known as a linguistic register. The register includes features that make communication more efficient in the mediated communication environment, like turn-taking strategies, as well as in-group features that mark the speakers as members of the speech community. Since all speech occurs in a social context, even the strategies for efficient communication must depend on social conventions being established. Borrowing and extending conventions from other known registers, like present tense usage in simultaneous sports commentary, is one means of creating shared understandings. Finally and more broadly, this book offers an in-depth review of different notions of community both online and offline, and situates ElseMOO against those definitions.

2

Welcome to ElseMOO

2.1 A Whirlwind History of TinyMUDs

A little bit of MUD history will set the stage for more discussion of the ElseMOO community. MUD history is difficult to come by, existing mainly in the memories of MUDders who were there, or in documents they have created for other MUDders.[1] Bartle 1990, a report on MUD servers for British Telecom, offers invaluable quotations from MUDders about their experiences on MUDs as well as some description of existing MUDs and their culture. MUD history is important to the members of the ElseMOO community (and thus to students of the community as well) because several of them started MUDding when social MUDs were just becoming popular, which gives them a pedigree as generic "MUDders" rather than simply "MOOers" ("MOOs," object-oriented MUDs, developed later). As in many communities, knowledge of community history and ancestry is a status symbol. Knowledge of the technical ancestry of MUD servers is also a status symbol, along with general technical savvy, particularly on ElseMOO. Another reason that the history of social MUDs is important is linguistic: many of the playful linguistic routines on ElseMOO reflect the history of ElseMOO, LambdaMOO, or MUDs in general. Many of them are related to or derived from linguistic routines found in a community known as the "Random and Moira" group, who are some of the earliest MUDders still active.[2]

2.1.1 TinyMUD, a Social Alternative to Scored Game MUDs

The genesis of "social" MUDs, in contrast to adventure-game MUDs, was the TinyMUD software. In 1989 Jim Aspnes developed TinyMUD at

---

[1]E.g., Burka 1993, 1995. Leong 1998 is a collection of Web pages for both MUDders and researchers.

[2]Some members of the "Random and Moira" group do hang out on DragonMUD, the oldest continually running social MUD in the U.S. (Clodius 1994).

Carnegie Mellon University as an alternative to the scored game that was MUD1, the first MUD. The original TinyMUD players are now known as "dinosaurs" (or just "dinos") among social MUDders, and many are still MUDding. According to one MUDder who started in 1990, how old you have to be to be considered a "dino" "depends on who you ask." Having appeared in early 1990 on any MUD makes you more likely to be considered a dino. Having been around from the TinyMUD start is a really impressive lineage, however.

In addition to eliminating infrastructure for gaming, TinyMUD allowed users to build rooms themselves.[3] Building, or adding rooms (and other objects) to a MUD database, often presents both social and technical problems for the MUD administrators and other users. A complicated, badly designed geography can be hard to visualize and hence hard to use. Burka (1995) reports in her history of early MUDs that ChaosMUD had a "weird topology that [wasn't] congenial to hanging out or building," one based roughly on a file-system metaphor, and it died as a result. Bartle (1990) is harsh on the subject of allowing anyone to build, and shows his stripes as a game designer:

> Game management is very difficult, however, since anyone, friend or foe, has full powers to add new rooms whether they have the slightest idea of what they're doing or not. This ensures that the only atmosphere a game possesses is that due to its players, and that any pretensions of consistency or depth swiftly disappear. Sadly, most people are not good room-describers (in the same way that most people aren't good novellists), and thus, although the quantity of rooms in a TinyMUD can be fantastically large, the quality is generally very low. [. . .] TinyMUDs are indeed limited only by the imagination of the builder - with heavy emphasis on the word "limited".

Bartle is accurate in his statement that unplanned building can damage an environment. Indeed, the original TinyMUD was famed for having one social hangout, the Rec Room, to which everyone wanted to attach their rooms. At one point, there were a staggering ninety-seven entrances to the Rec Room from players' private rooms.[4]

Building bloats a MUD's database and must be managed in some fashion, but I believe that, as Burka (1993) says, "one of the signs and side-effects of a successful MUD is growth, both in the size and population. A MUD where players can't build, or where what they build

---

[3]Bartle 1990 suggests it was inspired in part by LP MUD, another user-extensible server type in existence by then.

[4]See http://www.apocalypse.org/pub/u/lpb/muddex/exits.txt.

won't stay, occasions far less feeling of community investment or belonging than a community would desire." However, Bartle (1990) certainly wouldn't agree that building is necessary on a MUD, and even Burka (1993) points out that on TinyMUD, many people didn't build or explore, treating it as a "chat system with furniture." But "hanging out" is as much a part of MUDding as building and exploring is, as Burka (1993) says.

As I will discuss later, database growth and the administration of player building have been particular problems on LambdaMOO, where players may initially build a small number of objects of whatever kind they like. Ultimately an Architecture Review Board was created to set building policy and manage players' requests for additional building quota. ElseMOO, in contrast, had a relatively rigid policy toward building, with only a few users empowered to build. Toward the end of my research, the policies on ElseMOO were loosened in an attempt to foster more community feeling and a return to the creative roots of social MUDding.

Bartle concludes his summary of MUDs based on TinyMUD with his orientation toward gaming apparent again: "TinyMUD is not so much a [multi-user adventure] as a forum for conversation where participants have pinned short pieces of prose on the wall for the benefit of anyone with the inclination to read them. If this kind of [MUD] gets a strong hold in the USA, it could set the industry back several years." Ironically, most research on MUDs has focused on social and work-oriented MUDs, rather than game MUDs.[5] Researchers may operate from the reverse prejudice.

2.1.2 Variants of TinyMUD

Aspnes's original TinyMUD resulted in a real user community, and its members often helped design and run other social MUDs. Other MUD server types that soon followed include MUCK, MUSH, and UberMUD, which offer users different degrees of programmability. The TinyMUD server type also remained available and was used as the base for other MUDs.[6]

TinyHell, the second MUD using the TinyMUD server, was opened December 10, 1989. TinyHell became the first "Random and Moira" MUD, called after the character names of its administrators, who later ran many MUDs on which could be found members of the "dino"

---

[5]With the exceptions I noted in the previous chapter: Ito 1997; Ackerman and Muramatsu 1998; Reid 1996; Masterson 1996.

[6]A tree diagram of MUD ancestry is available at Keegan 1997.

community.[7] Then in March 1990, a collectively-run MUD based on a TinyMUD database variant opened, called Islandia. Random and Moira (who was then called Chrysalis) were among the committee of characters running it.

Dissatisfaction with the new MUD is remembered in Wetmore 1993. According to Wetmore's idiosyncratic, personal history of social MUDs, Islandia was "really starting to be a drag," in part because it was full of "furries" (anthropomorphic furry animal characters) having "tinysex." "Tinysex" refers to interactive typed erotic encounters on social MUDs.[8] Burka (1995) reports one definition of tinysex: "Tinysex is that act in which one or more players on a mud engage in a 'conversation' of sorts, where, by using descriptive phrases, their tinybodies seem to engage in an act which mirrors sex in reallife, for the implicitly agreed upon purpose of sexual s(t)imulation or gratification."[9] Kendall (1996) discusses a contemporary social MUD she calls AniMUCK that caters to users role-playing anthropomorphic animals, or furries; the characters are inspired by "Furry" fandom, an offshoot of comic and science fiction fandoms. AniMUCK generates controversy for several reasons, Kendall relates, including the fact that many character descriptions are overtly sexual (e.g., the seductive Puss-n-Boots character whose description Kendall quotes on p. 214), and tinysex is rumored to be a common occurrence on the MUD. Many current MUDders still react to furries the way Wetmore did to the furry newcomers on Islandia.

Bartle (1990) offers his opinion on Islandia, still a historically significant MUD:

Islandia started at Berkeley, but was moved to different sites as it increased in size. It was constantly added to, and grew to be huge. In the month of October, it had 1,503 players (from a total of 3,271) and 14,900 rooms - a phenomenal size for a [multi-user adventure]. However, of those 14,900 rooms, only 7,503 were used that month...[10] Islandia was a friendly place, with friendly people, and famed for its many beautifully designed rooms. Its maintainers scoured the database removing useless or incomplete creations, trying to keep

---

[7]At the time of TinyHell, Random's user had a character named Nightfall rather than Random.

[8]Activities associated with TinyMUD MUD users are often described by MUDders with the prefix "tiny" followed by a noun.

[9]Druid, one of the authors of this definition, reports that "it is possible to do calculus homework and have tinysex at the same time, if you type quickly." Many early MUDders, like MUDders today, were students or were multi-tasking as they MUDded.

[10]This seems to me a reasonably high percentage, although he presents it as if it were indicative of some flaw in the design or use of the MUD.

it to a manageable size and reasonably consistent. However, they finally decided to take the system down simply because, despite their efforts, it had grown too large; besides, they were wearying of trying to trim the database in the face of its relentless growth toward full capacity. The maintainers also felt that the game was too old. People were using the system as a means to annoy others, which was taken as a sign of decay. Since TinyMUDs offer no facilities for game management, this fate eventually befalls all such programs, except in the case where being nasty is the whole point of playing.

Bartle seems to be suggesting that the lack of game infrastructure results in social abuse of the MUD. Despite this missing game infrastructure, various technical and social administrative efforts have been made on social MUDs, the most famous of which is LambdaMOO's attempt at democracy, supported by a programmed infrastructure that allows users to vote on formal propositions. This infrastructure gives the population of users an opportunity to affect social policies on the MUD and also relieves the wizards of much stressful ad hoc policymaking.

In any case, BloodMUD, a parody of Islandia where anything was allowed, was opened March 1990.

The TinyBASE [TinyMUD] database was taken as a starting point, and developed along themes of blood, violence and sleaze. Rooms were deliberately corrupted by other players, with special attention giving to vandalising TinyBASE. BloodMUD was a reaction to the "nice" atmosphere that pervaded Islandia—and was a lot more fun to play. It finally disappeared when the database was accidentally deleted, but by then it had sunk into depravity. (Bartle 1990)

Bartle cites one player of BloodMUD saying, "BloodMUD was a fun place, near anarchy, as close as one could get. People did horrible things and generally broke MUD taboos whenever possible. It was not a MUD for socialisation or exquisite building, it was a MUD for being nasty and killing. ... In short, it was an excellent place" (Bartle 1990).

This quotation is interesting in that it mentions MUD taboos: community standards had been established and recognized on some social MUDs despite their short lifespans, and different MUDs were viewed as having different social contracts (cf. Curtis 1992). Furthermore, BloodMUD was created in reaction to another MUD, the way ElseMOO and many other MOOs were responses to players' experiences on LambdaMOO. Communities and sites are descended from other communities and sites in a traceable history. Explicit social contracts are written in response to prior MUD cultures on ancestral MUDs.

2.1.3   Flight from Newbies: the Random and Moira Gang

In the spring of 1990, TinyMUD was reportedly overrun with "newbies" who had a lot of tinysex (Wetmore 1993). The term "newbie" is common in other CMC forums as well; it refers to someone who is new to the technology being used (in this case, MUD software) or to the community, and who may not know the local social conventions. Anti-newbie and anti-furry sentiment increased on TinyMUD, possibly helping to solidify the "Random and Moira gang" who hung out on TinyHell. Although I wasn't there, it seems plausible to me that age discrimination—where "age" is meant in terms of experience MUDding—was an early force in group definition. The community response to newbies on LambdaMOO and ElseMOO more recently is similar to that described in Wetmore's 1993 history: criticism of the newer players' styles of interaction and their apparent interest in MUDding for the purpose of tinysex alone. Older players often avoid the high concentrations of newer players perceived as annoying or offensive, reinforcing the differences in their styles of interaction.

TinyHell was replaced by TinyHell II in the spring of 1990. Chaos, a programmable MUCK run by Random and Moira, was established in June of 1990. Programmability meant that players could create interactive toys and other objects, as well as just building rooms, as TinyMUD had allowed. This step forward led to new problems: for instance, one player created a listening device that allowed eavesdropping on conversations in other MUD rooms, to several people's horror.

Chaos was shut down, and the Random and Moira gang moved to Brigadoon MUCK in November 1990; then to Asylum in January 1991; to Dreamscape, an UnterMUD, in August 1991; then to Space Madness, a MUSH, in May 1992. Until recently the "Random and Moira" MUD was a MUSH I'll call Seashore, which opened in February 1994. This lineage illustrates that a MUD community may persist as a group beyond the lifetime of a single MUD. The Random and Moira gang, many of whom date back a long time in the history of social MUDs, are a particularly influential discourse group. Many of the routines and ritual jokes found on other MUDs, particularly ElseMOO, are descended from the Random and Moira gang's discourse practices.[11]

2.2   The ElseMOO Community

2.2.1   Who Are the ElseMOO MUDders?

According to Rheingold 1993, Bartle estimates 100,000 past and present MUDders worldwide by 1992, and Pavel Curtis estimates 20,000 active

---

[11]Thanks to Russ Smith for his memory of server history.

MUDders in 1992. ElseMOO was founded in 1992 as an offshoot of LambdaMOO.

Several regular users of ElseMOO (EM) have MUDded since at least 1990 (eight out of twenty-eight respondents to a survey I conducted in the fall of 1994). Tom, one of the founders of EM, told me how he got into MUDding. He and Ray were childhood friends, writing and playing computer games on their home computers as early as grade school. They ended up at different colleges, but kept in touch through email. In their freshman year of college, 1990, Ray sent Tom email about some things called MUDs he'd discovered on the Net. Tom checked out the TinyMUD descendants and disliked the command parsing, finding LP MUDs more sophisticated. When he told Ray this, Ray replied that it was the cool people on the TinyMUDs that he liked, not the technology itself. Tom gave them another try and started hanging out on TinyMUD Classic and Islandia. Ray soon discovered Stephen White's object-oriented MUD project called "MOO" and convinced Tom that object-oriented programming was interesting. Tom discovered the existence of LambdaMOO in January 1991; Ray considers Tom's dragging him onto LambdaMOO to be Tom's revenge for introducing him to MUDs. MUDs have been a social interest as well as a technical one for Tom and Ray and many other MUDders.

A handful of EM regulars consider themselves "MUDders" rather than specifically "MOOers," which many people who started MUDding on LambdaMOO or other recent MOOs consider themselves; Damon, Ray, Ted, Mike, and Sadness also hung out on Seashore MUSH, home of the Random and Moira gang, as well as on EM. The long history some of the EM people have on various kinds of MUDs, rather than just MOOs, predisposes them to think of themselves as generic MUDders. It's possible to become a "MUDder" after starting as a "MOOer," however. Sadness, an anthropology student at Stanford, started on LambdaMOO in 1993, began hanging out on ElseMOO in 1994, and then migrated to Seashore, while maintaining some presence on LambdaMOO and EM as well. She told me she used to think of herself as a MOOer, and now considers herself a MUDder. "MOO pampers you," she said; she enjoys learning the new, sometimes more awkward, commands on new server types. Almost everyone answering my survey considered themselves a regular on at least one or two other MUDs, and some maintained characters and popped in occasionally on up to eight other MUDs besides EM.

The median age of the twenty-eight survey respondents was 22.5, with the youngest two being 15 and the oldest being 34 and 44. There are about thirty-five regulars who might be considered "core" people,

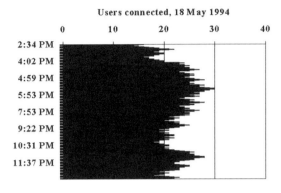

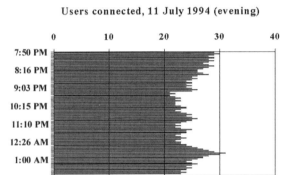

FIGURE 1 Number of connected users at recorded times

and another sixty or so who drop in regularly. On a normal day there are between twenty and thirty people connected to EM, although more than half may be idle (inactive).

The graphs in Figure 1 show the number of users connected at different times of day on particular days in 1994 (two years after the opening of the MOO). Curtis 1992 offers a similar graph of LambdaMOO in 1992 (also two years after its opening), which shows a more normal distribution around the afternoon hours, with a maximum of thirty-five users connected, and a minimum of twelve. I suspect that ElseMOO users tend to remain connected and idle more often.

Between a quarter and a third of the regular users are female. Most EM folks are either computer science students or professionals, and a few are unemployed. At least two-thirds of the regulars are students (undergraduates and graduates, some bored by and even failing their classes); a few are in high school. One or two of the younger ones have computer consulting jobs on the side.

When I asked how many hours a day they spent MUDding, only one of my twenty-eight respondents answered with a weekly rate instead (2–3 hours/week); the rest gave widely varying responses, from 1–2 hours per day to 12–14 hours. However, almost everyone agreed that their hours connected were not equivalent to their hours spent actively MUDding. Many of them give the MUD only partial attention while working at school or a job. Several MUD from home as well as work or school; others only MUD from home. Access hours differ somewhat, as a result, with some people being "night" people, and others being regularly connected all day from work but rarely at night. Before she graduated from Stanford, Sadness MUDded from her dorm late at night; her friends on campus thought she was weird, but she was having fun learning to program, creating her room and objects on LambdaMOO. She lost Net access when she graduated, and told me that MUDding was a student thing for her; but she was back online in a few months, with a public Internet service provider. She'd missed it more than she expected to.

Geographically, the EM crowd is diverse, hailing from places like Ottawa, Seattle (a small cluster there, with Damon, Penfold, Rick, and foliage), Newark (a larger cluster of about a dozen), Pittsburgh, Minnesota, and Australia. At the time of my survey, almost all of them had met one or more of the EM regulars or other local MUDders in real life, or wanted to.[12] A large MUD gathering occurred in San Francisco in the summer of 1993, where many LambdaMOO and EM people met for the first time. Mike, Penfold, Karen, ls (whose machine EM was running on), Kit, Jeani, Lenny, and Tom met for dinner and a trip to the Exploratorium. Photos of this event, like those of many MUDder gatherings, were posted on the Net.

2.2.2 Characters, Users, and Pronouns

Some discussion of the relationship between characters and users, and of the frequent identification of the two, will help readers understand the MUD dialogs in the rest of this book. In a MOO, all characters are technically objects, just like all scenery and all props. This means that they can be programmed and interacted with in various automated ways that I will illustrate later. Yet, because the user has no other representative in the MUD world, the character is strongly identified with the user. The simultaneous identification of and distinction between the real person and the character object are a complex matter. (Further dis-

---

[12]As of 1994 there were about a dozen people on EM who had met a "real-life" lover or partner on EM or another MUD.

cussion of this relationship can be found in Cherny 1995b.) Generally, it is not a question of pretended or playful identification when a user describes something that happened to her character as something that happened to her: her character is her in the context of the virtual world, and there simply aren't enough pronouns in English to differentiate the selves involved.

The complexity of the relationship that holds between a character and a user is illustrated in the dialog below (from Cherny 1995b). People greeted Karen, as usual, when she entered the room, only to find out to their surprise that this time she hadn't entered the room under her own volition:

1   Karen arrives from the eastern end of the patio.
2   lynn waves.
3   Shelley waves.
4   ls [to Karen]: Hi. I just walked you here at your
    request since you're in the car and nowhere
    near a computer on the net.
5   Penfold whuggles Karen.
6   Tom eyes Karen warily.
7   lynn eyes Karen and ls warily.
8   Tom says, "WHY"
9   ls says, "she, uh, thought it would be cool to hang
    out with you guys."
10 lynn laughs
11 Tom says, "BUT SHE ISN'T"
12 ls says, "oh, but she is."
13 lynn says, "hang out in scrollback?"
14 Penfold shakes Karen.

The user with character ls had been talking to his wife Karen (with character Karen) over their portable phones, and had told her about his conversation with their friends; she asked him to move (i.e., "walk") her character for her. (A "whuggle," as in line 5, is a virtual version of a hug; see Cherny 1995a and chapter 3.) ls's statement to Karen's character in line 4 sums up the confusing split reality shared by user and character: *I walked you (the character) here (the virtual room) at your (the user's) request since you're (the user) in the car (in real life).* Karen can be in two places at once, via her character and her physical body, and she can "hang out" even when she isn't at her computer looking at the conversation as it happens. She will be able to read it later, by scrolling back in her MOO window. The unusually explicit difference between Karen as user hanging out with friends via her character interface and

Karen's character hanging out without her "behind it" at the terminal was disturbing to the witnesses of the event, however. As Stone says, "In virtual systems, an interface is that which mediates between the human body (or bodies) and an associated 'I' (or 'I's'). This double view of 'where' the 'person' is, and the corresponding trouble it may cause with thinking about 'who' we are talking about when we discuss such a problematic 'person,' underlies the structure of most recent virtual communities" (Stone 1991, p. 87).

Ordinarily, people refer to their characters in first person, identifying their characters with themselves, but there are occasional moments when some users make a distinction between user and character explicit. One person who posts messages on public lists on LambdaMOO refers to her character, Dawn, as "the character Dawn" instead of "me" or "I." Others occasionally draw the distinction between themselves as typist and their character, usually to be amusing or to make a point (this example is from a signature on a message):

```
bella .... who wasn't, by the way, at that dinner.
neither was her typist.
```

The character may be considered a prosthesis, the external "I." It is unusual to refer to the character as distinct from the user in the discourse of the MUD. It creates a break in the usual understood state of affairs: that the user *is* the character, for purposes of isolating agency.

In this book, I will use "character" and "user" almost interchangeably, because characters are the user's placeholders in the MUD world. Sometimes users are also called "players," after early gaming MUD conventions.

2.2.3 Labels and Character Categories on ElseMOO

Aside from the categories of "MOOer" and "MUDder," there are other groups that ElseMOO members recognize: the programmers, the regulars, the newbies, the randoms, the guests, the refugees, the wizards, the "power elite." All of these labels have shifting denotations, of course, and not all refer to coherent groups.

The category of MUDder is one of the most problematic. In some contexts it means simply "one who MUDs," i.e., one who has a character on a MUD and has been active on a MUD for a while (more than a day). The stricter native categorization is about commitment to the medium and to a community. A MUDder is one who spends a significant amount of time per week (often per day) on MUDs, over some length of time.

Many people begin MUDding while they are in school, and lose Net access during the summer. This loss of access does not threaten their sta-

tus as MUDders (although it may weaken their ties to a community)—
it's an understood part of many MUDders' lives. MUDders aren't just
students, although many of them get initial access through university
accounts. The Seashore community illustrates the way that MUDding
can become more than just a student hobby; the Seashore group is older
than many other MUD groups, because the regulars started earlier and
many have continued to MUD since graduating. ElseMOO is also regarded by some of its regulars as hosting an older and more mature
MUD community than most MUDs.

Being a MUDder means not only knowing the commands of at least
one server type, but understanding the subtleties of social interactions.
A MUDder has been socialized in some MUD community, has learned
how to participate, may know some of the MUD's social history, and
has a sense of why MUDs are fun or possibly why they are being ruined
by newbies. Reactions to newbies often express cultural norms for interactions in a given forum. Newbies are new to the technology or the
community, and may illustrate their ignorance by having trouble with
the system's commands, violating local norms, or asking too many questions. Newbies are often expected to have a different sense of what is
fun about MUDs than older MUDders do; e.g., they are often assumed
to be interested only in tinysex. Newbies are seen as a threat to some
MUD communities when they are perceived as unwilling to respect the
community norms; their behavior may cause older (that is, more experienced) community members to avoid them and the public places they
frequent on the MUD. I discuss some of the criticism of newbie behavior
by older players on LambdaMOO below.[13]

"Programmers" are people with bits, or flags, on their character objects that allow them to program on a MOO. Also, more loosely, programmers are people who know how to program and do so on the MOO.
They often have a computer science background, although there are
many cases of non-technical people learning to produce fine MOO code.
Not all people who know how to program have a bit; on ElseMOO, the
giving out of bits to allow modification of the MOO has been intensely
political. I discuss some of the controversy surrounding the resource of
the programmer's bit below and in chapter 6. Programmers (in the sense
of people having a bit) are empowered to create objects on the MUD.
Such objects can be interacted with; they can embody MUD history or

---

[13]Interestingly, the only word that contrasts with "newbie" is "oldbie," which sometimes gets used for real old-time MUDders (often "dino" era). There doesn't appear
to be a label for non-newbies who aren't "oldbies" otherwise, although Upchuck on
LambdaMOO proposed variations of the term "elite" for older players, as I will show
in further discussion of the term "power elite" in chapter 6.

augment a conversation, like props. Programmers (in the general sense of people who know about programming) may have an advantage in the very technical discussions that often occur on ElseMOO. ElseMOO as a whole has a reputation for being a place where one can find smart programmers; several people on ElseMOO told me that they use it as a tech support line, or that they enjoy the technically competent population there. A few others bemoaned the technical discussion, saying it often went over their heads.

Guests are a troublesome category on many MUDs. Often MUDs have one or more guest characters available to people who don't have a character on the MUD. They don't require a password, and they often look generic, e.g., they are named "Guest" (or variations on the theme, like "Blue Guest," if there is more than one guest character). Guest users are often people investigating a MUD, who may later decide to get a character; they may not know the standards of behavior in the community and may behave abusively or obnoxiously. Bad guest behavior on EM has included paging all female characters to ask about mailing lists on oral sex, propositioning someone, and swearing, among other things. Obnoxious guests are "booted," forcibly disconnected from the MOO by a player holding special administrative powers. A booted guest may reconnect and continue the abuse, of course, unless a Community Group member blocks the user's site. ("Admin players" and the Community Group are discussed in chapter 6.) Occasionally multiple guests "attack" at once from the same site; EM regulars usually assume them to be a group of college kids in the same terminal room egging each other on with complete disregard for the MUD community. Guests are also occasionally people who have a MUD character, but want extra anonymity for an action or actions they don't want their character to be associated with (see chapter 6). Guests are therefore treated warily by many MUDders. On ElseMOO, guest site information (the Internet address from which a guest user was connecting) was made public in 1994, as a means of discouraging abusive behavior from guests. Site information reduces the anonymity the guest guise offers.

"Regular" is a term occasionally heard on EM, roughly synonymous with "ElseMOOer," one who frequents the MUD. There are different types of presences in the community, however, just as there are different styles of MUDding. Someone may be a regular but still feel unwelcome in a small group on EM, or be aware that there is a social network she has no access to, perhaps because she doesn't live in the same town that the other participants do. (Newark, for instance, has a large group of EMers who socialize online as well as "in real life.") Cliques are perceived to exist on EM just as in any community. I discuss these perceptions in detail in my discussion of the "power elite" and the Mouldy Couch Club. "Randoms" are players who are not recognized as being "one of us" or as being socially consequential; it's a term some EM people use, which may not be recognized by the whole community or any other MUD communities. Often randoms are new characters on the MUD, who are trying to become a part of the community or otherwise socialize there. A random is not necessarily a MUD newbie, just new to the community or to a social subgroup.

Wizards

The social structures on MUDs differ from the flat structures of newsgroup readers and posters (e.g., Baym 1995; Tepper 1997; Watson 1997) in that certain players are distinguished by their authority to modify the system infrastructure (much like the "listowner" who controls a mailing list's functionality). Such authority is granted and instantiated technically, not just socially. Wizards (also known as Gods on some MUDs) are characters that have administrative and technical powers over the MUD. Some of them have access to the computer files that make up the server and database; they generally are responsible, like system administrators, for the running of the MUD, for making backups of the changing database, for restarting it if it crashes. They have the ability to make significant changes to the MUD as well: they can create anything or destroy anything, including other players' objects or even other characters (Reid 1994b; Dibbell 1993; Ito 1997). Being a wizard is a technical matter of having a wizard bit, the flag on the character object that says it has the programming permissions of a wizard.

Ordinarily, users who have wizard characters also keep a non-wizard character, so that they don't accidentally delete something or read something private when they aren't intending to perform wizard tasks. On ElseMOO and LambdaMOO, the general population knows which non-wizard characters are controlled by the players of which wizard characters; in effect, the player (or user), rather than the character, is treated as the wizard, since the shared cross-character identity is known. I will discuss some effects of this conflation in chapter 6.

Being a wizard is often seen as either a "janitorial" duty (more often by wizards) or a privilege with power associated with it (more often by non-wizards). Wizards who don't make obvious use of their power or rarely do anything justifying having the bit are not often bothered by people wanting help with social or programming problems, and they are often not seen as socially influential or powerful. (See Reid 1994b for some discussion of how wizards are viewed on MUDs.) On Else-

MOO, where there are a lot of wizards because of programming projects that require wizard permissions, the bit itself does not automatically grant social status, although the person granted it must have achieved a certain status as a trustable programmer in the eyes of the other wizards. Instead, the wizards who are known to use their status to perform political or social actions (like "toading," the removal of troublesome characters from the MUD database) are seen as powerful. On EM, as a result of conflicts in 1993, the disciplinarian role that wizards often play was turned over to a committee partly composed of non-wizards, but to a large degree, EM regulars still equate wizardship with a disciplinarian role.

On many adventure MUDs, wizard status is earned by completing quests and winning battles (much as players advance in Dungeons and Dragons games) (Ito 1994). On social MUDs, however, wizard status is conveyed by another wizard, and so hanging out with the wizards and getting in their good books is jokingly advised in Burka 1993. For example, Tom, a founding member of ElseMOO, remembers that he was hacking on a lot of code that needed wizard permissions to install in the summer and fall of 1991 on LambdaMOO; he had been hanging out with the wizard Marie, in a room of hers called Hacker's Heaven, and joked that if she just made him a wizard she wouldn't have to keep installing his code for him. Indeed, the Archwizard soon invited him into his Den and told him Marie wanted to make him a wizard. Tom was surprised, and suggested that the promotion be delayed until after he had finished his college semester, so he'd feel more confident about his programming abilities and have more time. But one night in October, two players were maliciously teleporting other players around (i.e., moving their characters to new rooms). Marie deleted the characters from the database so their users couldn't reconnect. However, she was concerned that they would reconnect as new characters, and wanting to go to sleep, she gave the still-awake Tom a wizard bit so that he could take care of them if they returned. So although Tom's "wizarding" was originally suggested for technical reasons, social concerns brought it about, because of the interrelationship between the technical capabilities of wizards and the social needs of the MUD. Hanging out with the wizards and becoming known as a competent and presumably trustworthy person did, in fact, become a means to wizardhood for Tom.

Wizards' involvement in social matters differs from MUD to MUD, but on a great many MUDs, the technically elite wizards who control MUD resources also handle social problems, either because they are self-appointed governors or because other players come to them for assistance when a problem arises. Their ability to remove offensive players' characters from the database and block requests for new characters that originate from certain Internet sites is a key form of social control on MUDs, the underlying rationalization being "if you can't play by our rules you can't play at all." The "rules," however, are rarely formally recorded anywhere,[14] and wizards are constantly being accused of abusing their powers and making decisions arbitrarily as a result (Reid 1994b). The pressure on active wizards can be intense and lead to burnout, "an unacceptable cost for leisure-time activity" (Burka 1993). Many of the LambdaMOO wizards are now "retired" due to burnout.

One discussion on the mailing list *life-issues[15] on LambdaMOO illustrates the sort of backlash that can occur when wizards make decisions about what constitutes inappropriate behavior on a MUD. A player called Span had been "harassing" other players, and the wizards wanted to prevent him from connecting to the MUD but feared their decision would not be supported by the community. Finally Tom "toaded" him; that is, removed him from the character database with the "@toad" command. Toading is the virtual death sentence; the user can no longer connect to the MUD as that character.[16] And sure enough, this message appeared on the mailing list:

> While I was not particularly fond of span, I do not think he deserved to be toaded. Why? Because the action reeks of censorship, behavior control, intolerance, and paranoia from those on the Moo who have the most power. Span was annoying and verbally aggressive. But, the 'little people' on the Moo had to deal with span in a way somewhat reminiscent of rl [real life]. The 'little people' either stayed away from span, ignored him, locked him out, gagged him, argued against him, or just let him be. Yet the people on the Moo with the most power...perhaps those who interacted with span the least, did not see fit to deal with span in the normal social fashions. Those with the power on the Moo abused that power. Span was toaded because someone important didn't like him and Span said things that were unpopular. (Message 355 on *life-issues)

Another wizard responded sarcastically:

> It has come to my attention that some MOOers are unaware that the

---

[14] Although see http://www.godlike.com/mushman/wiz-ethics.html.

[15] The list name has been disguised at several informants' request. All mailing lists on MOOs are denoted with a preceding asterisk.

[16] Curtis 1992 discusses toading on other MUDs and LambdaMOO in particular. Rather than a simple transformation and limitation of player privileges, as it often means on other types of MUDs, toading on MOOs has come to mean the more severe removal from the database.

wizards sometimes make decisions quickly and which in some cases may be unfair. I apologize to those MOOers for this misconception. The wizards are not trained as judges and laywers and thus will not always be able (or, indeed, willing) to be completely fair. We apologize for the necessity of this. (Message 359 on *life-issues)

Since it is impossible for the wizards to be everywhere at once and intercede in every fracas, the fallback solution is to provide the population with the technical means to avoid unpleasant people and defend themselves, as well as to educate them about what behavior is considered rude or offensive on the MUD. On LambdaMOO, the document known as "help manners" describes community standards of behavior (I include it in Appendix A). Although it was primarily written by the wizards (Curtis 1992), several clauses have been added by the community via the LambdaMOO system of petition and then ballot. Examples of unmannerly behavior include moving other characters without permission, programming that requires a lot of computation (which will slow the MOO down), "spoofing" (producing anonymous utterances), and eavesdropping on others with programmed listening devices or by entering rooms silently (with no entrance message). In the spring of 1994, a clause about sexual harassment was added after lengthy debate about the definition of "netrape"[17] (cf. Dibbell 1993) and assault on the mailing list associated with the petition (see Stivale 1995).

In December 1992, after escalating social stresses that the wizards felt unprepared to handle, the LambdaMOO wizards retired from their social role with the Archwizard's announcement "LambdaMOO Takes a New Direction."

I believe that there is no longer a place here for wizard-mothers, guarding the nest and trying to discipline the chicks for their own good. It is time for the wizards to give up on the 'mother' role and to begin relating to this society as a group of adults with independent motivations and goals.
So, as the last social decision we make for you, and whether or not you independent adults wish it, the wizards are pulling out of the discipline/manners/arbitration business; we're handing the burden and freedom of that role to the society at large. We will no longer be the right people to run to with complaints about one another's behavior. (Message 537 on *life-issues)

With the wizards' retirement from social affairs, there was no formal

---

[17]Contrary to Stone's (1995) claim, the community is well aware of the problematic nature of the term and MUD researchers Pavel Curtis and Amy Bruckman were not the first to examine the use of the metaphor critically.

mechanism for players to resolve their own conflicts, particularly since technical solutions like toading, newting (temporarily preventing the use of a character), and site locks (which prevent anyone from connecting to the MOO from a particular site, such as AOL) weren't available to non-wizards. The celebrated case of Mr_Bungle's abuses and subsequent toading (Dibbell 1993) took place during the interregnum, the gap between control by the wizards and the institution of democracy with a system of petitions and ballots. Mr_Bungle was a character who attacked several other characters with sexually explicit, violent text throughout an evening. The victims requested his toading. TomTraceback, who ultimately toaded Mr_Bungle, says he did so by judging the public sentiment from posts on the *life-issues mailing list to the best of his ability.

Mr_Bungle was toaded April 1, 1993, and in May 1993 the Archwizard created a petition system as a way to establish community consensus on the MOO. The Mr_Bungle incident had established the need for a means to assess community feeling more systematically. Any user may draft a petition, and if sufficient numbers support it, it may become a ballot that all users can vote on. In the summer of 1993, an arbitration system was voted in; any player may invoke a dispute against another (e.g., for unmannerly behavior or perceived wrongs done), and a third party will be appointed to mediate. Disputes have been called against players on LambdaMOO for sexual harassment, for prolonged harassment with obscenity, for teleporting another character around without that player's consent, for shouting MOO-wide to all connected female characters, for misuse of another character's objects. Petitions have been drafted to reduce the lag on the MOO, to reduce the number of characters created, to revise the arbitration system, to institute term limits for members of the Architecture Review Board, which oversees building on the MOO. There has also been the occasional tongue-in-cheek petition, like *p:bat: "This petition proposes that each player be issued a wiffle ball bat (which IRL is a child's toy, a light, hollow plastic bat) with which they can beat other players. If you are beaten frequently enough by enough players, you get newted for a day" (Message 5236 on *life-issues).

The "Power Elite"

The close relationship between technical abilities and social influence on many MUDs is embodied in the notion of a "power elite," a category born on LambdaMOO in 1992. The "power elite," a term that has changed its denotation over time and on different MOOs, is often equated with the wizards who perform wizardly actions on ElseMOO. Some users of the term refer to the group of programmers (some of whom were wizards) on LambdaMOO who were the core of the group that founded ElseMOO. On LambdaMOO, where the term originated, it meant the group of programmers who were friends with the wizards. The concept of a "power elite" has been important to players on the two MUDs and has framed a lot of the political debate and cultural conflicts.

The term "power elite" dates back to the period of LambdaMOO history known as the Schmoo Wars. The Schmoo Wars involved conflict between characters interested in tinysex (or "netsex") and their opponents, a group that became known as the "power elite" (Amende 1993), in the wake of a technical innovation that supported the activity. In a sense, this was a conflict over values: what were the appropriate uses of the MOO? And there was perhaps some anti-newbie sentiment involved as well.

In 1992, Brine, a character on LambdaMOO notorious for his on-line sexual exploits, wrote a player class he called Schmoo, which had various attributes that supported erotic encounters. A player class is a type of character object that a user can choose (in object-oriented programming terms, the user makes the class her character's parent object and thus inherits the functionality of the parent object). The Schmoo characters had commands ("verbs") on them like "**dress**," "**undress**," and "**fondle**." Users of Schmoo characters could write descriptions of their characters clothed and unclothed, and their characters changed state when the proper command was invoked. Other commands were made available, like one that listed the genders of all players connected to the MOO. The Schmoos illustrate how a programmatic change to the environment can become a highly political focus for a MUD community. The users who chose to make their characters Schmoos became an identifiable group on the MOO, defined technically by their adoption of the character class and also symbolically by their conflict with their critics.

The "wars" were fought between the Schmoo players, whom Brine called "the Schmoo Love Cult," and a set Brine labeled the power elite (PE), a group of programmers on the MOO. Amende 1993 notes that the use of such labels intensified the dispute and made individuals with different views appear united when they really weren't. Brine believed that personal animosity on the part of the power elite motivated their dislike of his player class; some apparently found the programming job poor, others thought the netsex motivation behind the Schmoos was silly or even "repulsive." Penfold, one member of the PE, admitted to hating Brine, but also said "that wasn't the issue"; the Schmoos were. To further heat up the conflict, Brine kept lists of who became a Schmoo and who "defected." Schmoos reported "persecution" by hostile anti-

Schmooers and felt they had to "prove that they were interested in more than just netsex" (Amende 1993).

Brine's influence as a leader disappeared when he cracked a wizard bit (i.e., made himself a wizard by exploiting a security hole in the MOO server), crashed the MOO, and was toaded. Someone else took over technical maintenance of the Schmoo player class, and wizards and members of the so-called "power elite" created a way for players to add functionality to their characters without needing to belong to a player class.[18]

The term "power elite" is used in multiple ways—to represent the concept of a controlling group, and to refer to a particular group of people. The term has remained an important one on LambdaMOO and is also important on ElseMOO. Brine's use of the term was apparently originally meant to describe the enemies of Schmoos, whom he saw as wanting "to keep the power amongst themselves" (Amende 1993). The PE were supposedly the programmers who were friends with the wizards. Amende (1993) says,

> The members of the so-called "Power Elite," were all programmers who were friends with the wizards. They did quite a bit of programming, and did large projects that, for the most part, were either enjoyed by the MOO at large, or useful to the wizards in running the MOO technologically. Brine and some of the other Schmoos were quick to grasp the concept that this group of people were "evil" and "slimy"; that they "brownnosed" and "kissed up" to the wizards so that they too would have some power on the MOO. Oftentimes, the members of this Power Elite were approached by new players with programming questions, and although, for the most part the members of this group seemed friendly and willing to help, there were instances where a couple of the Power Elite members would seem rude, or stand-offish, or even condescending to the new player. The stereotype quickly spread that anyone who was caught with these people was actually "snobbish" and "elitist."

Although much of the Schmoo Wars was conducted in real time on LambdaMOO (and therefore is not recorded on mailing lists), a debate about the "power elite" and who they might be did appear on the LambdaMOO mailing list *life-issues. Some LambdaMOO posters in the fall of 1992 saw the power elite primarily as programmers:

> Power Elite is just a synonym for players who have been here a long

---

[18]Players can now make use of "feature objects," which give access to commands like the one the Schmoos used to list characters' genders.

time, so Know Lots About MOO. It's not some secret society of People The Wizards Like. (Message 50 on *life-issues)

Also "power elite" is a real term, it is not a "new" buzzword, it has existed longer than I have been here, and my object number seems to be one of the lower in this group. It refers to the "old" click of programmers who knew everything, and tended to look down on newer programmers for our stupidity [. . .] It is real! But the only ones who really seem to hate them are people who wizzed on other MOOs and asked one (or more) too many questions (I spaced mine out when I used to wiz *grin*) and those who just hate people who are in the "in" crowd. The "power-elite" are generaly nice people, and I am sure you have talked to more than one of them in the Living Room..... (Message 208 on *life-issues)

PE is not a player class. No one has ever given anyone else a power-elite bit. These people are *programmers*. Rather than spending their off hours bitching, they took the time to learn how to do something useful. Consequently, they have become known for their presence in the MOO community and their contributions to it. (Message 405 on *life-issues)

As the last poster above notes, the power elite were not a well-defined group like the Schmoos, since there was no technical delimitation of the group. The ambiguity of the term contributed to the conflict.

Although programming ability was seen by some as a requirement for membership in the power elite, social connection to the wizards was also important, according to other posters. The power elite were people deemed to have influence on the wizards and MOO politics generally, often as "oppressors." The context for the discussion about the power elite on *life-issues was a debate about how to take some social policing responsibility off the wizards: whether to create a subclass of wizard-like people who could help with disruptions, or to create better technical defenses like preventing teleportation and finding ways to silence obnoxious characters. Many people feared that creating a subclass of wizard-like folks would further empower the power elite, the natural choice for sub-wizardship (according to some)[19] to the extent that anyone agreed they existed.

The major concern expressed over this solution deals with class consciousness, and concern about the power elite becoming more en-

---

[19] Recall that "hanging out with the wizards" was believed to be one route to wizard status on social MUDs.

trenched, about the other players becoming more oppressed and feeling that they are second-class citizens on Lambda. This is a valid concern, but I feel the primary problems arise because of bad PR, and because, let's face it, there IS an 'inner circle' of old-timer players who DO have a better chance of being heard by the Powers That Be. (Message 166 on *life-issues)

The Power Elite, a term many people (including I) have been using quite freely, simply refers to a subculture within the MOO community which enjoys an amount of trust from and communication with the wizards. (Message 343 on *life-issues)

Anyone who says that PE is just a synonym for 'good programmer / helpful to comunity' is not thinking things out. There are many good programmers on here who are NOT considered PE [. . .]. Some of those seen as PE are, in fact, good programmers, but have not contributed greatly to the MOO community, at least if counted by useful-object-creation. To inject a little of my own opinions on PE-existence, to me it seems little more than a label for "well-known MOOers who usually align with the wizards." (Message 407 on *life-issues)

The group that I consider PE are newer than #20000, spend massive amounts of time in Hackers' Heaven, kiss wizard-butt, and say things such as "If you don't know how to program, we don't need you on this MOO." (Message 480 on *life-issues)

Several people on *life-issues assumed that the power elite were the wizards themselves, or the Archwizard's friends. Although one person insisted vehemently that they were trustworthy and helped the wizards out, others questioned just how helpful they were, and whether they were favored by the wizards.

You appear to be saying, here, that the wizards will not deal with members of the P.E. who violate help manners. I cannot offer direct witness on this, as I haven't really seen members of the P.E. *do* anything to people. [. . .] Perhaps the reason I haven't seen members of the P.E. abusing others is because that's how they *got* to be members of the P.E. - or on the other hand, because they *are* members of the P.E., they are much more aware of the wizards' power and the wizards' rapid reaction to abuse, and they have more to lose (being high-status P.E.ers) if they do something and get caught. (Message 331 on *life-issues)

I've been here long enough to notice, along with the existence of a power elite, an equally real sense of disempowerment that these people, with no more qualifications than anyone else except, perhaps, more advanced programming skills, friendship with each other, or slightly more seniority, are answerable to no one else. And although it is true that most of the PE become that because they are largely trustworthy, the case of the Exiled 7, (some of whom were friends of mine and, in my mind, did NOT deserve their lockout),[20] made me realize that the lack of due process here can have alarming implications. [. . .] The PE exist because they are "trustworthy?" Trusted by whom? Each other, presumably. Not, necessarily by me, I've seen too many PE-types who should know better being hostile, abusive, and generally rude for no particularly good reason. (Message 341 on *life-issues)

I respect their programming abilities, their contributions to the MOO, and I understand why they may be closer with the wizards. The way they act and treat other players I do not appreciate. I may be generalizing, but each one of the players that I (and most people) consider PE, I have personally seen treat non-PE in a condescending, overly impatient, and sometimes downright insulting manner. And this is when there are no wizards present. In the wizards presence, they behave properly, obeying 'help manners' very carefully. (Message 454 on *life-issues)

One wizard, Tom, apparently confessed to the existence of a PE with special privileged status on the MOO:

Under the current system, all players (except for #2 [the Archwizard] and to varying extents the wizards and the ill-defined Power Elite) have always been on a probationary period. (Message 314 on *life-issues)

Another wizard, Marie, posted her own definition of "power elite" and simultaneously defined a good citizen on the MOO:

Here's my definition of power elite: Someone who is sensitive to people in general, believes in and is willing to stand up for "Help Manners" and ideas of its spirit, technically competent or at least

---

[20]The Exiled 7 were seven characters toaded for abuse or hacking, who were later reinstated during the Amnesty period; further details in Cherny 1995d.

willing to read the help files instead of asking how to get the length of a list, willing to help others (or at least say RTFM) when they ask how to get the length of a list, has high moral standards, avoids taking advantage of people for personal gain, and owns up to errors they may have committed. In short, someone whom I would be proud to call "friend". [. . .] Oh, I nearly forgot. This isn't sufficient; in order to be a Power Elite on LambdaMOO, you must connect sufficiently often to be apprised of important events on LambdaMOO. (Message 338 on *life-issues)

One poster moaned, "People are starting to form little 'Power Elite'/ 'Non-Power Elite' Cliques. When are we gonna start acting like rational adults?" However, a vein of satire ran through the discussion, as is common on LambdaMOO lists.[21] Several people offered joke definitions for the power elite:

Hey, I found a new definition for Power Elite, from my discrete structures textbook:
"Maximal complete subgraph: subgraph of a graph G which is complete and contained in no other maximal complete subgraph of G. Also referred to in sociological applications as a clique." (Message 444 on *life-issues)

---

[21] One excellent example of this phenomenon occurred on the mailing list *p:antirape, when lidda suggested: "This discussion has gotten contentious nigh unto the point of incoherence. I propose that from here on anybody who posts here do so in limerick form if you oppose the ballot, and in haiku if you support it. That way we can at least all be amused, and the flames won't take up more than half a screen or so" (Message 523). The results were hilarious, including these:

From the thorny problem of MOO-rape
There seemed to be no escape
A problem so stinky
Needs a solution that's kinky,
So we bound ourselves up with red tape.
(Message 525)

haiku limerick
lidda's plan is cool except
it gives more space to
(Message 526)

cherry blossoms fall
the goldfish darts in the pond
VOTE YES OR DIE SOON
(Message 529)

So what criteria would people use? Some suggestions:
Player X eligible to be in the Power-Elite if:
================================

1. X is frenchtoast, or anyone who knows frenchtoast, or anyone who knows not to spell frenchtoast with a F. [. . .]
3. X is Brine, or anyone called Brine, or anyone who's pretty shit-hot excellent at MOO-code, but basically not the sort of guy that you'd feel happy to be dating your kid sister. [. . .]
6. X is the sort of person that routinely hangs about in Hacker's Heaven without looking out of place.
7. X is anyone that other players feel they can ask questions of concerning programming or other aspects of LambdaMOO life.
8. X is anyone in the list comprising TomTraceback, BerryBush, Garnet, and anyone else in that gang.
You know the ones I mean, er, yep, anyways... (Message 388 on *life-issues)

Another interesting subtext in some posts was the you-too-can-become-PE message. This vein of argument ironically reinforces the image of the power elite as the "middle classes," as one poster suggested, with its implication that people can work hard and become status-rich via knowledge and good moral qualities.

People get into the PE mainly by being reliable and trustworthy. (Message 331 on *life-issues)

If you don't like the difference between your 'power' and that of a PE, there's a quite simple solution. FTP parcftp.xerox.com and get the MOO programmers manual in /pub/MOO. Learn to program for yourself. And be willing to help others who also want to learn. I have never met a PE who has not been willing to help me as I slowly (and I mean SLOWLY) absorb bits of MOOcode. (Message 405 on *life-issues)

BerryBush (whom many considered "PE" and who later became a wizard himself on LambdaMOO in 1994) recoiled from the call to "disband" and disempower the power elite in some posts, saying, "It's a bunch of FRIENDS, for heaven's sake. It's not a bunch of evil would-be dictators. [. . .] How do you disband a group of friends anyway?" (Message 455 on *life-issues).

Finally, someone decided to do a survey of who players on LambdaMOO thought were power elite, and set up a voting machine in the LambdaMOO Living Room. When the votes were counted, the winners were BerryBush, Penfold, Mike, Ray, George, frenchtoast, and Apple-

Tise; as the creator of the voting machine said, "I don't think any of [them] are going to be surprised by their selection." Several posters who had remarked that they themselves were probably considered power elite did not show up in the top votes. The reporter of the votes only listed the top five slots (there were several ties), making up a rather small "middle class" if the power elite is akin to such a class on the MOO. Penfold, Mike, Ray, and George would later be founding members of ElseMOO. And the power elite would remain a category of some contention, although in a mutated form on ElseMOO.

2.2.4   Some History of ElseMOO

ElseMOO had a brief antecedent, "Distortion," a MOO project that lasted about six months in early 1992. Distortion had ten wizard-hackers, including Tom, Ray, Marie, Mike, Penfold, and Rick, who would later go on to hack on ElseMOO as well. Distortion was described as "technicalinnovationMOO" by Tom, a place to try out ideas for building a better MOO programming environment. LambdaMOO's database had grown by accretion rather than design, and didn't entirely follow an object-oriented philosophy (object-oriented programming is what distinguishes a MOO from other MUDs). The plan behind Distortion was to start fresh and build a new infrastructure. Distortion didn't last very long, however, partly because everyone lacked the time it required.[22]

In October 1992, a handful of talented programmers from LambdaMOO (including the Distortion folks named above) began ElseMOO, with the new goal of making a place for better building and coherent virtual reality design.[23] There is some disagreement about the date but it is "celebrated" as October 31, exactly two years after LambdaMOO began. There were almost a dozen wizards at the start. It was initially open by invitation only, because it was intended as a place for programming projects and MOO core database hacking, according to Tom.

Although Tom and Ray see EM as originally a place to work on building better text-based virtual realities, over time the identity of the MOO became more project-oriented (see chapter 6), as is now described in the document "help purpose":

---

[22]However, it did have a significant effect on MOO conversation patterns generally, since the folks from Distortion believe they invented the commands for directed speech ("lynn [to Tom]:   hi") and thought bubbles ("George .   o O (bleh)"), which have spread to most MOOs. See chapter 3.

[23]LambdaMOO was not feasible as a site for the kind of hacking the founders wanted to do, because by 1992 it supported a large community who wouldn't tolerate the breakages (times when the server was not available) that would be necessary during programming on core objects: parts of the programming infrastructure.

```
The ElseMOO Objective                    October 1993
```

EM is currently a place where a group of people does research and development into information structures, tools for collaboration, and cohesive simulated environments.

That is, we do cool things with networks and hang out on them.

Similarly, the text at the connection screen (see Appendix C) announces, "This isn't a game. It's a place where friends hang out and people work on various projects." Projects at EM include virtual reality design, network interfaces to MOO, improving MOO usability, and designing a structured information source (a hypertext relative called "jtext").

2.2.5 ElseMOO's Theme

The theme of EM's virtual geography is the town in Minnesota where Tom and Ray, who have known each other since childhood, grew up. Both of them have been computer literate since grade school, and both were fans of the text-based adventure games sold by Infocom (such as Zork). For Tom and Ray, the theme commemorates not just a place, but a childhood event. Sometime during junior high (around 1985), Ray was grounded by his parents. Ray played a pretend text-adventure game with Tom from home, over a BBS he had set up, with one of them acting as a player and the other giving made-up game feedback. The theme of the game was as realistic as EM's theme eventually was: Tom pretended to be the grounded Ray trying to sneak out of the house past his father. Ironically, years later, the character "Ray's Dad" would be an occasional visitor on ElseMOO, coming online as a last resort to track down his out-of-town adult son.

When Ray, Tom, and Pete, fellow Minnesotans and hackers on LambdaMOO, decided to start up a new MOO, Ray suggested the Minnesota theme and Ray's house became a central spot in memory of the BBS incident. The geography pays homage to the LambdaMOO antecedence, however. When a player, Kurt in this example, attempts to go "south" in the Living Room, a direction in which there is no exit, the system responds with "Kurt attempts to walk through the plate-glass windows! Fortunately, they're tougher than that," a replica of a message on LambdaMOO. In homage to the text adventure game inspiration felt by so many MUDders, Mike built a section of forest that replicates some scenery from a famous early text adventure game called ADVENT, and George built a small puzzle section. Despite the attempt to be as realistic as possible in EM building, Tom laments how difficult it is to capture real spaces in the simple database format of a MUD, and the realism isn't necessarily appreciated by Else-MOO inhabitants who have never seen the real places. "It's messed up," one player told me; "there are two patios." Real houses may have two patios, but in virtual reality two may seem redundant. Despite the original Minnesota theme, strange structures have grown on the Minnesota landscape, including Mike's House, located on "E. Some Tree Street" because Tom couldn't remember the name of the street when he drew Mike a map to build from;[24] a small quonset hut owned by Lenny; the Church of Etc.; and two habitable fruits in Jeani's kitchen, a pomegranate and a kumquat. The fruits particularly upset people concerned with maintaining the non-magical theme.[25] Despite the fruits, the document "help theme" forlornly insists, "The feel is modern and semi-realistic—there is nothing magical or really anachronistic." Some of the insistence on realism has been a response to the surrealism of LambdaMOO, which has a fairly permissive building environment and character types that include TV characters, vegetables, precious stones, insects, and alien monsters, giving little sense of coherence to the environment.[26]

While the theme may insist on realism, even the realistic parts are not all representations of reality—the footbridge in real life is a plank over a creek, yet on the MUD a popular party spot is the room Under the Footbridge. Although some people have seen the real geography EM is based on, most users don't know to what degree it's real or not; and even the realism in theme can't prevent the MUD-inherent feeling of

---

[24] "I don't remember the name of the street to the south, but it's probably named for some tree," his comment on the map says.

[25] From April 1994:
```
Mike says, "giant fruits."
Mike says, "with people living in them"
George says, "Nice and themely there."
Mike says, "yeah."
George says, "HUMANS DO NOT FIT IN FRUITS"
Mike says, "We've gone around and around about it, she somehow claims
they're themely or somehting."
Mike says, "At one point I suggested that it was all a hallucination, and
you had to take drugs to get in."
Mike says, "and like people outside just saw a bunch of people sitting
around with dazed looks on their faces."
```

[26] One non-MUDder friend of mine who peeked into LambdaMOO said it felt like "Joyce on acid."

"let's pretend" that all users have on MUDs, even if the pretense is of being in a real house in Minnesota. Everyone imagines the scenery very differently, often based less on the actual descriptions given to MUD locales than on their names or remembered subjective experiences. Under the Footbridge, which I imagine as dark, damp, and cold, is imagined otherwise by Karen and Shelley:

```
Karen sees it as shaded, but cool & green & lots of
  water running by to put feet in.
Shelley uses this place she used to ride her bike to
  and sit and read as her image of under the
  footbridge.
Karen doesn't have an image of it, just a feeling
lynn [to Karen]: I'm one who has an unpleasant
  association with it.... i used to think of it
  as the bridge a troll would hide under.
Shelley says, "cuz it was under a footbridge, and
  there was a rock there and the whole bit"
Karen giggles.
Robin doesnt think of it as dark, more shaded,
  covered out of the sun.
```

MUDs, like all texts, exist at the intersection of multiple subjective imaginings.

The EM theme document also states that "All characters on Else-MOO are expected to be humans—there are no space aliens, talking animals, or other creatures frequently found in other domains." A common response to the appearance of non-thematic new characters is the formulaic shout in capitals, "HUMANS ONLY," followed by an explanation of the theme of the MUD. The exchange below, which occurred in November 1994, brought up several philosophical questions about the virtual versus real location of the MUD and the ethnocentric assumptions inherent in descriptions. When you're on a MUD that runs in Newark that models Minnesota, are you in Newark or Minnesota? Should local customs apply to everyone who visits? Most MUDders would claim yes. Dragon came in with the description "A slightly draconic fractal. Or was that fractal dragon?"

```
Mike says, "HUMANS ONLY"
Mike says, "NO DRAGONS"
Dragon peers at Mike.
Mike says, "AT LEAST I'M A HUMAN"
Dragon says, "Actually, it doesn't say so anywhere in
  your description."
```

```
Mike says, "well, when everybody's human, you don't
    need to go around explicitly saying you're
    human"
Dragon says, "You don't?"
Mike says, "but the description generally implies it"
Dragon says, "Then how do you know I'm not human?"
Karen says, "you say you aren't"
Mike says, "because you're a fractal, or a dragon"
Dragon says, "No, my description merely says I'm a
    dragon."
Dragon says, "The chinese concept of a "dragon" does
    not necessarily exclude humanity."
Mike says, "this is minnesota"
Dragon says, "Don't attempt to label me because of
    your eurocentric mythos."
Dragon says, "No, YOU are in minnesota.  I am not,
    necessarily."
Karen says, "you are at EM"
Mike says, "this mud is minnesota"
Karen eyes herself warily.
Dragon glances at Karen, "Oh?  I thought it was in
    Newark."
Mike says, "the machine it's runnign on is in Newark."
Mike says, "the virtual reality is pretending to be in
    minnesota."
Dragon says, "My, you have a surprisingly flexible
    notion of location."
Mike says, "And you're spoiling its pretension."
```

Billock, who is known as a black Labrador dog on LambdaMOO, has an ElseMOO character reminiscent of his LambdaMOO one that maintains the EM human theme: "A large black man from Labrador who loves to play ultimate frisbee."[27] lew, who is a 3-inch "superbunny" on Seashore MUSH, plays a homeless person when he visits EM, wearing a reference to his usual character: "Six feet tall, blond, unshaven. lew is apparently a street person. He wears raggedy tennis shoes, dirty jeans, and a white t-shirt with a rabbit drawn on it in blue Marks-A-Lot (tm)." Mike defends the way theme is upheld: "well, it's not like we @toad non-humans, we just pester them a lot."

The decision to discourage non-human characters was motivated by

---

[27]This, incidentally, is the only racial reference in a description on EM that I know of.

a few concerns. One was a techno-aesthetic one that Ray calls "the Goodyear Blimp problem." Movement in and out of MUD rooms is signaled by exit and entrance messages that are printed on the screens of the players who are occupying rooms adjacent to those exits. The text of the messages is usually written by the creator of the exit, and is fixed. When the means of locomotion is unusual, the predetermined message may be weird or inappropriate. On LambdaMOO, there are a number of "wanderers," autonomous non-player objects that roam around the landscape; one is the Goodyear Blimp. When the Goodyear Blimp "wandered" into Marie's Hairstyling Salon, the message triggered said, "Goodyear Blimp goes to have its hair done," clearly a ludicrous message.[28]

Along with feeling that non-humans weren't technically supported by MOOs, Ray felt that non-humans were rarely role-played well in MUDs, and admits that he "probably mistakenly felt that people interacted more positively when they were talking to players identified as human."

Perhaps because of the realistic geographical theme and humans-only requirement, ElseMOO became a place where many people use their real names (or realistic names, anyway) and make their real email addresses or other information available on nametags their characters carry. The wizards, who emphasize the realistic geography, were the strongest proponents of real names; many other players use their character names from LambdaMOO or other MUDs they frequent. Continuity of characters across MUDs is important for many people. Folks from LambdaMOO who know EM people in that context, but want to fit in with the realism of the theme, occasionally choose to use their real name on EM (or another real-sounding name, as opposed to a fantastical one) and add their LambdaMOO name to their alias list. (The alias list holds other names that can be used to refer to the character; frequently typos or short forms of the name are on it, as well as nicknames and in-joke labels, like "omelettehead," or "GrinningEvilMike."[29]) In my early days on EM and LambdaMOO I spent a lot of time checking people's aliases on EM in order to see who they were in the LambdaMOO political arena.[30]

---

[28] I had a similar problem with a soap bubble object on LambdaMOO that "clambered up" trees.

[29] Ito 1997 discusses titles earned on combat MUDs, which contrast in interesting ways.

[30] Since there was so much overlap between LambdaMOO and EM, at least in early 1994, it was not uncommon for LambdaMOO visitors on EM to assume that everyone on EM was active in LambdaMOO politics. Several people tried hard to place me as someone on LambdaMOO under a different name, not guessing that I was there under the same name and not politically active.

Other character norms are unstated but pervasive. Character descriptions on EM are generally short, often combining physical description with other pithy comments. Hacker cultural references abound. New characters with flirtatious or fantastical descriptions are generally pestered (with intent to discourage) as well. For instance, the humorous description on the new character Buddy, below, did not go over well. (In this example, the lines of text after the **look** command are Buddy's self-description, and the next set of lines are extracts from an ElseMOO discussion of that description.)

```
>look buddy
Quite handsome, with large muscles and a devilish
grin. You can tell he is very intelligent, and
are dying to hang out with him. You can tell he
loves girls with red hair and German beer.

Buddy would like honest opinions on his bogus desc.
lynn hates it actively.
Damon is dying to hang out with you? fuck no, he is
  not
Damon says, "red hair and German beer"
Buddy wonders why... it's a joke.
Damon says, "niiiice"
Jerry thinks it sucks, Buddy.
Bryan says, "red German hairy beer"
Damon holds up a sign reading "1.2"
```

Of course, such criticism does not always go over well. EM has a reputation for being hostile to strangers, which may be due to the regulars' attempts to defend the group identity and cultural norms. In response to the criticism of his description, Buddy responded, "Maybe I should just be my asshole self. I'd fit in here...!" But shortly after this exchange, Buddy stopped coming to EM.

The stress on realism in character identity and description on ElseMOO contrasts with the picture of postmodern identity play on MUDs painted by, for example, Bruckman 1992, Turkle 1996, Allen 1996b. Although these works do not insist that role-playing or complex character construction are norms on MUDs, they focus on aspects of identity play that are not prominent on ElseMOO. Bruckman 1992 and Turkle 1996 both suggest that role-playing on MUDs may be a therapeutic opportunity for identity exploration. They present interviews with MUD users who play characters with different personality types online and who find these useful in exploring aspects of their identities.

Bruckman sees MUDs as "rich psychological play spaces" (p. 22), citing Erikson (1985), who discusses playful situations as safe spaces for self-exploration. Turkle (1996) describes cases in which MUDders felt empowered by their online identity play, and also cases in which the players felt they had wasted their time or reinforced aspects of their personality that they liked the least.

Curtis (1992, p. 8) describes player descriptions on LambdaMOO that he believes contain a degree of wish fulfillment ("I cannot count the number of 'mysterious but unmistakably powerful' figures I have seen wandering around in LambdaMOO"). He notes that despite such character descriptions, most players are not performing a significant amount of role-playing, and says that players appear to tire of such efforts quickly. He speculates that the non-fantastical theme of LambdaMOO doesn't make such character portrayal easy. (Schiano 1997 also notes that most users of LambdaMOO don't use multiple characters or create multiple identities for their characters.) In contrast, social role-playing MUDs like PernMUSH, based on Anne McCaffrey's dragon novels, present contexts and fantastical themes where "in-character" portrayal is the norm.

Another apparent norm on ElseMOO is that the regulars on EM do not play characters of a different gender than their own. Perhaps because everyone treats the MOO as an extension of real life, or because many people have met other players in real life, it would be hard to maintain a gender-swapped character.[31]

2.2.6   Projects on ElseMOO

EM was intended to be an informal research MUD for a bunch of friends interested in developing text-based virtual realities. One of the first projects on EM after it opened in the fall of 1992 was the development of a MOO-gopher, instigated by a researcher named Lenny. MOO-gopher

---

[31]For some interesting discussion of this behavior on other MUDs, see Kendall 1996; McRae 1996; Bruckman 1992, 1993; Curtis 1992; Reid 1994b. Some researchers, e.g., Jacobson (1997), have assumed that it is simply impossible to be sure of the genders of users of MUDs, and have therefore expressed doubts about the validity of much work on gender in MUDs. But in many of the more tightly knit communities, the regular users have either met one another in person or spoken on the phone, or know someone who has first-hand knowledge of other users. Violations of trust and misrepresentation of self have an impact on the community. The processes of ethnography, of becoming a part of a community, meeting people online and face-to-face, hearing their speculations about one another both online and in "real life," all contribute to the researcher's certainty that players are or are not gender-swapping in a particular community. Judging from my research and my conversations with other researchers pursuing MUD ethnography, I believe the incidence of gender-swapping in MUDs is much smaller than one might expect from the amount of literature dedicated to the topic.

allowed people to jointly interact with gopher, an information storage and retrieval service on the Internet, inside a MOO. The MOO-gopher interface is either a MOO room or a portable slate that can be used privately (or collaboratively if it's dropped in a room). Lenny advertised his gopher work on a Usenet gopher group in early 1993. Lenny said in his post, "I thought this was an interesting way of linking the 'interactive community' of MUDding with the 'information retrieval' space that gopher represents. It's interesting watching people in a gopher room help each other find something (and get in each other's way)."

The gopher announcement attracted biologists who were interested in the possibilities of MUDs for collaborative work and information retrieval. Although EM had not advertised an open-door policy, in early 1993 there was an influx of new users. A post on a biology newsgroup applauded the possibilities of MOOs (despite the title "A Cynic looks at MOO") and invited folks to investigate the work at ElseMOO:

Although the MUD/MOO environment was created for games, a number of computer scientists have noticed that the same human interaction that made them so attractive as games could be harnessed for work. Furthermore, the customizability of the MOO lends itself to the modification of the game environment for practical ends. When such modifications are worked out, MOOs promise to provide yet another efficient, low cost way for scientific communication. MOOs could replace scientific meetings!

Meanwhile, as the biologists set up shop, the gopher work led to more successes. Tom, whose small college in Minnesota was considering banning MUDding, was invited by Lenny to co-author a paper on the MOO-gopher work, partly to give his MUDding some research credibility. In February 1993, Lenny came to Minnesota for Gophercon '93 (a conference on gopher applications) and got a tour of the real scenery EM's geography was modeled after. Tom and Lenny gave an impromptu talk about the MOO-gopher and won the "coolest new application of gopher" award, a stuffed gopher. In August 1993, Tom and Lenny presented a paper on MOO-gopher at INET '93, the annual conference of the Internet Society, in San Francisco.

Another network success for EM was in becoming the first MUD on the World Wide Web, January 25, 1993. In June 1993, EM appeared in the "What's New on the WWW" listings of the National Center for Supercomputing Applications: "If you haven't tried it yet, take a look at the Web server running inside [ElseMOO]. See particularly the object browser. (For those unfamiliar with the term, a MOO is a 'consensual text-based virtual reality', aka MUD or Multi-User Dungeon, wherein people interact with one other in a computer-enabled world. Since these systems commonly feature rich and extensible programming environments, it is possible to build Web, Gopher, and other servers (and clients!) directly into the online virtual world.)" During 1994, when I was doing my research, many guests appeared who had wandered in from ElseMOO's Web page, which had been publicized by the NCSA's report.

ElseMOO was running on Ray's machine at Midwest University in early 1993, but a bad experience with a system administrator (who killed the process) made the EM wizards look for more stable options. Karen, a grad student at a Newark university who had found EM via the gopher work, introduced her husband ls, a system administrator at Random Newark University, to EM; he offered the MOO a site. Shortly thereafter the Newark migration began and continued till 1995. Ray, bored at Midwest, moved to RNU in the fall of 1993. Pete went to RNU for graduate school in the winter of 1993, and Tanya, his girlfriend at the time, went with him. George started at RNU in the fall of 1994, and Ted took a job as a system administrator in Newark then too. Unhappy in her minimum-wage computer support position in Tennessee, Shelley moved to Newark in the winter of 1994, where she knew many EM folks already and had more career options. Tom began graduate school at RNU in January 1995. Mike began graduate school in the fall of 1995 at RNU, after a few years working as a programmer in California. Marie has been working in Newark since 1988 as a software engineer. At least a dozen EM regulars are in Newark now, a significant percentage of the roughly sixty regulars on the MUD; most of the Newark folks may also be considered among the "core" regulars, who number about thirty-five and are connected almost every day for several hours.

ls, as well as being a friendly system administrator, was actively interested in using MUDs for computer-supported cooperative work (CSCW); he opened his own MUD for system administrators at RNU in 1993. In connection with a government-funded lab, he started a full-scale computer-supported cooperative work MUD-based project similar to that described in Curtis and Nichols 1993; several EM MUDders worked on the project. Ray is working on another CSCW-MUD project for a company in Newark. Shelley has been developing MUD environments for teaching in. EM itself, with its project orientation, has created something close to an occupational community: "a group of people who consider themselves to be engaged in the same sort of work; whose identity is drawn from the work; who share with one another a set of values, norms and perspectives that apply to but extend beyond work related matters; and whose social relationships meld work and leisure" (Van

Maanen and Barley 1984, p. 287). Unlike most occupational communities, however, EM was self-motivated; hacking has always been both an avocation and an occupation for the programmers involved. Tom, Ray, and Pete reminisced fondly about the hours spent having design and technical discussions at a diner called Perkins in Minnesota during their early college years, illustrating how inseparable their social and technical lives were.

2.2.7 ElseMOO's User Culture

Although ElseMOO was founded by LambdaMOOers, it maintained a strong identity of its own, distinct from the culture on LambdaMOO. In this section, I discuss some of the ways in which the MUD was used on a daily basis, including what users reported they liked or didn't like about EM. The mundane daily life of users and their characters on EM was as much (or more) a part of the culture as were the historical incidents I discuss in later chapters. Some of the issues that were important to EM users during everyday use of the MUD centered on conversation: size of the group, quality and type of conversation, attitudes toward public versus private conversations.

What Do People Like Here?

Several recurrent themes emerged from my 1994 survey of EM regulars regarding their likes and dislikes about EM. I also gleaned some helpful insights about responses to the MOO culture from a public discussion independently started by Karen on the ElseMOO mailing list *chitchat in 1995.

A few women explicitly mentioned liking the harassment-free environment, with no players seeking netsex encounters and conversations that did not feature sexually suggestive jokes. EM has a documented policy of not tolerating sexual harassment at all; guests who make suggestive remarks are booted. The document outlining acceptable behavior on the MOO, "help manners," says, "Harrassment of other players will not be tolerated. Emoted violence and obscenities are considered inappropriate in the social context of EM. [. . .] It isn't reasonable to ':kiss' or ':hug' folks you don't know."[32]

Other people mentioned liking the adherence to theme in the geographical design: "I like that the MOO hasn't grown exponentially. I like that most if not all of the rooms are part of some designed in topological interesting-ness. I think Karen said it first and Brine echoed it and I'm gonna say it again. Stuff here isn't just thrown up, it's designed and

---

[32]The notorious "netrape" incident described in Dibbell 1993, which involved friends of EM users, as well as other less publicized incidents, contributed to this policy.

engeneered for fun and pride. People build parks that are *used*. People are getting things done here." The limited programmer policy bothered a few people, however, and one suggested relaxing it and having an area open for people to build in.

To a lot of people, the "maturity" and general intelligence of EM residents makes the place attractive. The fact that EM is perceived as "elitist" by both insiders to the community and outsiders was a plus for some and a minus for others: "people who go out of their way to be jerks on a regular basis get kicked off"; "we're evilly elitist so we can throw out annoying guests without fear of retribution"; "NO NITWITS/MORONS/SCHMUCKS/etc... or at least less of them"; "Unfortunately, there is a definite sense of elitism here, which still exists despite recent gradual improvements. EM [. . .] deserves its ivory tower reputation, but that's another reason I like it—I get to hang out with the Virtualeratti"; "I don't like the antisocial attitude we all have. It scared off my favorite MOO pal from here"; "Sometimes I don't like the way people are treated; but I'm as much a perpetrator as anyone. (There's a real harsh attitude against people who don't behave exactly in the same rigid social patterns that others do)"; "Outsiders see Else as a sterile, cold, elite hangout for extremely technical people who don't care about other people. I see Else as a warm, valuable, intelligent, engeneered work/play area. People come here to relax and learn and the marks they leave are consistently positive." Several people felt that EM suffered from excessive "clubbishness" or "cliquishness," especially on the part of the "old-timers."

A large number of survey respondents commented on the technical knowledge of the EM residents, saying for the most part that it was a place to learn, "clue-dense," and for one, "my primary tech support line." A few people complained that the geek talk went over their heads or was occasionally annoying.

The EM linguistic culture was mentioned several times. One woman told me she finds group humor fun, mentioning routines (e.g., roll calls, see chapter 3) and conventional utterances in particular (although those are my technical terms for the speech behaviors she described). Another said, "Perhaps the thing that made me hang out in the first place [. . .] is that I'm fascinated/entertained by the culture ... the rituals, the in-house humor, the language play." She elaborated on the play: "the unexpectedness, the mutability, the constant shifting [. . .] language play taking off from a mundane remark or typo or misreading." She provided an example of such play (which may not be particular to EM, but is representative of some interactions she finds fun). This example includes several discourse phenomena I discuss in chapter 3, including "null-emotes" (line 2), the "**eye**" command (lines 3, 8), and byplay emotes (line 14):

```
1  lynn says, "what brings you two to EM?"
2  Shelley
3  Shelley eyes herself warily.
4  Conner [to Shelley]: So, what's up with that?  Why
   did you do?
5  lynn says, "Yes, Shelley is a big crowd drawer."
6  Mike says, "SHELLEY HAS BIG DRAWERS"
7  Mike says, "oh"
8  Severn eyes Mike warily.
9  Shelley | !. lynn says, "Yes, Shelley is a big
   crowded drawer."
10 Conner read that as "Yes, Shelley is a big clown
   drawer."
11 Shelley says, "oh cripes"
12 lynn hehs.
13 Conner is obsessed with clowns, and, well, Shelley.
14 Conner hands Shelley floppy shoes.
```

On MUDs (and indeed on other parts of the Internet), textual interactions are often quite different from the sorts of verbal interactions people encounter or expect face-to-face. This fact may lead the visitor to conclude that they are entirely escapes from real-world norms and conventions, rather than places with their own norms. Many MUD speech activities have evolved to express community membership and to play within the medium's affordances. Verbal play, despite being play, is still communicative and often has a serious effect on interpersonal relationships, however. On EM, people hug and "whuggle" (a virtual interaction similar to a hug, see chapter 3), playfully drop nuclear bombs on each other, set each other on fire. These colorful actions have real impacts on their relationships. MUD actions are often symbolic expressions of meaning, some more bleached and routinized than others: a MUD "hug" is something close to a real-life hug, although more virtual hugs occur between people in EM than between those people face-to-face; while "accidentally setting someone on fire" in EM, a ritual utterance, is usually intended humorously but may be used to indicate affection or mark that some relationship exists between the two players.

Not everyone was happy with EM, and some people quit coming there. It is overwhelmingly easy for a quiet player who doesn't come often to disappear without being missed, having hardly made any impact on the regulars at all. Jones 1995 questioned what commitments people have to one another in virtual communities; the disappearance of players can sometimes go unnoticed for a long time. Occasionally a regular also stops coming to EM. Ted quit coming because he found himself fed up with MUDding and the social situation on EM: "I was spending too much time online in general and it was causing me to be irritable and I left because the time spent online was becoming less and less interesting and fun. [. . .] I would actually get *extremely* angry at certain people and aquire a very pissy and annoyed attitude. I had lost any interest in being open minded during a conflict. It went from 'Well, OK, I may be wrong about this, let's see what he/she has to say...' to 'Holy *christ* this person is stupid. WHY do I even bother coming here anymore. I hate most of these idiots.' It was a point in EM's history where there were a lot of newbies coming around, and my sense of territory was being perturbed." He later came back to EM, and remains ambivalent about the place and his reasons for MUDding: "I came back to EM [. . .] because it was something to do when I got really bored (which at that time in my life, was very often). I simply gave it a rest for awhile and decided it was the only steady thing that was available to do when bored stiff. As much as I want to say that I didn't come back because I missed anyone there, I'm pretty sure there were a few people I wanted to talk to."

Other folks have left EM because of loss of Net access, or some change in lifestyle that is dramatic enough to make them quit MUDding for a time. Ellen rarely MUDs much anymore because she is now married to Kurt, whom she became close to during the Mouldy Couch Club days, which I discuss in chapter 6; real life has superseded MUDding somewhat. She also has no Net access from work. She admits to missing her friends on EM.

Daily Conversation

To a visitor on a MUD, conversation appears to be the main occupation of the regulars. Certainly programming, writing mail to mailing lists, and exploring geography or playing with programmed toys are part of many people's MOO experience, but real-time conversation is definitely a central component for most players. Topics discussed in parties I was in during my research included novels, Web page design, the date rape policy at Bryn Mawr, body piercings,[33] S&M, films, food (recipes are occasionally exchanged), comics, Star Trek, Unix system se-

---

[33]Several EM regulars have piercings.

curity, programming by demonstration, AI, bots in MUDs,[34] gif images of MUDders posted on the Net, posts on LambdaMOO mailing lists, income taxes, idiot bosses, idiot users, core hacking, job interviews, music recommendations, how rude player X is, whether the Community Group can be overridden by the Steering Committee, visiting Seattle, how Karen and Penfold met in Chicago's O'Hare airport, newbie behavior, the piles of snow outside, cats with pedigrees and without, kitten antics, industrial MUD projects, articles about MUDs, MUDding too much, anti-depressants, Netrek, Doom, Myst, bad graduate advisors, meeting MUDders on conference trips, mediation on LambdaMOO, guest booting, ColdMUD development, role-playing MUDs, and cultural differences between LambdaMOO and EM.

One woman told me she likes "intellectually stimulating parties. So I like it when smart people who are interested in vaguely the same sorts of things I'm interested in are all hanging out. Even if they're chatting about packing for their move to New York, some interesting tidbit always comes out about the geologic properties of the place, or internet connectivity en route, or whatever. Stuff that I find fun and interesting." Another EM regular commented on how he is both entertained and informed by MUD conversation: "When I mud during the day, I'm MUDding from work, and usually use mud conversation as an escape from work, something to do while I'm waiting for a compile or when I'm stuck on a problem. In this mode, I usually value it as a source of entertainment, although I often can get information from it as well, not only things like help with programming problems but also things like what's happening in the world (I don't read a newspaper or watch the news on TV, so muds are my primary source of news about current events) or just what's happening in my friends' lives."

Along with the usual daily interactions, there are occasionally special events on EM. Tom wrote a program that allows text-based adventure games to be played on EM, with multiple participants, rendering the traditionally single-player games multiplayer. Although too many collaborators can make the game confusing, watching the play is fun. In the summer of 1994, a series of "programming picnics" were organized for Sunday afternoons, at which MOO projects could be worked on and discussed. Two holidays are informally celebrated on EM, April Fool's Day and Christmas. On April Fool's Day, 1994, players spontaneously reversed the spellings of their characters' names. On April Fool's Day,

---

[34] "Bots" are robots, in this case small programs, that operate autonomously, used either for simple functions like mapping, dispensing MUD currency, and taking messages, or as non-player characters in combat MUDs (Smith 1995).

1995, players connected to discover themselves inside the fish tank in the EM Living Room, with Karen's MOO kittens transformed into catfish. For Christmas, 1994, Shelley made a Santa who would take Christmas wishes from people, which was immensely popular.

More mundanely, people occasionally MUD together while watching TV, creating a social situation out of a solitary one. The practice of MUDding from work, with the MUD connection in one window or buffer and a programming project or other work in another, serves a similar function. People often narrate their real-life actions as they perform them (see chapter 5). Occasionally people MUD from the same physical location and narrate what others are doing (Newark MUDders manage this since so many are associated with the same university). Exchanging Web URLs and looking at them in real time together is another popular activity. Discussion of programming problems is of course a very frequent use of the MUD. EM has a reputation as a good place to go to ask technical questions, particularly questions about the MOO programming language.

"Parties"

EM is used on a daily basis to chat and program on. Most users connect, list who is on the MUD and where they are, and join a "party," a group of people talking. Some users connect and pick somewhere quiet to idle. By using a login watcher to see who connects, one can keep track of friends, perhaps page them hello when they connect. Idle people are usually working in real life, but will later read the text of MUD conversation stored in their buffer. In mid-1995 there were complaints that EM was "IdleMOO," because often more people were idle than active. Despite such complaints, maintaining a presence on the MOO, even if mostly idle, is important to a lot of people.

Some people prefer large, active parties while others prefer smaller groups and quieter conversation. MUDding styles differ, and frequently the people who have their attention divided while MUDding (because they are at work, for instance) are less keen on large parties, where the conversation moves quickly. Quickly moving conversation is sometimes considered "spam," not in the current sense of junk email but in the broader (original) sense of garbage text or online noise. Samples of people's opinions on parties and smaller groups from surveys I conducted in MOOmail show that people find the experiences of different-size groups qualitatively different: "My favorite are usually smaller parties with more intelligent conversation about something specific, rather than just random chatter. Although a massive spammy party can kinda be fun at times too." Recognition of idle behaviors also affects the experience of group sizes: "I like parties, because on EM that's the only way you can guarantee continual conversation, or that someone will always be listening to my ranting"; "I guess my favorite group size is four or five. Fewer than that and it devolves into an idle party. More and it acquires a moron whose wit is less than adequate." Some people have definite dislikes for larger groups: "I don't like parties; I increasingly find the signal to noise ratio getting worse and worse. The only time I like them is when I'm in a really silly spammy mood and need to relax, in which case it's nice that you can say almost any stupid word play thing and it will fit in. I still like that best when it's with the oldtimers, though— Pete, George, Tom, Penfold, etc."; "I avoid parties when I'm at work cuz I usually don't have the bandwidth to spare on them, and when there is someone that I generally talk to specifically, party conversation just gets in the way. Plus I hate people." (This last remark is probably mostly a joke.)

Almost anyone is welcome in a party situation, but joining a small group requires some confidence that your presence will be welcome: "I prefer groups of people and 'parties' is almost always the first command I type when I log on. I find them to be more comfortable because I don't have to know the people as well as I do when it's a small group." The "**parties**" command shows a formatted list of the groups on the MOO:

```
West patio --- 3 seconds idle, 8 people (3 idle):
   lynn, Shawn, Egypt, Border, and Marie (and
   Honda, Scott, and Ray)
Tennis courts --- 14 minutes idle, 2 people (both
   idle): (Brillo and Jon)
Patio --- 20 minutes idle, 2 people (both idle):
   (Hilary and Sandy)
Ray's sunroom --- an hour idle, 2 people (both idle):
   (Pete and Lenny)
4 parties found.
```

The Living Room is the standard party spot on EM, but other places may host impromptu parties that have accreted from smaller gatherings of people trying to avoid the big group or just talk quietly with friends. Ray has joked that there are three types of parties on EM: the Living Room, not-the-Living-Room, and about-to-become-the-Living-Room. Ray's "not-the-Living-Room" descriptor is apt because often people specifically avoid the current party place, for instance if they are trying to remain idle while they are working or doing something else offline. At any point, however, "not-the-Living-Room" may become "about-to-become-the-Living-Room" if someone joins someone who is

People in 2 party spots, 3 June 1994

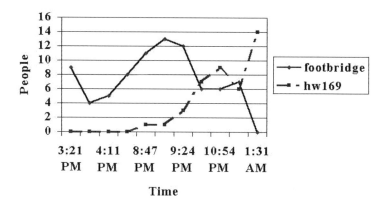

FIGURE 2 Number of users in two "party" spots

alone. Curtis 1992 refers to "social gravity," the phenomenon of people drawing more people in a MUD. Two people alone together are often assumed to be having a private conversation (particularly if they are a mixed-gender pair), and often someone wanting to join will page first to see if joining is acceptable; but once three are gathered, the seeds for a party are there, and other people will join with no warning. Sleep called such gatherings "flash parties" after Larry Niven's term "flash crowd," coined in one of his science fiction stories.

Figure 2 shows the activity in two ElseMOO rooms from midafternoon to late in the evening. For most of the day, Under the Footbridge was the main party spot ("the Living Room") but by evening an alternative party spot, Highway 169, had developed. By the time I disconnected at 1 a.m., Highway 169 was the new hot spot. In fact, it was the group of me, Tom, and Ray actively chatting in Highway 169, and the fact that fully half of the occupants of Under the Footbridge were idle around 9 p.m., that resulted in Highway 169 looking appealing. By 10:00 p.m., all of the active people from Under the Footbridge had joined the Highway party (Figure 2 only shows total occupants, not idle vs. active occupants). And by 10:00 p.m., Tom and I had left the Highway party, and Ray had fallen idle.

"Spam" is a highly subjective term, and party conversation that appears witty and fun to one person is annoying spam to another (Marvin 1995). Tom and other old-timers occasionally wondered if a "lambdafication" of EM was occurring, in which tetchy old-timers avoided newbie parties deemed "spammy" in favor of private quiet conversation with a few friends. On LambdaMOO, small groups may meet in locked rooms, but on EM, with few private or lockable rooms, an endless social tide results, as people flee from parties that accrete around them. (Tom used to notice the sudden growth of a group around him, announce "flash party," and then leave suddenly, occasionally disconcerting friends like Ray who wanted to speak to him; Ray told me he often didn't notice a party had become spammy until Tom left.) Another means of avoiding some of the spam that develops in parties is by aggressive gagging of individuals (or gagging of objects on which commands reside, like the Antisocial Feature I discuss in chapter 3). The "**gag**" command allows a user to filter out utterances from specific people, effectively rendering them invisible. (Use of this command is ordinarily undetectable to the person "gagged," but variations have been tried that alert the audience and/or the gaggee.) The subsequent creation of a command to list the players most often gagged on EM caused definite unhappiness for a time; while it's usually unclear whether someone's departure from a party is due to your conversation or some other need (like real-life distraction), it's harder to overlook the fact that you are being routinely gagged by ten people you thought you were hanging out with.

On EM, with few private rooms, the public geography gets appropriated by individuals and places become associated with them. Shelley idled in the laundry room in Ray's house; Penfold used the space Under the Footbridge. People who built their own rooms (usually because they were wizards, or part of the early MOO design group) used those (ls's Skate Shop, Rick's dead room). A few lockable rooms have been created, since the need for truly private conversation does arise. Two-person private conversation is possible with "whispers" or "pages" (discussed below), but sometimes people prefer to "talk out loud" or include more people yet still retain privacy. The Church of Etc. is a lockable room (the lock was created by Mike, for a private conversation with me). But the politics of using a locked room for a private party on EM are delicate; if someone knocks on the door, an occupant runs the risk of being seen as unfriendly or exclusionary if she doesn't let the knocker into the private party. In September 1994, a reporter came to interview Ray about the history of EM, and a party gathered around them. Most people were listening to the conversation and adding to it, but some of those present were offering off-topic commentary on their real-life work tribulations or making other non sequiturs. In an attempt to avoid this spammy distraction, the people concerned with the interview moved to the Church, but everyone else followed and was allowed into the room, rendering the move and lockable door useless.

Use of Whispers, Pages, Asides

As I discussed above, the geography of the MUD is used to restrict and control access to conversation, although there are few means to enforce this on EM because of the lack of lockable rooms. Players join attractive parties and leave spammy ones; when they flee crowds, smaller groups accrete around them. There are two other ways to control access to conversation: "pages" and "whispers" allow private exchanges between two players on the same MUD.

A whisper is a private comment to another character in the same room. People may whisper to express irritation or make a private joke during a public conversation, or to carry on a parallel private conversation. On ElseMOO, the etiquette for whispering is complex: players whispering usually have to be on fairly friendly terms, otherwise the whispering feels inappropriately imposing, as if it were an attempt to create greater intimacy than is wanted. Guests who attempt to whisper are generally asked to speak out loud.[35] Prolonged whispering makes some people uncomfortable because it can be inferred that it's occurring if the public conversation lags and someone checks whether the room occupants are idle; active but silent characters are often concluded to be whispering (or paging someone in another room). Some players deem it rude or exclusionary.[36]

Paging, a private conversation mode between two players who are not in the same MUD room, is also very common on EM. Paging is a particularly good way to keep a relationship hidden, since two characters do not betray their interaction by being in the same room (see Cherny 1995c for discussion of whether paging threatens the virtual geography metaphor). For some people, there is a difference between whispering and paging: you don't have to be on as familiar terms with someone to whisper with them as you do to page, since whispers are often comments on conversation going on in the room. Paging requires starting a new conversation with someone elsewhere, stepping out of the room-as-common-context metaphor on the MUD. Paging is therefore more of an imposition.

It took me a month or two of regular MUDding on EM to discover

---

[35] From "help manners": "speak out loud to people you don't know, rather than paging or whispering."

[36] One exclusionary command available on Seashore MUSH (but not EM) is "**mutter**," which all but one specified player sees, allowing players to exchange remarks about an excluded other.

how prevalent whispering and paging are. Much of the MOO's interpersonal drama and gossip occurred in these undetectable modes, as I discuss in chapter 6. An observer who was not a participant on the MUD would not realize this.

Less common but still related, "asides" are exchanges between any number of players "multi-MUDding": comments about events on another MUD they are simultaneously connected to. Multi-MUDding on ElseMOO was fairly common; users may connect to more than one MUD at a time, paying split attention to several buffers.[37] Although some players see pages and whispers as "non-VR" because they have no real-world analog (since they allow unobservable private conversation), the facilities are regularly used on MUDs. I haven't heard the practice of multi-MUDding and aside-making criticized in these terms, perhaps because the facility lies in the capabilities of the computer and the client program, rather than the embedded virtual world's design.

EM folks used to "crash" a party on another MUD occasionally and use the EM buffer to make comments about the activity on the other MUD. The word "asideMOO" (which may have originated on Distortion, EM's predecessor) is used by some EM folks to refer to a MOO one uses to make comments (asides) on another concurrent MUD conversation. One of the most hilarious examples of this occurred one day in February 1994 when a group of EM folks went to the LambdaMOO Coat Closet (the initial connection point on LambdaMOO), where a bunch of guests were trying to pick each other up. BerryBush, who was visiting on EM, brought his character FabulouslySexyBimbo into the Closet to impress them. We laughed on EM over their attempts to get to know "her" and each other.[38]

Mailing Lists

The facility for asynchronous conversation is an important one for both LambdaMOO and ElseMOO politics. It also provides yet another way for users to experience some MOO communities: posting on and reading

---

[37]Schiano (1997) does not find evidence of significant experience with other MUDs among the subset of the LambdaMOO population that she studied. LambdaMOO's population as a whole is significantly different from that of ElseMOO, because LambdaMOO was often publicized, making it readily accessible to first-time MUDders, while ElseMOO was relatively difficult to find. The ElseMOO population for the most part had experience on other MUDs and many of them started on LambdaMOO. To find ElseMOO at all, MUDders would have to hear about it from a friend or find the Web page.

[38]It's a truism among MUDders that a sexy female character is probably not operated by a female user (Bruckman 1993; Smith 1995; Kendall 1996).

mailing lists. A significant amount of ElseMOO conversation was about mailing-list activity on LambdaMOO. The facility for mailing lists was added to LambdaMOO in 1991, and ElseMOO always had them, although they were less active given the difference in size and political process on ElseMOO. On LambdaMOO, the MOO-internal mailing lists are the main site of activity associated with the democratic process and disputes between players: lists are associated with all petitions, ballots, and disputes. Mailing lists are also dedicated to a large numbers of more general social topics, from *life-issues to *bay-area-mooers to *smut to *literature to meta-lists like *best-of-lists. Following the traffic on even a small number of lists can be a full-time pursuit; *life-issues, for instance, often produces twenty to forty messages a day.

As Watson (1997) comments, the posters on newsgroups—and MOO mailing lists—are often seen as representative of the group as a whole, perhaps erroneously. He estimates 3300 posters out of an audience of 50,000 reading the music fan newsgroup he studied. Nevertheless, those posters are taken as representative and have had an impact on "real-world" concert policies because they are seen as representative of the online group as well as offline fans.[39] On LambdaMOO, posts on a mailing list were instrumental in influencing a wizard's decision to toad one notorious abusive character. As I discussed earlier, TomTraceback decided to toad Mr_Bungle based on his reading of public opinion as expressed on the mailing list *life-issues.

The difficulty of gauging opinion accurately from a mailing list is one reason the petition and ballot system was created shortly thereafter. However, mailing lists remain a critical part of the democratic infrastructure. Asynchronous communication in the MOO (mailing lists and personal mail) makes it possible for political action (and other interest-oriented discussion) to go on without anyone missing it through not being connected at the right time. Important meetings still occur in real-time synchronous mode, such as discussions between mediators and disputants, but for a population the size of LambdaMOO's (six thousand characters registered as of March 1994), "town meetings" of all interested parties would be impossible. Campaigning for ballots and petitions (and for membership on the Architecture Review Board) does

---

[39]I use quotes from posts on mailing lists to support my own generalizations about the communities because the mailing lists provide the only record of many events and cultural attitudes. It is true that some very large number of LambdaMOO players pay no attention to the mailing lists, neither reading nor posting. Their experience of the MOO is as a real-time interactive space, and I have no access to their responses to or involvement in politics on the MOO for most events.

still occur in real time; the Living Room on LambdaMOO is a popular site for political conversation.

Contrary to arguments in Kiesler, Siegel, and McGuire 1984 that CMC allows more voices to speak, mailing lists on LambdaMOO are dominated by a few individuals. This fact is also noted in Watson 1997; the highest-volume posters are seen as taking up more than their share of space and "bandwidth" on the newsgroup he studied. Similar findings about domination of the group by a posting minority have been reported in Sutton 1996 and Herring 1993, among others. To verify my sense that certain voices dominated some lists, I calculated some statistics for participation on the *life-issues list on LambdaMOO for the period from September 15, 1994, to December 31, 1994, as shown in Table 2. 1501 messages were posted, by 182 characters using 233 character names (many characters have the ability to change or "morph" to another name and appearance at a single command). There were five high-volume posters, amounting to 35.5% of the total words and 353 messages. The highest-volume poster (Dawn) was over twice as prolific as the next highest (TQ).

TABLE 2 Highest volume posters on LambdaMOO *life-issues

Poster	Words	Percent of Total Words	Messages
Dawn	26232	13.8%	107
TQ	11496	6%	63
Mouse	10672	5.6%	64
Fooey	9875	5.2%	60
Mutey	8770	4.6%	59
Brine	3798	2%	58

Certainly, on LambdaMOO many players recognized the disproportionately high volume of posts from certain players:

Dawn demands more than her fair share of our attention here perhaps, but I am a lot more worried by the demagoguery of Fooey or Mouse. (Message 5234 on *life-issues)

A petition (*p:pace) was drafted by Mouse in November 1994 to address the problem (he was fully aware that it would limit him as well): "The overall aim of this petition is to encourage more thought between posts, and to permit those who don't log in as often or type as fast to get a word in edgewise." The petition didn't reach ballot because it failed to garner enough support.

It was my impression that many of the LambdaMOO veterans who founded ElseMOO spent far less time socializing on LambdaMOO in public rooms during 1994 and far more time reading political lists (or *life-issues) and dispute lists instead. This may have been partly due to the perception that the newbies flooding the MOO were spammy and uninteresting, as well as the fact that their friends were no longer hanging out regularly in public. Private parties in locked rooms or paged conversations happened occasionally. Even newer LambdaMOO users admitted to a similar evolution of use on LambdaMOO:

> At first, I experimented with The Living Room, then the Hot Tub (Thanks, Marie!), then spoofing (I still get a kick out of spoofing...), then moosex, and then, I discovered *life-issues. I rarely leave my room anymore, unless one of my RL friends is on here and wants me to @join em. I love the mailing lists [. . .] but I always look forward to *life. I look forward to the different petitions and ballots that *life talks about and I love reading the mailing lists on them. (Message 5223 on *life-issues)

One woman on EM told me, "At LM, I sometimes get together with my close friends, and we chat quietly. Often, I read mail—part of the pleasure I derive from MOOing involves watching the flux and movement of that indefinable 'social ambiance' that is painted by the largest mail lists." Another says he just uses LambdaMOO for "mailing lists and looking at interesting objects" other people have built in MOO code— in other words, as a browsable database rather than a site for interaction with other users directly.

2.3 Conclusion

From the beginning, different MUDs had different goals, cultures, and behavioral norms. Early TinyMUDs faced the same conflicts over geography and building that the more recent MOO communities of LambdaMOO and ElseMOO have faced: unconstrained building can lead to confusing geography and database bloat, as well as threatening the theme of the MUD. Early TinyMUDs also experimented with different systems of government and more or less explicit social contracts for player behavior, but many details have been lost because of the lack of records. Existing records (generally informal histories by participants) tell us that areas of contention on early TinyMUDs included newbie behavior, the pursuit of tinysex, and "furry" role-playing. It's also clear that MUD communities sometimes span multiple MUDs, and MUD users participate in multiple communities. The Seashore community has remained a fairly consistent group over the lifespan of at least seven MUDs.

ElseMOO, the site of my research, was founded in 1992 by several active LambdaMOO users. Many EM users remained active on LambdaMOO during my research, and the political dramas on LambdaMOO were a regular topic of conversation. Despite this close relationship, the two MOOs differed in several important respects: size, political infrastructure, attitudes toward programming and building. ElseMOO was significantly smaller than LambdaMOO, with around thirty people connected daily, in contrast to the hundred or more connected to LambdaMOO. LambdaMOO also had a huge number of registered characters, partly due to the publicity it received in the popular press. ElseMOO was run by small committees (the Steering Committee and the Community Group), while LambdaMOO offered a baroque system of ballots, petitions, and mediation of disputes between players. Much of LambdaMOO's political activity occurred on mailing lists internal to the MOO database, and browsing these lists was a regular pastime for many ElseMOOers. A recurrent debate on one of the popular LambdaMOO mailing lists centered on whether there was an identifiable group of privileged MOOers on LambdaMOO, a "power elite." The members of this group, if it existed, were thought to be friends of the wizards, good programmers, occasionally arrogant, and wielding power on the MOO. Several LambdaMOO users who may have been "power elite" were founding members of ElseMOO, and several wizards from LambdaMOO were active members of the ElseMOO community. ElseMOO has a reputation as a technically sophisticated community, as well as exclusionary and elitist. As I discuss in chapter 6, ElseMOO's reputation was sometimes painful for ElseMOO regulars as well as outsiders.

While LambdaMOO allowed a good deal of building and programming, ElseMOO had a much more restrictive policy, and most users never programmed or built additions to the MOO geography. Nevertheless, technical discussions were common and it was known as a place where good MOO programmers hung out. Because few users had private MOO rooms, most private conversations occurred in two-person paged conversations rather than in private, locked rooms as is common on some other MUDs. Certain individuals, in particular some of the founding programmers, did have their own private rooms, however. There was undeniably a class difference of sorts based on character age, programming permissions, and technical abilities.

Other important facets of the ElseMOO community include the emphasis on the use of human characters (rather than role-playing animals or other fantastical figures) and the sedate suburban geography described in the virtual landscape. Not only did most users have human characters, but a significant percentage of users had characters based on their real lives and were not role-playing or attempting to disguise their identities. As far as I know, none of the regulars were gender-swapping.

Many of them had met face-to-face at conferences or when visiting other towns. Several of them were in fact involved in romantic relationships with partners they had met on ElseMOO or another MUD. ElseMOO was a part of real life for most of its regular users, not an escapist fantasy world.

3

Features of the MUD Register

Damon says, "anyone who doesn't think we speak some strange separate dialect has been smoking crack."

As I discussed in chapter 1, mediated communication situations may give rise to particular registers, or language varieties adapted to the situation of use, which may also mark insider status in a community. That the ElseMOO community sees itself as possessing a particular linguistic repertoire is illustrated by the fact that in 1994 they made an attempt to document their "jargon" and in-jokes.[1] This attempt was met with some criticism by a few insiders; Henry, for instance, complained, "What good is it having personality if you're just going to explain it to everyone? People don't walk around with books about themselves saying 'This is the slang I use, these are my mannerisms, this is how I act.' Part of getting to know a person or place is learning all these things about them. By handing anyone who wants it a complete list of everything that makes EM unique you're threatening the uniqueness. [. . .] I can see explaining some things..like obscure acronyms and such..but coming out and explaining ROLL CALL and loses and things like that..little inside jokes and personality traits of EM..is just silly, in my opinion."

Ferrara, Brunner, and Whittemore (1991) suggested that computer-mediated communication, because it is written, may be related to the note-taking register, but may also show similarities with the mediated IART (amateur radio) and CB registers in that it is more or less interactive. Ferrara, Brunner, and Whittemore's data on CMC showed similarities to the note-taking register (Janda 1985) and sports commentary in the kinds of simplifications used. Unstressed pronouns, articles, and finite copulae were omitted. Subject phrases were also regularly dropped.

---

[1] The documentation project never went very far, unfortunately.

Their data also showed creative spellings involving fewer keystrokes, e.g., "nite" for "night," clippings like "info" for "information," and the use of symbols in place of words, e.g., "&" for "and." These shortenings and simplifications were apparently produced to speed up communication.

Missing from the Ferrara, Brunner, and Whittemore study, however, is a convincing analysis of the speakers as a speech community, since their data was gathered in a laboratory experiment.[2] In this chapter I look at the features of language use in ElseMOO, both as responses to the medium and as indicators of community membership. Primarily I focus on syntactic, morphological, and lexical patterns, as well as routines (Coulmas 1981) and conventionalized utterances. The history of the community and contact with other MUD communities provide inspiration for many of the conventional or ritual expressions; Seashore MUSH, the current home of the "Random and Moira gang," is particularly influential on the ElseMOO community, because the memberships overlap. Furthermore, the programmability of the MUD environment both affects and reflects the discourse practices of the community.

3.1 Syntactic and Morphological Phenomena

There are several types of syntactic and morphological phenomena in the MUD register of the EM community, including verb formation, deletion of prepositions and copulae, limited reduplication, and reduction of words to contracted forms in formulaic utterances. Most of these occur in fairly limited environments, or quickly become associated with particular words or types of utterances, however. In some cases (like deletion of prepositions), the forms appear to have evolved to make typing easier or faster, but in other cases (like the verb formation process that occurs with interjections), the amount of typing is not reduced. In some of the contractions, the intent seems to be to mimic the kinds of phonological processes found in casual oral speech. Articles are rarely deleted, except in formulaic contractions.

Notably, all emotes of action occur in the simple present tense, third person. This is similar to the use of the present tense in sports commentary speech, also known as the reportive register (Ferguson 1983). I examine emotes in more detail and discuss the semantics of MUD present tense in chapter 5.

3.1.1 Verb Formation

In one type of verb formation, an emoted verb is formed out of something often "said": e.g., instead of "Tom `says, "cool"`" Tom expresses his re-

---

[2]For more discussion of their data, see Cherny 1995d.

sponse as "Tom cools." These verb-creations are usually derived from short, frequently produced utterances, usually interjections or acknowledgments, like "uh oh" or "oh." In several of these cases, a preposition has been dropped as well.

(1)   a. Tanya eeews anne
      b. Mike cools. "multi-user cecil?"
      c. Carl cools, care if I html-ize it?
      d. Jon acks news
      e. Kelly ews. "That's kinda gross"
      f. Anthony ohboys...things are gonna get confusing now.

There are occasional examples of longer utterances (this was collected for me by a user who found it odd herself):

(2)   Pete actuallies, calls NES once he gets contact info from johnf

The **say** gloss of this one might be something like "Pete says, "actually, I'll call NES once I get contact info from johnf."" (Note the use of the simple present tense "calls" for future intention. I will discuss this in chapter 5.)

The verb form "ohs" has undergone another mutation for some users, becoming "ose," perhaps because of its apparent phonological similarity. Often exclamatory sound-effect utterances get inflected: "eees," "eeps," "arghs." The abbreviation for "be right back," "brb," is occasionally tensed as an emote: "George brbs." I don't believe I have ever seen a past tense version of one of these "verbed" utterances.

3.1.2   Contractions

There are other phonologically related word formations in the register. Some formulaic lexical items apparently result from the reduction of articles or other contractions. "Dunno," for instance, is a common form for "doesn't know" or "don't know," as is "onna" for "on the."

(3)   a. Lenny bops you onna head.
      b. anne gonna go see _in the name of the father_ tomorrow night.
      c. Jon punches lamba onna nose
      d. Ava gonna be a freshman again if she's lucky
      e. Pete dunno. Marie is prolly gonna yell at him for posting.

"Gonna" (from "going to") is a common form as well. anne's and Ava's deletion of the finite copula in the position before "gonna" in Examples 3b and 3d is not a habit shared by all (or performed consistently):

(4) a. anne is gonna doze off here soon.
    b. Marie is gonna introduce him to moo in a year.
    c. Kurt's gonna go talk to Colm in private.
    d. Penfold is gonna fight this in the debugger until
       luunchtime.

Some of these contracted forms occur even when there is no article to reduce. This suggests that some users view them as new lexical items, usable outside their derivation environment. According to Tom, the "runs atta" form was popularized by a character on Seashore MUSH.

(5) a. Ted sees no mjr onna Seashore
    b. Jon runs atta Ted.
    c. Ted runs atta Damon
    d. Sandy nods atta Kelly.

Attitudes about language have occasionally surfaced in response to innovations in the MUD register. On LambdaMOO, for instance, during a discussion about "proper" speech versus colorful innovations, several people agreed that roleplaying a particular character might require innovations, like "Hey youse! Get yer mitts offa me!" (Message 2435 on *life-issues). One user posted that she preferred emotes to be grammatically correct (as opposed to mimicking oral speech patterns, as **says** often do) (Message 2436 on *life-issues). However, she modified her point to add, "Just to clarify that last (parenthetical) statement, the same rule about purposefully incorrectness applies to emotes, as far as I'm concerned. Thus I forgive myself using :pat and :bop which use the fictional word, 'onna.' :)" (Message 2437 on *life-issues). The usages that have become fixed are often more acceptable than random new innovations.

3.1.3 Deletions

Unlike in the data described in Ferrara, Brunner, and Whittemore 1991, subject deletion is not common in my MOO data; but since the MOO server inserts the character name as the subject in **say** and emote commands, there aren't as many opportunities for it as there were in the Ferrara, Brunner, and Whittemore discourse. (Alternatively, one might argue that the speaker-as-subject is always deleted by the typist because it is inserted by the MOO server.) Here is one case, however.

(6) Sleep waves bye. Gonna go bang his head on zmodem
    for a little longer.

Deletion of prepositions in some frequent utterances is common:

(7) a. Jon laughs lynn, nods
    b. Henry nods George.

c. anne giggles illon.
d. Karen giggles Rick
e. Jon waves Sandy, btw

However, these forms have dropped in frequency on EM since the introduction of the Carpal Tunnel Syndrome Feature, which provides shorthand commands for these utterances, outputting a full form of the sentence including the preposition. Ironically, the shorthand forms for these utterances are themselves even further contracted, although the output appears fully formed.

Example (8):

```
>nd tom
lynn nods to Tom.
>gg tom
lynn giggles at Tom.
>wa tom
lynn waves to Tom.
```

Figure 3 illustrates how the ratio of the use of the shorthand CTS commands that output "nods," "grins," and "giggles" to typed-out (emoted) utterances using those verbs increased over time in my logs, suggesting that the use of the commands was spreading to more people. To generate the statistics, I considered only forms that used complete prepositional phrases, not forms without arguments. Canonically formed utterances with correct punctuation and prepositional phrases were counted as CTS uses, while forms without prepositions but with objects, or without final punctuation, and forms with additional material (e.g., "Mike nods, grad students tend not to, he's noticed."), were counted as typed utterances. I considered only utterances with prepositional phrases because I hypothesized that longer utterances are harder to type out without making deviations from the CTS canonical form, so the CTS-produced and typed-out forms should be observably different.

I hypothesize that it is easier to use the CTS command than to type an entire phrase, and that its adoption will be driven primarily by economy, rather than by preference for the unabbreviated prepositional phrase form. Supporting this hypothesis is the fact that another utterance commonly used as a back channel (like "nods," "grins," and "giggles") that does not appear on the CTS command set—"laughs"— does not show full canonical forms (like "lynn laughs at Tom.") more frequently, as did those I concluded were output by the CTS commands. If it were simply the case that people began regularly typing out canonical, "correct" forms rather than using the command set, phrases other

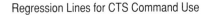

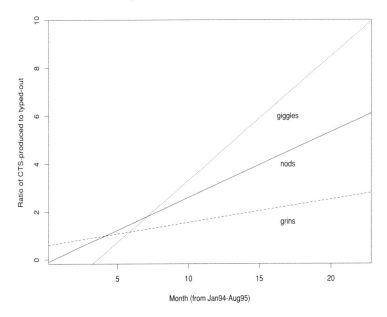

FIGURE 3 Regression lines for ratios of hypothesized CTS phrases over phrases typed by hand, over a period of 20 months

than those produced with the command set would also exhibit this positive correlation over time; but they do not. Although several people have complained about the ungrammatical reduced forms, I conclude that economy overrides any linguistic prejudice against them.

Another frequent conventional abbreviation is the dropping of the finite copulae from predicative sentences and progressives (or occasionally future progressives):

(9)   a. Shawn HONGRY
      b. Penfold bad mood
      c. Karen checking email while ls unpackes!
      d. anne going to bed, kids.
      e. Rick getting there.

3.1.4   Reduplication

Not all morphological and syntactic phenomena are abbreviatory, however. There is a limited amount of reduplication, particularly for activities:

(10) a. Ray nodsnods Shelley
      b. Will nodsnodsnods, he's real weird very often
      c. Damon nodnods
      d. Jon sorta nods Nat, but nodsnods Penfold, too
      e. Pete waveswaveswaves!
      f. Colm laughlaughs.
      g. Jon coolscoolscools vat 3.3

A few individual creative variations exist, like

(11) Shayne nodditynodnods.

Pete is particularly associated with the production of triple-forms like "waveswaveswaves," leading to this innovation on Colm's part:

(12) Colm laughslaughspeteslaughs

Reid (1994b) calls such cases "verbverbing," claiming they are frequent on MUDs generally, and explains them as textual descriptions that imply repetitive actions. Via, a long-time MUDder who has played on many types of MUDs, reports reduplication being used by one old-time MUDder in particular:[3]

Via remembers nodsnods from EONS and EONS ago on
<shudder> furrymuck when he briefly had a
character there
Via says, "As a matter of fact, lynx, the original
<as far as I know> used to use nodsnods"

Reid's examples show the tense marking only on the outside (i.e., reduplication, then tense marking, in procedural terms). The cases I have seen most often on EM have the tense marking occurring before the reduplication, so that it appears on both (or all) verbs. My interpretation of the reduplicated forms on EM is not of repeated or longer-lasting actions, but of more emphatic ones. Pete is said to "convulsively wave" by folks who know him in real life, which is the image the triple form evokes for them. This reduplication seems to occur only with a subset of common activities: some, but not all, of the conventional actions and back channels that I classify as Type 1 and Type 2 emotes in chapter 5.

Another form of emphasis consists of using all capital letters, which is also common on bulletin board systems, Usenet, and Internet Relay Chat (IRC), and in email more generally (Carey 1980; Danet, Ruedenberg, and Rosenbaum-Tamari 1998; Marvin 1995).

---

[3]FurryMUCK is particularly associated with tinysex and cute furry animals. I believe there are a lot of linguistic innovations within that community in particular, although I don't know the extent to which they spread to other MUD groups, since many MUDders are prejudiced against furries (Wetmore 1993).

3.2 Abbreviations and Shortenings

Use of abbreviations and shortenings in a register is very much culturally conditioned. Although many abbreviations are common on EM, certain outsider forms are sneered at: e.g., "u" for "you," "r" for "are." Table 3 explains some common abbreviations on EM. Many of the abbreviations are shared with Usenet or general hacker culture (see, e.g., Baym 1995; Raymond 1991; MacKinnon 1995), although others are specific to EM (e.g., "tinflm").

TABLE 3   Some abbreviations on ElseMOO

atm	at the moment
brb	be right back
btw	by the way
bbs	be back soon
bbl	be back later
bbiaw	be back in a while
convo	conversation
filfre	feel free
irl	in real life
rl	real life
ivr	in virtual reality (on a MUD)
vr	virtual reality (on a MUD)
lr	Living Room
LOL	laughs out loud
GOL	giggles out loud
rotfl	roll on the floor laughing
oic	oh, I see
wtf	what the fuck
rtfm	read the fucking manual
sb	scrollback (verb and noun)
tinflm	this is not fucking LambdaMOO

Like other registers (e.g., CB use of the "ten code"), the MUD register has developed special vocabulary to refer to frequently occurring events or objects. "Spam" is large amounts of unwanted text on one's screen;[4] "mav" (used as a verb and a noun) is a mistaken modality usage in a MUD conversation, so called after a character in MUD history who said material intended to be whispered (Smith 1995); "dinos" are long-time social-MUD MUDders, usually TinyMUD users from about 1990, some of whom are a subset of the Random and Moira gang on

---

[4]The term is in common use on Usenet now, but many MUDders believe it originated on MUDs.

Seashore MUSH; "to idle" is to become inactive on the MUD; "to wake" is to become active after being idle. Some of the terminology is very EM-specific: people who come from LambdaMOO to EM when LambdaMOO is down or inaccessible on the Net are often called "refugees"; the group of old programmers from LambdaMOO who founded EM are often called the "power elite" (see chapters 2 and 6 for discussion of the history of this term); and "random" is sometimes used to describe a MUD player who is either unrecognized or more specifically not "one of us."

One discourse habit derives from a command in the MOO text line editor, which in turn is based on a Unix editor's command for string substitution, s/<oldstring>/<newstring>. In Example 13, George corrects his mistyping after the fact using the "s//" notation.

Example (13):
```
George thinks Tanya of anne was interested, so hasn't
    done anything.
George s/of/or
```

It is also often used to make a comment on someone else's text. Here Mike equates May's response to online harassment with typical unenlightened suggestions about offline harassment.

Example (14):
```
Marie got all terribly emotional in the cyberspace
    panel and nobody understood her.
Shayne chuckles.
lynn [to Marie]: is that the one where May was saying
    women should log off if they are harassed?  I
    heard it.
Marie nods.
Mike s/log off/go home and lock the door/
```

Other programming notation is also used occasionally, like "!" to mean "not." Some abbreviations or short forms originate from more than just a desire for economy. There is a cultural history, shared between MUDs, for a few of them. The word "filfre" (short for "feel free") is adapted from an Infocom text adventure game; such games were popular with many MUDders.

Influence from the old MUDder community on Seashore is felt strongly on EM, since several regulars are members of both MUD communities. "Oit is biig" is short for "oh, it is big," and the "oit" part is used more generally in other constructions, like "oit is lame," for instance. In the conversation below, Tom tells me that the power elite in particular are prone to pick up forms used by the Random and Moira gang, who hang out on Seashore now.[5]

Example (15):

```
Tom says, "do you know about 'oit is biig'?"
lynn doesn't know where it came from, no.
Tom nods.
Tom says, "someone on dreamscape or whatever the
    current random and moira mud was"
Tom says, "um, this is severalth-hand, so it'll be
    inaccurate"
Tom says, "was exploring an lpmud"
Tom says, "and found a room with a description roughly
    like"
Tom | You are in a room.  oit is biig!
lynn laughs
Tom says, "so, uh, this was found amusing"
Tom says, "and propagated"
Tom says, "to EM/lm power elite, as happens fairly
    often"
Tom says, "(we got (and mutated) roll calls from them,
    for example)"
Tom thinks.
Tom Traceback says, "and of course there are now a
    million variations on it"
Tom says, "it's part of the repertoire"
Tom says, "so one day, brad jackson logs in here"
lynn nods?
Tom says, "and he's been in contact with ray on the
    phone, or maybe this was after ray went down
    there for a quarter"
Tom says, "but anyway, he says something like 'ohhhhh,
    it is biiiig'"
lynn sniggers.
Tom says, "and someone says 'well, i guess now we know
    how ray pronounces 'oit''"
Tom "village elder" Traceback
```

In sum, use of abbreviations and shortenings is highly culturally de-

---

[5] Tom is also known as TomTraceback (or Tom Traceback), and special code on his character causes the system to refer to him more or less randomly by one name or the other.

pendent. Misuse or use of forms not accepted in a particular community marks one as an outsider.

3.3 Routines

Routines are standardized, frequently uttered formulae in a speech community; Coulmas (1981, p. 3) suggests that they are "highly conventionalized prepatterned expressions whose occurrence is tied to more or less standardized communication situations." "Competent language use is always characterized by an equilibrium between the novel and the familiar. In every society there are standardized communication situations in which its members react in an automatic manner. Routines reflect, in a sense, a conception of the social system, and their importance for socialization as well as secondary acculturation is quite obvious, because routines are tools which individuals employ in order to relate to others in an accepted way" (p. 2). Routines (cf. "interaction rituals" in Goffman 1967) give us a sense of membership in a community and a sense of confidence and behavioral certainty. Routines may be idiomatic frozen expressions, or just oft-repeated formulae that can only be explained by referring to contexts of use. Politeness behavior, openings and closings (Schegloff 1972), turn-taking mechanisms, gambits that signal floor-taking attempts (Coulmas 1981), and phatic phrases may all be routinized. Kuiper 1996 distinguishes rituals as routines that are perceived to have cultural or social significance. I will use the terms "ritual" and "routine" more or less synonymously, since all the routines I discuss are socially significant.

Kuiper 1996 studies the special formulaic speech of auctioneers and sportscasters. Their speech is highly routine, governed by sequencing rules and marked by extreme fluency and chanted or droned intonation. The extreme time pressures of production (and the distraction caused by non-speech activities the speaker is performing) lead to the use of formulaic speech in those contexts. MUDders are also under production pressures, in that they are typing their speech, trying to follow a conversation, and possibly distracted by the real world as they MUD. Although the time pressure on MUDders is nowhere near what it is on auctioneers and simultaneous sportscasters, speech in the MUD register is nevertheless fairly routinized. Unlike auctioneer and sportscaster speech, however, it is routinized less at the discourse structure level than at the utterance level (probably because the speech events are less formal and the conversation is highly interactive). Many routines in EM are ritualized, conventional utterances intended to facilitate social interaction in the MUD, acting as openings or closings, back channel responses, or familiar jokes.

Creativity in language sits at the intersection between grammatical and social rules and innovation or novelty (see Kuiper 1996). Routines evolve, conventions change; individual creativity may affect the development of a community's speech. Play in online communities is documented by Danet, Ruedenberg, and Rosenbaum-Tamari 1998, Ruedenberg, Danet, and Rosenbaum-Tamari 1995, Myers 1987a and 1987b, Reid 1991, and Baym 1995, among others. Ruedenberg, Danet, and Rosenbaum-Tamari see IRC as inherently playful, providing the "perfect insulation to maintain a play frame," "keyed" as play (Goffman 1974) and set apart from the serious world in various textual ways. IRC itself is nonserious, they claim, full of users trafficking in artificial identities and ASCII wit.

ElseMOO, despite its status as a research-oriented MOO (not a game by most community members' definitions) and as an extension of many people's real lives, nevertheless has a significant amount of textual play in it. Many routines in EM are playful, particularly the ones I describe in this section. Often routines record events in the community's history, which are re-enacted as playful rituals. Although Coulmas (1981) expresses doubt that two-person routines constitute routines at all, it is clear from the interactions in the EM community that local creativity and innovation, even between just two people, are the sources for routines adopted by the community at large.

3.3.1 Some ElseMOO Routines: Flirt, Under, Dance, Loses, YER MOM, WITH GUNS, Etc.

I discovered one ElseMOO routine in a surprising manner. I was one of a group of people who were multi-MUDding, connected to both LambdaMOO and EM, using EM to talk about what was happening on LambdaMOO. Our characters were in the Coat Closet on LambdaMOO (the initial connection point for many players) laughing at guests, and I accidentally made a typing mistake, saying, "`lynn stand next to Shelley`." Shelley responded, "`Shelley flirt with lynn`." The explanation was forthcoming on EM:

Example (16):
```
Shelley [to you]: see, once everyone in the EM lr was
   hard-idled, and when Karen woke up later on,
   she saw a guest had come in, and she had these
   lines:
Shelley says, "The guest stand next to Karen"
Shelley says, "The guest flirt with Karen""
```

```
Shelley says, "The guest has disconnected."
Damon laughs
Shelley [to you]: so when you said 'lynn stand next
   to shelley,' i though you knew about the rest
```

The lack of tense on the verbs, a particularly newbie-like mistake, as well as the cursory attempt at flirtation, also newbie behavior, made the event amusing and memorable. Various funny variations on this routine have occurred, including

Example (17):

```
Shelley [to Karen]: Hey, baby, been here before?
Shelley eyes herself warily.
Karen stand next to shelley
Penfold flirt with couch
```

Similarly, one of the routines recorded in the short-lived EM Jargon project is the "under" routine. In this routine, a character disconnects upon hearing the word "under." Here is the Jargon project explanation:

Example (18):

```
UNDER.
======

So one day some people were making random conversation
in the living room or somewhere, and Sleep said
something like "These jokes are going over my head." and

   Tom [to Sleep]: Under.

and then immediately

   Sleep has disconnected.

And Mike said "Whoa." and decided to test this by
saying "Under." to someone else, who promptly
disconnected.  This was the earliest known example
of disconnection mimicry (see 'help
disconnection-mimicry').  It was something of a craze
for a while, but it doesn't always work these days.
```

(Sleep's abrupt disconnection was probably due to network problems.) The "under" routine rarely occurs anymore, however. I only discovered its existence when Karen whispered that I should disconnect because a visitor to EM had said "under"; the explanation followed.

The "dance" routine allows users to report their actions or feelings in a creative and individual, though routinized, way. It probably originally began in the dino community; lew, a dino on Seashore MUSH, thinks he saw a version on TinyMUD Classic in 1990 ("people doing the 'took-my-last-final-dance-of-joy'"). Doing "the guest dance," when a guest appears, is a related form. The humor in these lies in the use of text to suggest something neither physically described nor easily imaginable. Some examples:

(19) a. Karen does the i-got-to-meet-another-EM-person dance.
      b. Tom does the 'i'll never go home again' dance
      c. Henry does the Emacs Is Too Huge dance
      d. Ray does a little dance of gloating around Pete
      e. Mike does the something really silly and too long to be adjectived dance
      f. ms does the dance of impending ingestion.
      g. Shelley does the 'oi am fidgety' dance
      h. Ray does the @gag dance
      i. Shelley does the 'one week from thursday' dance, which is a variation on the '9 days' dance.
      j. Ted does the 2 SPARCs on my desk dance.
      k. Tom does a little identity-crisis dance
      l. Kurt does the green card dance.
      m. Henry does the hongry hongry hippo dance
      n. Carl does a little, 'there is now a proto linked list' dance
      o. Ted does the dance of plentiful milk.
      p. Henry does the 'i ate too much pasketti' dance.
      q. karne does a hello dance.

In the MUD medium, users may type simultaneously but not be aware of their comments' redundancy until one of them finishes and presses RETURN. The "loses" routine is a standard response to having typed something that another person has just said; it's a means of maintaining involvement despite the redundancy of one's text, or of getting "credit" for a similar utterance (Susan Herring, personal communication). Ordinarily, a user types "loses" at the point at which she receives the text from another user that renders her comment redundant. In Example 20, Mike received Ray's message (line 5) as he was typing line 6, whereupon he interrupted himself to announce that he had lost, and sent the line.

Example (20):
```
1 Ray should prolly see this movie
2 Via [to Ray]: which mivoe?
3 Ray says, "considering the soundtrack has the best
  U2 song ever"
4 Via oof.
5 Ray says, "_Until The End Of The World_"
6 Mike says, "Until the loses"
7 Mike guessed right though.
```

"Loses" is related to the "wins" routine, in which two people say identical things, but the first person to say it "wins" and often announces the fact. The other "loses." The wins/loses labelings are also common on Seashore MUSH, and probably other MUDs as well. In Example 21 Shelley and Ted both null-emote, a routine I discuss below, illustrating that it's the speech act, rather than the content of the utterance per se, that's at stake in winning and losing.

Example (21):
```
anne says, "what the hell is wrong with my spacebar?"
Shelley
Ted
Ted LOSES
Shelley WINS
```

The "blose" verb is a related lexical form. It comes from the "b" in "bye" plus "loses." This form frequently occurs when a player disconnects and another player fails to say goodbye in time.

The "YER MOM" routine is a playful insult in which someone borrows someone else's verb and inserts "YER MOM" as an argument. Some examples of YER MOMisms (occasionally spelled "YR MOM" as well):

Example (22):
```
Marie [to Tom]: You're preaching to the choir.
Penfold says, "actually, he's preaching to the
  acolytes."
Tom is preaching to YER MOM.
```

Example (23):
```
lynn is fixated on MOOers food habits irl.
Tom is fixated on YER MOM.
```

Example (24):

```
Ted | gcc -g -o test -DYRMOM test.c
```

The predictability of many utterances is the origin of the "etc" and "ohnevermind" routines. In the "etc" case, someone doesn't finish typing an entire line, because the rest can be inferred.

Example (25):

```
Mike demangles Henry's neck.
Ted was never aware of there being a category for
  Professional Writers
Ted says, "does that make me a Professional MUDder?"
Mike thinks it's a stretch to call a "Trek Writer" a
  pro
Henry killed Mike!  Mike has left.
Mike laughs.
Henry kills Mike for demangling him, not for etc.
```

Here we can infer "not for thinking it's a stretch to call a Trek writer a pro."

The "ohnevermind" completion is often used in place of spelling out and completing an old MUD routine; here Henry and Jubilee start "roll calls" (discussed below) but don't finish them:

(26)   a. Henry STUPID CHILD Rohnevermind
       b. Jubilee IS NOT JUST TURTLE GRAPHICS ROLLohnevermind

Of course, "ohnevermind" is associated not just with routines, but with predictable or bad-taste jokes as well. In Example 27, Ray suggests that Tom might want the CG rubbed. (The CG is the Community Group, described in chapter 6; "rubbed" may mean "rubbed out.")

Example (27):

```
Tom says, "so could someone who has time and working
  hands take charge of hounding the cg into
  making a decision and sending a letter?"
Ray [to Tom Traceback]: you want us to rubohnevermind
```

The "YER MOM" (or "YR MOM") utterance is routinized enough to be completed with "ohnevermind."

Example (28):

```
Jon dreams in YER MOhnevermind
```

Kendall (1996) describes a common routine called an "objoke" that persists in the dino community on Seashore and has spread to the EM speech community: "a common form of word play is the 'objoke' (short for 'obligatory joke'). Objokes are puns based on word endings" (p.

210). For example, if lew says, "HEATER VENT," the "-er" ending triggers a common joke response:[6]

Example (29):
Parker says, "heat 'er vent? I hardly know 'er"

This is often abbreviated to "I hardly." On EM, the shortened form is more common.

Example (30):
Henry says, "GOTCHER? I HARDLY."

Example (31):
Ellen [to Jeani]: Oh. God forbid, you'd loiter.
Mike hardly etc

The origin of the "WITH GUNS" ritual utterance gets retold occasionally. Many people don't know the origin of many speech routines on EM but use them anyway, as George does below in line 1. In typical fashion for them, Ray and Tom perform the origin story together. (AppleTise is a character on another MUD.)

Example (32):
1 George clubs Ray WITH GUNS
2 lynn says, "where'd the WITH GUNS thing come from?"
3 George says, "the cannon?"
4 Ray says, "no"
5 Tom says, "noooo"
6 Tom says, "AppleTise"
7 Ray says, "let Tom tell THE STORY"
8 George shuts up.
9 Tom says, "he was explaining to us about how he had
   this cool idea for a game"
10 Tom says, "like, a real-world game, a board game"
11 Tom doesn't remember if he was planning on making a
   mud version of it or what
12 Tom says, "anyway, we asked him to describe it, you
   know, what it was like, and his first
   attempt to explain it was"
13 Tom says, "something to the effect of"
14 Tom says, "'it's like candyland, but with guns'"
15 lynn heheh
16 Ray says, "and of course tom ALL CAPS'd it"
17 Tom says, "which provoked the instant and

---

[6]The use of capitalization is sometimes a part of the routine, in that it draws attention to the "-er" ending and prompts for the response.

```
     irresistible reaction 'candyland WITH
     GUNS'"
  18 Bonny shoots a hole in your lollipop!
  19 lynn nods solemnly.
  20 Tom says, "which phrasing then became universally
     applicable"
  21 George WITH GUNS
```

The "cascading quote" routine involves players' repeatedly "pasting," or copying into the conversation, material already pasted by another player, creating a long chain of pasted comments. The vertical bar, or pipe, indicates a paste.

Example (33):
```
Mike ON THE CREEK ROLL CALL
foliage (distracted)
Tom grins.
Mike | Mike ON THE CREEK ROLL CALL
Mike | foliage is floating in the creek.
Tom | Mike | Mike ON THE CREEK ROLL CALL
Shelley | Tom | Mike | Mike ON THE CREEK ROLL CALL
```

3.3.2 Roll Calls

The "roll call" routine is particularly popular on EM. To start one, a character announces a roll call in capital letters, and the characters present who feel they fit the subject or attribute in the name of the roll call answer with their names on a line alone, by "null-emoting" (in this context, the virtual equivalent of raising their hands or saying "here").

According to lew, a dino from Seashore MUSH, the first roll call routine originated as a way to identify who was logged on and active on a MUD in 1990 where disconnected characters were listed in a room's contents along with connected characters. "Back on Islandia, which ran under one of the TinyMUD versions, when you did a 'look' in a room, it listed everyone there, regardless of their logged-in status. In the Islandia treehouse or town square, this list could get huge, making it almost impossible to tell who was 'really there.' The first roll call occurred in the Islandia treehouse, when it suddenly occurred to me I had no idea who was there so I didn't know what to start talking about. So I just emoted 'ROLL CALL' and then null-emoted (probably the first intentional null-emote) and most of the awake people immediately realized the 'rules' and followed suit" (personal communication).

Roll calls are fairly common routines on EM. In the first line here, Pete quotes a character from another MUD after the vertical bar:

Example (34):
Pete | Blotchy_Guest says, ''Don't you oppress me! I
  have freedom of expression so I can do
  whatever I want here, you fascist running dog
  power elitist!''
Pete giggles
Karen eyes Pete warily.
Pete FASCIST RUNNING DOG POWER ELITIST ROLL CALL
Pete
Jubilee
Karen ?
ms [to Jubilee]: You wish.

When I was learning the conventions on EM, and emoted a "yup"
after my name instead of null-emoting for my first roll call affirmative,
I was chastised for violation of the "roll call protocol." Roll calls even
occasionally appear in modified form in MOOmail. This exchange occurred recently on *chitchat, the general social list on EM. (Egypt is a
character.)

Message 466 on *chitchat:
Date: Thu Jul 27 17:39:42 1995 EDT
From: Karen
To: *chitchat
Subject: baiii

ls and i are heading to switzerland this evening.
we'll be gone for two and a half weeks. see you
later...
karen

Message 467 on *chitchat:
Date: Thu Jul 27 17:40:51 1995 EDT
From: Largo
To: Karen and *chitchat
Subject: Re: baiii

> ls and i are heading to switzerland this evening.
> we'll be gone for two and a half weeks. see you
> later...

TAKE US WITH YOU

```
Message 468 on *chitchat:
Date:     Thu Jul 27 18:21:44 1995 EDT
From:     Kelly
To:       *chitchat
Subject:  re: baiii

Huh. He's in Hawaii, and he wants to go somewhere
cold and neutral.  Whatever.
------------------------
Message 469 on *chitchat:
Date:     Thu Jul 27 19:47:33 1995 EDT
From:     Ray
To:       *chitchat

COLD AND NEUTRAL ROLL CALL
------------------------
Message 470 on *chitchat:
Date:     Fri Jul 28 23:58:42 1995 EDT
From:     Egypt
To:       *chitchat
Subject:  roll call

Egypt
------------------------
```

3.3.3 Null-Emotes

Roll calls evolved into more general "null-emotes" on EM.[7] With the null-emote, a character can playfully identify with other objects, locations, people, or even processes or events. Null-emoting also provides an excellent example of the jointly constructed nature of discourse in the MOO—an audience can metaphorically seize someone's remark and turn it into the first part of a joke, entirely rewriting the speech event as play. However, the null-emote as such does not usually key a free-for-all play event; it's usually just a quick aside.

In the most straightforward examples of non-prompted null-emoting, a character answers a question with his name on a line alone, implying that the character is the answer to the question. In Example 35, Tom suggests that he is what is weird. Similarly, Ray is why Seashore sucks, Tom is Will Couch, George is where Tanya should deposit Shelley, and Fred is how fucking long it takes 1.1.45 to compile on a 386/40.

---

[7] Not everyone enjoys them, however; Mike finds them highly annoying.

Example (35):
Lenny says, "what's weird?"
Tom

Example (36):
Ted explains to Woodkey why Seashore sucks.
Ray

Example (37):
lynn says, "who's Will Couch?"
Tom

Example (38):
Shelley needs to find out where Tanya should deposit
   her tomorrow night.
George

Example (39):
Rob says, "how fuckung long does it take 1.1.45 ro
   compile on a 386/40"
Fred

The null-emote is fundamentally a joke; a null-emoter, through her response to a question intended to evoke an informative response, subverts the discourse in a playful manner. (The traditional excuse for producing a null-emote is "Oh, I thought it was a roll call.") The joke often lies in the improbability or impossibility of the character really being the answer to the question. Clearly, "Fred" is not a reasonable answer to a question about how long compilation takes. However, like all good textual play, the null-emotes that come close to being possible "true" responses are often the most humorous. For example, Ray is a character on the MUD Seashore; Ray therefore may be implying that he is in fact one reason Seashore sucks. The speech activity of a null-emote implies jest, but the context he performs it in renders his response ambiguous and the humor more subtle.

Null-emotes seem to be appropriate in most question contexts: who, what, where, why, how. The null-emote phenomenon, however, is semantically complex. Null-emotes also occur in the context of an embedded question, an indefinite, or a plural:

Example (40):
lynn wonders what she came here for.
Shelley

Example (41):
George pssst, "I think Penfold has something hanging
from his nose."
Shelley

Example (42):
Tom says, "i was trying to think of behaviors you
could disallow programmatically without just
removing programmer bits from everybody"
Ray

Example (43):
Honda | There is an open ballot on which you have not
yet voted:
Penfold

Example (44):
Del says, "gameboy??"
Ted

Again, in the examples above, the null-emoter is not intending her character name to be a serious response to the embedded question or open proposition. Penfold implies he is an open ballot to be voted on, but he is not necessarily associated with any real ballot; Ray implies he is a behavior that can be disallowed programmatically, and Ted suggests he is a gameboy, but they are not trying to be sensible or accurate.

In semantic terms, the null-emote seems to function as an assignment of a value to an available argument position, i.e., it suggests that an individual could satisfy the predicate denoted by the indefinite or plural ("satisfy" in a playful, nonrealistic sense, clearly). This analysis is supported by a rarer form of null-emoting, in which the character is apparently intended to control either an empty subject position or an adjective's argument position. (In Example 46, I use an ASCII representation of a cartoon thought bubble or balloon. This form was invented on Distortion, the predecessor to EM, by Mike and Ray; it has since spread to other MOOs and even Seashore MUSH. The command "**think**" will produce the bubble design, or it can be manually typed as an emote.)

Example (45):
Will tries to do that thing with @describe here as
"This is a nice place. [couch] Blah blah blah
etc." Oitis HARD.
Will says, "Or at least, comes out really ugly."
Border

Example (46):

```
lynn . o O ( making love in the afternoon )
Tom
```

The adjective and the participial phrase semantically represent one-place predicates of individuals, thus allowing a similar binding of their argument position (loosely speaking, they are missing something, and the character name provides it). Tom is making love in the afternoon; Border is ugly.

Interestingly, textual adjacency[8] is needed for a null-emote to feel "successful." The "presentation" of the speech act apparently matters a lot. Line 2, below, prevented a good null-emote opportunity.

Example (47):

```
1 Kit [to Henry]: so what do you operate?
2 Jon says, "It was all that rain talk"
3 Largo hehs.
4 Largo [to Jon]: You spoiled the most purest of
  null-emote opportunities for that. I hope
  you're satisifed.
```

Other cases are group participation events, where either multiple responses are appropriate or a null-emote is actually expected. Tom pokes Penfold in Example 49 because he expected a null-emote and didn't receive it immediately.

Example (48):

```
Tom | Two members of your company are invited to
  attend at no cost.
Ray
Patrick
Tom | If you would like additional members of your
  company to participate, the cost will be $200
  per person. Non-Forum members may attend for
  $500 per person.
lynn
```

Example (49):

```
Tom | 1. Good interactive stories emerge from:
Tom pokes Penfold.
Penfold
Tom . o O ( whew )
lynn says, "Blatant NULL-EMOTE prompts"
```

---

[8]Or nearness, in some topic-driven sense; one informant pointed out that intermediate text is okay as long as it doesn't distract from the null emote, as in Example 49.

The null-emote speech event is one clear way in which the audience participates in defining and changing the speech context, and it illustrates how characters can briefly alter their own character's significaton, to fit themselves into the conversation under different temporary identities (cf. the discussion of text and audience in Brenneis 1986). Interestingly, the habits of online discourse can become real-life habits as well. And they can undergo translations: the null-emote appears among some MOOers in real life, translated into a physical gesture (like a slight hand-raise) during conversations or while listening to talks or television. It survives as a physical, bodily involvement in a discourse, suggesting that for these MOOers the body is involved in identity. Among a few other MOOers, however, null-emoting in real life consists of saying their name. (EM community members tell stories about almost or actually null-emoting "in real life" during conversations with non-MUDders, who of course have no idea what this behavior means.)

3.3.4   Xythian-Completion

A variation on the null-emote speech event is known as "Xythian-completion," after a character on LambdaMOO (who also has a character on EM).

Example (50):

```
Ray says, "I think it's in question whether DAWN knows
    what the ballot says"
Bonny giggles.
Ray says, "xythian-complete at will"
```

Possible Xythian-completions for this context might be:

```
in question whether LYNN knows what the ballot says
```

or

```
in question whether DAWN knows what lynn says
```

In Xythian-completion, aka "x-completion," a character name replaces a noun, or sometimes another part of speech, in a phrase or sentence. Like null-emotes, Xythian-completion is not intended sensibly, and the fact that grammaticality is lost (for instance, when a character name replaces a part of speech other than nominal) is another indication that this form of play is not meant to be understood as sensible speech behavior. In Example 50, Dawn and lynn do not need to have any connection in real life or on any MUD; the Xythian-completion is solely a text game involving identifications "on the fly" in the course of interactions among the EM community.

Since many members of the EM community also frequent LambdaMOO, I have occasional examples from LambdaMOO as well. Example 51 shows an automatic message on a locked room on LambdaMOO that is triggered when an uninvited guest tries to enter the room. Ray parodies it with Xythian-completion, asking the readers to imagine him as a stretching wall.

Example (51):
```
The wall twists and groans as it tries to force itself
  into the shape of Khaki_Guest. With a crack it
  snaps back into shape.
Ray snaps back into shape.
```

Example (52):
```
Conner nods. i know. was wondering what this license
  thing entailed, then.
Patrick
Border says, "not necessarily v.32, etc"
Conner says, "hm."
v.Patrick
```

In Example 52, Patrick Xythian-completes into "v.32" and the readers imagine a "v dot Patrick." This is an example of a type of Xythian-completion that occurs frequently, in which a character name is embedded in punctuation, especially odd punctuation. According to one informant, this was the probable origin of Xythian-completion; it was intended to draw attention to odd typographic entities, and has since become generalized to include name substitutions elsewhere. (There is some disagreement among the population about its evolution, however.) Here Tom Xythian-completes into "–core=":

Example (53):
```
Phred [to Vermont]: how would I invoke it?  'gdb
  core'?
Vermont [to Phred]: gdb ../../bin/driver
  --core=mudlib/core
Henry says, "--core= is optional there"
--tom=
```

Finally, a rarer form of completion results when a character responds to something unspoken in the context and substitutes her name into it, as in line 6 below. The number for film listings is 777-FILM, which is what foliage is Xythian-completing into.

Example (54):
```
1 foliage [to Damon]: hey. yr alive. what time would
  you want to go?
```

```
2 Damon [to foliage]: late
3 foliage [to Damon]: i.e., do you have a paper, can
  you tell times?
4 Damon [to foliage]: no, but i can call the theatre,
  hang
5 Damon says, "oit is buusy"
6 777-FOLIAGE
```

External texts are borrowed from to provide context for Xythian-completion as well. Example 55 shows Ray reciting quotes from *The Hitchhiker's Guide to the Galaxy*, substituting himself and Tom for the characters in the book in lines 6 and 10.[9]

Example (55):

```
1  Tom . o O ( *three* ray? )
2  Ray is confused
3  Tom too!
4  lynn says, "'ray' is a mass noun? there are three of
   it?"
5  Tom nods solemnly.
6  Ray says, "'The' Ray? No, just 'A' Ray, didn't you
   hear I come in six-petc"
7  Tom says, "what's that from?"
8  Ray says, "Zaphod"
9  lynn says, "oh yeah."
10 Ray gets stranger things than Tom free in his
   breakfast cereal.
```

3.4   Play with Modality

Danet, Ruedenberg, and Rosenbaum-Tamari 1998, Ruedenberg, Danet, and Rosenbaum-Tamari 1995, and Reid 1991 report significant ASCII play in IRC. They illustrate users communicating actions or sound effects marked by asterisks, e.g., "*grins*," "*bang*." Emoticons, sideways facial expressions like ":-)" denoting amusement, irony, unhappiness, etc., are popular on IRC as well as in other parts of the Internet (Baym 1995; Mason 1990; MacKinnon 1995; Reid 1991). Use of capitals to express force or emphasis is also common (Carey 1980). In a description of play on IRC involving smoking (see Carlstrom 1992 for an interesting parallel in a MUD), Ruedenberg, Danet, and Rosenbaum-Tamari (1995) describe the use of text symbols to evoke the sounds of inhalation:

---

[9]Tom points out that this is an odd example, given that characters do not usually Xythian-complete with other characters' names. Ray is a particularly good friend of Tom's, which may excuse the liberty.

Line 107 <Thunder> sssssssssssss *passes joint to
         lucia*

A mix of actions and "speech" on the same line is common in IRC:

Line 127 <Kang> thankx dude *puff* *hold*

Conventions for describing "actions" appear to differ somewhat among individuals. Ruedenberg, Danet, and Rosenbaum-Tamari note, "*Puff* and *hold* may be either nominalizations or infinitives, the names of the actions, or even first person verbs with the pronoun 'I' deleted." Other IRC users use third person inflected verbs, with the subject deleted (since it is unambiguous, one presumes). Many use brackets instead of asterisks to set off the actions, e.g., "<g>" for "grins."

A guest coming to EM reportedly said, "this is just like IRC <g>.. with fun things to do." Bonny, a regular, responded, "except we don't say <g> here."[10] The emote command obviates the need for such abbreviated descriptions of common actions. In the EM discourse community, the use of emoticons is restricted to a few individuals (contrary to Reid's 1994b claim that they are "legion" on MUDs, suggesting that particular communities differ). Sadness, for instance, has a personally distinctive one: "=)". Smiling faces, or "smileys," are the most commonly occurring, when they occur at all; few people use more complex or obscure ones. (The availability of ritual utterances that perform the same types of mitigation or metacomment precludes much use of smileys, I suspect. The "eye" command may substitute for much of the effect of a smiley. See section 3.5.1.)

ASCII play does occur, as well as play based on knowledge of programming notation or MOO language conventions (see Marvin 1995). Here Idan and frogd play with the syntax for setting a MOO property, and George muses, in a thought bubble, that "warm" is not equal to "hot."

(56) a. Idan @set me=bloodthirsty-women_with_high_heels_ok
     b. frogd.sarcastic = 0;
     c. George . o O (warm != hot)

An ASCII arrow is often used in play as well:

Example (57):
The corporate guest says, "where is everyone from?"
Henry <- NJ
lynn <- at Stanford
Rick <- was at Stanford...

---

[10]This exchange was added to the Welcome Message, which is how I know about it; see Appendix C.

```
Henry <- idiot who's last educational triumph was
  probably 6th grade
Mike [to Henry]: WHOSE
Henry [to Mike]: SEE!
```

Use of capitals for emphasis, or to simulate shouting, is common.

(58) Devil says, "ITS ALL FROGDS FAULT, STRING HIM UP
      WITH AN ENDFORK"

Example (59):

```
lynn [to Illon]: just noticed you were at UMist.
Henry is not well.
Mike says, "UMIST ME HAHAHA"
Mike is not well.    --Henry
Ted HAHAHHAHAHA
Henry HAHAHAHAHAHAHAHAH
```

The "HAHAHA" formula for maniacal laughter is common, as is the more sinister form "BWAHAHA" (according to Ray, "BWAHAHAHA" is dino in origin; he says, "imagine Vincent Price laughing").

Other forms of ASCII play occur as well. (In Example 60, lines 2 and 3 were typed by Ted and Pete respectively, using the "spoof" command, which allows an utterance to appear without the author's name at the front.[11])

Example (60):

```
1 Freddie has a headache this big: {            }
2 and it has Ted written all over it
3 ... And it has 'Pete' written all over it.
4 Pete LOSES
5 Freddie ha
6 Ted WINS
```

Aside from simple ASCII play, more complex forms of response to the modalities available have evolved. The emote, in particular, allows a lot of flexibility; several discourse behaviors have evolved out of a response to the interplay between "speech" and emotes.

One is the practice of quoting a single word or short phrase from someone else's text (or one's own) as a way of highlighting it, stressing its inappropriateness, or indicating a sense of irony at the speaker's

---

[11]It is clear that the authors were Ted and Pete, because otherwise the author's name would be appended to the end of the line after hyphens, as in Example 59. Spoofs are possible with no attribution at all on LambdaMOO; see Marvin 1995 and Cherny 1995b.

choice of words. Here Mike expresses his disbelief that the client needs an event system, and Ellen disagrees with PBMax's generalization.

Example (61):
```
Rick [to Mike]: needs an event system and some way to
  tell the client that the utterance is from a
  particular person.
Mike "needs"
```

Example (62):
```
PBMax [to Penfold]: Not many *wanted* him around, but
  everyone was too afraid to DO anything about
  it.
Ellen "everyone"
```

In another type of modality play, an exclamatory utterance surfaces as an emote, but untensed, e.g., "Karen eep." This is probably intended to suggest urgency or fast, emotional response.

Example (63):
```
Tom incidentally has probably broken 'home' for
  people who live underground.
Karen eep
```

```
(64)  Tom aieee as he discovers how the secret tunnels
      connect to the sandcastle
```

Tom's "aieee" above simulates a wail or scream. (Interestingly, I have only one case of "aieee" appearing with the tense morpheme but dozens of untensed examples, which I suspect is because the exclamatory force is weakened by tensing it. Addition of complex modifiers apparently doesn't have that effect, as Example 64 indicates. I do find occasional examples of it as a **say**: "Mike says, "aieee."")

The use of formulaic sound effects is pretty common on EM. "Mmm" and its variants are usually joking signs of approval, possibly related to "yum"; "eeeee" and "aieee" are screaming or keening sounds of distress. I haven't seen many uses of "rrrrrr" or "errrr."

Example (65):
```
Tom says, "there used, btw, to be a five-letter fetish
  around these"
Tom says, "e.g., eeeee, aieee, mmmmm, rrrrr, errrr"
Tom says, "arrrr"
Tom Traceback says, "arrgh"
lynn says, "oh, odd."
Tom says, "that's decayed over time, but some of us
  are still pretty rigorous about it"
```

```
Tom uses mmm, generally, though.
lynn says, "interesting."
lynn says, "how did they start?"
Tom says, "they started with eeeee"
Tom says, "which started with me saying it"
Tom <- proud originator of too many moo speech patterns
```

Performance is often keyed by the use of an emote followed by a quotation. The lack of a **say** verb keys it as not a "real" utterance by the player, but a performed one. Here Tom is reporting what is going on in real life, his hearing about Pete's day, and in line 2 he is performing it for the listeners in the MOO. Ray joins in by playing off the sound of "helpless" with "hapless."

Example (66):
```
1 Tom hears about Pete's "really productive day".
2 Tom "I think I sent about... three pieces of mail
  and... talked to a couple people."
3 You say, "heh."
4 Tom just nods his head in helpless approval.
5 Ray nods his head in hapless approval.
```

In Example 67, George is keying his comments as playful, not serious, by "yelling" in capitals, eyeing himself, and using emotes to "quote" fictitious text in lines 10 and 15. The discussion is about where guests should be when they connect to the MUD (and "wake").

Example (67):
```
1  George says, "EM SHOULD CHASE GUESTS AWAY"
2  George says, "THEY SHOULD WAKE UP IN HELL, not some
   COZY SEWER"
3  George eyes himself warily.
4  ls laughs
5  della peers at George suspiciously.
6  della says, "whee!"
7  George says, "ThEY SHOULD WAKE UP WHERE THEY ARE IN
   A COLD DARK SEWER _AND_ CAN GET RUN OVER"
8  George . o O ( subway )
9  Tom giggles at George.
10 George "Woops, you didn't get off the rails in
   *** time!  disconnected ***
11 della thinks maybe she's glad she wakes up
   someplace cozy
12 ls says, "or we could build a really comfy hotel
```

    room and pamper then and make them feel all
    cozy"
13 Will says, "They should have to solve a puzzle to
    get to the main MOO."
14 ls says, "AND THEN SKEWER THEM ALIVE WHEN THEY WALK
    OUT."
15 George "A hot spear runs you through. Ow. You'd
    feel pain, but you're dead."

Play is keyed in Example 68 by the lack of **say** in line 6 and the use of sound effects (similar to those used on IRC).

Example (68):
1 Largo nods, saw the Space Shuttle one time in
   Vt...tiny little light that cruised across
   the sky.
2 Narcotic says, "get out the rifle"
3 Henry says, "you could see a launch from here some
   time this past winter..looked like a big
   meteor going the wrong way"
4 Will hehs.
5 lynn doubts she'll make it.
6 Largo *THUNK*.....[thud]....."What happened?"
   "WHO WAS THAT MASKED SPACE SHUTTLE?!?"

There are other means of signaling jest; spoofs, which are utterances without the author's name prepended, are often intended jokingly. On EM, if the name of the character who authored the spoof is mentioned in the spoof, no attribution is shown; otherwise, the author's name is appended after the spoof. In Example 69, Kit pastes text from another source and everyone else comments on it. Ray spoofs in line 6 in response to Penfold's "bet we can break it."

Example (69):
--------------------- Kit ----------------------
> Remote Tele-Excavation via the Web
>
> An inter-disciplinary team at the University of
> Southern California is pleased to announce Mercury
> Site, a WWW server that allows users to tele-operate
> a robot arm over the net. Users view the environment
> surrounding the arm via a sequence of live images
> taken by a CCD camera mounted on a commercial robot
> arm. The robot is positioned over a terrain filled

```
> with sand; a pneumatic system, also mounted on the
> robot, allows users to direct short bursts of
> compressed air into the sand at selected points.
> Thus users can "excavate" regions within the sand
> by positioning the arm, delivering a burst of air,
> and viewing the newly cleared region.
--------------- Kit stops pasting ---------------
1 Penfold says, "heh"
2 lynn says, "weird"
3 Penfold says, "bet we can break it"
4 Karen hehs.
5 Ted excavates Penfold with a puff of air.
6 Somewhere in California, a small robot melts down.
  Nobody notices until Monday.      --Ray
```

Greeting rituals are particularly routinized. Waving is common when someone enters a room, but variations on the theme have developed. On Seashore, "shouting" an entering character's name in capitals is common, and this is often done on ElseMOO as well. On EM, the "null page" and a null directed speech utterance are two fully phatic forms that play with modalities available in the MOO. Several people greet one another with "null pages," or pages with no content at all, often upon connection to the MOO: "Tom pages, """ The null directed speech greeting gradually evolved:

Example (70):
```
Honda recalls the evolution:
Honda [to Penfold]: PENFOLD!
Honda [to Penfold]: !
Honda [to Penfold]:
lynn says, "heh."
Honda says, "minimalism at work."
```

Honda understands the null page as an oriental-style bow, he says, while Karen finds it bothersome because it appears that the "speaker" has nothing to say to the other person.

Directed speech is also used for humorous, performed displays, as when Penfold, who was eagerly waiting for a flight to arrive, said, "Penfold [to time]: pass." Speech may be similarly directed to people who aren't present in the room, as a means of performing an attitude or opinion: "Xavier [to user]: why are you being so stooopid??"

Another minimal form is the "said" question mark, which expresses general confusion or questioning. Here I ask (or wonder) what is causing Tom's sigh:

Example (71):
Tom sighs.
lynn says, "?"

In sum, the types of textual expression in the register make use of the keyboard symbols as well as the commands for "speech" in the MUD. Emotes, **says**, directed speech, and spoofs expand the range of variations on meaning that can be signaled in the discourse. The adept speaker of the community's register learns to recognize even slight deviations from the "standard" uses of these commands as meaningful once they become systematic. The availability of multiple, flexible ways of communicating invites users to innovate, and the community may adopt their innovations into its linguistic repertoire. Despite being limited to simple text, MUDders can express themselves subtly and fluently.

3.5 Antisocial Commands

In the programmable environment of a MUD, discourse may be partly automated. According to Reid 1994b, adventure MUD players get access to the emote command only in certain "emote rooms"; elsewhere, specific programmed "verbs" allow limited actions. Reid reports, "Thomas Gerstner, who is associated with an adventure-style MUD named 'Nemesis', recently circulated the results of a tally showing how many times each command was used. Over a period of 250 days, and with an average of twenty players connected at all times, players on Nemesis invoked a 'feeling' command every thirty seconds." The most popular commands were those reported in Table 4. Ito (1994) lists "soul" commands for the combat MUD she participates in, which appear analogous.

TABLE 4 "Feeling" commands used on Nemesis, from Reid 1994b

smile	89089	laugh	34063	kiss	12212
bow	50138	wave	30875	shrug	10849
shake	46312	giggle	20145	kick	9504
greet	46152	sigh	19222	poke	9307
grin	46046	hug	19220	chuckle	7401
nod	42385	wait	13550	french	6773

MOOs often have programmed "verbs" for social interaction available to users on Feature Objects, which may be subscribed to using the "**@addfeature**" command. The verbs may be humorous programs such as "bonkers," which cause the bonked character to appear to recite lyrics from Disney songs, or they may be simple conventional commands much like the "feeling" commands on combat MUDs, often referred to on LambdaMOO as "social" commands. The purpose of social commands is usually to reduce the amount of typing needed: if I type "smile" on a MUD with an appropriate social command, everyone around me sees "lynn smiles." More elaborate output is also possible. Reid (1994b) gives an example of output from "french" on an adventure MUD called "Revenge of the End of the Line"; if a character named Fred typed "french Ginger," the command's output to Ginger would be:

```
Fred gives you a deep and passionate kiss...   It
   seems to take forever...
```

On EM, the Antisocial Feature has the main collection of "social" commands, although the original purpose of the command set was to automate a very antisocial, unpleasant set of utterances. These commands are records of community in-jokes or ritual phrases that communicate a listener's response and affect. For instance, if I want to indicate that I think someone is behaving oddly, I may "eye" them "warily" using an Antisocial verb:

```
1 >eye tom
2 lynn eyes Tom warily.
```

As shown in line 1, I type the Antisocial verb, followed by the name of the person I want to "aim" it at, and the message shown in line 2 is seen by the occupants of the room I am in. I could also produce line 2 with an emote, of course, but the verb provides a shorthand input form. A new player on EM (or another MUD with such commands) usually learns to emote these utterances first, unless she has investigated the feature objects that can be "added." As a player becomes more sensitive to the interactions in text, she notes that no one ever appears to make mistakes or variations in typing certain ritual utterances, and this consistency is a clue that there is some partially-automated means of producing them (Doheny-Farina 1995). Users may ask someone what feature object they need to add to obtain the shortened forms, or the information may be offered when a typing error shows that they are using a plain emote instead.

Several of the commands on the Antisocial Feature are historically related to the combat MUDs' feeling commands; several EM folks thought that "poke," "shake," "glare," "worship," and "point" may all have been inspired by LP MUDs or diku MUDs. Other common commands shared between combat MUDs and LambdaMOO and EM include "nod," "wave," "laugh," "grin," "sigh," and "giggle," and these probably evolved on both types of MUDs independently; greetings and emotes that function as back channels (see section 4.4; also cf. Schegloff 1982) or affect displays are common routinized utterances. The Carpal Tunnel Syndrome (CTS) Feature Object, which provides shorthand verbs for often-used utterances, includes the ritualized back channel and greeting emotes that are not included on the Antisocial Feature; the output verbs it provides include "nods," "hehs" (a laugh sound), "waves," "giggles," "grins," "smiles," and "?" (which suggests a questioning look). The CTS verbs were created by a few players who were experiencing repetitive stress injury and needed to reduce the amount of typing needed for conversation; routinization and the establishment of ritual expressions may be motivated not only by the need to save time and signal in-group status, but also by the need to preserve one's health.

Around December 15, 1994, Tom installed a counter on the Antisocial Feature to assess which commands were used most often. As of January 12, 1995, the highest counts were

eye	1789
whuggle	909
poke	512
shake	476
peer	247
kill	81

By August 17, 1995, the difference between the top commands had changed a bit:

eye	14410
whuggle	12966
poke	4885
shake	4427
peer	2886
kill	845

I'll first discuss "eye" and "whuggle" in detail, and then the origins of a handful of other commands.

3.5.1 Eye

The "**eye**" command was the genesis of the Antisocial Feature. Tom began "eyeing" things "warily" because it seemed like an amusing appropriation of a literary convention. The history of the feature's creation was told to me by Tom and Ray, talking in tandem, as they often do.

Example (72):

```
Ray says, "tomtraceback wanted to eye people"
Ray says, "but he felt compelled to make an overly
  complicated object to do it"
Tom eyes Ray warily.
lynn hehs.
Tom eyed people a lot.
Tom then made a simple verb on himself to do it.
Tom then was coerced by Brew into making it a feature.
lynn says, "so other people wanted to do it too? hence
  brew etc?"
Tom then had to make it more complex so he didn't keep
  on writing the same code over and over.
Tom [to lynn]: i guess so
```

The code Tom refers to is the programming that allows new verbs to be added to the feature, along with each verb's "help" message and "no-args" message (the error message that is printed when a user doesn't supply an argument, a target for the verb output). Other people on EM have modified the feature; Penfold added authorship tracking in 1995, so that the name of the character adding a new utterance can be recorded for historical purposes.

The story of the origin of **eye** is accompanied by amused recollection of the Archwizard on LambdaMOO reacting to all the "eyeing" that was going on. (In this conversation #0 is the System Object, #1 is the Root Class on a MOO, part of the technical infrastructure of the MOO server, and #2 is the Archwizard.)

Example (73):

```
Ray remembers Archwizard saying: "that will be enough
  of the eyeing, thank you"
Ray says, "when people were eyeing #0 #1 #2"
lynn hehs.
Patrick chuckles.
Tom hehs, had forgotten that.
Patrick eyes Ray warily.
Karen says, "archwiz remembers that too"
Ray remembers Honda pasting the line at Ray, actually
Karen says, "that's where i heard the story"
```

When used on another character, the **eye** command indicates amused wariness, uncertainty of another speaker's intent, or disapproval. An explanation for the use of **eye** came out in a discussion of how to use "**ceye**," an Antisocial command that "continues" the "eyeing." In lines

8–10 Ray demonstrates, by spoofing Tom (i.e., speaking as him), a situation in which he would eye Tom (for his liking of an unlikable computer language) and then use the **ceye** command to continue to eye him warily.

Example (74):

```
1  Ray says, "ok, ceye"
2  Ray continues to eye Tom warily.
3  Ray says, "useful when someone is doing a lot of
   eyeing warily"
4  lynn nods to Ray.
5  Tom says, "well"
6  Tom says, "not so much 'a lot'"
7  Ray says, "well"
8  Tom says, "I like tcl" --Ray
9  Ray eyes Tom warily.
10 Tom says, "but it's not as nice as perl" --Ray
11 Ray continues to eye Tom warily.
12 lynn hehs.
13 Tom says, "as when you eye someone for acting
   untoward, and they continue acting
   untoward, and you have to eye them loses"
14 Tom lol at the example.
```

Other examples of using **eye** to communicate affect responses to other players are shown below.

Example (75):
```
Henry says, "woah, cool, i just shot a pencil like
   30'"
Bryan eyes Henry warily.
```

Example (76):
```
lynn says, "who is this guy, anyhow?"
Henry [to lynn]: shelley will forward all his messages
   to you
Shelley [to lynn]: heh
Shelley eyes Henry warily.
```

Example (77):
```
anne should have gone to japan to pick up cute figure
   skaters with new great hair.
Henry eyes anne warily.
Henry [to anne]: were you recently given the opportunity
   to got to japan and show off your hair to figure
   skaters?
```

The **eye** command is often used to eye oneself warily, in a manner I consider pre-emptive; it alerts other players that the speaker is being ironic, non-serious, or extreme in some manner and is fully aware of it. This use of **eye** may in fact replace the use of smileys in some cases, which as I noted don't occur often on EM.

In Example 78, Bryan eyes himself for his parody of Tonya Harding. In response to his mention of Harding, I use the Antisocial command "**break**," which originated as a warning about programming work under way, to playfully "break" one of the things I am carrying. Jon responds with a YER MOMism.

Example (78):
```
Bryan wonders what the Tonya Harding doll is gonna be
   like if they make one.. She skates around, a
   lace breaks and she bawls the whole time
   swinging a lead pipe?
Bryan eyes himself warily.
>break virtual
You break the virtual onion ring, so don't use it.
Jon giggles
Jon breaks YR MOM, so don't use it.
Jon eyes himself warily.
```

As the playful conversation continues, Jon uses the sarcastic formula "nods solemnly," anne quotes the "a it" in Henry's remark to draw attention to it, and Shelley is sarcastic in response to Jon's rationalization. She then eyes herself warily, both making the sarcasm plain and mitigating it.

Example (79):
```
Henry [to Jon]: hey, don't go callin' my mom a it
Jon nods solemnly.
anne "a it"
Henry nods solemnly.
Jon used "it" on purpose, to try to make it a little
   less offensive.
anne [to Jon]: how...sensitive of you.
Shelley [to Jon]: o, and it helped muchly
Shelley eyes herself warily.
```

Eye has spread to several MOOs (see Doheny-Farina 1995, for instance, who mentions its appearing on MediaMOO; several LambdaMOO and EM people were influential in the evolution of early discourse on MediaMOO).

3.5.2 "Whuggle"

The second most often used command on the Antisocial Feature is an eminently social one called "**whuggle**," which Ray was initially afraid to put on the feature because it was too "nice." A whuggle is a purely virtual interaction that, for most people, has the connotations of a hug.

Because of its popularity on EM, I was quite surprised to discover that whuggling originated on some "Random and Moira" MUD ages ago, not on LambdaMOO or EM, although I have heard people say that they've never seen whuggling happen as often elsewhere as it does on EM. A dino from Seashore suggested that it may have come from another form (like "sbuggle") originally, and metamorphosed into "whuggle" over time. Tom thought it might originally have been an abbreviation for "wyld huggle."

In this discussion about the addition of **whuggle** to the Antisocial Feature, Tom and Ray try to remember if it was deemed unacceptably "nice" on EM at first, and whether the sarcastic use of **whuggle** (which Tom is particularly associated with) originated with the dinos.

Example (80):
```
Tom remembers Mike being upset about it or something.
Ray remembers Tom being somewhat upset about it
Ray says, "or at least me thinking that"
lynn says, "too nice and warm and fuzzly?"
Tom says, "here, anyway"
Karen nods.
Tom nods to lynn.
Tom says, "not antisocial"
Ray remembers thinking that Tom was trying to destroy
  the warm and fuzzy usage of whuggle by using
  it sarcastically
lynn says, "so was Tom's use of it as sarcastic the
  source of that use?"
lynn loses
Ray can't remember
Ray could swear he picked it up from tinymud dinos
Tom says, "yeah"
lynn starts back in shock
Ray says, "both the nice and sarcastic usages"
```

A whuggle is often used to greet close friends when they enter a virtual room. A new character on EM has it explained to him in the conversation below.

Example (81):
Buddy still wants to know what a whuggle is.
[. . .]
Mike [to Buddy]: it's like a hug
Jerry [to Buddy]: find the root word!
Rick says, "and like a wave..."
Mike says, "and like a pat on the head"
Buddy hides his face.
jill says, "but you can do it to inanimate objects not
  here too."
Damon says, "sorta like hug crossed with .001
  strawberry shortcakes"
Mike says, "and it's often used sarcastically."
Rick says, "smaller than a breadbox."
jill hugs REM. No.
Rick says, "and less threatening."
Damon says, "so, nonlethal in small concentrations"
Mike says, "on inanimate objects, for instance"
Jerry | WHUGGLE : We HUG in Graphically Lame
  Environments
Buddy whuggles all.
Buddy says, "I get it."

It may also be used sarcastically, especially on inanimate objects.
Examples of characters whuggling inanimate objects are shown below
(some of these were probably intended sarcastically).

(82) a. Rick whuggles reference-counting.
      b. George whuggles his new headphones.
      c. Largo whuggles AIX-dependant code.
      d. Pete whuggles politics

Hugs and whuggles occur mainly during greetings but also during
other interactions, often as a sign of affection or support. In one case,
after a woman had to kick an annoying character off the MOO, another
woman hugged her supportively and she returned the hug. Another
example is shown below. This conversation occurred right after Shelley
told a long, very amusing story about a bad experience she had had
while going home that night.

Example (83):
Shelley scrolls back and realizes she spammed.
Mike ? Shelley
Kelly [to Shelley]: Yes, well, we did too.
Shelley [to Mike]: okay, talked a lot

Mike [to Shelley]: we enjoyed the story.
Mike whuggles Shelley.

Although whuggling can involve inanimate objects and can be sarcastic, one character takes interpersonal whuggles seriously enough to find them offensive when unwanted, as shown below. The "**kill**" command's formulaic output in line 3 is related to player killing on combat MUDs (Reid 1994b); it usually expresses nothing more serious than criticism. (Although the command's output message says "Ted has left," in fact Ted is still present. On some MUDs—and for some players on EM who select that option—killing sends a player to the room designated as their "home.")

Example (84):
1 Ted whuggles George.
2 George [to Ted]: HEY NO WHUGGLING.
3 George killed Ted! Ted has left.
4 Ted whuggles George.
5 Ted whuggles George.

In another instance, a woman who was whuggled by a male character protested vehemently that she had been whuggled just because she was a woman.

Example (85):
1 Patrick waves to everyone and whuggle Marie and
   Karen.
2 Marie kills Patrick.
3 Marie chants, "Support a whugglee's right to
   choose!"
4 Karen too chants, but has told Pat he could whuggle
   her, so.
5 Marie gets disgusted
6 Marie thinks Donn is a nice male sounding name, so
   it's eir male morph on lmoo.
[She changes gender and name here.]
7 Donn [to Patrick]: OK, take that! You whuggled a
   BOY!
8 Donn [to Outsider]: I'm pissed because Patrick chose
   to whuggle me based solely on my apparent
   gender at the time.
9 Donn says, "So, I changed it."
[. . .]
10 Donn nods Out. But it's *frigging EM here* I

```
shouldn't have to put up with LM stule
sexism bullshit.
11 Donn style
```

(A morph is like a secondary character owned by the original character. "Eir" is a third person possessive gender-neutral pronoun used by some MOOers. "LM" in line 10 refers to LambdaMOO.)

Several characters have argued that it is offensive to be whuggled by people they don't know well. One male whuggled by another male protested afterward that there should be a protocol for whuggling: a character would carry a list of acceptable whugglers, and if she is whuggled by one of them, then the result would be a mutual whuggle event, "X and Y whuggle."[12]

The manners guide, which characters can see by typing "help manners" in the MOO, proscribes random hugging (and other overly familiar behavior):

```
Behavior that would be rude 'face-to-face' is rude
here, too. It isn't reasonable to ':kiss' or ':hug'
folks you don't know.
```

It would be overly simplistic, however, to assume that the standards of real-life interactions apply transparently in virtual reality; the existence of a purely virtual interaction like whuggling is enough to debunk that notion. Plenty of behavior involves a fantastical component, as the following examples of Antisocial verb output illustrate.

```
(86)  a. Ellen swings her Ellenaxe at the couch, the
         large-scale projects whiteboard, and the conference
         hall lobby.
      b. Bryan accidentally sets fire to Mike.
      c. Ray takes off and nukes LambdaMOO from orbit.
         "It's the only way to be sure."
```

Hugs do occur between characters who don't know each other in real life, and they are not always viewed as offensive. The etiquette involved seems to require that both parties feel affectionate toward one another. "Help manners" may even be intentionally disregarded:

Example (87):
```
Marion would hug Jon if it weren't against
Help-Manners.
Marion strangles help manners and hugs Jon, whom she
doesn't know from Adam.
```

---

[12]A couple of people have since implemented something like this.

In Cherny 1995a I discuss the gendered nature of whuggling. A woman is almost four times as likely to initiate a whuggle event on EM as a man. Women are three times as likely to whuggle men as they are to hug them, but they are equally likely to hug as to whuggle other women. Why? It may be that the whuggle is seen as a "safe" form of affection in the MOO, while a hug has potential real-life significance. Men get whuggled, therefore, rather than hugged; other women, "safer" objects of affection who won't "take it the wrong way," can receive hugs.

This observation tallies with comments made to me in a survey on whuggling. "To me, whuggling males, females, etc, is not that much different in itself, but it seems to be used much less between two males, just like a hug, and likely for exactly the same reason, whatever that might be"; a whuggle is "kinda like a hug, but you can do it to people you don't know very well, and you can do it to people whom you'd never hug IRL. I think it's physical, but it implies a state of emotional well-being or something. Like you wouldn't necessarily whuggle someone you were mad at"; "For me it's an abstraction meaning a safe show of affection or caring."

Survey responses included several folk etymologies that affected (or reflected) how people imagined it:

- "I think of it as a bear hug that's also accompanied by jostling the person about — kinda make believe you're an agitator on a washing machine. A hug and a wiggle — that's where I thought it was derived, actually."
- "I have NO IDEA what it means. I have CONSTRUCTED a def'n of a cross between a wink and a hug."
- "I heard somewhere it's from 'warm hug'..."
- "Some people say it's like a hug with a wiggle."

For most people it is something like a hug; but for several people it is quite abstract and has different meaning in different contexts. One day Karen emoted that she was "whuggled" by her real kittens. Upon reflection, she said, "when I first emoted :is whuggled by kittens, I realized that there was an emotional feeling to whuggling that the kittens were conveying to me physically. When I say they whuggle me, it means they come up and nuzzle my nose with their noses or heads, and basically greet me in kittenish ways. That got me to thinking about whuggling people in vr. At first I thought it's just an emotional thing—greeting between two people who are close friends—with no particular physical component. I realized when I thought it, tho, that a whuggle is when you come up to someone and pat em on the shoulder or touch eir arm when greeting. Not a hug, but a touch that indicates more closeness than a simple wave or handshake would. It's to a different degree with different people, just like hugs are different." Another woman, on the other hand, told me she has no real-life correlate for it: "no RL correlating thing; in fact, when I meet people IRL whom I whuggle here, I miss the whuggling, and I wish there were some small physical-contact thing we could do to acknowledge the fact that we are whugglers." It's interesting that so many people conceptualize a whuggle as physical, despite the virtual world it occurs in and the fact that it evokes no single, simple physical action.

Creative play with routines is common. Karen and Ted evolved their own greeting ritual using food additions to "whuggle."

(88) a. Ted whugkarenfeedsM&M
      b. Karen whugted with cheesecake with rasberry melba
         sauce!
      c. Ted whugkarenrealbigandgivesherabrownie
      d. Karen whugtedandbrowniesharesicecreamm
      e. Ted whugkarenbutdoesn'tgettoooclosebecausehemaybesick

3.5.3   Histories of Other Antisocial Commands

There are 144 commands on the Antisocial Feature Object, recording general MUD history as well as personal history of the people empowered to add to it (ten players who happen to be wizards, as of August 1995). The origins of many commands have become unclear or been lost; most players on EM who use the commands don't know the origins of more than a handful of them. Their use is routinized, just like the use of the YER MOMisms and objokes, which aren't programmed. The fact that these commands are programmed and recorded in a fixed state prevents them from being forgotten entirely, unlike some routines that come and go in MUD discourse (the "under" ritual, for instance, is no longer common among the MUDders I know). Rather than remember the entire phrasing of a complex utterance, a player need only remember the verb (or look it up in the commands on the feature) to use an Antisocial command. The commands are generally not transparently related to their output, and the help messages aren't that helpful either, so a good deal of in-group knowledge or experience is required to use them correctly.

I've loosely grouped various Antisocial commands according to whether they are derived from the personal history or experiences of a player, programming references, associations with a particular character, dictionary definitions, meta-play on the Antisocial Feature itself, dino or combat MUD history, or EM history. The stories of their origins are quoted from an interview I did with Ray, Tom, and some other players about them. More examples can be found in Cherny 1995d.

Personal History

Several commands come from personal experiences of the wizards or regulars on the MUD.

Line 1 below results from Ray's typing "bad george." The "**bad**" command was inspired by interactions in real life between George, Karen, and Julius. Even the authors of these commands occasionally have a hard time remembering their origins, as this case illustrates.

Example (89):
```
1  Ray [to George]: Bad George.
2  lynn says, "what's the bad one from?"
3  Karen says, "george"
4  Karen says, "well, Julius"
5  Karen says, "the two of them kept saying it to me
   irl" [ . . . ]
6  George doesn't remember why
7  George says, "oh!"
8  George says, "yes!"
9  Karen says, "playing cards here at my house"
10 George says, "it was bad Karen"
11 Karen [to Julius and George]: Bad Julius and
   George.
```

The "**cathedral**" command (whose output is shown in line 2) comes from a line Tom saw in a newspaper article.

Example (90):
```
1  Ray says, "cathedral"
2  Ray comes down on Tom like a ton of cathedrals.
3  Tom remembers CALLING SOMEONE UP ON THE PHONE to
   tell them about this.
4  Ray thinks that was from some book
5  Tom says, "no"
6  lynn [to Tom]: this? cathedral?
7  Tom nods.
8  Tom says, "not the command"
9  Tom says, "the thing it came from"
10 Tom says, "op/ed piece in the mpls star tribune
   (although it may have been from elsewhere)"
11 Tom says, "about ummmm abortion"
12 Tom says, "an abortion clinic shooting had
   occurred"
```

```
13 Tom says, "some catholic priest had publically
   endorsed the shooting"
14 Ray laughs
15 Tom says, "and, said this columnist, the catholic
   church hierarchy 'came down on him like a ton of
   cathedrals'"
```

Ted told a story once about a visit to the cable company, which resulted in the "**cable**" command (whose output is shown in line 1):

Example (91):

```
1  Ray sits there taking his finger across Tom's neck
   saying gleefully, "I'm slicing your throat!
   yesss I am! Pooky wooky! I'm slicing your
   throat!" as if it's a game.
2  Ray says, "from Ted's story from going to the cable
   company and sitting in line"
3  Tom | With whom did you wish to play decapitation
   games?
4  Ray says, "some mother was doing this to their
   infant"
5  lynn [to Ray]: at the cable place?!
6  Ray nods
7  Tom thinks he made the command out of it.
8  Shawn [to Ray]: redistribution of wealth from the
   people who can afford cable to theripists..
9  Tom says, "Ted was as i recall not pleased"
10 Tom thinks it gave him the creeps.
```

In line 3 above, Tom shows the "no-args" message, the message printed when "cable" is typed with no argument. The no-args messages are often amusing jokes in themselves. Note that this recording of Ted's experience in a command was not at his own request or suggestion, and he is not one of the players empowered to add to the Antisocial Feature; the players who are empowered to add to it make their own decisions about what to record. They don't see themselves as "recording" an event so much as creating amusing text messages.

Programming References

The "**c**" and "**gcc**" commands (whose outputs are shown in lines 2 and 8, respectively) are references to the programming language C and to a C compiler. In line 9 below, I invoke the command **gcc** on myself, and its output appears in line 10.

Example (92):
```
1  Ray says, "C"
2  George causes C to whomp Ray without mercy.
3  Ray hates that one
4  Ray thinks it's just stupid
5  George likes the blank message.
6  lynn says, "from a miserable programming
   experience?"
7  Ray guesses so, but it's not as clever as :gcc
8  Ray.c:1584: warning: passing arg 2 of 'George' from
   incompatible pointer type
9  >gcc me
10 lynn.c:1584: warning: passing arg 2 of 'herself'
   from incompatible pointer type
11 Ray | >gcc
12 Ray | Make who look like a broken select call?
13 lynn hehs.
14 George LOL
15 Ray says, "actual error message from compiling, um,
   Tk?"
```
Ray illustrates the "no-args" message of the **gcc** command in lines 11 and 12. Interestingly, Ray thought, wrongly, that he had made the command. George later explained that he made it when someone was pasting error messages into a MOO conversation.

A few other commands have their sources in sarcastic references to online documentation. "Rtfm" is a standard hacker acronym for "read the fucking manual."

Example (93):
```
Ray says, "aha, here's a cool one: direct"
Ray directs George to the fine documentation while
   chuckling madly.
Ray says, "clear roots in rtfm"
```

Characters As Commands

Several ElseMOO commands are named for characters, to immortalize some utterance of theirs that particularly appealed to an Antisocial author. Some characters on LambdaMOO are also represented by commands producing utterances that are associated with them.

Here folks discuss the "**via**" command, named for Via, an EM regular. Its output is shown in line 2.

Example (94):

1 Tom [to Via]: hey, what is the story behind the
  'via' command? we couldn't remember.
2 Penfold inflicts serious virtual harm on himself.
3 Via [to Tom]: I was sitting there with a bunch of
  folks in the living room, and Largo was
  being his usual self, and I couldn't think
  of a good comeback for one of the things he
  said
4 Via [to Tom]: so I threatened to inflict serious
  virtual harm on him! folks proceeded to
  guffaw, and George made it into an
  antisocial
5 lynn hehs.
6 Tom nods.
7 Via [to Tom]: which is why Largo usually greets me
  with that one :)

Similarly, the "**dana**" command (whose output is shown in line 1 below) is due to the teleport arrival message on a LambdaMOO character. The teleport arrival message is printed to the room Dana teleports into, to announce her arrival. On many MUDs, such messages are customizable. The page-echo message is the message a player sees after paging someone, also often customizable.

Example (95):

1 Ray screams 'NO NO NO ANYTHING BUT Tom'
2 Ray says, "on lambdamoo, Dana had a teleport-in
  messsage that was something like:"
3 Ray | A strangler with a slashed up face drags Dana
  in, who is screaming 'NO NO NO ANYTHING BUT
  Living Room'. He deposits her, dusts his
  hands and walks off with a smug smile.
4 Ray says, "anyway"
5 Ray thinks a lot of people liked the message, in
  general, but the bad caps made everyone
  laugh
6 Ray says, "oh, and the no-args message was one of
  her page_echo messages"
7 Ray | I am not interested in hearing from you, Dear
  Ray.
8 Ray thinks that was the story

The "**anton**" command originated with Anton's work on ColdMUD, a new MUD server type. Line 1 shows the result of Patrick's typing "anton Ray."

Example (96):

```
1 Patrick [to Ray]: I find your current work on high
  performance server architectures to be
  trite and insignificant, not to mention
  that it's probably something really stupid
  that you had to use big words to make sound
  interesting.
2 Patrick [to Ray]: 'anton' came from anton coming
  back after not playing with coldmud for a
  long time and everyone busting him on it.
3 Ray [to Patrick]: and it's actually from anton
  complaining that we were being too fawning
  about how cool what he was doing was
4 Ray says, "and Ted saying that to anton"
```

Not only are regulars and LambdaMOO characters immortalized, but one "random" named Sam is as well. Tom created this command (whose output is shown in line 2), inspired by the silly laugh and emoticon.

Example (97):

```
1  Ray says, "aha, here's a cool one: Sam"
2  Ray kicks Tom in the head. TEE-HEE :)
3  Ray suspects some random named Sam wandered on, did
   this to someone, and then was immortalized
4  Patrick | "Sam" is not the name of any player.
5  Tom says, "did this to himself"
6  Patrick says, "mebee someplace else. Seashore or
   soemthing."
7  Ray [to Tom]: really?
8  Shelley kicks lynn in the head. TEE-HEE :)
9  Shelley says, "oh, that's rude"
10 Tom says, "Sam was trying to get attention"
11 Ray | >Sam
12 Tom says, "it was the TEE-HEE that really got me"
13 Ray | I AM Sam!!!!
14 Tom says, ":)"
15 Tom says, "he said that, too"
```

Lines 11 and 13 illustrate the command's no-args message.

Dictionary Definitions

A few commands are simply dictionary definitions of the words that form the command; Ray's typing "eviscerate Tom" results in "Ray deprives Tom of vital content or force," "darn Tom" results in "Ray mends Tom with interlacing stitches," "despite Tom" results in "Ray vexes or injures Tom spitefully." Ray condemned all of these as "lame." They are rarely used.

Meta-References to the Commands

A few commands refer explicitly to the commands themselves. One day Karen was "getting pounded on by feature verbs, so thwapped someone, and without any silly feature." I imagine "thwapping" to be roughly like swatting someone. Now that emoted thwap is in fact on the Antisocial Feature as a command: "Ray thwaps Karen, and without any silly feature."

Dino and Combat MUD History

Along with the host of commands that may have come from LP MUDs or other combat MUDs ("**poke**," "**shake**," "**worship**"—traditionally done to wizards, who are known as "gods" on many combat MUDs—"**glare**," "**point**," etc.), the "**greet**" command comes from the dino community's ritual greeting.

Example (98):
>greet tom
lynn says, "TOM"
>greet! tom
lynn [to Tom]: !

The "**greet!**" command shown above is the more minimal form evolved on EM between Penfold and Honda, on the way to the fully minimal null directed speech greeting, "lynn [to Tom]:".

Similarly, the "**bwaha**" command produces the evil laugh common among the dino community: "Ray [to himself]:BWAHAHAHAHAHAHAHAHA."

The very amusing "**tangle**" command originated in a reference on Space Madness (a Random and Moira MUD that several EMers hung out on) to tangled social relationships. Damon is responsible for its output: "Ray entangles Tom in a hugely complex multiparty relationship with no obvious resolution."

The "**bonk**" command outputs both an action and an attributed "response" from the targeted character: "lynn bonks Tom. He says, "Oif!"" This records a ritual interaction among old MUDders (see "bonk/oif" in Raymond 1991).

On LambdaMOO, the bonk ritual became the genesis of "bonker" objects. According to Tom, "bonking" used to be an online ritual performed between two characters; one would emote that she bonked the other, and the bonked person would say an "oif" in response. Players tried to maintain a universal balance of bonks and "oifs." Then a wizard (Brew) on LambdaMOO made objects that performed the entire ritual, no longer necessitating the "oif" response from the bonked party. Finally the "oifs" were replaced by customizable bonker responses. This is an example of an old object bonker in action:

```
Ray bonks lynn with bonker....  lynn says, ''Oif''
Ray hands you bonker.
Ray says, ''note that that bonker was #7072 when #7072
    was max_object() :-)''
Ray says, ''oit is oold''
Ray says, ''bonk Ray with bonker''
>bonk Ray with bonker
You bonk Ray with bonker....  Ray says, ''square stinks
    wastes months played hourly''
```

Because of special code on his character object, Ray produces a customized response to being bonked: a "word square," an utterance in which the number of words in the utterance equals the number of letters in each word. Such word play is popular on EM.

Nowadays most bonkers on LambdaMOO are just commands ("verbs") a character can use to produce silly output. The Disney bonker on LambdaMOO, for instance, causes bonked characters to appear to spout lines of Disney songs. Other bonkers produce lines from sources like Zippy the Pinhead.[13] The evolution of bonking from a routine that was manually typed to a programmed action and object artifacts is similar to the evolution of other routines on MUDs. Looking at the playful artifacts on MUDs is a good way of getting an understanding of local culture and history. In section 3.6 below, I discuss more use of objects as records of MUD history.

Other ElseMOO History Sources

There are other sources in EM history for commands. For instance, the "**berries**" command originated in an entrance message on a room in the Park on EM. The message announces a player's entry to the room thus:

---

[13]The Hacker's Dictionary says this of "bonk": "In the {MUD} community, it has become traditional to express pique or censure by 'bonking' the offending person. Convention holds that one should acknowledge a bonk by saying 'oif!' and there is a myth to the effect that failing to do so upsets the cosmic bonk/oif balance, causing much trouble in the universe. Some MUDs have implemented special commands for bonking and oifing" (Raymond 1991).

"Kit arrives from the southeast, looking like he has just seen some berries."[14] The output of the **berries** command is "Ray [to Kit]: You look like you've just seen some berries!"

The "**losebutwin**" command is related to the winning and losing routines on EM and other MUDs. Its output is "Tom says, "Tom Traceback loses to the system object, BUT WINS because he FUKN SAYS SO.""

The "**grak**" command originated from a post on the mailing list associated with the role-playing game (rpg) run on LambdaMOO. In line 2 below, Ray demonstrates the command output (for "grak tom"), and in lines 3 and 4, the no-args message. Interestingly, Penfold and Tom aren't entirely sure who made it.

Example (99):

1 Ray says, "grak"
2 Ray swings his Rayaxe at Tom.
3 Ray | >grak
4 Ray | Grak? What an odd thing to type. Seek counseling.
5 Penfold says, "lambdamoo rpg"
6 Penfold <--
7 Penfold says, "some post on *rpg-s had 'Grak swings his Grakaxe at Frebble.'"
8 Ray nods, Brine had a monster named Grak, with a weapon called a Grakaxe
9 Ray says, "oh, hm"
10 Ray thought the monster was real
11 Penfold says, "it prolly was"
12 Penfold only knew about it from the post, and btw interpolated 'frebble' there
13 Tom says, "Grak was real"
14 Tom says, "but it came from the post"
15 Tom says, "which didn't just mention that line, but had it LOTS of times, in somebody's scrollback log"
16 Tom says, "which was intended to demonstrate some problem, but to me was just really funny"
17 Penfold nods at Tom, plausible

---

[14]I was told,
Ray says, "from the silly exit message in the park that none of us could figure out what to make say"
Tom still totally loves that entrance message.

```
18 Penfold [to Tom]: wait, did you add grak?
19 Tom says, "Penfold pointed it out to me"
20 Penfold gets himself and Tom confused.
21 Tom says, "and i think we both decided to make it a
   command, after goofing off with it for a
   while"
22 Tom says, "'goofing off' => figuring out the best
   message for it, too"
```

Several movie references are found in the Antisocial list, as well: references to lines in *Johnny Mnemonic, Aliens,* and *Barton Fink.* Ray relates the output of the "aliens" command (in line 1 below) to general EM history and the view that the EM power elite "rule LambdaMOO from orbit":

Example (100):

```
1 Ray takes off and nukes himself from orbit. "It's
  the only way to be sure."
2 Ray says, "related to filament's RULE LAMBDAMOO FROM
  ORBIT quote"
3 Tom [to Ray]: and 'aliens'
4 Patrick [to Ray]: uh... Aliens ?
5 Ray [to Patrick]: right, original source material
```

Typos are occasionally institutionalized in ritual utterances. The "cyc" command ("Ray cycs Karen warily.") is due to either Tom or Penfold regularly typoing "cyc" instead of "eye." Similarly, the ritual emote "hsm" ("Tom hsm"), which signals that a player is thinking about something said, apparently originated as a typo of "hms" among the dinos. Ritual typoed greetings between Karen and Tom are also common.

In sum, the Antisocial commands record many snippets of history and relations both within the MOO and with other MUD communities. However, as historical records they are not particularly robust, and several origin stories are lost or fragmentary. When I interviewed several EM wizards about the commands' origins, a large group of players interested in hearing the stories gathered, indicating that they are a matter of curiosity and cultural interest.

3.5.4   Uses of the Antisocial Commands

Although many commands have the character of in-jokes, most of the EM regulars know neither the jokes nor the origins of the commands, yet use them anyway for their intrinsic humor. Antisocial commands are used as joking asides in conversation and as weapons in occasional

"Antisocial" wars, playful routines in which commands are traded back and forth among multiple participants, occasionally aimed at objects on the MUD as well. I give an example of such a speech activity in section 5.1, when I discuss byplay. These ritual interactions resemble ritual performed insult exchanges in some speech communities (e.g., "playing the dozens" among African American youth, Kochman 1972).[15] Because of the formulaic nature of the Antisocial utterances, the activity resembles the "quotefests" that occur on Seashore; MUDders there save quotes from one another's discourse that are amusing, bizarre, or suggestive, and often resurrect them months or years later to paste them into the MUD during ritual quote exchanges. In both the Antisocial command wars and the quotefests, the intent is humor and play, not offense, although many of the Antisocial utterances are insulting or otherwise unpleasant. Abrahams (1992) discusses the nature of insult performance: "Insults are primarily improvised, fixed-phrase formulas and are most powerful when they are employed at points of greatest stress in community life. Insulting is usually a responsive activity, arising in verbal competition [. . .]. Traditional rivals have often developed an extensive repertoire of insults that are called forth under licensed conditions when members of the two groups meet" (p. 146). Although the Antisocial command wars are somewhat similar to the performances Abrahams describes, the Antisocial commands are not used in any real combative situation; use of them immediately keys an exchange as play. Furthermore, their frozen, programmed output precludes the sort of improvisation that is valued in rituals like "playing the dozens."

Antisocial commands are special on EM in that they are visible long-distance, across room boundaries, and visible to all in the "target" room, unlike pages or remote-emotes.[16] As a result, long-distance public displays of affection, affect, or greeting occasionally occur. In Example 101, Tom enters the room my character is in, coming from the Living Room; George eyes him warily from the Living Room, an action visible to all the characters there as well as in the room Tom has just entered. (George may have eyed him for an abrupt departure without a goodbye.)

Example (101):
You hear someone walk onto the bridge.
Tom swings down from the top of the bridge through the
   gap.
From the living room: George eyes Tom Traceback
   warily.

---

[15]I am indebted to Tari Fanderclai for this observation.
[16]Remote-emotes are paged emotes, which also show the speaker's location: "(from the living room) Shelley eyes you warily."

Tom sits on the large sandstone rock beside Karen.

In this next case, I paste a remote-emote from Shelley in line 1, to allow Penfold to see it. Penfold eyes us both warily, which is visible to her and to the occupants of the room she is in (signaling to them that something may be going on in pages), she responds by poking us, and I poke her back remotely (the tilde allows reference to a character in a different room).

Example (102):

```
1 lynn | (from the living room) Shelley bites you!
2 Penfold eyes Shelley and you warily.
3 lynn says, "well."
4 lynn says, "she waved too."
5 From the living room: Shelley pokes Penfold and you.
6 >poke ~shelley
7 You poke Shelley.
```

Some players consider such uses of the Antisocial Feature spammy and pointless. They believe that only the player "targeted" with the command should be able to see its output, despite the fact that the commands are usually used as intentionally public performances of interaction.

3.5.5 Negotiation over Antisocial Discourse

Negotiation over what is on the Antisocial Feature is complicated; currently only most of the wizards (Tom, George, Damon, Penfold, Sleep, Mike, Ray, Rick, Pete, and Jubilee) are able to add anything to it. Marie has been vocal about disliking the Antisocial Feature, and considers it just as spammy and unpleasant as the bonkers used on LambdaMOO, which many people feel contributed to the "old-timers" leaving the noisy public areas (see chapter 2). Certainly it is true that parties can degenerate into primarily Antisocial exchanges, but it's also true that several commands on the feature, like "**eye**" and "**poke**" (to get another player's attention), are regularly used for complex communicative functions, so generalizing about the commands is problematic.

Tom sees the Antisocial Feature as a historical record and a personal one, too, although many others have contributed to it over the years. In Example 103, he refers to the suggestion that the "," command, a shorthand for the "<-" notation, be added to the Antisocial commands, a suggestion he doesn't approve of.

Example (103):

Tom [to lynn]: note btw that i always get irritated
    when people comes up with suggestions like ",
    should be on the antisocial feature" (which

happened _very_ early in EM history) or "let's
have the antisocial feature but call it
something else"
Penfold [to Tom]: let's have the antisocial feature
but have it make toast
Tom says, "oh, just because the name 'antisocial
feature' is not insignificant"
Tom says, "oh, or "let's have the antisocial feature
but get rid of all the messages that aren't
nice""
Ray nods
Freddie says, "yeah"
Tom as the author feels uh uh well, offended anyway.

Despite complaints about violence and spamminess, the only things
that have been changed on the feature since its creation are the "oral"
commands, which were removed during what Penfold calls "The Great
Oral Purge," apparently because of their sexual overtones.

Example (104):
Penfold says, "with the exception of the Great Oral
Purge?"
Tom was uneasy with the purge, but not for the same
reason.
lynn says, "oral purge?"
Penfold nods.
Tom felt like the commands were lame, regardless of
whether they were antisocial.
Penfold says, "well, they were, yeah"
Tom [to lynn]: the "bite" and "eat" and "suck"
commands got removed.
Tom says, "is that the right list?"
Ray thinks that's right
Penfold says, "just because they didn't do anything"
Penfold nods
Penfold says, "lick"
lynn says, "i don't see why they're so much worse"
Tom says, "because i don't use them"
Penfold says, "because they're lame"
Ralph says, "because all the rest are in-jokes"
Ray says, "because this is a family moo"
Ray dunno
Penfold says, "and specifically because of the sexual
implications"

```
lynn says, "violence is ok, sex isn't"
Penfold says, "sure seems that way, doesn't it?"
```

Although occasionally controversial or disturbing in their content, the Antisocial commands are a distinctive part of the EM linguistic repertoire. Other MUDs have similar customized command sets, and often there is some overlap in the commands due to the players' multiple community memberships or history on other MUDs; the **eye** command, for instance, is found on several other MOOs. The Antisocial commands reflect the fact that the programmable MUD environment provides the means to permanently record cultural references and facilitate rituals, as well as the opportunity to create new rituals and add to the shared culture by providing new commands that may become popular. The linguistic culture is partly a culture of technology use, since knowing commands is a component of producing the community's language.

3.6 Objects As Conversants

Objects frequently have commands on them that output some information to the occupants of the room when someone interacts with them. For instance, if I want to sit on a chair, I can type a command:

```
>sit on chair
lynn sits on the folding chair.
```

Objects may generally only be interacted with if the player's character is in the same room as the object. The Antisocial commands and the Carpal Tunnel Syndrome commands discussed earlier are available anywhere.

Objects also serve as a record or embodiment of history, giving a permanence to some events. Stories are associated with some objects: their reason for creation, their origin on other MUDs, their original author. The high5ing glove on EM is a copy of an object made by the character lew on Dreamscape, an old Random and Moira MUD. The glove is used to congratulate someone. Mike uses it below in lines 4–7 because Henry comes up with a clever name transformation to apply to Mike during a game inspired by a children's TV show.[17]

Example (105):

```
1 Mike takes a AI from his chest and turns Henry
  into a hairy!
2 Henry takes a FA from his chest and turns Mike
  into a fake!
```

---

[17]The copyright notices were attached when the glove was copied by a character on EM, with lew's permission.

3 Delak takes a GA from his chest and turns Finder
  into a gander!
4 Mike picks up the special high-fiving glove
  and slips it onto his hand. (c) 1992 lew industries.
5 Mike leaps up into the air and high5s Henry with
  a resounding >THWACK<.
6 The high-fiving glove on Mike's hand glows gently
  for a moment, then returns to normal.
  (c) 1992, lew industries.
7 Mike suddenly flings a large glove to the ground
  and shouts, "I CHALLENGE YOU, BENJAMIN J.
  TOAD!" You nod your head in solemn approval.
  (c) 1992, lew industries.

The entire interaction, from picking up the glove to flinging it down,
is a programmed script on the object, and is generated by typing the
command "**high5** <someone> **with glove**").

The vase in the EM Living Room dates back to a joke on ChaosMUD
in 1990, in which a vase object transmitted everything said in the main
party spot into another room. Apparently the original joking line for
the vase worked like this: "thelfar speaks into the vase. "lew
suspects."" It evolved into a message referring to (secret) agents. Now
on EM, discussion of agents in the Living Room is likely to cause someone
to type the command "**identify** <someone> **to vase**," resulting in the
output message visible to all in line 8 below:

Example (106):
1 Mike says, "which one?"
2 lynn highly recommends it for a giggle.
3 lynn [to Mike]: "What's An Agent, Anyway?"
4 Kit walks in from the sunroom.
5 Shelley waveys Kit
6 Ted | lynn [to Mike]: "What's An Agent, Anyway?"
7 Ted | Kit walks in from the sunroom.
8 Ted whispers into the vase, "I think Kit is an
  agent."

(In lines 6 and 7, the vertical bar represents a "paste," indicating that
Ted is quoting the previous lines 3 and 4. He brings the earlier text back
into focus to motivate his action in line 8.)

Often new commands or objects on EM are the subject of play for
a time. The creation of a topic-marking facility for MOO rooms in
late 1994 provided one such opportunity for play. Ordinarily, a player
can designate a room's conversation as being on a particular topic, and

the message displayed describes a groundskeeper putting up a sign with the topic label on it. (When a player lists the "parties" on the MUD, the topics associated with each party are also displayed. Rarely are they serious, however.) The topic can be changed, or the sign can be removed. Here Tom and Ray play with the topics during our discussion of the history of the Antisocial commands.

Example (107):

```
Tom covers the topic sign reading 'where did all of
   the antisocial commands come from?' with a
   slip of paper reading 'me'.
Ray pulls the top sheet off the topic sign.
```

Below is an excerpt from some extended play with a Christmas tree object on EM. There are several commands on the tree, including "**shake**" and "**clap**." When someone shakes the tree, random ornaments fall off. One of the ornaments is a Lego toy resembling Tom. After the Tom ornament fell on the floor, there were two "Tom"s in the same room (the character and the ornament object). It became difficult for the MOO server to parse commands correctly, and people pasted in the error messages that the server sent them.

Example (108):

```
Ray walks up to the tree and SHAKES IT VIOLENTLY.
The tree shakes and shivers, and Tom just falls off
   onto the floor.
Ray giggles
Penfold | You see no "tom at ray" here.
lynn laughs too
Ray says, "now we have a problem,"
Ray | You haven't specified which "tom" you mean.
lynn | Which tom do you mean?
Penfold argh
Ray | You see no "tom ornament" here.
lynn says, "too many Toms!"
Ray picks up Tom.
Ray | Tom (aka #1371 and lego tom)
Ray puts Tom in the Christmas tree.
Penfold says, "lego my tom"
lynn says, "leggo my Lego Tom"
Bonny eyes Ray warily.
lynn [to Penfold]: hrmph
Ray puts the annoying electronic bell in the Christmas
   tree.
```

```
Penfold ornament
Robin claps at the Christmas tree. Clap, clap!
The lights on the Christmas tree burst to life.
```

Few players are empowered to create objects on EM. Only players with programmer bits and sufficient building quota may do so. As discussed in chapter 2, EM has fairly restrictive policies on building and on the distribution of programmer bits, which has caused some friction on the MOO. As one person told me, "as for small incidental objects, people with programming bits create them [. . .] to augment social interaction. People without prog bits can't. That's a bit arbitrary." People with programmer bits may not only make objects that record history or become community play props, but may perform on-the-fly object jokes: Rick said he was eating onion rings, I asked for one, and he made a virtual onion ring object and gave it to my character. Similarly, on LambdaMOO one day, George made a "movie picker" object to solve a debate between me and Tom about what movie to see in real life. On EM once, a player made a herpes object in order to be able to give herpes to another character. An emoted "Sondra gives you herpes" is not nearly as successful a joke as one involving a "real" MUD object.

3.7 Human Toys

Other automation appears in MOOs. Characters themselves may be automated in interesting or amusing ways. The character ls, for instance, has code that automatically moves him out of crowded rooms once they get too "loud"; he also has code that automatically null-emotes for him if he hears certain question words. Other sorts of minor automation on LambdaMOO include "idle twitches," which look initially as if they were said by a person, but are actually just triggered by mention of the character's name in its vicinity while it is idle. Line 2 below is Ray's idle twitch. (Note that "you" in line 1 refers to the user, not the character, which is sitting there in the room with my character.)

Example (109):
```
1 lynn [to Ray]: so when you come back, I have a
  question...
2 Ray lies, "I'm awake, I'm awake!"
```

Code that functions even when a player is not connected is illustrated below, sent to me by one of the participants. The character Tom has a bit of code that removes people from his MOO room when Tom's user is not connected, by first trying to move them through the door, and if it's locked, ejecting them. In Example 110, Tom forgot about this and invited others to stay after he disconnected; the character Ray was automatically ejected to his own home, where his idle twitch then went off. Ray's user saw this exchange in his scrollback later. (From the point where "Tom stirs" in line 6, all activity was automated.)

Example (110):

```
1  Tom says, "filfre to hang out here until my parents
   get home"
2  Penfold says, "should we sneak out?"
3  Tom has disconnected.
   < disconnected: Tom. Total: 156 >
4  Penfold leaves too!
5  Penfold goes home.
   < disconnected: Penfold. Total: 156 >
6  Tom stirs, opens his eyes, and notices there are
   people in his room while he's trying to
   sleep.  He quickly ushers you outside.
7  The door seems to be stuck. You get a little
   claustrophobic.
8  Tom frowns.  "You're still here?  Well, if asking
   politely doesn't work..."
9  Ray's Home
10 Ray's home is a biology lab taken over by scores of
   slightly obsolete computers: Apple IIs,
   first generation PC clones and an Amiga
   1000.  [ . . . ]
12 Ray (#3920) arrives.
13 Ray lies, "I'm awake!  I'm awake!"
```

The word "filfre" in line 1 is an abbreviation for "feel free." Line 9, the announcement that Ray's character is now in a new location, indicates that he has been ejected from Tom's room. Line 12, the actual arrival message, triggers his idle twitch in line 13, because idle twitches respond to mention of the character's name.

Some users have special "verbs," or MOO code, on their characters that allow other people to "do" things to them, producing amusing output. Some users call this "human toy" code, although the character, not the human body, is the locus of the interaction. Tom, for instance, has a "throw" verb on himself that allows people to throw him around, and that generates a random exclamation from Tom. (The character's code, not the human typist, produces the "ooch.")

Example (111):

```
>throw Tom at bed
You throw Tom at an old-fashioned bed.  Tom is now
   slumped over an old-fashioned bed.
Tom says, "Ooch!"
```

The character Pete on EM produces nonsense utterances when "poked" or "kicked"; some of those utterances actually originated on LambdaMOO, recorded by an object in the Living Room (a Cockatoo bird, which babbles things it has heard LambdaMOO characters saying in the past). Pete simulates bird-behavior in response to being poked and kicked, and then spouts messages recorded by the object on LambdaMOO, shipped to EM by network link (lines 3 and 6). This example was collected while Pete was idle (i.e., his character had been sitting there inactive because the user was busy in real life).

```
1 >poke pete
2 Pete shifts about on his perch and bobs his head.
3 Pete squawks, "BRB - gotta help out somewhere else"
4 >kick pete
5 lynn kicks Pete.
6 Pete babbles, "long time Listen, Purple, Dharma is
  away from his keypad right now, I guess. you hold
  tight and work on that beer; I be right back!"
```

In a rather extreme example of cyborg metamorphosis, Shelley turned herself into a human appliance while she was programming a washing machine object for EM. In line 3, Berke activates her, and she continues to converse normally while her code simultaneously generates output messages that are appropriate to a washer working.

Example (112):

```
1  Berke says, "Hey, are you a washing machine?"
2  Shelley says, "no...i was messing with the washing
   machine adn copied the verbs that worked to
   myself so i wouldn't have to start over if
   i screwed up."
[ . . . ]
3  Berke hands Shelley four quarters and a pile of
   dirty clothes, and presses the button on
   Shelley's left shoulder.
4  You hear Shelley fill with water.
5  Berke hee
6  Karen hehs.
7  Shelley giggles.
8  Shelley makes a clunking sound.
9  Shelley begins to jump around the room, agitating
   the clothes.
10 Berke lol
11 Shelley will take it off soon.
```

12 Shelley stops and you hear water draining.
13 You notice that Shelley is beginning the rinse
   cycle.
14 Berke [to Shelley]: So add an 'unplug shelley' verb
   which will shut the washing machine off.
15 Shelley goes silent for a moment, then suddenly
   begins to spin round and round, water
   spraying everywhere.
16 Shelley [to Berke]: yeah...i'm just waiting to have
   someone jump me about turning myself into a
   toy.
17 *PING*
18 Shelley drops a pile of clean, wet clothes. You have
   a feeling she's kept at least one sock, though.

(In line 10, "lol" means "laughs out loud.") Note that Shelley wonders whether she has crossed into a territory that isn't acceptable for the regulars on EM. She was eventually asked to make herself incapable of talking during washing machine behavior, because the mix of characteristics (human and appliance) was disturbing on aesthetic grounds.

3.8 Conclusion

The register that has evolved in EM shares features with other registers in mediated communication situations in which speakers of the same register are communicating with one another, like CB (Powell and Ary 1977) or amateur radio (Gibbon 1985); simplifications to speed transmission (deletions, contractions, acronyms) and special vocabulary for commonly occurring events and objects are prevalent. Unlike in the Interactive Written Discourse described in Ferrara, Brunner, and Whittemore 1991, subject and article deletion rarely occur, and unlike in IRC (Reid 1991), emoticons are rarely used.

Unlike the subjects used for the Ferrara, Brunner, and Whittemore 1991 data gathering, the speakers of EM form an elective discourse community, sharing history together and with other MUD communities. They have a strong perception of EM as a speech community, with conventional routines and utterances that are specific to them or shared with LambdaMOO and Seashore MUSH. Some routines evolved in response to the medium ("loses/wins," "etc"), but most are historical records of speech patterns on other MUDs, showing in particular the influence of the old "dino" community (a subset of the group on Seashore MUSH), or of events on EM or LambdaMOO. Individual creativity sometimes results in new routines or conventional utterances.

There is a close interaction between linguistic conventionalization and programming on ElseMOO. A routine may be programmed into an Antisocial command, or it may become the output of a command programmed on an object. Part of "speaking" the register involves knowing the commands that produce ritual utterances. The recording of routine utterances on objects and as commands no doubt preserves them in the discourse, as well. Although anyone may theoretically be influential on the speech patterns of the community, only a handful of people are empowered to add to the Antisocial commands or to build objects. The power structure that I describe in chapters 2 and 6 has a subtle but definite effect on the speech of the group; people who might be considered the "power elite" are influential not only as innovative MUD speakers (e.g., Tom's "eyeing" and "aieee"), but as programmers and wizards who can build records of the speech of themselves or others on the MUD or invent new textual devices for communication (e.g., directed speech, thought bubbles).

4

Medium Effects: Turn-Taking and Back Channels

We saw that ElseMOO users use special language that reflects their history together as well as properties of the medium (text-based, typed interaction). It's clear that text-based computer-mediated communication does not offer the same rich communication channels available in face-to-face conversation. Yet text-based communication is both useful and productive in the MUD community, despite the poverty of the text channel. How does text conversation differ from face-to-face conversation? How do users have to adapt to make it comfortable and to avoid misunderstandings?

Opportunities for smooth turn-taking, interruption, requests for clarification, and speaker change are important for successful communication (Clark and Brennan 1991). Feedback signals of understanding and attention, which have been called **back channels** (Yngve 1970), have also been deemed important in conversation (Clark and Schaefer 1989). This chapter explores the effect of the MUD medium on turn-taking and back channel behavior during conversation, suggesting that users adapt their communication practices to the demands of the medium.

4.1 Interactivity

The concept of **interactivity** is a recurrent one in literature on human-computer interaction and mediated communication systems. Rafaeli (1988) theorizes interactivity as "an expression of the extent that in a given series of communication exchanges, any third (or later) transmission (or message) is related to the degree to which previous exchanges referred to even earlier transmissions" (p. 111). The interactivity of a message thus depends partly on the interactivity of earlier messages. As a concept, interactivity applies to any communication situation, whether mediated or not. He cites Goffman's (1957) notion of "reciprocally sustained involvement" (p. 50), which more loosely characterizes it; a press conference, for instance, even with questions from the audience, is rarely interactive, since follow-up questions only rarely build on the relation between previous questions and answers.

Interactivity in Rafaeli's sense certainly depends greatly on the communicative competence of interlocutors, particularly in unfamiliar communication situations. The ability to turn-take successfully on the telephone, for instance, depends on becoming comfortable with the lack of visual feedback; for some people this is harder than it is for others. Additionally, the speech event of a phone conversation requires being able to negotiate technology-determined rituals like openings in which the caller is not immediately identifiable to the person called (Schegloff 1977), since visual identifications aren't available. Some callers may assume that a small voice sample is sufficient for identification, while others may provide more verbal information; the opening sequences can be said to be "recipient-designed" (Schegloff 1977) based on assumptions about an interlocutor's knowledge and abilities in the phone context.

All conversation is usually recipient-designed, when it is cooperative; we may assume this is true of highly interactive communication as well. As Whittaker 1994 says, feedback is critical for interactivity, since feedback enables speakers to recognize when their message has been understood (Clark and Schaefer 1989) or when a repair is needed, aiding in further recipient-design.

4.1.1   The Importance of Interface and Infrastructure

In order to study the interactivity of a system, we have to understand the effects of system characteristics on message exchange. Discourse patterns are related to the technical affordances of a system as well as to the contexts of use.

Baym 1993 gives examples of how particular resources affect cultural formation in the Usenet newsgroup community on rec.arts.tv.soaps. The details of the network infrastructure (and commonly shared features of newsreaders) significantly affect users' experiences of the community. The ability to identify posters and follow "threads" (topics) across time is important in the asynchronous medium, where multiple topics may be active at once (Black et al. 1983). Other small system details can be extremely important. Baym quotes a user comparing the free-flowing creativity on Usenet with what Prodigy's infrastructure allows:

Prodigy posters do not have the ability to include parts of previous postings in their posts and therefore it is much more difficult to carry a thread along as the sentiments of the original posts are lost in the discussion. Also, prodigy posts are often much shorter, due to the fact that reading and writing multiple pages is very slow. (Baym 1993, p. 147)

Usenet is an asynchronous communications system: users are not interacting in real time, but are reading and posting to persistent databases of posts. In a synchronous system like a chat system, users are connected and communicating at the same time. There are a wide range of possible synchronous systems. As Kiesler et al. (1980, p. 75) point out for the conferencing system they used, "there is [. . .] a definite 'asynchronous' quality even to 'synchronous' computer conferences." In their system, a user cannot compose and read messages at the same time, so a significant time lag between message-readings is introduced if a user wants to post a message. This situation does not hold for MUDs.

We need to specify system characteristics more finely than the distinction between synchronous and asynchronous systems if we are to understand interactive behavior in the system. There have been several attempts to classify media systems according to different sets of characteristics (e.g., Paisley and Chen 1982; Daft and Lengel 1984; Rice and Williams 1984; Oviatt and Cohen 1991a; Clark and Brennan 1991; Whittaker 1994).

Daft and Lengel (1984) organize media according to "richness"; media are characterized according to how fast feedback occurs, which channels are used, whether "sources" are personal or impersonal, and what language types (body language, natural language, or numeric language) are available. The telephone, characterized as "richer" than written documents, is described as offering "fast" feedback, an audio channel, a personal "source," and natural language. As Heeter (1989) points out, the components are not independent: the possibility of body language is dependent on the visual channel. Other components may vary within a medium, for instance the personal or impersonal nature of the source message. It is unclear how "rich" a formal telephone call is.

Rice and Williams (1984) describe media systems in terms of channel limitations, channel redundancy (the possibility of having the same message in two or more channels, e.g., spoken words also appearing in text form), the potential for interactivity (immediate two-way exchange), social presence according to users' judgments, privacy as judged by users' senses of whether "outside" individuals can monitor, and the "familiarity" of the system according to users' judgments. Since Rice and

Williams include three categories that depend on users' judgments of a system, it is difficult to use their criteria to assess systems in the literature that haven't been supplemented with data from user questionnaires. Clark and Brennan (1991) provide a rich set of criteria for describing media systems. They identify "eight constraints that a medium may impose on communication between two people, A and B" (p. 140):

- co-presence: A and B share the same physical environment;
- visibility: A and B are visible to each other;
- audibility: A and B communicate by speaking;
- co-temporality: B receives at roughly the same time A produces;
- simultaneity: A and B can send and receive at once and simultaneously;
- sequentiality: A's and B's turns can't be put out of sequence by intervening turns from other people;
- reviewability: B can review A's messages;
- revisability: A can revise her own message privately before sending it to B.

Face-to-face communication, therefore, has co-presence, visibility, audibility, co-temporality, simultaneity, and sequentiality. Video conferencing has all of those but co-presence. A computer conference, they say, has co-temporality, sequentiality, and reviewability.

Although more descriptive than other researchers' sets of media characteristics, Clark and Brennan's list contains some redundancy and some inexplicable points. Since visibility is a category, it is unclear what else co-presence offers; and since co-presence is a property not of mediated communication but of face-to-face communication, it seems unhelpful as a system characteristic. The visibility category does not allow for visual displays of anything other than another speaker, so that it cannot take into account systems in which users share a drawing space or other workspace (e.g., Whittaker, Brennan, and Clark 1991), or systems in which users are represented by graphic figures or "avatars" (e.g., Morningstar and Farmer 1991). For greater generality, channels and the type of their information content should be specified. The granularity of messages should also be specified in connection with the revisability criterion; generally a message is revisable up to its transmission grain size. Email messages, large-grained, are revisable within a single message; Unix **talk**, with every character transmitted, is not revisable (except at the character level perhaps, although all mistakes and revisions are visible).

4.1.2 Defining MUD System Characteristics

Despite my criticisms of these categorizations, I acknowledge that a concise description of a media system needs to specify such attributes. However, it should be kept in mind that the social context of use affects both system design and emergent use patterns (e.g., message storage facilities may be added to a system if not all users can be online when transmission occurs in some setting; see Dourish 1995 and Baecker 1993 for references to related literature). Even describing system characteristics is difficult without making reference to use patterns based on larger social context issues. The media characteristics I propose, therefore, are not technological determinants of behavior, but are themselves partly determined by user behavior.

I'll describe communication systems by using the following set of features: message granularity, the possibility of message storage, the temporal structure of communication, available channels, and related interface characteristics.

Message granularity refers to the size of transmissions and relates to how real-time a medium is: small message size is usually related to spontaneous, real-time (synchronous) communication, which allows little revisability. Both technical and social issues are related to granularity: technically, when is a message transmitted; and socially, how large are the message chunks in practice? Technically, a message might be transmitted in characters, in lines, or in some other arbitrary size. Usually the transmission command is related to the buffer size: character-by-character transmission (as in Unix **talk**) doesn't require the user to issue a transmission command, while line-by-line transmission may take a simple RETURN command to send (as in a MUD). Socially, users generally send larger messages when they are less likely to get responses quickly: more is accomplished in a single transmission, and the resulting speech exchange is often less interactive, with subsequent long messages less related to preceding messages.

Whether message storage exists (and for how long) suggests whether the medium is intended to support real-time activity or asynchronous browsing. Large granularity combined with message storage, as in Usenet or mailing lists, tends to reduce the amount of interactivity, since more topics are covered in a single message and more time tends to pass between exchanges than in a synchronous forum. However, the possibility of storage doesn't necessarily result in non-real-time communication; email exchanges can be carried on between two people connected at the same time, and may be quite short, similar to real-time chatting. The possibility of storage can change social expectations; Zuboff (1988) describes email being used in accountability games, with off-the-cuff responses being taken as more serious than intended, and people "covering their asses" by producing email evidence for all decisions (cf. Markus 1994).

Describing the temporal structure of the medium doesn't solely mean distinguishing between synchrony and asynchrony (real-time and non-real-time), but also involves what Clark and Brennan called "simultaneity": is a channel two-way? If it's two-way, interruptions can occur in real-time interactions, allowing for a higher degree of interactivity. Additionally, Clark and Brennan's sequentiality should follow. The two-way channel only becomes important in synchronous, very small-grained communication. Asynchronous communication will not result in simultaneous use of the channel, which a two-way channel allows. Synchronous large-grained communication may result in overlaps, but the large grain size will reduce the likelihood of overlaps and the usefulness of overlap for repair attempts (Sacks, Schegloff, and Jefferson 1974), thus reducing interactivity. As an example of interface characteristics affecting use, consider that Unix **talk** is two-way: input comes in simultaneously with output, character by character. However, the split-screen interface reduces the impact of interruptions significantly; the channel does not have to be "fought" for, which means both interlocutors may continue transmitting if they wish, or if they don't notice the other typing. It takes some skill to learn to use the split-screen format and maintain interactive, recipient-designed conversation.[1]

Channel characteristics need to be explicated in more detail than has been done in the literature I've reviewed so far. The interface channels that connect users communicating through a media system may provide more information than simply audio or video. Their potential for transmitting other forms of information must be specified. Habitat, a multi-user environment in which users are represented by graphic "avatars," is another type of mediated communication system (Morningstar and Farmer 1991). The interface is graphically visual, but the visual channel does not connect the users directly. MUDs do not generally use graphics or audio, but some industrial MUD projects are adding video and audio channels to the text interface (Curtis and Nichols 1993).

---

[1]The Rafaeli 1988 definition of interactivity doesn't allow for simultaneous transmission, only for a sequential exchange. This is perhaps an artifact of considering face-to-face conversation as ideal, where the floor must be negotiated for as a resource and simultaneous exchanges may signal problems with floor negotiation. Despite this reliance on face-to-faceness, I accept that if two interlocutors are significantly overlapping there is less interactivity, although it is clear that some overlap is normal in face-to-face conversation; cf. Goodwin 1986, Edelsky 1993.

One of the possible effects of mediated communication is a feeling of **telepresence**, of being in a third world created by the media system (e.g., Morningstar and Farmer 1991; Dourish and Bly 1992). Steuer 1992 describes telepresence as the experience of being in an environment created by a communications medium. Even simple text environments can evoke a feeling of telepresence, as evidenced by posters on BBSes who report a sense of place (Steuer 1992, Stone 1991). With greater sensory vividness and a more interactive interface, this experience of presence is intensified. The sense of "interactive" that Steuer refers to is different from the notion I invoked from Rafaeli 1988. I have retained an emphasis on message transmission because of my linguistic interests; but the interface focus of Steuer's discussion is clearly valuable in explicating the feeling of engagement and immersion that a system may evoke in its users. The interface characteristics of concern to me, then, are the sensory channels that either give a "direct" link to an interlocutor or support a sense of telepresence and specifically of **co-presence** in some mediating third world. I'll leave these characteristics vague, but refer the reader to Steuer's (1992) discussion of speed, range of manipulability, and mapping of controls (particularly metaphoric mappings, e.g., wheel controls for vehicle manipulation) that affect telepresence sensations.

The list below summarizes the media characteristics I've discussed, as they apply to MUDs. All of these properties have some bearing on the interactivity of a medium (in the message transmission sense). The list combines social and technical aspects of a system's use, and is not meant to eliminate the context of use or details of the interface from consideration.

- message granularity: any length line may be sent, but in practice utterances are between about five and thirteen words long
- message storage: real-time conversation is usually saved only in a user's local buffer (and not saved beyond a session); mail may be stored in an internal MOO database
- temporal character: synchronous (i.e., used in real time, except for mailing lists), but not two-way
- channels: visual (text only)

In sum, MUDs (in their main mode of use, real-time synchronous conversation) may be characterized as having generally small-grained messages, usually from a word to a clause in length, which are ordinarily not stored by the system, although users maintain local buffers of "scroll-back." Real-time message transmission is buffered a line at a time; the user transmits by pressing RETURN. Message granularity in the synchronous conversation mode is actually largely up to users, who learn to respond dynamically to the constraints of the context, as I discuss in this chapter. Long messages decrease the sense of co-presence and awareness of others in the medium, by decreasing the real-time feel (since composing a long message takes more time). MUDs are synchronous but not two-way channeled, so interruptions cannot occur in the form of overlap. All MUD communication occurs in text, but users report a strong feeling of telepresence, probably due to the highly interactive environment and the fact that the MUD database models a physical world that can be interacted with using text commands. Asynchronous modes of communication in the form of mailing lists and private mail exist in some MUDs as well, supporting larger-grained messages that are stored in the MUD database.

4.2 Previous Literature

According to the literature on computer-supported cooperative work (CSCW) and CMC, one major problem posed by mediated interactions is difficulty with turn exchange and conversational floor control. Some authors advocate strict one-at-a-time speaker/actor roles (Novick and Walpole 1990), while others condemn this structure as too restrictive (Ellis, Gibbs, and Rein 1991; Beaudouin-Lafon and Karsenty 1992). Woodburn et al. (1991) found that strict sequencing in dyadic (two-person) text-based CMC situations increased the amount of time required to complete a task, and users generally preferred to determine their own strategies for turn-taking. In the full-duplex split-screen connection they studied, users liked being able to see messages being composed character-by-character, and could frequently begin answering in parallel.

Control flow depends heavily on properties of the medium. McKinlay et al. (1994) note that properties of CMC may offset some of the problems that increased group size causes in face-to-face situations; because of the permanence of the medium, users depart from serial turn-taking and adopt topics in parallel (cf. Black et al. 1983; McCarthy et al. 1993). Face-to-face models of turn-taking may not be appropriate for CMC situations, they conclude.

Black et al. (1983) studied turn-taking in email discussions compared to classroom conversations. They found that the time delay in email resulted in multiple topics (or "multi-threads") being pursued in parallel, instead of one at a time as in face-to-face conversation. Real-time messaging, in their study, displayed single-topic threads, like face-to-face conversation. They also found back channeling to be minimal in email, resulting in "dangling" conversations with no closure.

McCarthy et al. (1993) report on text-based conferencing in which users can only see contributions after a typist presses a "send" key. Since composition was not visible and upcoming messages were not signaled, users missed contributions or wasted time typing what another user had already sent. Users were also unsure when another user was "listening" and available for conversation. Timely repair mechanisms were also missing, leading to persisting misunderstandings. McCarthy et al. conclude that message structuring to help with signals of understanding (e.g., back channel response buttons), to establish referents, and to enforce response to queries might be helpful additions to text-based CMC systems.

Oviatt and Cohen (1991a, 1991b) found that keyboard communication of instructions to assemble a water pump resulted in fewer back channels, longer turns, and fewer clarifications or interruptions. The medium was deemed less efficient than the interactive speech medium, since the task also took longer to complete. However, the task involved was a complicated manual one, so the keyboard modality was not optimal in any case. Their finding is also predicted by Clark and Brennan (1991), who attach high cost to reception, production, and speaker change in the keyboard modality.

In the sections below, I challenge some of these conclusions, in particular the claims that fewer back channels necessarily result from keyboard interactions, that longer turns result, and that repair is impeded by the medium. I also discuss the effect of the permanence of the medium on the topic threading, and show that multi-threading is still common, despite the real-time nature of the conversation in MUDs. Contrary to the finding in McCarthy et al. 1993, users in MUDs have adapted to the problems caused by the one-way channel, in which messages are not received until a user finishes typing and sends them. Their adaptations include sending smaller-grained messages and using frequent back channels.

4.3 Turn-Taking in the MUD

The entire notion of turn-taking as a process in conversational interactions stems from an "economy" model of conversation, in which all interlocutors want access to the floor and must negotiate for it. Turn-taking as conceived in Sacks, Schegloff, and Jefferson 1974 is an aspect of synchronous communication, in which all potential speakers have access to the channel at once, and ideally, for processing reasons, only one speaks at a time. It is viewed as a competitive process.

Process aside, the turn itself is a matter of some theoretical and empirical concern. Goodwin (1981, p. 18) discusses examples like this:

Example (1):

```
1 John: Well I, I took this course
2      (0.5)
3 Ann:  In h ow to quit?
          [
4 John:     which I really recommend.
```

Silence within a turn is usually called a "pause," while silence between turns is a "gap." The silence in line 2 above is classified differently by the different speakers: for Ann it is a gap, but for John it is a pause. John's continuation in line 4 reveals that he was not finished with his turn, but to Ann, he appeared to be. Her line 3 therefore becomes an interruption, since John is not finished.

Is the turn an intentional unit? John's intention was for lines 1 and 4 to constitute a single turn. However, for Jaffe and Feldstein (1970), what occurs is the turn structure; they simplify the procedure for determining "possession of the floor" according to which speaker is speaking. Simultaneous speech they resolve by fiat: a "speaker switching rule" is invoked to determine who wins the competition. Although such a process may be useful descriptively, it is apparent that turn-taking and turn-identification are complex processes that are problematic for speakers as well as discourse analysts. As Goodwin (1981) suggests, the turn itself is a matter of empirical and analytic concern, rather than just a predefined category useful in analysis of other structures.

Murray (1989), in a discussion of a computer messaging system and turn-taking, considers the turn an intentional unit. Turns may be made up of utterances and messages; a message is the line of text sent by the message system (which has an upper limit on the size of messages), and an utterance consists of the messages sent by a speaker between messages from other speakers or the system. In Example 2, P and T are different speakers:

Example (2):

```
T1: IF YOU HAVE A NAIVE USER WITH A HOME TERMINAL, YOU
    REALLY HAVE A PROBLEM
P1: It's not just home terminal ted, it's the whole
    general question of orderly
    communications/information for users.
T2: I THOUGHT THE OLD STUFF WAS PRETTY WELL
    DOCUMENTED.
P2: ... batch going away is a case in point, we've got
```

```
          to provide info -- rather detailed info ahead
          of time.
      P3: yes, and i want to put out similar documentation
          for home terms.
      P4: also batch.
```

Messages P1 and P2 are a turn, to Murray (1989, pp. 324–325), because P2 is an elaboration of P1, and does not refer to T2's content. P3 and P4 are part of a new turn. P2, P3, and P4 are all one utterance, because they were sent without interruption. Turn allocation does not occur as it does in face-to-face speech; parties can take turns at will.

In the discussion that follows, I will use the term "utterance" to refer to Murray's "messages": what a user sends in a single command line (using emote or **say** or another communicative command) to the MOO server. Each utterance appears only after a user finishes typing and presses RETURN, whereupon the network transmits the utterance to the server and to the other connected users. There is no constraint on message length in MOO, unlike in Murray's message system; users determine their utterance (or message) length based on the demands of the conversational context.

Because the size of an utterance is entirely determined by a user, I believe it to be difficult to separate out an intentional turn unit that is different from the order of speakers that appears on the screen (which is in part determined by the server and network timing, and thus out of a speaker's hands anyway). "Interruptions" clearly do not have the status they have in face-to-face speech, since overlap is not possible. If a speaker chooses to express a point in several small utterances, another speaker may take turns in between, at any point, and they are not as potentially damaging to the flow of conversation as they are in face-to-face speech. An analyst might choose to say that each utterance ends with a turn completion point or a "transition relevance point," but since any other speaker may speak at any time, with her utterances showing up between other speakers' utterances as the network feeds them out, transition relevance points do not seem an appropriate notion for the medium. (I will expand on this topic in the next section.) I believe the topic-driven notion of holding the "floor" is more relevant here than the idea of "turns" as intentional units, given that multiple speakers may all type at once in the MUD medium (Edelsky 1993; Shultz, Florio, and Erickson 1982; Hayashi 1991). I will elaborate on this after discussing the process of turn-taking described in Sacks, Schegloff, and Jefferson 1974 and contrasting MUD conventions with it.

For the sake of discussion below, I will consider any stretch of utterances by a single typist before another typist's utterance(s) to be a turn. So in Example 3, lines 1–2 are a turn, lines 3–4 are a turn, and so forth.

Example (3):
```
1 Ted runs around in circles
2 Ted says, "I get to meet mi-cheeEEEeeele"
3 Karen hehs.
4 Karen says, "you could've two days ago,
  but noooOOooo"
5 Ted shakes Karen.
6 Karen grins.
```

4.3.1 Sacks, Schegloff, and Jefferson 1974 Contrasted with MUD Turn-Taking

In face-to-face conversation, Sacks, Schegloff, and Jefferson (1974) observe, speaker change recurs. Overwhelmingly, one party talks at a time. Moments when there is more than one speaker are common in face-to-face conversation, but brief. On the MUD, speaker change occurs if both parties are active at once. Sometimes people leave messages for an idle person in her buffer, which she will see later, taking advantage of the persistence of the conversation in the client. Interaction in real time is the norm, but it is not necessary. It is trivially true that only one speaker speaks at a time in the MUD, since only one person has access to the channel at once. No text can overlap, although speakers may be typing at the same time. The order of utterances can be mixed up, however, if someone is responding to a remark that has since been superseded by another remark, and the response appears to follow the wrong utterance.

Unlike in face-to-face conversation, multiple threading can occur in conversations in the MUD, as Black et al. (1983) describe occurring in email conversations. MUD conversation is more like the real-time messaging system that Black et al. looked at and found lacking in multiple threading, however. Since in face-to-face encounters speech participants are usually involved in only one encounter at a time, Black et al. conclude that time delay causes the multiple topic threading. Since MUD conversation shows some multiple threading, I conclude that it is the persistence of text on the screen that makes multiple threading possible (as well as the lack of interruptions due to the one-way, half-duplex mode), rather than the time delay. McCarthy et al. (1993) and McKinlay et al. (1994) support this claim. MUD conversation does not generally show multi-topic utterances as Black et al. (1983) observe in email messages. Each utterance is primarily on one topic and directed to one person.

Example (4):

1 The Swedish guest says, "how do I get out?"
2 Tom [to Shelley]: so woj said something about dinner
3 lynn says, "@quit"
4 Shelley [to Tom]: cool, i was hopgin he'd find you
5 The Swedish guest says, "thanks"
6 Mike says, "happy birthday!"
7 Shelley is still waiting for her orders
8 Shelley grins.
9 Shelley [to Mike]: thanks
10 Mike | The guest [to swedish guest]: ok
11 Tom [to lynn]: so the big deal about amulet, if it
   delivers, is portability
12 Mike [to Tom]: you put him up to that, I bet
13 The guest leaves the library to the east.
14 lynn nods to Tom.
15 Tom says, "well, that combined with a high clue
   quotient on the part of the designers"
16 Tom laughs at Mike.

In Example 4, several conversations are occurring at once. I answer the guest's question about how to leave in line 3, and she thanks me in line 5; Tom and Shelley discuss her birthday dinner plans; and Mike, referring to a private joke with Tom about directed speech, quotes from an earlier line in the conversation with a "paste" (vertical bar) and then refers back to the line with a deictic pronoun in his next utterance, line 12. Meanwhile, another conversation starts up between Tom and me about a graphic user interface toolkit called Amulet. Such multi-threading is reminiscent of collaborative floors in Edelsky 1993.

In face-to-face conversation, transitions from one speaker to the next with no gap or overlap are common. A slight gap or overlap or neither characterizes the majority of transitions. (Yngve 1970 appears to conclude otherwise, although that conclusion is based on a much smaller sample.) In a MUD, timing is unreliable, so close timing only occurs if both parties are active and responding immediately to each other's comments. There is usually a small gap between an utterance and the response to it, however, due to the need to type the whole utterance before sending it to the server.

In face-to-face conversation, turn order is not fixed, but varies. Turn size also varies. Turn size and order vary in the MUD too. Interestingly, short turn size often makes conversation more interactive. An example of short turn size follows:

Example (5):
```
1  Tom says, "ROBOT KIDS"
2  lynn says, "?"
3  Tom says, "hm, you didn't hear about that
   one?"
4  lynn dun think so
5  Tom unfortunately doesn't remember it very
   well; Shelley or Jon might well have a log.
6  Tom says, "i'm sitting around in my room on
   lambdamoo one day"
7  Tom says, "and some guy teleports in"
8  Tom says, "because i'm a wizard"
9  Tom says, "and introduces me to his rl
   fiance"
10 Tom says, "and i kind of watch helplessly"
11 Tom says, "as the situation gets weirder and
   weirder"
12 Tom says, "and at one point he's asking me"
13 lynn nods.
14 Tom says, "or telling me"
15 Tom says, "that he and his fiance would like
   to use lambdamoo to create robot kids"
16 Tom says, "it's that weird, and he's not
   self-conscious about it at all"
```

Tom appears to break his utterances at what would be prosodic boundaries in oral speech, or what Sacks, Schegloff, and Jefferson might consider transition relevance points. However, as mentioned above, this notion does not map well onto MUD conversation, since any speaker may begin typing an utterance during any other speaker's utterances, and no overlap occurs. My back channel nod in line 13 could have occurred anywhere between his numerous utterances. However, Tom breaks his utterances at very different places in the next example. The context for the discourse below is a discussion of the origins of EM, which was supposedly inspired in part by interactive fiction ("the i.f. stuff"; like Zork and other text-based adventure games). A new character had just entered the room, and some discussion of his unusual name, Michele-America, followed.

Example (6):
```
1  Joe [to Michele_America]: has anybody talked
   to you about how disorienting your name
   might be?
```

```
[ . . . ]
2  lynn [to Tom]: what do you work on when you
   work on the i.f. stuff?
3  Tom says, "i was talking about the history of
   EM and stuff, M_A"
4  Michele_America says, "oh... yes, you're
   right but this is my name. :)"
5  Tom [to Michele_America]: well, there's this
   long-time regular user here named Michele,
   so your name kind of gives us a jolt
   because of its obvious similarity.
6  Penfold says, "and 'america' is kind of an
   unusual last name in the USA"
7  Michele_America says, "yes... my name is
   Michele because i'm italian. but i live in
   Portugal."
8  Tom [to lynn]: ha. building and its
   infrastructure--integration, english
   stuff. and occasionally we talk about
   agents or weather or simulations or
   something, which i think would also
   contribute.
9  Michele_America says, "and the America is
   because my great-grandfather was an
   emigrant in the USA. :)"
10 Tom says, "but as you know, we generally
   devote almost no time to actually building
   stuff, so that leads to a reputation for
   being against or uninterested in it, and
   so on and so on and so on"
```

Tom seems to break his utterances in Example 6 when he begins
speaking to a new person or makes a new point, rather than at clause
or phrase boundaries as in the previous example. This makes the interleaved conversation easier to follow. Notice that in line 8 he uses
directed speech (aka "stage talk") to establish who he is speaking to,
since gaze is not available. (In MUDs without this capability, a speaker
generally needs to address an individual by name.) He does not redirect
his remark in line 10, and we assume he is speaking to the same person
as in his previous line 8.

In face-to-face conversation, the length of a conversation and its topic
are not specified in advance. This is true in the MUD as well. Further-

more, there are communicative options other than **say** and **emote** in the MUD, allowing distinctions and input sources not possible in face-to-face conversation. In Example 7, Tom pastes text from another source in order to illustrate what he is trying to program.

Example (7):

```
Tom says, "suppose i have oh here"
Tom | (define-macro (define-binding object event
  . program)
Tom | '(set! (cmds object) (cons (lambda ()
Tom wants that to be (lambda () thestuffin'program'
```

The "thought bubble" is another frequently used textual device in the MOO: "Karen . o O (once)." The Antisocial commands, or interactions with objects, all involve communicative behavior that is further mediated by the MUD server, producing "utterances" not typed directly by the player (see chapter 3).

In face-to-face conversation, the relative distribution of turns is not specified in advance; it is an interactional achievement. This is true in MUDs as well. The number of parties in a conversation can vary both in face-to-face conversation and in MUDs. There is some evidence that when there are more than six speakers talking within one minute, the number of words per minute that can be produced and understood drops. The graph in Figure 4 shows dense, representative, one-minute time slices[2] from conversations with different numbers of participants, analyzed according to median number of words in the minute, number of utterances per minute, and words per utterance per minute. The number of utterances per minute climbs as more speakers participate (upper right graph), while the number of words per utterance decreases (lower left graph). The intersection of the two tendencies results in a high point at six people, for words produced per minute (upper left graph). The final box in the lower right shows the number of cases used for each data point; it is very difficult to find examples of more than seven people talking during one minute. There are certainly cases of seven or more people being active in conversation at once, but usually not all are speaking frequently enough that they show up within a one-minute time slice.[3] For conversations like those, it becomes difficult

---

[2]My logs are time-stamped. In order to generate the data for this and other graphs, I used Perl scripts to parse my log files. The choice of one-minute increments was based solely on the fact that my logs were marked at one-minute increments.

[3]The single point for ten speakers is anomalous in several ways: it is rare for ten people to be active, and this particular case was an interview situation in which a journalist was asking about the history of EM and its relationship to LambdaMOO.

even to identify active participants, since many people may only speak occasionally.

The explanation for this pattern probably lies in constraints on production and perception. Users are typing while they are reading, and in fast-moving conversations, it can be difficult to produce timely utterances if one types long ones (the time it takes to read a conversational context and to type a response is the minimum time delay before anyone sees it). Shorter utterances are not only faster to produce, they are easier for an audience to read, as well. (See Kuiper 1996 on time pressures and the formulaic speech of auctioneers and sportscasters. He suggests that some formulaic speech, such as weather forecasts, is recipient-designed to improve the hearer's comprehension.)

Figure 5 shows a graph of turn sizes in a long conversation (98 minutes) between me and Tom. The histogram below it shows the distribution of different turn sizes. Figure 6 shows similar data for a group. In Örestrom's 1983 study of the turns in the London-Lund corpus of spoken face-to-face conversation, he found that two-thirds of all turns were below 20 words long, and the median turn length was 13 words. We can see that well above two-thirds of the MUD turns were less than 20 words long. Figure 7 shows the mean turn length in both dyadic and group conversations that were not restricted to occur within any time unit.

I considered six conversations of six or more people speaking contrasted with eight conversations of two people speaking. The number of turns in the dyadic conversations ranged between 32 and 285, with a total of 961 turns considered; and the number in groups of six or more ranged between 169 and 458 for each conversation, totaling 2519 turns. The graph shows the means for the turn lengths in each conversation type. The average of the mean turn sizes for dyadic conversations is 11.9 words; for groups, 6.8 words. (The average of the median sizes for dyads was 8.8 words; for groups, 5.5 words.) The difference is significant between dyads and groups.[4] The comparatively large deviation in the data points for dyadic conversation (3.65 versus 1.14 for group data) is probably because differences in speaker involvement in the topic of conversation are reflected more in two-person conversations. In groups, individual differences in concentration on the topic are less noticeable.

The conversation was therefore more focused than is usual for large party discussions, with a single topic controller most of the time.

[4]For a t-test ($t = 3.284, p < .008$). Since the deviance for the two groups is not close, I also tested with a Mann-Whitney rank test and achieved significance at the 5% level. (In a comparison of turn size medians between the two types of conversation, significance is achieved at $p < .05$.)

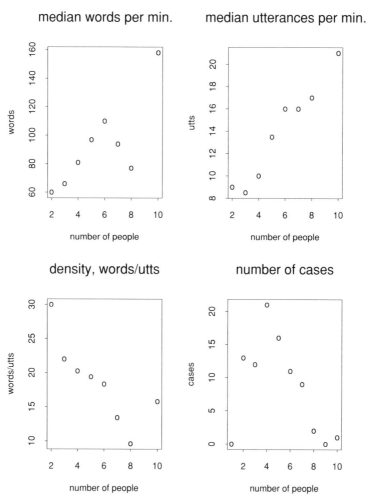

FIGURE 4 One minute time slices during conversations with different numbers of conversants

The lower left cell of Figure 4 is most relevant in a comparison of the results in Figure 4 and Figure 7. The average words per utterance in one minute will be the same as the words per turn in the minute if the turns are assumed to be only one utterance long. (In the conversations used for the graph in Figure 4, turns were on average 1.64 utterances long for dyads and 1.16 utterances long for groups.) The higher values in the Figure 4 graph probably represent the difference between my selection of very dense time slices and the averages over an entire conversation. Very dense (i.e., fast-moving) slices were chosen for the computation of Figure 4 because intermittent activity and idleness are common on ElseMOO (where people often split their attention between the MUD and work). Conversations may be dropped and picked up hours later, which makes calculations of speech production rates difficult. The requirement that all speakers in the groups considered be active within the one minute was an attempt to avoid "idleness" effects, as was the choice of dense time slices (especially in the case of smaller groups, where all might be active during the minute but still be relatively inactive in the conversation).

These findings about turn size contradict the prediction in Clark and Brennan 1991 and the findings in Oviatt and Cohen 1988 that turn size should be longer in keyboard modalities than in voice. There may be a difference because the task-oriented exchange in Oviatt and Cohen 1988 resulted in long one-sided explanations, rather than highly interactive spontaneous speech. Users adapt their communicative behavior for the medium: smaller turn size, hence smaller-grained messages, increases interactivity, the degree to which messages may be related to earlier messages. Shorter messages allow more opportunity for back channels and repair, as I discuss in the next section.

Talk can be continuous or discontinuous in face-to-face conversation, where interruptions may occur. This is also true in MUDs, but in different ways. People can be interrupted "in real life," but the interruption isn't visible in the MUD the way it is in face-to-face speech. Conversants need to plan for this eventuality. Example 8 illustrates a person distracted during conversation. The connection messages give an indication of the times events occurred. In line 7, Daphne notices that Mike is "at work" and therefore vulnerable to interruption.

Example (8):
```
1  Mike says, "I might end up in Newark for grad
   school."
2  < connected: 'drew (#2533) on Mon at 14:50.
3  Daphne says, "Really? Which one?"
```

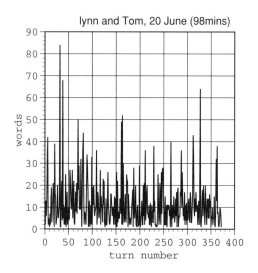

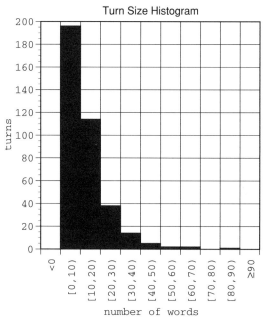

FIGURE 5 Plots of turn size in dyadic conversation with histogram of sizes

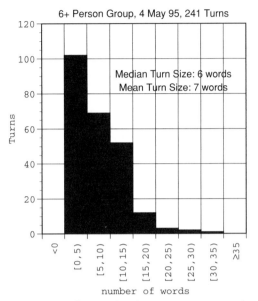

FIGURE 6   Histograms of turn size in group conversation

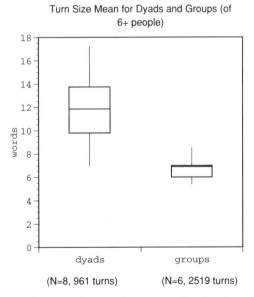

FIGURE 7   Distribution of mean turn sizes for dyads and groups

4 Daphne says, "I like that this moo starts out on a
   highway"
5 Daphne says, "Wow, you're a wizard? Oh yes, you told
   me that but I'd forgotten. Can you make me
   a programmer?"
6 Daphne pokes Mike
7 Daphne says, "Hm, you must be at work"
8 < disconnected: Honda (#82) on Mon at 14:55.
9 < connected: a Canadian guest (#2019) on Mon at
   14:56. On-line: 27. >
10 Mike blinks.
11 Mike says, "Hi, sorry, yeah, people came in
   to ask me a question."

Turn allocation techniques are obviously used in face-to-face speech.
A current speaker may select another speaker, or speakers may select
themselves. Use of an adjacency pair is one way of selecting another
speaker.[5] The first pair part, e.g., a question or an invitation, requires a
response from another speaker, an answer or an acceptance or rejection.
Other examples of adjacency pairs are greeting/greeting, request/grant,
and offer/accept sequences. A speaker may use an address term (such
as a name) or gaze to select the next speaker, along with the first pair
part. Failure to respond to the first pair part is seen as the responsibility
of the speaker selected for the turn.

In a MUD, adjacency pairs exist, but silence is not attributable to
the respondent. As mentioned, an interlocutor may have been called
away suddenly and be unable to answer. Use of the directed speech
option functions like naming an addressee, to help pin down the intended
respondent in an adjacency pair. (In contrast, Murray 1989 described
messages sent to only one person and suggested that naming functioned
in other ways when it occurred). It also functions like eye contact.

Example (9):
Ray [to Tom]: cafe
Tom [to Ray]: ok, can i demo ~zork to lynn first?
Ray says, "sure"
lynn says, "yay"

Confusion does occur when a speaker uses a second person pronoun
and the intended referent is not clear from context, however. Note Shelley's use of directed speech to clarify her reference here.

---

[5]Yngve 1970 mentions that this is not a neat phenomenon, however; speakers may
ask questions but retain the floor through subsequent utterances before turning it
over to a respondent.

Example (10):
Shelley says, "wait, you're not goign now?"
Tom says, "who?"
Shelley [to Tom]: you, to the mfa place

Other-initiated repair will select the previous speaker in face-to-face conversation. This may take the form of partial or full repetition of previous utterances, usually with question intonation, or questions about the content of a previous utterance. In Example 11, from Sacks, Schegloff, and Jefferson 1974, p. 717, Lori asks a question that selects Ben as the next speaker; it is his responsibility to clarify his previous utterance.

Example (11):
Ben: They gott-a garage sale.
Lori: Where.
Ben: On Third Avenue.

In a MUD, intonation isn't available, so questions must be explicit. Other-initiated repair does select the previous speaker. Here Hacker asks Ray clarifying questions, which he answers.

Example (12):
Ray builds the education offices
Hacker says, "This is such a good idea."
Hacker says, "Where are they Ray?"
Ray says, "by the pond"
Karen thinks it's a clumsy implementation tho
Karen [to Ray]: in moocity?
Hacker says, "Pond is w or e of LM?"
Ray says, "east"
Hacker says, "Oh, along the brown path then?"
Ray says, "yeah"
Hacker says, "Gotcha."

In face-to-face conversation, self-selection occurs during a pause, when the first starter gets the floor. (Similarly, in classroom situations, the first hand up usually gets to speak first.) Sacks, Schegloff, and Jefferson (1974) point out that the need for planning utterances leads to the use of appositional beginnings like "well," "but," "and," and "so..." Speakers use these as pre-starts (the way tags are post-completers) to get the floor. They then create an utterance that projects their turn length. Using question words indicates a question is coming, for instance; intonation can also signal the size of the upcoming turn.[6]

There are many appositional beginnings in MUDs, despite the fact

---

[6]Yngve (1970) apparently disagrees, however, about the importance of signaling

that speakers have more time to edit their responses and must plan their utterances in order to type them out. The appositional starts may be used to mimic face-to-face conversation processes, or to affiliate to previous turns. Brine, a LambdaMOO regular who visits on EM occasionally, pointed out to me recently that ElseMOOers quite often use "so" to begin a new topic. In Example 13, Tom uses a free-standing appositional start at line 3, possibly to signal that more is coming.

Example (13):
```
1 Tom is thinking about putting a realtime
  parties tracker into loon.
2 lynn says, "what would that do?"
3 Tom says, "well"
4 Tom says, "initially, just maintain a window
  that shows you roughly what 'parties' does now"
```

"Turn-constructional units" are employed in face-to-face conversation. Turns can be projected to be one word long, phrasal, or sentential. Turns are usually attempted at "possible completion points" in sentences, clauses, and phrases, and after some single words. Turn-completion points are normally syntactically sensible. In the examples below from Sacks, Schegloff, and Jefferson (1974, p. 721), the overlaps occur at possible turn-completion points.

Example (14):
```
George: I saw em last night [at um school
Henry:                      [They're a riot.


A: Well we just wondered,
A: We just came in from Alexandria,
A: just got home
A: and [these winds were so bad we're gettin' scared
  again, heh
B:    [Mm hm,
B: No, [we doh-
A:     [And we wondered whether we should go to a motel
  or something.
B: No, you stay right where you are.
```

Back channels (which I discuss in detail later) and repair attempts occur at possible turn-completion points (or "transition relevance points"), according to Schegloff 1982.

---

turn size. He notes that interruptions do occur when turns are syntactically or intonationally incomplete.

Speakers in the MUD have the option of "interrupting" by speaking at any point during another's talk; rather than overlap, their utterances will be interleaved with the other speaker's utterances. Back channel responses, or utterances that appear to function similarly, are often offered during another person's stretch of talk. Repair attempts for both content and disorderly talk also occur.

4.3.2 Repair Mechanisms

Repair mechanisms exist in both MUD discourse and face-to-face conversation for dealing with turn-taking errors and violations. In face-to-face conversation, the repair inventory includes interruption markers ("excuse me"), restarts, repeats, and premature stopping. The repair mechanisms in the MUD differ slightly because of the lack of a two-way channel in the medium. The "loses" routine (discussed in chapter 3), which is similar to premature stopping, is one common response to discovering that another speaker has already typed what one is typing; the user types "loses" instead of finishing her utterance, and then sends the text to the server anyway.

Responses can get disorderly and require explicit "fixing." In Example 15, Karen's back channel response to "cool" appeared after the next remark from Damon, changing the entire meaning of her nod. Karen straightens the confusion out by telling him what she was nodding at. (Note the dropped preposition, a very common convention.)

Example (15):
```
Karen [to Damon]: inspection cuz buying a house.
Damon [to Karen]: aha! cool!
Damon says, "wait, you're rich?"
Karen nods solemnly.
Damon says, "house + boston -> rich, right? ok, just
  checking"
Karen says, "uh"
Karen says, "no, i nodded cool."
Karen grins.
ls says, "houst + boston -> newly poor"
```

Utterances are also re-ordered by pasting lines of text from other sources. In Example 16, Shelley pastes a line from earlier in the conversation that she didn't get to respond to, so that she can respond to it properly as innuendo. (Line 2 is a "spoof" by Mike; he typed a question that he expected Sadness to ask. The appended "--Mike" alerts everyone that it is not actually Sadness who is typing.)

Example (16):
1 lynn [to Mike]: we can do it later.
2 Sadness says, "can you go bowling with us on
  Thursday, Mike?" --Mike
3 Mike says, "Why sure, I'd love to."
4 Sadness says, "oh gee."
5 lynn snorts.
6 Shelley | lynn [to Mike]: we can do it later.
7 Shelley woo
8 Sadness laughs.

In Example 17, Tom uses a paste from an earlier context to explain what his pronoun "this" referred to in line 4.

Example (17):
1 Rob [to Tom]: if they don't know about quitting then
  they're likely best off using@quit
2 Tom [to Rob]: um, thanks.
3 Mike [to Robin]: What's new?
4 Tom isn't quite sure what he's supposed to conclude
  from this.
5 Mike says, "From what?"
6 Tom | Rob [to Tom]: if they don't know about quitting
  then they're likely best off using@quit

In sum, the turn-taking methods and methods for repair of disorderly turns in the MUD are different from those in face-to-face conversation, but clearly related. Conversation can be orderly or disorderly, and if it is disorderly, repair mechanisms come into play that are specific to the medium. They include signals of premature preemption, explicit explanations of disorderly lines, and pasting utterances into the conversation at a later point.

4.3.3   The Shared Floor

Models of turn-taking that apply to face-to-face conversation do not map well onto the MUD medium, however. Given that there is no competition for the channel per se, but rather competition for attention or control of the discourse, notions of shared or collaborative floor (Edelsky 1993; Shultz, Florio, and Erickson 1982; Hayashi 1991) seem to be more helpful than the standard turn-taking literature. These notions also appear more useful for theorizing multi-threaded topic discourse.

Edelsky (1993) relates dissatisfaction with the Sacks, Schegloff, and Jefferson 1974 turn-taking model even for studying face-to-face conversation. The model does not account for different speaker perceptions of "interruption" behavior: cases where multiple overlapping speakers are "on the same wavelength," for instance. Simultaneous talk in Edelsky's group data sometimes seemed interruptive and sometimes seemed more collaborative. Edelsky criticizes the turn-taking literature for focusing on one-at-a-time speech between dyads or in institutional settings like classrooms or therapy sessions. Phone conversation has been another source of data for conversation analytic studies of turn behavior, despite the (largely unspecified) effects of the medium on the interaction. Most of these studies do not acknowledge a speaker's own intuitions about having the turn, and certainly in the conversation analysis tradition the analyst's intuitions are no more valid (Jefferson and Schenkein 1978).

Edelsky goes on to define a turn as "an on-record speaking [. . .] behind which lies an intention to convey a message that is both referential and functional" (1993, p. 207). Floor is "the acknowledged what's-going-on within a psychological time/space" (p. 209). Clearly these are difficult to determine from the observer's perspective, but they allow for the existence of non-floor-holding turns, a concept that appears to be needed for the analysis of back channels. Edelsky then proposes the existence of both collaborative floors and single floors. Morganthaler (1990) proposes, as an intermediate type, the interleaved floor, in which individual identifiable speakers jointly work out a topic (distinguishable from a collaborative floor because single speakers are not identifiable in the "babble" of collaborative speech).

In looking for alternative characterizations of talk, Shultz, Florio, and Erickson (1982) expand on notions of participant structures (Philips 1972) and define four types of "floor" at family dinners. Hayashi (1991) builds on their work and Edelsky's, describing the floor as a community competence, which is cognitively developed while participants interact, providing a continually updated context for each subsequent interaction. Floor reflects social concerns like solidarity and power, cooperation and conflict, and the like, as well as more operational notions like topic change and support. Hayashi (p. 8) categorizes the following types of floor:

> Single conversational floor:
> > Single person floor:
> > > Prime-time at a time floor
> > > Speaker-and-supporter floor:
> > > > Less-active interaction
> > > > Active interaction
> > > Non-propositional floor
> > Collaborative floor:
> > > Ensemble
> > > Joint floor

Multiple conversational floor:
Side floor and main floor
Main floor in parallel

At the broadest level, there is either a single main floor or there are multiple floors. Where there is one floor, that floor may be constructed either by one person in the main, or by multiple parties. A single main speaker may hold the floor and be seldom interrupted, as in sermons or lectures, and thus hold a "prime-time at a time floor." When listeners interact with the speaker, the interaction may create a speaker-and-supporter floor. With more-active interaction, simultaneous talk and overlap occurs, as well as back channel responses; with less-active interaction, back channels occur but there is little overlap or simultaneous speech. "Non-propositional floors" occur when speakers entirely pre-occupied with their own thoughts briefly create a self-centered floor that has nothing to do with listeners and the ongoing floor.

Collaborative floors result from multiple speakers contributing at once to the floor. Ensemble floors result from little simultaneous talk; the group achieves a rhythm with close timing, as they attend to a common goal and the topic at hand. Joint floors, on the other hand, show sudden topic changes, overlap and interruption, and turn failures. Finally, a multiple conversational floor occurs when multiple floors occur at once and subgroups form. These may occur in parallel (when speakers share multiple topic goals), or one may become a side floor. Side flooring may constitute an interruption to the main floor.

Not all the distinctions can be appropriate in a medium like a MUD, in which overlap is not possible. Subgroups also cannot be formed with physical proximity or volume adjustment, so if they do form, they must be purely topic driven. Modifying the list for what might be possible distinctions in a MUD, we see:

Single conversational floor:
Single person floor:
Prime-time at a time floor
Speaker-and-supporter floor
Non-propositional floor
Collaborative floor
Multiple conversational floor:
Side floor and main floor
Main floor in parallel

Interestingly, perhaps because there are few formal speech events in MUDs, I cannot identify examples of prime-time at a time floors in EM. Fanderclai (1996, p. 240) refers to attempts to lecture in the MUD medium and floor control attempts generally when she describes "the uselessness of delivering a lecture in what is designed to be an interactive environment, and the irony of programs that silence people in an environment that can let everyone talk and be heard at the same time." The medium is far from ideal for formal lectures or debates; without non-intrusive visual feedback, it is disconcerting to speak for any length of time to an audience that does not respond.

Speaker-and-supporter floors are common in dyadic situations, where listeners provide back channel responses regularly, and one speaker may be dominant. In Example 18, Tom is the main floor holder, with lynn, Ray, and Patrick being supporters.

Example (18):
```
Ray says, "you're talking about CSL the VR space?"
lynn says, "see paul's paper on video connectins and
   space etc."
Tom thinks things are going well, anyway, in general.
Tom [to Ray]: well, not "csl" per se.
lynn is relieved by that.
Patrick ahs.
Tom says, "in fact, we're probably going to get rid of
   the virtual representations of each of the
   kind of corporate structures"
Tom says, "create more anonymous spaces, which may
   eventually be appropriated and sometimes
   named"
Ray
Tom says, "emphasis on providing a variety of types of
   space, and finding out which ones get used"
Tom eyes Ray warily.
lynn nods, great.
Tom [to lynn]: i showed them your map.
```

Non-propositional floors are very common in MUD conversation, particularly because people are often prone to narrate their actions in real life as they occur (Type 4 emotes, discussed in chapter 5). Frequently these narrations or side comments are not intended to start a new conversation topic. On the other hand, frequently they are intended to do so, and they just aren't picked up by anyone. Who has the ability to start a new topic, who is likely to be responded to when they speak, has a lot to do with power and social influence in the community, I suspect, but I have not analyzed the question systematically. (I have heard some complaints from newcomers about being "ignored" when they ask questions or make comments.) In Example 19, Dorian is asking about the history of EM, and Ted is talking off-topic about something at his job. (I do not mean to imply that Ted has no social influence; on the contrary, he is one of the more influential speakers as far as linguistic innovation goes.)

Example (19):

```
Dorian [to Tom]: Cool stuff without programming? How?
Karen [to Ray]: didn't you call it a party?
Ray says, "well, yeah, that was my operational
  analogy"
Ted . o O ( cu -l /dev/cua0 9000000 ? )
Ray says, "EM was a big really long house party"
Tom says, "Ray drew an analogy to a party on several
  occasions"
Tom says, "this doesn't mean it was one, it meant it
  shared characteristics"
Dorian [to Tom]: Characteristics such as?
Ray says, "mind you, we had disagreements on what this
  meant and whether it was valid"
Tom [to Dorian]: for example, in a perfect world, you
  would be able to make a dog and train it to do
  tricks without ever having to use eval or set
  properties.
Tom +" "
Ted is not real excited about editing 198 records by
  hand out of userbase, nope.
Tom [to Dorian]: characteristics such as "if
  somebody's obnoxious, youmake them leave".
Ray says, "people you know show up, hang out at your
  place"
```

Collaborative floors are common. In Example 20, the thread about Shelley becoming different appliances is jointly developed by all. Shelley is explaining why she copied verb code (the "start" verb) from her washing machine object onto herself, and thus has become the appliance (as discussed in chapter 3; see Cherny 1995b for a discussion of automation and cyborg identities).

Example (20):

```
lynn [to Shelley]: so when we agreed to take over the
  appliance project, I am not sure this is what
  I thought would happen with it.
Shelley [to lynn]: well, this all started becasue i
  was working ont he washer and didn't want to
```

lose the part of the start verb i had right
lynn nodsnods
Shelley [to lynn]: then someone tried to start me and
was disappointed
Tom [to lynn]: i was thinking that as she makes more
appliances she should repeatedly take on the
characteristics of her latest work.
Shelley [to lynn]: so i added the missing properties
Kelly nods, hopefully when you're done you can stop
being a washer and re-create the actual
washer.
lynn says, "oh, cycle through the latest appliance."
lynn cools

Although the lines above are relatively long, it may be interesting to note that Edelsky (1993) found an average turn size of 6.5 words in collaborative floors; in Figure 7 I showed that group turn size is about 5.5 words in EM. Most group situations are collaborative or multiple floor situations.

Since subgroups aren't easy to identify within a conversation (because there is no visual or spatial dimension), the differences between side floors and parallel main floors are hard to identify. As a participant in the event, I would claim that the interaction between the guest and the regulars about code, in the middle of an ongoing interview conducted by Dorian, constitutes a side floor in Example 21.

Example (21):
Karen [to Dorian]: what's your book going to be on?
Ray was thinking Lotus Notes, but either would do
Dorian [to Karen]: Everything in the MOOniverse,
basically.
Karen [to Dorian]: big book
Ray spends way too much time thinking about Lotus
Notes at work
Ray says, "it is Evil"
The corporate guest says, " do you guys see some one
here that may be interested in helping a guest
with a code problem?"
Dorian grins Karen. "I'm working on narrowing it
down. But something like a
history/ethnography/travelogue."
Karen [to the corporate guest]: ask away...
Ray [to the corporate guest]: hm, well, just ask

Side floors might also be constituted when whisper conversations start between two participants in the main floor. It is fairly common for a secondary whisper conversation to start and even to address the same topic as the main floor, although privately.

A parallel main floor example is below. In the midst of a conversation about stalking, a conversation about a file system is occurring between Pete and Molly.

Example (22):

```
Harry says, "What's a good way to get rid of some
    boring, very cute girl who's stalking you?"
Harry says, "Kill."
anne says, "the kiwi margaritas at that place are so
    nummy i might just die."
Molly [to Harry]: Kiss her.
lynn [to Harry]: ask her to leave you alone.
Pete [to Harry]: give her my phone number
Pete eyes himself warily.
anne says, "ask ted."
Molly hehs.
Molly eyes herself warily.
The guest says, "hi robin"
Robin lol vange.
anne says, "give her my phone number."
The guest smiles
Pete [to Molly]: what does df say about the disk?
Pete says, "owait, i spose it doesn't mount so you
    don't KNOW."
Robin [to Harry]: whyforyouwanttogetridofher?
anne [to Robin]: cause she's boring.
Molly [to Pete]: Not mounted eh.
anne says, "if she was cute and interesting, he'd have
    married her already."
```

In sum, various types of shared floors are possible, but the distinctions among face-to-face situations that Edelsky (1993) and Hayashi (1991) bring out are not all available, because of the lack of overlap in the medium. Multiple participant floors are in fact easier to achieve than they are in face-to-face conversations, given this lack of overlap. The common multi-threaded conversation identified in Black et al. 1983 and noted in McKinlay et al. 1994 may be analyzed as an example of multiple floors occurring at once.

Despite this array of floor types and the earlier discussion of repair mechanisms in MUD conversation, I do not mean to imply that floor manipulation is simple or painless. A MUDder recently wandered onto an academic MUD and spoke about a log she read of a group of teachers discussing ways to use the MUD in teaching: "It's been my most chillingly RL-like experience on a MOO so far, watching the meeting dynamics and seeing what was said. [. . .] My overwhelming feeling was of being in a stuffy room in some vaguely uncomfortable sort of chair with a bunch of very stuffy people, the women having to get their comments in edgewise while a man felt it necessary to be a very hands-on moderator and two other men argued ubiquitously about their pet point long after the others seemed to want to move on" (anonymous personal communication).

Fanderclai 1996 refers to automated control devices for floor control in classroom situations. There is an example of voluntary use of real-life meeting tactics in a MUD meeting in the log of a discussion on TinyHell II, from early 1990.[7] A moderator called on characters who raised their hands (or paws, as the case was):

Example (23):
Stewy opts for giving Random the floor before
  answering fur.
fur says, "like i said earlier, i can ask someone to
  go with mee to eat, so that makes it more
  social"
Random says, "You can do that anyway."
LongThorn raises his hand, now.
Moira raises her hand too.
Random takes advantage of having the floor to answer
  fur. :)
Stewy pulls out his notepad to record the queue of
  speakers.
Random says, "I should point out that if people (ie,
  The Public) really had ANY interest in more
  realism in muds, they'd bonnie well use the :
  command to simulate realism more often. It is
  my observation that (with the possible
  exception of tinysex :)) this is rare indeed."
fur raises his paws.
Random says, "I distinctly recall having a spaghetti
  dinner on DaisyMud."

(The ":" command is the emote command's shorthand.)

---

[7]At http://www.apocalypse.org/pub/u/lpb/muddex/reality.txt.

MUD conversation can seem chaotic to new users, especially when more than six players are talking at once and the screen scrolls quickly. When there is a particular goal or topic to the conversation, the spontaneous mix of conversational threads (which is particularly conducive to textual play) can become even more confusing. The conversants on TinyHell II probably made use of the recognized real-life conventions of hand-raising and moderation because they were attempting to discuss one topic and wanted to maintain focus.

In sum, face-to-face models of turn-taking don't apply well to MUD conversation. In MUD conversation, speakers make use of various textual devices for repairs and establishing context and addressee, in the absence of visual or auditory channels. Conversation may be multithreaded and many types of floor structure are possible.

4.4 Back Channels

Gumperz 1982 notes that back channels represent "one common way in which conversational cooperation is communicated and monitored," and may include nods or other body movements, or interjections like "ok," "aha," and "right" (p. 163). Study of email messages (Black et al. 1983) has found back channels to be significantly missing; study of ISDN half-duplex video connection interactions has similarly found far fewer back channels than are found in face-to-face or full duplex video (O'Conaill, Whittaker, and Wilbur 1993). I maintain that back channels do occur in MUD discourse and are indeed important for determining the attention state of an interlocutor, as well as establishing whether speaker intentions have been understood. In a text-based medium where no physical cues are available, and interlocutors may be called away from their terminal at any moment, these are particularly important; back channel emotes and **say**s play a large role in achieving mutual understanding among users and facilitating a sense of co-presence (cf. McCarthy et al. 1993, where co-presence was hard to achieve).

Schegloff (1982, p. 77) reviews the literature on back channels briefly:

The most common term now in use for such items, "back channel communication," was introduced by Yngve (1970), and includes a much broader range of utterance types, including much longer stretches of talk. The term "back channel" has been adopted by Duncan and his associates (for example, Duncan and Fiske 1977), together with the broadened definition of the class. Duncan and Fiske (1977, pp. 201–202) include not only expressions such as "uh huh," "yeah," and the like, but also completions by a recipient of sentences begun by another, requests for clarification, "brief restatements" of something just said by another, and "head nods and shakes."

In this literature, they have been variously claimed to signal ongoing attention (Fries 1952, p. 49), to signal attention and understanding of what is being said (Georgedon 1967, p. 44), and "to provide the auditor with a means for participating actively in the conversation, thus facilitating the general coordination of action by both participants" (Duncan and Fiske 1977, pp. 202–203).

Schegloff points out that back channels in face-to-face conversation occur at possible turn-exchange points, until the speaker is obviously done and needs some other response. He considers them "continuers," since they are abdicators of the turn exchange that otherwise might occur; the listener signals with them that a speaker may continue with an extended discourse structure, which the listener recognizes is in progress. Example 24 is from Schegloff 1982, p. 82.

Example (24):

```
1  B: I've listen to all the things that chu've said,
      an' I agree with you so much.
2  B: Now,
3  B: I wanna ask you something,
4  B: I wrote a letter. (pause)
5  A: Mh hm,
6  B: T'the governor.
7  A: Mh hm::,
8  B: -telling 'im what I thought about i(hh)m!
9  A: (Sh:::!)
10 B: Will I get an answer d'you think,
11 A: Ye:s,
```

Note that after line 4, Speaker B paused, and a back channel was produced, enabling her to continue. At line 10, Speaker A is finally ratified as the next speaker.

The "confirmation feedback" discussed in Oviatt and Cohen 1988, important in task-oriented phone conversations to communicate understanding of goals, would also be considered back channels under most definitions. Grosz and Sidner (1986) discuss them within the larger category of "cue words" showing understanding of discourse structure. Grosz and Sidner also looked at task-oriented dialogues; Example 25 is taken from an expert-apprentice dialogue (Grosz and Sidner 1986, p. 186). The "ok" in line 5 below is considered a cue word, as is the "now" in line 6, which would not be considered a back channel by any definition.

Example (25):

```
1 A: One bolt is stuck.  I'm trying to use both the
     pliers and the wrench to get it unstuck,
     but I haven't had much luck.
2 E: Don't use pliers.  Show me what you are doing.
3 A: I'm pointing at the bolts.
4 E: Show me the 1/2" combination wrench, please.
5 A: OK.
6 E: Good, now show me the 1/2" box wrench.
7 A: I already got it loosened.
```

Schegloff (1982) focuses on nonspeech sounds like "mm hmm," which he claims are used instead of longer forms like "I am listening" that would be more turn-like. However, they are conventionalized sounds that are well recognized by a community. The frequency and type of back channels across cultures and across speech events within a culture may differ, often dramatically. White (1989) discusses the greater frequency of back channels in Japanese speech, for example. Debates, class lectures, and ceremonies differ in their turn-taking structures and therefore in their back channel type and frequency from those in dyadic conversations, which I will focus on now.

Duncan (1973) uses the term "back channel" to include non-turn material that shows the speaker how his turn is progressing for his listener, but he also includes "sentence completions," "requests for clarification," and "brief restatements," which for others would be full turns (e.g., Duncan and Niederehe 1974). In Yngve's (1970) original discussion of back channels, he makes clear that there are different types of back channels, along a continuum from nonspoken attentive gaze, to nods, to murmurs, to short questions, to sections of talk as long as "filling in needed personal background so that the person having the floor could continue" (p. 574). He thus distinguishes between turns and "having the floor," and considers much of back channel activity to consist of turn-taking.

As pointed out in Coulthard 1977 and Goodwin 1981, there are differences of opinion over what constitutes a turn. Nods and other gestures are not usually considered turns in their own right, but murmurs of assent, or noises of the sorts Schegloff (1982) discusses, are more questionable. As noted, for Schegloff it is important that the set of utterances examined are not full turns. Longer utterances ("I understand," "I am listening") could perform some of the same functions, but he maintains that the short forms are used because they are not full turns. The nonlexical status of the sounds he examines also prevents them from being heard as turns, despite their well-recognized conventional forms.

4.4.1 The Functions of Back Channels in MUD Discourse

In a MUD, back channels are full turns, since they are utterances like any other, and there is no "background" effect. Yngve's (1970) and Edelsky's (1993) distinction between "turn-taking" and "having the floor" is correct for the MUD discourse: a speaker may "have the floor" in some topic-controlling fashion, and choose utterance and turn size according to other factors, like how crowded the room is and how much interleaved talk there is. A speaker might similarly choose to provide feedback to another speaker, choosing not to change the topic.

In the discourse of the MOO, the routine utterances that I will call back channels are slightly different from those found in face-to-face conversation: they include some nonlexical imitations of speech sounds or laughter ("Tom hehs"), and some lexical descriptions of behaviors that are back channels "in real life" ("lynn nods"). They also include conventional misspellings of other conventional forms (the back channel "hsm" came from a typo of the back channel "hms") and other conventional typing shortcuts (e.g., "oic" comes from "oh, I see").

Examples of back channel use in a MUD conversation occur in lines 3, 9, and 13 below.

Example (26):

```
1  Tom says, "only in look_self"
2  Karen says, "cool"
3  Karen nods.
4  Karen thot so, but
5  Karen says, "oh"
6  Karen says, "there was another reason"
7  Karen sigsh
8  Karen wanted name ^j----^j desc
9  Tom says, "huh"
10 Karen
11 -----       --Karen
12 Karen's description
13 Tom nods.
14 Karen says, "now i can't"
```

Karen is trying to describe how she wants some text to be laid out: lines 10–12 are her attempt to graphically represent the fields she wants, which consist of a name, a line of hyphens, and a description underneath it. (In line 11, the MOO server appended her name to indicate that she was the author of that "utterance.")

Conventional expressions of puzzlement, as in line 9 above, are examples of "other-initiated repair" as discussed in Schegloff 1982. Since

Schegloff suggests they occur at the same points in conversational interaction that back channel utterances might occur, I class them together
with the other utterances I consider here (although Schegloff's analysis is quite different ultimately, because he is not interested in creating
a single general category). Longer, less conventionalized examples of
repair initiation are not included, however (contra Duncan 1973 and
Duncan and Fiske 1977), because of the difficulty of coding and searching for them automatically in the data. Affect signals or assessments
like laughter (or the textual expression of it) are also considered to be
in the supercategory of back channels for purposes of this chapter, for
the same reason that short other-initiated repairs are. Additionally, I
believe that affect responses in MUD discourse function very similarly
to the other types of back channel responses: they show attention and
comprehension by registering appropriate emotional responses.[8]

Explicit back channels are used with great frequency among the Else-
MOO population. Some of the more frequently used utterances have
been encoded in easy-to-type commands that both document and encourage their use. In particular, the Carpal Tunnel Syndrome Feature
command set (described in chapter 3) is regularly used on EM; it makes
available several of the regularly used back channels. For instance, if I
type the "**nd**" command from the CTS command set, everyone in the
room with me sees the output "`lynn nods`," which often indicates that
I am attending to or understanding what has been said to me. Other
utterances in common use on the CTS command set include "**gg**," which
outputs "`lynn giggles`" (if typed by me), "**h**" for "`lynn hehs`" (simulation of laughter), "**gr**" for "`lynn grins`," "**sm**" for "`lynn smiles`,"
and "**/**" for "`lynn says, "?"`" (which approximates a questioning look,
according to users' interpretations). The CTS command set was created
by two users in early 1994, and in mid-1995 it was being used by approx-
imately one-third of the regular population; the remainder use emotes
for these routine utterances, e.g., by typing "`:nods`" at the prompt.

The back channels I considered in the MOO discourse are listed below; all are conventional forms used by the community.

nods, hsm, hms, hmm, hrm, oh, oic, ok, ah, yeah, yes, ?,
giggles, laughs, grins, smiles, hehs

In a later section, I consider some particular subcategories of back channels.

---

[8]Note that line 5's "oh" is not a response to a remark from Tom, but is volunteered
independently, indicating that Karen has thought of something that she wants to
discuss. This would not be considered a back channel, therefore (see Heritage 1984).
My automated statistics generation process is not sensitive to such differences in use,
unfortunately, and would classify it as a back channel.

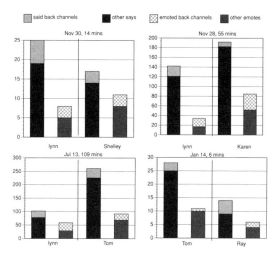

FIGURE 8   Ratios of emotes, says, emoted back channels, and said back channels

Some of these occur as either emotes or **says**, e.g., "Tom `hmm`" or "Tom **says**, `"hmm"`," an alternation that may be due to their onomatopoeic non-lexicality. ("Tom `says`, `"nod"`" would normally be inappropriate, however, and is classified as a "mav" by the community, so called for a character on another MUD who regularly made modality errors in conversation; Smith 1995. However, I have seen such **says** done consistently and apparently intentionally by players from Seashore MUSH.) Graphs of the number of emoted versus "said" back channels in four conversations of different lengths between two people each are shown in Figure 8. Note that in some cases the number of emoted back channels is almost equal to the number of "said" back channels. This result differs from the finding in Black et al. 1983 for electronic mail, where there were few back channels because of the lack of real-time responses. Black et al. (1983, p. 62) claim that "the conversational 'back channeling' associated with verbal discourse is minimal in discussions which use computer terminals, creating 'dangling conversations.'" MUD conversations do not "dangle" the way email or computer messaging (Murray 1989) conversations do. It is clearly necessary to differentiate between synchronous, small-grained communication by terminal and asynchronous larger-grained communication.

Despite problems with turn-taking models as predictors of their placement in MUD discourse, there are obviously some regularities in back channel use in MUDs. In this rather focused discourse, notice that Karen and Tom produce them at the same points: in lines 3–4, after a point has been made, and then again at lines 10–11, after an expansion on another point. I produce one at line 8, agreeing with or acknowledging Tom's comment in line 7.

Example (27):

```
1  lynn says, "cuts are followable in films,
   but I started wondering about them in the
   context of muds and teleporting"
2  lynn says, "without visual links, you lose
   relationship between spaces"
3  Karen nods solemnly.
4  Tom says, "hmmmm"
5  lynn says, "and it could be done badly in
   a cd rom game too, no doubt"
6  Karen hears the mop, is so happy
7  Tom found some of the cuts in myst confusing.
8  lynn nods.
9  lynn says, "but it's still so slooooowwwww even
   with them"
10 Tom nods.
11 Karen nods.
```

Schegloff (1982) points out that back channels are normally taken to indicate agreement, among other things. He suggests that they imply agreement because they occur in the same places as other-initiated repairs, yet they aren't repair attempts. Their use as continuers in an ongoing discourse, passing up the opportunity for repair, implies listener agreement. Clark and Schaefer (1989) similarly propose that they behave as acknowledgments or agreement markers.

Back channels have been argued to show attention as well (e.g., Yngve 1970). Schegloff points out that back channels are at best "claims" of attention, which is different from "evidence" of it. This distinction may be important in a MUD, particularly where people are working while talking, and cannot always give their full attention to the text window. The persistent nature of the text, as well as its non-intrusiveness, allows for more casual involvement with it. Users can delay their experience of the conversation if they need to read it later in their buffer, something not possible with real-time audio or video, where a speaker expects more or less instant feedback. Full attention of the sort required in most face-to-face conversations is therefore not required in the MUD.

In Figure 9, I plot the course of two sides of one long conversation on June 20, 1994. The left axis measures the number of utterances in each time period (since the last period), as indicated with the solid line, and

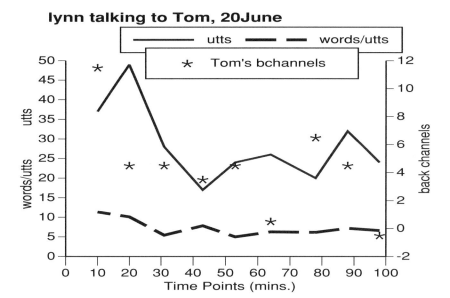

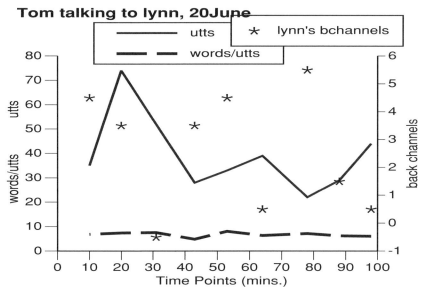

FIGURE 9 Graph of rates of utterance overlaid with back channels

the rate of speech, as calculated by words per utterance in the period, indicated by the dotted line. When a speaker is relatively inactive in conversation, there is a low utterance count (see time 43 minutes). A higher rate of words per utterance indicates that longer utterances are being produced (see time 10 minutes on graph **lynn talking to Tom**). Time increments are about 11 minutes. The star symbols show the number of back channels received from the interlocutor during each time period, measured along the right axis. In other words, the graph of **lynn talking to Tom** has Tom's back channels plotted over it.

In their analysis of task-oriented conversation, Grosz and Sidner (1986) found that cue words like "ok" and "yeah" showed comprehension of a speaker's goals. Schegloff (1982) suggests that back channels are often "continuers," abdications of a full turn from a hearer, which essentially give permission to a speaker to continue developing a complex discourse structure like a narrative. If back channels were only functioning as indicators of comprehension of a speaker's plans or as responses to the development of an extended discourse structure, there should be fewer back channels during periods of little interaction. However, periods with low utterance counts for both conversants (43 minutes, 78 minutes) nevertheless show the presence of several back channels from the interlocutors. (The inclusion of some repair and affect responses in my counts ought not to prejudice the results, especially if both those categories of response are similarly associated with complex discourse structures; see below.) The appearance of these signals in such periods probably indicates that a potential interlocutor is attending and may be available for more extended conversation.

It is difficult if not impossible, however, to totally distinguish between "acknowledgment" functions (Clark and Schaefer 1989), which indicate understanding, and "attention" functions alone, since the attention markers are always occurring in response to utterances and may perform both functions. In the next section I break down back channels by type more thoroughly, but each type may still perform multiple or ambiguous functions. The lack of correlation between back channels and periods of increased utterance rate, however, suggests that their function as "continuers" is not the whole story. The conversants in this phatic, largely non-task-oriented conversation are in a "continuing state of incipient conversation" (Schegloff and Sacks 1974, p. 262), analogous to that achieved in the two-party situations Goffman (196, p. 102) describes: "communication arrangements that seem to lie halfway between mere copresence and full-scale co-participation."

In the following excerpt from the period around the 43 minute mark, the conversation has moved off the previous topic, which was a somewhat tense one, and the interlocutors are registering their continued alertness, even while they document their actions in real life. In lines 1–2, I illustrate that I am reading email in another window and paste a section from one message. After a desultory exchange on that topic, including a back channel at line 6 indicating comprehension, Tom begins playing with names in thought bubbles (lines 7–9) and then reports singing, a common practice while listening to music and MUDding at the same time. I respond with back channel responses in lines 12 and 14, initially indicating I am still alert, and then acknowledging receipt of information, before making another desultory conversational offer in line 15.

Example (28):

```
1  lynn sees OJ all over the popcult list,
   of course.
2  ------------------- lynn -------------------
   In any case, thanks to OJ, Al, and the LA
   chopper teams and reporters for providing
   all of us cult studs folx with yet another a
   perfect Baudrillardian moment...
   ------------- lynn stops pasting -------------
   Done @pasting.
3  Tom says, "al?"
4  lynn dunno.
5  lynn says, "media coverage somehow.''
6  Tom says, "ah"
7  Tom . o O ( oj et al )
8  Tom . o O ( woj simpson )
9  Tom . o O ( homer j simpson )
10 Tom [sings]: who throwed lye on my dog?
11 Tom wonders if he could fall asleep.
12 lynn says, "hmm. go home and sleep.''
13 Tom is home.
14 lynn says, "oh."
15 lynn says, "I wonder why I keep dreaming
   about food."
```

Line 12's "hmm" is part of a larger turn. MUD back channels do not have to be separate turns, and as we saw, turn status is hard to define in a MUD.

Narrative emotes (Type 4, in chapter 5) of what is happening "in real life" or elsewhere are common during semi-idle periods. Narrative emotes tell the listener that attention may be split and how. Here is a another example from around the 43 minute time; note that lines 5–6 are a split turn.

Example (29):

```
1 Tom [sings]: i live
2 Tom [sings]: where it's
3 Tom [sings]: graaaaaayyye
4 lynn gets another random guest 'hi' on lm.
5 Tom says, "hm"
6 Tom says, "do you answer these?"
7 lynn says, "the other day I did, but I am
  not today."
```

The distribution of back channels during periods of mutual rapid, dense conversation suggests that some of their functions in periods with less conversation (marking attention, showing understanding or confusion, providing assessment like laughter) are being taken over by other types of utterances (or by longer phrases that I am not counting in my analysis as back channels). The number of back channels given by speaker A to an interlocutor B generally increases when B's number of utterances increases, but often stays low if instead A's utterance rate increases in parallel (see time 21 minutes and 63 minutes on Figure 9). If A's rate increases too, A is not being a passive listener, but is involved actively in the conversation, which may result in fewer back channels. In Example 30, from around the 60 minutes mark in Figure 9, the confusions are cleared up with explicit questions, rather than conventionalized shorthand utterances like the single question mark or "huh." (The "ow ow ow" utterance in line 5 means that it's harder to type comfortably at home.)

Example (30):

```
1 Tom thinks about when he'd wake up if he
  went to sleep now, and whether it'd be
  safe to bike.
2 lynn says, "bike where?"
3 Tom says, "work"
4 lynn says, "how hard is it to work from
  home?"
5 Tom says, "ow ow ow"
6 Tom says, "plus, i can't do any interesting jupiter
  stuff"
```

In sum, there are frequent back channels in periods of only desultory interaction, and the back channels appear to function generally as evidence of continued attention, necessary in a text-based medium where an interlocutor may be invisibly called away or not attending. They may decrease when more substantive means of registering attention and understanding are used, in periods of more active participation.

4.4.2   Situated Back Channel Functions

As noted in the conversation analysis literature, different back channel utterances may perform slightly different functions, and back channels may behave differently in different contexts. Jefferson (1981) suggests that "mm hmm" is a passive recipient token, while "yeah" implies its producer may soon take the floor. The "hmm" utterance or emote (and variants "hsm," "hms," and "hm") in the MOO is not equivalent to the "mm hmm" utterance; it probably functions similar to "hmm" in some "real-life" conversation, which represents a sign of thought or discomfort with an interlocutor's previous statements, carrying a suggestion that an explanation of the cause of discomfort or other further comment will be forthcoming. In Examples 28 and 29, "hmm" was accompanied by further comment. In Example 27, while Tom did not respond further immediately after his "hmm," he was the next speaker on the topic. In a non-response situation, "hmm" (or this variant, the tensed "hms") functions as a sign of internal disquiet:

(31)   Honda hms, that URL doesn't seem to work..

If there is no accompanier to "hmm," a question may be forthcoming from an interlocutor. In Example 32, I said "hmm" about the guest's wandering behavior. Tom didn't make the connection and asked about it. (Of course, the specific function of the back channel as representing disquiet is not established by this example; it may simply be that its nature as a back channel requires that there be an item to be responded to, which was not clear in this non-conversational example.)

Example (32):
[at 4:00 P.M.]:
A guest scrambles up from the ditch at the east side
   of the road.
The guest descends into the sewer.
A guest emerges from the drain.
The guest scrambles down into the ditch to the east.
[at 4:01 P.M.]:
lynn hmm
Tom says, "?"
lynn says, "just that guest being so crazed"
Tom nods.

The "nod" may function passively as a token of understanding or agreement, with no further comment expected, or it may perform as a required turn, indicating "yes," in which case it is not precisely a back channel (although my automated search code will classify it as one). The cases in Example 33 contrast with the uses of nods in Example 27, where they were not necessary responses, but signaled continued attention and/or agreement. (Note that in "real-life" conversation, a nod without a vocal acknowledgment in this situation would be rude.)

Example (33):
Ray says, "incidentally, nv works multicast
  on linux"
Ray tested last night
Honda [to Ray]: That's video stuff?
Ray nods
Honda [to Ray]: Ron Frederick's package?
Ray nods
Honda [to Ray]: Cool ..

These functions of nod responses as full turns (here, second pair parts in adjacency pairs) highlight their underspecified, interactional meaning. In periods of little conversational action, they are indicators of attention, with some suggestion of agreement; in answer to questions, the agreement meaning becomes prominent and they can perform a turn. This is consistent with Clark and Schaefer 1989, where back channel utterances function minimally as indicators of attention, and may also be acknowledgments (which are continuers, in Schegloff's [1982] sense), or even more significant contributions. Gricean cooperative principles help make the interpretation of the nod into an appropriate response to a question.[9]

In Table 5, I outline a more detailed categorization of utterances that function as back channels, affect responses, or repair initiators. I believe it is difficult if not impossible to separate affect out from the back channel function in this medium, since an appropriate emotional response to a turn (e.g., a laugh) indicates both attention and understanding just as well as a nod does. Furthermore, the distinction Goodwin 1986 makes between continuers and assessments—that the former occur between turns, and the latter overlap turns—is not available in the MUD

---

[9]Grice (1975, 1978) identified basic maxims of conversation that underlie cooperative use of language. According to his maxims, conversational participants speak sincerely, relevantly, and clearly, and provide sufficient (but not excessive) information (summarized in Levinson 1983, pp. 101-102). Hearers assume that speakers adhere to these maxims and interpret contributions as relevant, sincere, and informative.

medium, where overlap cannot occur. However, I have here labeled them as different types. "Status" indicators are the explicit acknowledgment utterances like "yeah" and other-initiated repair utterances, which may be emoted or "said."

TABLE 5 Back channel types

Type	Examples
Affect	lol gol grin smile laugh heh giggle hee frown sigh eyes
Nod	nod
Status	hsm hmm hrm ? ok yeah yes uh um err hms

Figure 10 illustrates breakdowns of the number of each type in twenty-minute conversations for dyads and groups, two conversations of each type. It appears (predictably) that affect responses increase in large group conversation, while the number of status indicators decreases. This is probably a function of the party atmosphere, in which it is harder to have a focused conversation and account for misunderstandings.[10]

A representative slice of party conversation with affect back channels is below. Note how many parallel conversations are occurring, too. (In line 24, "gol" stands for "giggles out loud.")

Example (34):

1 Tom is simply ignoring George now that he's still
   held at arm's length.
2 Freddie finally got his pepsi
3 Freddie says, "well slice actually"
4 Karen [to Shelley]: yay
5 Karen . o O (orange sherbert)
6 Freddie [to Shelley]: but you haven't read them yet
7 Shelley [to Freddie]: then how do i know they're
   good?
8 George whuggles Tom.
9 Freddie [to Shelley]: how do you know they're good?
10 lynn says, "awww."
11 Freddie nopds

---

[10] Although the contexts are not directly comparable, O'Conaill et al. (1993) found an average of seven back channels in twenty minutes of ISDN video, as compared to 30.5 in LIVENET video and 60.8 in face-to-face conversation. Classification and identification of back channels in those media are a very different challenge from that of analyzing them in the textual interactions my Figure 10 represents, however.

```
12 Tom whuggles George.
13 Tom grins.
14 Bonnie blinks
15 Freddie nooooods
16 Shelley [to Freddie]: cuz i read em, doof
17 Shelley giggles.
18 Bonnie hehs, gets nominated for ARB
19 Bonnie eyes herself warily.
20 Karen hehs.
21 Tom HASSLED GEORGE INTO WHUGGLY SUBMIShm, that
   sounds a little weird
22 Freddie [to Bonnie]: did you really?
23 Karen eyes Tom warily.
24 George gol
25 Bonnie nods to Freddie.
26 Bonnie says, "bizarre"
27 Karen . o O ( too weird )
28 George mmm, ARB
29 Freddie says, "wow... everybody is"
30 Tom | You have new mail (172) from ARB Petition
   Core Object (#5250).
31 Bonnie nods.
32 Karen [to Freddie]: what, weird?
```

In summary, different back channels may perform different functions, highly contextually determined. In the MUD medium, where no overlap is possible, differences between continuers and assessments may not be possible to establish. Affect signals function as back channels; in large party situations, there are more affect utterances than in dyadic conversations and there are fewer status indicators of (mis)understanding.

4.5 Conclusion

Consideration of turn-taking and back channel usage are important in analysis of the register features of the MUD discourse, since they are critical aspects of interaction in the medium as a whole. Understanding the properties of the communications medium is a necessary first step toward understanding how turn-taking here differs from that in face-to-face conversation.

Face-to-face models of turn-taking do not map well onto MUD turn-taking, because of the lack of simultaneity in the medium. Overlap and interruption do not occur in the way that they do in face-to-face conversation. Since speakers do not need to negotiate for the turn in MUD

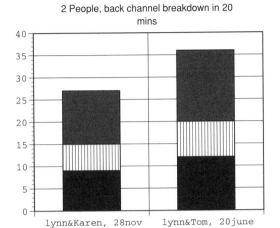

2 People, back channel breakdown in 20 mins

- status
- affect
- nods

lynn&Karen, 28nov   lynn&Tom, 20june

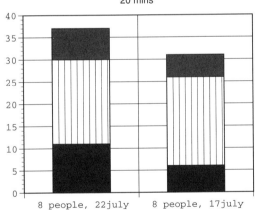

Large Parties, back channel breakdown in 20 mins

8 people, 22july   8 people, 17july

FIGURE 10 Types of back channels in dyadic and group conversation

discourse, but rather for possession of the floor in a more topic-focused manner, theories of floor are more fruitfully considered. The notion of the collaborative floor is particularly useful, since multiple topics are often handled in parallel in the discourse of the MUD. Furthermore, turn size is generally shorter than it is in face-to-face conditions, contrary to predictions in the literature. Users adapt to the medium and learn to produce smaller turns in order to maintain interactivity and a sense of co-presence.

Finally, the general distribution of back channels in several MUD conversations shows that they are used for maintaining a sense of co-presence and awareness in a conversation, not just for signaling comprehension, assessment, or recognition that a complex discourse structure is under construction. Although each back channel response may perform slightly different functions, as a class they share some characteristics: they are conventional, often non-lexical, responses used by the community in similar places in the conversational interaction. Some of them describe non-linguistic actions like nods or laughter. MUD conversation does not map well onto turn-taking models of face-to-face conversation, since turn boundaries are problematic to define, so the placement of MUD back channels is not easily described in terms of transition relevance points. However, their overall distribution suggests that they increase when an interlocutor's rate of speech increases, unless both speakers become very active in parallel. Otherwise, their occurrence in periods with relatively low utterance rates suggests that they help maintain a sense of continued conversational context and co-presence even when focused, topic-driven conversation is lacking.

5

Emotes and the Simple Present Tense

As I showed in chapter 3, the MUD community uses a particular register that differs from ordinary spoken and written language in several respects, including the use of simple present tense, which resembles that found in sports commentary register (e.g., Ferguson 1983; Kuiper 1996) and other related registers (cf. Thorne 1988). Most studies of register have not included analysis at the level of semantics (e.g., Ferguson 1964, 1977, 1983), although many point out impressionistically that tone, rhetorical style, point of view, and use of metaphor may differ in special registers (e.g., Carter 1988; Thorne 1988; Houghton 1988). In this chapter I categorize emotes into five types (conventional actions, back channels, byplay, narration, and exposition), describe contexts of their use, and discuss ways in which present tense is used in ordinary, non-MUD speech. I then discuss the semantics of the use of present tense for emotes in the register, including an informal analysis of the impact of verbal aspect on the interpretation of MUD emotes.

5.1 Emote Types

The emote, which many chat programs do not offer, makes the form of communication in social MUDs particularly complex.[1] The emote is used for ritual actions of several types, which I will discuss in this section.

Reid 1994b includes some history of the emote (called **"pose"**) in

---

[1] A variation on the emote is in fact available in Internet Relay Chat (apparently added since Reid 1991), but reports on its popularity differ greatly. The emote command in IRC also differs from the emote in MUDs in that in IRC, the emote command requires more effort to use than the unmarked **say** utterance; extra typing is required to label an utterance as an action, while in MUDs the two commands require the same effort.

TinyMUD. The evolution of the command illustrates the interaction between user innovation and technical development. Programmable MUDs are in many respects constantly evolving systems; the emergent user culture affects what commands are available. One way in which the culture becomes reified in the environment is through the creation of objects and commands that make ritual utterances easier to execute. The emote (or pose) command was a basic initial case of this. As Smith says, quoted in Reid 1994b:

> On TinyMUD, there is a 'rob <player>' command, that allowed you to attempt to steal 1 penny from said player. However, said player could prevent this by @locking themselves, and then they could set a @fail and an @ofail message on themselves. The @fail message is displayed to the person doing the robbing, the @ofail is displayed to everyone else in the room with the robber's name prefixed.
>
>
> Example:
> @fail me=Moira slaps your hands.
> @ofail me=gets his hands slapped by Moira.
>
> Bozo types> rob moira
> Bozo sees> Moira slaps your hands.
> Everyone else sees> Bozo gets his hands slapped by Moira.
>
> As it happens, if you're not @locked, the @success and @osuccess messages get displayed in the same manner if you are robbed. In not a whole lot of time at all, people started MANUALLY setting their @osuccess to a 'posed' command and robbing themselves—they usually were @locked to themselves, which is a TRUE lock, so only they could set off that message. Example:
>
> @osucc me=falls over laughing.
> rob me
> I see> Moira stole a penny from you!
> You stole a penny from Moira!
> Everyone sees> Moira falls over laughing.
>
> Ta-da, a pose!
>
> This is, as you can imagine, a horribly blunt way of doing poses, as each time you have to reset your @osucc. After about a week

of this, Wizard (Jim Aspnes) gave up and added the pose (aka ':') command.

Smith describes players creating the first poses by setting messages on their characters that contain the desired pose (e.g., "falls over laughing"), and then triggering the message by using a command that outputs the message. As she says, this is a circuitous way of simulating another modality. Evolution of the **whisper** and **page** commands followed similar routes (Smith, quoted in Reid 1994b).

Emotes are usually in third person, but the first person authorship and third person presentation occasionally make pronoun usage confusing and irregular. People often do not maintain third person, especially when other pronouns are involved, or after sentence boundaries. (The second sentences in 1a and 1b below may be "speech" intentionally non-quoted; people often leave off the quote marks when they mix emotes and "speech.")

(1) a. Rick ohwows at lynn. someone who might actually
       be within 1000 miles of me..
     b. Rob speaks about Multiple parentage. Okay, who
       can I marry?
     c. BerryBush BAHs Billock for having already signed
       Garnet's petition, so I can't effectively ask him
       to do so.

Second person pronouns are often ambiguous and confusing to a room full of readers. In Example 2, George berates Shelley for using second person in emotes, and other people play with second person in response. ("Sb" in line 1 refers to scrollback, the text of previously occurring MUD conversation.)

Example (2):
1 Shelley paged you but you musta had too much sb to
   notice
2 George [to Shelley]: Don't use "you" in emotes.
3 Shelley uses George in emotes then
4 Tom [to Shelley]: use "you" wherever you like.
5 George [to Tom]: NEVER USE "you"
6 della uses you!
7 Rob thinks you're stupid.
8 Rob eyes himself warily.
9 Shelley says, "if you'd been keeping up it would
   have been all fine and clear"
10 Rob | :thinks you're stupid.
11 George [to Shelley]: If you had used "bonny" rather
   than "you" it would've been clear, too.

Additionally, the emote is often used to mix action or narrated material with material that would otherwise be "said," such as intentional dysfluencies and addressee indicators.

(3)   a. `Mike nods to Karen, it's a mess.`
      b. `Hacker will go for a drive inna night-time. TOO`
         `BORED TO MOO NOW.`
      c. `Ellen remembers reading, ummmmmm, some Jack London`
         `short story in 7th grade.`
      d. `Tanya could tell you some stories Shelley`

For the purpose of examining the role of the emote in the MUD register, I divide emotes into five broad categories in terms of their role in determining the content and structure of conversations, shown in Table 6.

TABLE 6   Emote types

Name	Type	Example	Tense
Conventional Action	1	`Tom waves.`	Present
Back Channel	2	`Tom nods.`	Present
Byplay	3	`Mike pastes Tom's lips.`	Present
Narration	4	`ls packs for his trip.`	Present
Exposition	5	`Tom hated that movie.`	Any

The first type consists of conventional "actions" like waving when entering a room, poking someone to get their attention, blinking to announce that one is "awake" in the room again after a period of idleness. The second type includes reactions during conversation that communicate continued attention or understanding, similar to back channels in face-to-face speech, like "`lynn nods`" or "`lynn grins.`" The third type comprises joking byplay during conversation, often meta-discourse commentary, like "`Shelley hands some prepositions to Jon.`" The fourth type includes emotes describing actions occurring in real life, as a kind of narrative commentary; these often explain periods of idleness. Unlike the first four types described, which all occur in simple present tense, the fifth type consists of emotes of internal or factual background, in which other tenses may occur. These may represent states of mind; for instance, "`lynn hated the film.`"

5.1.1   Conventional Action

Although many utterances are ritualized in the ElseMOO discourse, this first category of emotes is what I will call "conventional" or "ritual" actions. Most of them are actions that are classifiable loosely as conversation openings or closings (Schegloff 1972, 1977; Schegloff and Sacks

1974). This category includes "hugging" or "waving" to someone when they enter or leave the room, "poking" someone to get their attention, "idling" when one is leaving one's terminal and not able to participate in conversation, and "blinking" or "waking" when one returns to the MUD window and becomes active again.

I will focus mainly on greeting and leavetaking, since they are used most systematically. I will also include "said" greetings and goodbyes (including conventionalized forms like the "null page" and null directed speech), to simplify the analysis. Examples of greeting waves follow.

Example (4):
```
Bonny wanders in from the eastern path through
   the parsley trees.
lynn waves bonny
Bonny waves.
Tom says, "this maroon shirt frightens me"
Karen waves.
```

Satire is one of the best ways of finding out what a community recognizes as conventional behaviors or categories. George, one of the regulars on EM, wrote satiric regulations about proper etiquette in certain situations. These regulations are considered satiric because they are exaggerated prescriptions of behavior that has evolved over time. No user is expected to follow them as stated. In fact, although giving a reason for departing is considered polite if you have been active in the conversation, reasons are not always given; and there is no even close approximation to the second point under Leaving.

Example (5):
```
Leaving:
1) Say goodbye and/or wave.  A reason why is
optional.
2) Wait for at least 2 members of the social
setting to acknoledge that you are leaving or 5
mins.
3) Leave.

Entering:
1) Wave
2) Say hello or hi (optional)
See Regulation 2131.GO for information about
saying goodbye or greeting people entering the
social setting.
```

Contexts for Conversation

The importance of such conventional actions for the community should not be underestimated. They help define and structure interactions, particularly at the margins. They serve as signalers of contexts for potential conversations. Laver (1974, p. 233), in an examination of phatic communication, notes that much of it is heavily conventionalized or ritualized, and that it frequently occurs at the margins of interactions, establishing contexts and relationships, facilitating "psychologically comfortable transition from silence to interaction, and then from interaction to silence." Firth (1972, pp. 29–30) says that "greeting and parting is often treated as if it were the spontaneous emotional reaction to the coming together or separation of people, carrying overtly its own social message. But sociological observation suggests [. . .] that for the most part it is highly conventionalized [. . .]. In a broad sense greeting and parting behavior may be termed ritual since it follows patterned routines; it is a system of signs that convey other than overt messages; [. . .] and it has adaptive value in facilitating social relations."

Examination of greeting waves and other forms of greeting reveals complex attitudes toward the "geography" and toward idle behaviors. In most cases, a character entering a room on EM waves to or otherwise greets the room's occupants, and the active occupants usually greet the entering character in return.

Although statistics are of only limited use when behavior is complex and situated in a natural context rather than a controlled laboratory setting, I present a few numbers to illustrate the point. In two days (sixteen hours) of logs and seventy-one cases of characters entering a room I was in, in fifty-four of the cases (76%) the entering character issued a greeting. (I considered only cases of regular community members who know the conventions in this investigation.)

Cases in which no wave or hello is issued upon arrival can either be dismissed as simply "rude" or examined, situating the actions in their contexts, to find a deeper organizing principle behind the use of greetings (see Schegloff 1972 for an example of this strategy, examining cases of unusual speaker order in phone greeting sequences).

In a large sense, connecting to the MOO means entering a potential conversational context. Since many people use login watchers, which alert them to connections and disconnections, greetings upon connection, rather than just upon entry to a room, are possible. (The login watcher is perhaps parallel to a ringing phone in Schegloff 1972, although the login watcher provides only an announcement of presence; generally, though, greetings in MOO differ from phone greetings in that no identification of the person "calling" is necessary, since the name is trivially available. This situation parallels some examples mentioned in Tang, Isaacs, and Rua 1994, where Caller ID was available, and greetings were reduced to "Hi, Ellen" from "Hi, this is Bob," for instance).

Greetings that do occur immediately upon connection happen in long-distance pages (since few people gather in the room that serves as the connection point). The possibility of long-distance communication expands the notion of conversational context beyond the room one is in; as a result, the borders of conversations are more flexible, and this may explain deviation from the standard greeting upon entry to a room. Example 6 illustrates greeting immediately upon connection. The first line was printed by my login watcher. After seeing the connection information, I paged hello at the > prompt and received a hello in response. Penfold then joined the party, but did not repeat a greeting.

Example (6):
```
< connected: Penfold (#83) on Mon at 20:37. On-line:
  27. >
Tom dunno yet, is looking.
>page penfold hi.
Your message has been sent to Penfold.
Tom says, "his ongoing problem, he's now blaming
  Delta for it?"
lynn says, "what prob?"
Tom says, "he had a dispute with maryanne"
Tom says, "the fish was selected to mediate"
lynn says, "oh that, yeah."
Tom Traceback says, "he was also mloses"
Penfold pages, "hi."
Tom doesn't think he likes facial hair.
Penfold arrives from the eastern end of the patio.
Tom says, "except penfold's"
Tom eyes himself warily.
```

In fact, in several cases, joiners who didn't greet seemed to have been involved in paged conversations with members of the group before joining them. The general greeting on entry to the room would have been somewhat redundant. Other non-greeters appeared to be people who were not intending to participate, just to idle in the midst of a group. A few others were people who had joined other groups before and greeted people there; perhaps they felt that an initial greeting to people upon arriving on the MOO was enough for the day. Overlap in the membership of the different groups probably was a factor as well.

(In "real life" it also becomes awkward to repeat hellos to people one has already greeted.)

Departures As Closure

A close look at departures supports some of the basic conclusions above about conversational contexts. I showed above that some people view connection as an opportunity for greeting, even across room boundaries, which ordinarily define the contexts for conversations. Disconnection in a room counts as a departure from conversation, and hence may require a goodbye, as Shawn's departure shows.

Example (7):
```
Karen eeep a spider
Tom eek a mouse
Shawn [to Karen]: mmm nice juicy spiders
lynn [to Karen]: keep it away from me....
Tom says, "why are wohwait"
Shawn bye
Shawn has disconnected.
```

However, not all disconnections are preceded by goodbyes or waves; long-idle users may just disconnect suddenly, may be kicked off by a firewall logging them out after a certain idle period, or may be bounced off by call-waiting seizing their phone line. When active people leave a room with no wave or bye or statement of intent to go, it is generally seen as odd (often, on EM, the departing character will be "eyed warily," signaling unease); but if someone relatively idle walks out or disconnects without any warning, it is not so disconcerting. The reaction to the departure is dependent on the conversational involvement of the person.

Out of thirty-nine departure events in sixteen hours, in twenty-three (59%) the departing player said goodbye in some way. Nine of the other sixteen departures were caused by disconnections. Seventy-six percent of arriving characters greeted those already there; idling habits or connection problems appear to explain the disparity between greetings and goodbyes.

Of the sixteen who left with no goodbye, ten were idle for at least five minutes before their departure. One or two others appeared to be having connection problems. Three cases of departure from the room when the character had been idle for less than a minute appeared to be instances of people trying to avoid "spammy" (noisy) crowds; in two of those cases, paged conversation continued with them after they left. Another one left quickly to get something from an adjacent room and returned immediately—with no goodbye or hello at each juncture, probably because his participation was merely suspended momentarily.

One of the idlers entered without a greeting and idled the entire time he was present in the room, then left with no goodbye; his lack of an entrance hello may have been an indication of his intent to just idle in the room.

Leaving or joining a group normally requires an active (non-idle) human agency, which is expected to conform to social norms when entering a conversational context. Social norms usually involve greetings and closures. Disregarding those norms, by entering or leaving without appropriate greetings or goodbyes, may signal a lack of interest in participating in the conversation (and hence an interest in idling). The option of long-distance paged greetings expands the conversational context from the room to the entire MUD, and makes not greeting upon entry to a room also a viable social option. Technical concerns like connection problems may also excuse or explain flouting of the norms.

In her discussion of computer messaging, Murray (1989) hypothesizes that closings don't occur in her data because other media take precedence over the computer conversation, because neither party has anything new to contribute to the topic, or because the initial reason for opening conversation has been resolved. While silence in MUD conversations does result from real-life interruptions, it's not appropriate to say that the other media take precedence, precisely; generally someone interrupted "in real life" returns to the MUD conversation afterward. Lack of new information or resolution of the conversation's purpose as reasons for concluding conversation presuppose a very different, purely task-oriented use of the medium, which is not true for the community on the MOO I observe. People in EM are in a social context, occasionally having technical, task-oriented conversations there; the social framework is not forgotten when the task is concluded, however. Clearly, the motivation for use of a communications medium has a large role to play in the way it is used, and the results in Murray 1989 do not carry across to MUD interactions.

5.1.2 Back Channel Reactions During Conversation

The second class of emoted utterances consists of simulated back channels during conversation, like "lynn nods" and "lynn giggles." These are highly routinized and conventional as well; several "said" back channels are equally conventional (e.g., "lynn says, "oic"," short for "oh, I see").

I discuss back channels in detail in chapter 4. Their existence suggests that assumptions by early computer-mediated communication researchers that the limited channel necessarily results in a reduced sense of social presence (Short, Williams, and Christie 1976) or in less feedback (Daft and Lengel 1984, 1986) were premature. Evidence for the importance of these utterances can be found in the fact that many of them have been translated into shorthand commands on the Carpal Tunnel Syndrome Feature to make them easier to type. Users adapt to the medium and adapt the medium to their use, as other CMC researchers (Hiltz and Turoff 1981; Walther 1992) have suggested.

5.1.3 Emoted Byplay

Byplay emotes usually occur in a multi-party, joking context. They serve a function similar to that of back channels in that they signal attention to conversation, but they may involve other characters in a more phatic, often teasing manner. Sometimes their imagery is quite violent or unrealistic (e.g., "Karen detonates a low yield nuclear device over Penfold"), but they are understood to be just play, given the conversational context in which they occur (see Cherny 1995a, 1995c). The overall impression these actions give is of a cartoonish unreality, a rubberiness of boundaries. An example occurs in line 3 below.

Example (8):
1 Tom says, "....can you speak, Mikey, without paste?"
2 Kit [to Tom]: EAT MY PASTE
3 Mike pastes Tom's lips together.

Play in the MOO is a highly cooperative behavior, usually happening during multi-person conversation and often triggered by or directed at objects in the environment. Objects and their modes for interaction form a partial conversational context, which distinguishes MUDs from IRC and most other chat environments (Holmes and Dishman 1994; Danet, Ruedenberg, and Rosenbaum-Tamari 1998; Evard 1993).

Interactions with objects in conversation may consist of interactions with "verbs" (MOO commands) on objects (discussed in section 3.6), references to objects using Antisocial commands, or references to imaginary objects conjured during the discourse (including bodies). The real world may also be referred to in a joking manner.

Interactions with Objects

The character's dual identity as user and as object to be played with is the source of many joking exchanges (see Cherny 1995b). Several commands on EM produce a random list of characters and other objects in their output; for instance, if I typed the right command, people in the room with me might see a (nonsense) output utterance like the following.

Example (9):
lynn thinks we should have some kind of INTELLIGENCE
     TEST to get in here so people like Tom, the

```
Library Browser, the Last Exit For The Lost, and
the Generic Combination Lock can't BLUNDER ALONG
and BOTHER ALL OF US AGAIN.
```

("The Library Browser," "the Last Exit For The Lost," and "the Generic Combination Lock" are objects in the MOO, randomly picked to parallel "Tom," the name I passed to the command I typed.)

Programmed objects can be props for group play. Objects in the environment that cannot be interacted with via code on them can nevertheless feature in group play. Often they are targeted with the Antisocial commands. One day's humor revolved around vilifying the trees someone had put in the park. Most of the actions or quotes directed to the trees originated from the Antisocial commands (some of which were invoked by me at the prompt, e.g., "shake" in line 12). Jon initially keys his behavior as play by directing his Antisocial "invite" command to the tree objects in lines 2–3.

Example (10):
```
 1  Jon stands up from the tree stump.
 2  Jon [to the trees]: Come to Perkins!
 3  Jon [to a tree]: Come to Perkins!
 4  Jon giggles
 5  >!The trees groan and pull their roots out of
    the ground; they advance on Jon threateningly...
 6  The trees groan and pull their roots out of the
    ground; they advance on Jon threateningly...
    --lynn
 7  >eye me
 8  lynn eyes herself warily.
 9  Ray giggles
10  Ray nails a tree down.
11  Jon detonates a low yield nuclear device over a
    tree.
12  >shake trees
13  lynn shakes the trees.
14  Ray spraypaints "WAKE UP" on a tree in dayglo
    orange.
15  Ray giggles
16  Jon takes off and nukes a tree from orbit. "It's
    the only way to be sure."
```
(In line 5, I "spoofed" the behavior of the trees, which resulted in the line shown in 6, with my name appended as the author of the spoof.) This

play interaction with the trees lasted about fifteen minutes, evoking gales of laughter and worries about what workmates might think of the typists' hysterics. In lines 6–19 of Example 11 players report they are laughing out loud ("LOL") or "howling," a conventional expression inherited from Seashore MUSH.

Example (11):

1   Ray pokes a tree, the Rosette Feature Object, the West, and Rimmer and asks them about their pronouns. They consider themselves, and decide they like them, because they are theirs.

2   Janus . o 0 (But what did they smoked? A tree ?)

3   George says, "ANTISOCIAL PARTY"

4   Border blinded a tree and Ray with science!

5   Ted said, "Captain!" A tree, the trees, and Pete's radio said, "wot?"

6   Ted LOL

7   Ray HOWLS

8   lynn too

9   Shelley too!

10 Jon also!

11 Ray says, "this is bad because I've got the video camera on"

12 George [to a tree, under the footbridge, and the string utilities]: Not to be unprofessional, but PBTHBTHBTH!

13 lynn laughs at Ray

14 George whines at a tree, the verbname attribute, the Generic Tutorial Exit, and J. Text.

15 Shelley says, "this is bad because we're in a crowded lab"

16 Ray turns off the camera

17 Ted screams 'NO NO NO ANYTHING BUT tree, trees, nametag, west patio, and Gelfin'

18 George says, "this is badowait i'm alone"

19 Jon [to a tree, the trees, the hammock, and the grass]: Have fun playing GOD on your new little MOO. Maybe you can get some respect there. I doubt it, though.

20 Shelley sends the users awaowait

21 Border [to a tree, the grass, and Jon]: GET A LIFE.

22 Ray just keeps on laughing
23 Ray mumbles that he likes a tree and the Generic
   Gopher Slate here instead of the library.
24 Hacker . o O (These people will never take over
   LambdaMOO, 'cause they're too wacked!)

(Note Hacker's comment in the thought bubble in line 24, referring to the popular conception of EM as a political force on LambdaMOO.) This interaction with the trees was almost entirely produced by using Antisocial commands directed at them (and other random objects on the MOO). Interspersed among the actions with the trees are reports of real-life actions (Type 4 emotes), like Ray's turning off the video camera pointed at him, and reports of imaginary real-life actions, like Shelley's sending the users away from her crowded lab. In the next subsections, I'll consider the use of emotes for improvised play and reports of imaginary real-life actions.

Interactions with Imaginary Objects

Contextual suggestions may briefly evoke imaginary objects in the discourse, producing a cartoon-like atmosphere at times. Play with these unreal objects is often collaborative, as in this case, in which Marie responds to the gift of imaginary flowers.

Example (12):
Marie [to Patrick]: caller is "this" from the calling
   verb. You sure you want caller and not caller
   perms?
Patrick ose!
Patrick duhs.
[at 2:49 P.M.]:
Patrick YAYS.
[at 2:50 P.M.]:
Patrick pulls a handful of roses out of the air and
   presents them to Marie in appreciation of her
   help.
Patrick feel st00pi, to.
Patrick kicks his silly S1 keyboard.
[at 2:51 P.M.]:
Patrick [to Marie]: thanks.
Marie stops and smells the roses.

Often such actions are a sort of brief aside or meta-discourse comment.
   It is out of the ordinary for characters to indulge in extended, solitary interactions with imaginary objects, as occurred in Example 13, when

a guest on the MOO enacted a biker persona fantasy at length. Note the regulars' critical response. One person suggested the guest go to LambdaMOO instead, that he'd fit in better there.[2]

Example (13):
```
The Canadian guest lights smoke:
Tom eyes the Canadian guest warily.
lynn backs away from smoking.
[at 2:10 P.M.]:
Karen too!
Karen is allergic
The Canadian guest removes whisky bottle from pocket
    and takes a long hit:
The Canadian guest throws smoke out window and returns
    bottle to pocket:
Robin says, "hey how was the brunch thingy?"
[at 2:11 P.M.]:
Tom [to Robin]: ask bean
The Canadian guest runs hands threw greay hair:
Robin [to Tom]: okay.
[at 2:12 P.M.]:
Karen whispers to lynn, "what a dea guest"
Robin [to lynn]: fil is pretty normal...
Karen whispers to lynn, "what a dear guest, that is"
The Canadian guest removes biker jacket:
Tom [to the Canadian guest]: out of curiosity, why are
    you using : to end sentences?
Karen too Tom!
Karen was just typing it
lynn grins.
The Canadian guest drops jacket on floor
Robin hehs.
[at 2:13 P.M.]:
Tom says, "what floor?"
Karen [to Canadian guest]: did you notice we're in a
    ditch?
The Canadian guest bottle in jacket breaks
Karen says, "there's no floor or window"
```

---

[2]I've left in the time stamps, because one of the things I found odd about the interaction when it happened was how much time the Guest took between each emoted action. The impression given was of grim, plodding determination.

```
Tom eyes the Canadian guest warily.
lynn eyes the Canadian guest warily.
Robin peers at the Canadian guest suspiciously.
The Canadian guest says, "when you drink and smoke as
   much as me, you loose track of things""
[at 2:14 P.M.]:
Tom feels like he's witnessing a really clumsy strip
   tease.
```

Tom later told me that the annoying aspect of that guest's interaction was his lack of interest in or reaction to the other players in the room. It also appeared to be significant to the regulars that the guest did not pay attention to the characteristics of the room they were in, which was a ditch at the side of a road. Play with imaginary objects usually occurs within a larger discourse context, involves multiple parties in the creation of the fantasy, and often involves the characteristics of the room as well. Other characteristics of his interaction that mark him as an outsider include his peculiar punctuation (he is unaware that he doesn't need to end his **say** in a MUD with quotes, for example, and he seems to believe that an emote using a ":" requires another colon at the end of the typed text) and highly elliptical speech (deletion of articles is not common among speakers of the EM register).

Play like this, which does not involve programmed objects, resembles mime. If the objects of the MUD are analogous to the physical world and can behave like props in play, play without them is solely conjured by imaginary textual gestures that are highly contracted and focused, similar to mime. "Mime condenses time. Mime cannot take a long time to explain something; it has to be clear immediately. [. . .] Mime uses space in a condensed and economical manner as well. It creates the illusion of an expanded space that has volume, mass, and thickness [. . .]. The mime sculpts the volume and size of what he or she portrays" (Royce 1992, p. 194).

During play in a MUD, a single utterance may tell an entire story, particularly if it is highly ritualized, like this Antisocial command: "`Jon takes off and nukes LambdaMOO from orbit. "It's the only way to be sure.""` The player does not leave the MUD room, but the boundaries of time and space seem to stretch to allow the imaginary event. When play is collaborative, multiple authors attempt to improvise a narrative together; see Kolko 1995 for some discussion of this type of phenomenon, which rarely happens for extended periods of time in EM.

Imaginary Actions in "Real Life"

In another subcategory of byplay, a character describes what she could be doing in real life. These actions don't involve the virtual environment. The most common, perhaps, is "LOL," which stands for "laughs out loud," but frequently the speaker is not in fact laughing audibly in real life. It is certainly difficult to tell to what extent reported real actions are really occurring; but in at least one instance, Tom's typist was revealed by another MUDder in the room with him in "real life" to be quite silent despite the reports of "Tom LOL" in the course of MOO conversation. Another possible case is a joke prompted by MOO conversation context:

(14) `Damon writes down "keep lights on when with inga"`

These emotes are often distinguishable from those that do narrate real actions by the fact that they are responses to the on-going MOO conversation. Still, affect responses like "LOL" remain ambiguous, situated between imaginary and actual real-life actions.

5.1.4 Narration of (Non-imaginary) Real-Life Actions

The next type of emotes are genuine narrations. It is quite common for users to document in real time their actions in real life, while they MUD, in a manner similar to simultaneous sports commentary. In Example 15, ls packs his computers for a trip while MUDding. (A "duo" is an Apple portable.)

Example (15):
```
ls starts packing for his argonne trip.
[ . . . ]
ls pulls out his second duo.
lynn says, "you have two?"
paul [to ls]: show-off
ls says, "uh, yeah."
```

In some cases, users of narration emotes may be motivated by a need to explain their distraction, lack of timely response, or departure from the MUD conversation; in other cases, they could be providing conversational openers. However, some users seem to connect solely to document their daily work actions, hardly noticing remarks directed to them or conversation around them.

Interestingly, emotes about real-life actions occur in simple present tense, as if the actions are going on simultaneously with the typing. In some cases there is genuine overlap. For instance, evidence that the activity of talking to Brock continues beyond the typed narration in line 1 below is found in line 2, where Shelley describes how Brock sounds (present tense).

Example (16):
```
1 Shelley talks to Brock.
2 Shelley says, "he sounds, um, i dunno...disappointed
  or something."
```
Perhaps oddly, simple present tense can also be used to describe events that have already occurred in real life.

Example (17):
```
Marie wakes, scrolls, giggles "$code_utils:boot_player_
  if_needed"
```
In this case, Marie describes waking after being idle, reading her scroll-back in the MOO window, and giggling at a programming line quoted in scrollback. Her narration of the entire sequence of events occurs in one line. We interpret these as sequential actions because narrative time is understood to progress with each verb that reports an achievement or accomplishment in a sequence (Dowty 1986). I discuss the semantic properties of events in the present tense in MUD register in section 5.4.

5.1.5 Emotes of Background or Exposition

Background and expository emotes differ from the other types in that they need not be in the simple present tense; they are usually statements about the speaker's attitudes, beliefs, or background relevant to the conversational context. They fit seamlessly into conversation as if they were uttered as **say**s: they can be responded to as if they were "spoken" as **say**s, and they can occur in response to **say**s. Often they show first person speech-like properties, such as being directed to another speaker, containing second person pronouns, and even showing dysfluencies similar to those frequently intentionally introduced in **say**s. Line 5, below, is an example.

Example (18):
```
1 lynn [to Damon]: so Kit thinks you and I would be a
  cute couple.
2 Damon says, "um"
3 Damon says, "how nice"
4 lynn laughs.
5 Damon hasn't, well, met you, lynn
```
The choice of emote modality over **say** modality for an utterance is no doubt significant, but a complete analysis of the difference in meaning remains for future work. I suggest that it has something to do with tone, via a manipulation of perspective. The omniscient narrator's voice suggested by third person is more distanced, and perhaps feels more

authoritative. However, some users make use of the emote modality for long stretches of conversation, like Marie below.

Example (19):

```
Marie wants chocolate and M&M's make her teeth
  hurt.
Marie's house mate is allegedly buying instant
  chocolate pudding at the store.
lynn says, "switch to fudge."
Marie nods.
Marie has been eating hot fudge topping straight
  out of the jar :-)
lynn says, "aieee, wow."
Marie might be out of it now tho.
Marie is like hardcore.
```

5.1.6 Frequency of Each Type

Figure 11 indicates the relative frequency of the different kinds of emotes in conversation. I compare three conversations among large groups of people with three others between two people. Playful byplay emotes (Type 3) are more common in multi-person parties than in the more sedate conversation that occurs between two people alone, and emoted back channels occur more often in dyadic conversation. Note that expository emotes occur with about the same frequency in both types of conversation. (Since Type 1 emotes, or conventional openings and closings, only occur at the boundaries of conversation, I have excluded them from this chart.)

Figure 12 shows the ratio of emoted actions to **says** in two other conversations, among two and three people.[3] Note that several people use emotes almost half the time.

5.2 Other Uses of the Simple Present Tense

The types of emotes I discussed above are repeated in Example 20. Types 1–4 represent actions; Type 5 represents internal states of mind or background history, among other things. The emoted actions are in present tense. (An action not in present tense would be classed as Type 5.)

---

[3]Since I was logging, I appear in both conversations.

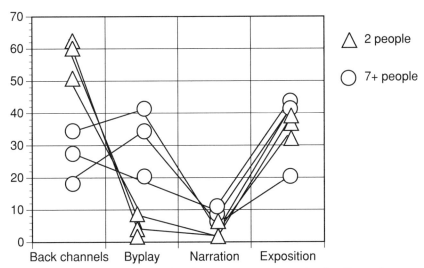

FIGURE 11　Percentages of different emote types in dyadic and group conversations

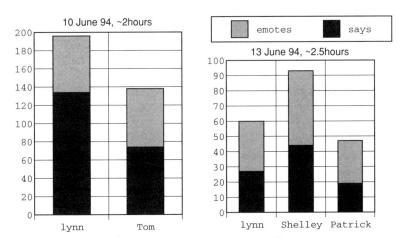

FIGURE 12　Ratios of emotes to says in conversations

Example (20):

Name	Type	Example	Tense
Conventional Action	1	`Tom waves.`	Present
Back Channel	2	`Tom nods.`	Present
Byplay	3	`Mike pastes Tom's lips.`	Present
Narration	4	`ls packs for his trip.`	Present
Exposition	5	`Tom hated that movie.`	Any

Narration emotes (Type 4) describe events that are occurring more or less concurrently in the real world, while the Type 1–3 emotes describe events that occur solely in the unreal, or imaginary, MUD world. The utterance in some sense "creates" the event.

One possible explanation for the prevalence of simple present tense is that the convention is inspired or otherwise historically based on the fact that the MUD system's responses to user commands (such as a navigation command, like "go north") are messages in simple present tense. The messages in Example 21 are output presented when users type commands to interact with the virtual geography or objects.

(21) a. `Guest steps off the catwalk.`
b. `Ferris heads for the eastern end of the patio.`
c. `Plaid_Guest wanders up the street to the west.`
d. `Tom picks up TomTraceback's Business Card.`

Some system messages use forms other than the simple present, however.

(22) `Tom has disconnected.`

A historical explanation is not enough to account for the persistent use of present tense in the MUD discourse. Furthermore, the simple present tense is not used only in system messages; it also occurs in casual conversation where ordinarily (in non-MUD discourse) the present progressive or past tense might be used.

Uses of the simple present tense in non-MUD registers have been discussed in the linguistic literature on tense and aspect. Leech (1971), Kuhn (1989), and Binnick (1991), among others, survey how the present tense is used in English.

The simple present indicates that an utterance is true at the present time (with stative verbs):

(23) a. I am sick.
b. John loves Mary.

It is used for habitual or "freqentative" events (generally with non-statives):

(24) a. Dogs chew on bones.
b. Whenever he calls, he sits close by the fire.

It is also used for "gnomic" facts, or what is true at all time for all readers:

(25)   Milton defends the freedom of the press in his *Areopagitica*.

It is used in performatives:

(26)   a. I hereby christen this ship the *Marie Belle*.
       b. I promise to write.

Smith (1991, p. 153) points out that the simple present is used for sentences describing perception and mental achievement: "they constitute reports of instantaneous events, reflecting perhaps the special immediacy of perception."

(27)   a. I see the moon.
       b. I feel the current of the river.
       c. I understand.
       d. Oh! I see!

It can be used for future time when the action is considered part of a plan "already fixed."

(28)   I start at Oracle on Monday.

The simple present also refers to future time when it occurs in clauses with *I hope, as soon as, before, until*. (Present progressive can also denote the future: "I am leaving on Monday.")

"Reportive" (or sometimes "reportative") use of present tense is usually associated with sports commentary register or the "patter" of demonstrators (Leech 1971; Kuiper 1996). For instance, a sports reporter narrates actions as they occur, in a manner similar to the narration emotes in the MUD register.

(29)   Napier passes the ball to Attwater, who heads it straight into the goal!

Binnick (1991, p. 248) points out (somewhat confusingly) that "the reportative use has two subspecies that differ: the more 'narrative' use actually involves the moment of the speech act, whereas the reportative does so only nominally. The latter is rarely if ever used of the actual present moment, for obvious reasons. It occurs in titles, in captions on photos and pictures, in stage directions, and the like. In this sense the usage is quite like the historical present."

Stage directions use the simple present. Smith (1991, p. 154) cites the opening directions of *Mourning Becomes Electra*:

(30)   Berke and Minnie come forward as far as the lilac clump...

The "dramatic" present, also known as the conversational historical present (CHP), is used like the past tense. Wolfson (1982) found that the CHP alternates with past tense in performed narratives, organizing a story into episodes. She concludes that the present tense is used deictically, with temporal adverbs and other devices situating the time of the present tense events.

(31)   So I am walking down the street, and this guy says to me....

Captions on photos in the press often occur in simple present tense as well, as do the headnotes of chapters or texts (Thorne 1988). Chapter 1 of *David Copperfield* is headed

(32)   I am born.

Leech (1971) points out that in books the present tense is often used to convey the sense that the work as a whole is existing at a present moment. Therefore, past tense and present tense are both acceptable for references to earlier chapters:

(33)   The problem was/is discussed in chapter two above.

Perhaps similarly, "verbs of communication" allow present tense, as if the "communication is still in force for those who have received it" (Leech 1971, p. 7):

(34)   a. Joan tells me you're getting a new car.
         b. The ten o'clock news says it's going to be cold.

Some of the uses above describe events related more directly to the speech time (e.g., reportive uses) while others are tied to a contextual time that may be past (e.g., historical present, synopses) and might be said to act deictically. A complete analysis of the present tense's usage must make clear how the speech moment (i.e., the present moment) and the reference time are related. In the MUD register, Types 1–3 emotes are directly tied to the speech time, much as performatives are, while Type 4 emotes (Narration) are related in the way that reportive speech is tied to the speech time: they describe an action as it occurs elsewhere or just after it occurs.

5.3   Performatives and MUD Actions

The emoted actions of Types 1–3 initially suggest the sort of speech acts that Searle (1969, 1989) and Austin (1962) discuss, called "performatives." Performative speech acts are utterances that usually occur in the first person, simple present tense, indicative, and by their utterance perform some action: e.g., "I hereby pronounce you man and wife" or "I promise I won't spend that dollar." Despite being in the simple present, they do not describe habitual or generic actions; they describe an event that occurs at their time of utterance and by virtue of their utterance. Emoted actions seem to be related to this class of speech acts, albeit in third person, conjuring events as "events" solely by their utterance. (I follow Searle 1989 in not including indirect speech acts in my discussion here.)

Intentionality is a major component in Searle's 1989 account. He argues that a class of verbs with intentionality as a component must be recognized; that one cannot perform a performative action without intention to do so. "Manifestation of the intention to perform the action, in an appropriate context, is sufficient for the performance of the action" (Searle 1989, p. 551). Furthermore, the performative verbs are self-referential, in that they describe their own actions and execute them at the same time. If I say, "I promise to come home at noon," I both describe the content of my promise and make it.

Searle concludes that the explanation for performatives does not lie in the meaning of the verbs, but in the world itself. "If God decides to fry an egg by saying 'I hereby fry an egg,' or to fix the roof by saying 'I hereby fix the roof,' He is not misusing English. It is just a fact about how the world works, and not part of the semantics of English verbs, that we humans are unable to perform these acts by declaration" (Searle 1989, p. 554).

It is tempting to conclude that the world of MUD conversation is one in which we humans can do so. Every uttered action is understood to occur at its utterance, in the context of the MUD conversation. There is some evidence that users view such emotes as events that "happen" (even if only as a communicative action) as soon as they are emoted; they are thus nondeniable, like performatives. One woman described to me her distress at being hugged by a guest she didn't know and then her attempt to negate the event:

Example (35):
1 The guest hugs Karen.
2 Karen is NOT hugged by Guest.

Despite her attempt in line 2 to retract the hug, another character later referred to "the guest who hugged her," suggesting that he perceived it as nondeniable, or at least, nondeniable by her. In some sense, the action occurred as soon as the message showed up on people's screens.

One problem Searle (1989) and Verschueren (1994) tackle is why there are no performatives for verbs like "hint," "boast," or "lie," which sound as if they ought to parallel verbs like "promise" and "order." Searle concludes that they cannot be used performatively because they imply that their actions are not performed explicitly and overtly, which is required of performatives. Verschueren expands this into a theory about distance between the description of the action and the action the utterance performs. In the utterance "I lie to you that I am done with my Ph.D.," the action performed is the lying about a proposition, and the description is the statement that it is a lie. He claims there must be no "distance" between the two in order for the utterance to be performative. To claim to "lie," for instance, is to describe an action negatively valued and insincere; the choice of the word "lie" creates an evaluative distance between the description and the action intended, causing the performative attempt to fail. "I order you to go," on the other hand, succeeds because the action is an order, and the description is of an order as well, with no evaluative distance or insincerity implied.

Interestingly, there are occasional uses of verbs like "lie" in the discourse of the EM community:

(36) `Ray lies, "I'm awake, I'm awake!"`

In fact, this utterance probably succeeds partly because in fact it is not uttered by the user of the character Ray; it is an idle twitch, a programmed, automatic response. (Idle twitches were discussed in chapter 3.) In fact, his character *is* lying, as the utterance states. Any negative evaluative distance in this case is confined to the third person description of action, rather than the utterance "I'm awake" itself. That description is important for communicating that the utterance is not an ordinary one typed by an active user. Indeed, most "hearers" recognize its automated status. (See Cherny 1995b for more discussion of agency and automated actions.)

Note that this utterance would not succeed as a simple **say** from Ray's character: "`Ray says, "I lie, I'm awake."`" The third person emote allows a distance between the description and the action that is not allowed in first person performatives, where the two must coincide. The perspectival distance allowed by emotes complicates and enriches the sorts of actions that can be undertaken in the text conversation.

Verschueren (1994, p. 5) discusses some speech acts that are not first person simple present tense, which he calls semi-performatives:

(37) a. Le porteur déclare etre majeur. [The holder (of this ticket) declares that he/she is over 18.]
  b. You are dismissed.
  c. Passengers are warned not to lean out the window.
  d. I am asking that you to do this for me, Henry, I am asking for you to do it for me and Cynthia and the children.

Example 37d (which he takes from Searle 1989, p. 537) he dismisses as not containing the "content" of the request, and therefore calls it a description of the request rather than a making of the request itself.

There appear to be similar cases in the MUD discourse, as shown in Example 38.

Once we expand our focus to include emotes in Types 3–5, it appears that a simple performative analysis for all emotes is not sufficient. The MOO example below consists of a description of action:

(38) Ted says one thing, then the opposite, and
      aggressively asserts that both are true. He then
      annoys you for a while, just before boasting
      of his SPARCbook like you care.

Ted describes himself as "boasting," but he is in fact describing an action he is not explicitly performing (since one cannot boast solely by saying that one boasts), which puts this example in the category of semi-performatives like Example 37d above. Emotes like this are a common occurrence, some of them more explicitly performative than others. The more performative types include "note," "observe," "ask," "tell," and "wonder," which usually take a proposition as a subordinate clause, unlike the boasting case above. The proposition appears to accomplish the action, unlike the subordinating verb on its own.

(39) a. Sandy notes that the power elite IS NOT linked...
      b. Shelley observes that she's about conferenced out
         and would really like to go to the espresso bar
         across the street and talk about something else.
      c. Marie thanks lynn for signing

The "boasting" example is not alone in its meta-discourse character. In Example 40, Tom describes the preceding conversation in line 9.

Example (40):

1 You see a car scream by on the road, you hear a
   SLAM, and Mike zings into the ditch and
   lands with a painful THUD.
2 Ray laughs
3 Tom says, "zing"
4 Ray says, "THUD"
5 lynn says, "THUD"
6 Mike says, "WHAM!"
7 lynn [to Ray]: hmmph
8 Shelley says, "THUD"
9 Tom and Ray and lynn reenact the event.
10 Ray wins by virtue of only being a few yards
   away from em.ccs
11 lynn [to Tom]: using Mike.
12 Tom [to Ray]: It must be a real pain for you

```
not to be able to blame lag when you lose
anymore.
```

(Em.ccs is the machine that the MOO resides on, and Tom refers to network lag in line 12.) Note that Tom describes the reenactment in present tense, suggesting that it is not over. Note also Ray's use of the "wins" routine in line 10, referring to getting his "THUD" out before mine. He has already won, but he describes the event in present tense. Present tense seems to be fine for actions that have just ended as well, as we will discuss below. Performatives normally do not describe events after they occur.

Considering the range of "action" types that are performed in third person simple present tense emotes, many of which describe either ongoing or concluded events, it seems that a simple performative analysis of emoted actions is not going to account for all cases. Whatever "semi-performatives" amount to, these emotes may indeed be of that type; however, a more fruitful avenue to explore is the relationship between present tense and discourse semantics generally.

5.4 Aspectual Classes and Tense

Aspectual class interacts with interpretation of sentences in the present tense. In a non-MUD "normal" register, simple present tense can only be used with stative verbs, since the present is understood to imply truth at the moment of speech, which only statives allow. In Dowty's (1979, 1986) analysis, the truth of a sentence is relative to an interval of time. A stative is true over an interval, as well as at all subintervals of time down to moments.

(41) a. John loves Mary.
      b. John knows the answer.

Non-states take on habitual readings in present tense. Activities describe an action going on for some interval of time. For Dowty, an activity is implicated if a sentence is true over an interval and over subintervals down to a certain size.

(42) a. John runs every Tuesday.
      b. John giggles when he reads the comics.

Accomplishments describe a behavior culminating in another state or in the creation of an object. An accomplishment is true over an interval, but false over all subintervals.

(43) a. John ran a mile.
      b. John built a house.

Achievements describe punctual events, like reaching the top of a mountain, or waking. They are similarly false over subintervals.

(44) a. John reached the top of the mountain at 5:55 PM.
b. John died.

Dowty (1979) collapses accomplishments and achievements into one category, often called "telic" events, and defines the aspectual classes as follows:

(45) a. If α is a stative predicate, then $\alpha(x)$ is true at an interval I just in case $\alpha(x)$ is true at all moments within I.
b. If α is an activity verb or an accomplishment/achievement verb, then $\alpha(x)$ is only true over an interval larger than a moment.
c. If α is an accomplishment/achievement verb, then if $\alpha(x)$ is true at I, then $\alpha(x)$ is false over all subintervals of I.
d. If α is an activity verb, then if $\alpha(x)$ is true at I, then $\alpha(x)$ is true over all subintervals of I that are larger than a moment.

In other words, statives are true at moments, as well as over intervals, while activities and accomplishments and achievements are not true at moments, but are true over intervals. Hence non-statives in simple present tense in ordinary registers are interpreted as habitual, rather than as being true at the moment of speech. Activities are only true down to a certain interval size; if *John runs* over some time interval, Dowty considers him not to be running at the moment of speech, at which he is perhaps raising his legs or puffing instead (both parts of the running, but not the activity itself).

5.4.1 The MUD Register Data

Type 1–3 emotes in MUD conversation usually have no referent in the real world. Type 4 emotes refer to actions in the real world, narrated as they occur, suggesting a similarity to reportive uses of the simple present tense. To properly consider the range of interpretations of the simple present tense, we must examine emotes referring to both the MUD world (in which play, back channels, and ritual greetings and closings occur) and the real world. I will call the MUD world the *irrealis*, or unreal, world.

Statives

In MUD register uses of the simple present tense, statives do occur. In this example, "irl" stands for "in real life," which means in the real world.

(46) `lynn finds ben okay irl, just very earnest`

Here is an example of a state of mind that is based on MUD world referents. (Max is a robot dog that roams the MUD.)

(47) Tom wants to be able to page Max.

It is difficult to find a state that is true in one world (or frame, Goffman 1974) and does not correspond to anything in the other, since most are states of mind. A state that might be argued to hold in the MUD but not in the real world is described in the message a user sees upon entering a room occupied by another character. Not uttered by a person, the message in line 6 of Example 48 displays a character's virtual presence; the user may not be "there" at his desk in real life, but the character is "there" in the room anyway. (In this example, I typed the command to join Tom at my prompt, and my character was moved to the location of Tom's character, The Ditch at the Side of the Road. Entering the ditch, I see a description of the "room" in line 5 and an announcement of which characters are present in line 6, the line of concern here.)

Example (48):
1 >join tom
2 You push the manhole cover aside and squint in the
  light...
3 The Road
4 The Ditch at the Side of the Road
5 Mud, frozen lifeless grass, and litter from the
  passing traffic fill the depression at the
  side of the road.
[. . .]
6 Tom is here.

In Example 49, the states are certainly not intended to be "real," and may be assumed to be MUD world states only.

(49) a. Kurt is really George.
      b. Tom is really Karen's Penfold.

A diagram illustrating the interpretation of statives with respect to the time of speech is given in Figure 13. The speech time is represented as a tick mark on the time line, labeled r_s, with the state holding around it for some indefinite length of time.

Non-statives may have a habitual or generic meaning, as in an ordinary, non-MUD register, but this is a less common interpretation. See line 3 below.

Example (50):
1 Ray [to lynn]: See, it's easy to tell the difference

between me and Tom. He actually gets things
done around here.
2 lynn [to Ray]: and you boot people. heh.
3 Tom boots people too, but only after asking about
eight other people if he should.

MUD world, Real world

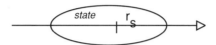

FIGURE 13 Statives in MUD and real worlds

Activities, accomplishments, and achievements often appear to occur
without the habitual reading they have in "normal" discourse, as shown
below.

Activities

Interpretation of activities ranges from a very short-term perfective or
completive reading to a longer-term, more imperfective reading. Greetings or affect responses to conversation in the MUD world frame are
read as short-term actions, as in lines 2 and 4:

Example (51):
1 Ava walks in from the sunroom.
2 Ava waves.
3 Colm says, "aVa!"
4 Ava smiles.

The normal interpretation of affect responses like "Tom giggles" in
conversation is that the events they report go on for a very brief period,
and end with the utterance. This effect must be overridden with explicit
statements of ongoing action, as in line 4 below.

Example (52):
1 Bryan bleeps, ".- -. .... .- -- ... --- ..- - -
.... . .-."
2 Largo eyes Bryan warily.
3 Bryan guesses not.
4 Largo continues to eye Bryan warily.

In Example 53, Tom "wakes," blinking, after being idle in the room
and announces that a fight (semantically, an activity) is going on in
real life in the background. No start or termination time is implied.

Significantly, the "where" query in line 7 results in an identification of the world Tom intends the activity to be interpreted in, in this case, "rl" or "real life."

Example (53):
```
1 [at 5:39 P.M.]:
2 Tom blinks.
3 Tom whuggles lynn.
4 lynn whuggles Tom.
5 [at 5:40 P.M.]:
6 Tom and Carl and George fight about @gag.
7 lynn says, "where?"
8 Tom says, "rl"
9 Tom is mostly ignoring them.
```

In the normal English register, the activity would be reported in the progressive: "Tom and Carl and George are fighting about @gag." The progressive is acceptable in the MUD register as well.

The simple present "talks" can be used the way the progressive "is talking" would be used in normal registers. Evidence that the activity of talking to Brock continues beyond the typed narration in line 1 below is shown in line 2, where Shelley describes how Brock sounds (present tense).

Example (54):
```
1 Shelley talks to Brock.
2 Shelley says, "he sounds, um, i dunno...disappointed
  or something."
```

Real-world activities may also be short-term, with accomplishment-like interpretations, however. Example 55 shows how complexly real-world activities are reflected in the MUD world: after his laughter in the real world, Ray reports "Ray laughs" in the MUD. The understood duration of both events is short-term, since normally laughter does not continue for long periods during conversation in the real world. In Example 55, Tom is in the same room as Ray is in real life. He reports his own "watching" activity in line 2 after the event he is watching has occurred—Ray's typing of "emote laughs."

Example (55):
```
1  Ray laughs
2  Tom watches Ray document his laughter.
3  Tom says, "mudding with people in the same room is
   weird"
4  Ray laughed before typing :laughs
```

```
5  Tom nods.
6  Ray thought he did
7  Ray says, "wait, now I'm confused"
8  Tom eyes Ray warily.
9  Ray says, "which world is the real world?"
10 Ray eyes himself warily.
```

My sense is that there is a strong pragmatic effect influencing the interpretation of real-world activities. A longer-term activity that would not allow MUDding during it, like "lynn brushes her teeth," would have an inceptive reading, while short-term activities usually have a completive reading. But it is hard to know how to distinguish the inceptive readings from the future intention readings discussed in section 5.4.4.

I give diagrams for the preferred interpretations of activities in the MUD world and real world in Figure 14. Despite the importance of pragmatics in their interpretation, I represent activities in the real world as ongoing around the time of speech, which is a tick mark labeled r_s. Activities in the MUD world are punctual, occurring with the moment of speech (which I represent as a tick mark just at the end of the activity blob). (Alternately, one might represent the moment of speech as a blob identified with the activity event blob, but this seems less intuitive.)

Real world

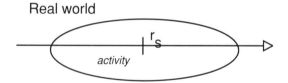

MUD world

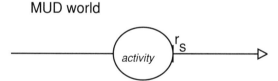

FIGURE 14 Activities in MUD and real worlds

Accomplishments and Achievements

The MUD register appears to parallel the sports commentary register in its use of present tense accomplishments and achievements to describe events that have already occurred in real life. Most such sentences in the MUD register refer to events that have just occurred.

Users are most likely to interpret the real-world accomplishment sentence below as meaning that the action is completed. The next most likely interpretation is that the event is ongoing at the time of typing.[4]

(56) Bryan writes to a user.. "What the hell are you
       compiling that takes 20 minutes a shot?"

Playful actions especially feel "just completed," even if the action described, which is understood to be unreal, might take a long time to perform in reality. ("Stuffs him into the weather map" is probably an accomplishment.)

Example (57):
Harry grabs hold of Henry and stuffs him into the
   weather map.
He switches Henry into the firing chamber of the
   weather map and yanks the firing cord. KABOOM!

Although it is not spoken by a user, the following message appears after a character enters the Living Room on the MUD, and probably represents an accomplishment.

(58) Kurt walks in from the sunroom.

In this example of a real-world achievement, Brett is not likely to be spewing cherry coke as he types the present tense statement in line 8, nor is he announcing an intention to do so in the future. The event is understood to have just occurred, probably simultaneously with the laughter reported in line 5.

Example (59):
1 Tom says, "and have the say command always just
   print 'A cockroach click-clicks.'"
2 Bonny giggles.
3 Egypt [to lynn]: I was doing Rikki Tikki Tavi and
   Watership Down...
4 Phred thinks another FurryMUCK based in MOO would be
   neato.
5 Brett LAUGHS
6 Bonny says, "DISNEYMOO"

---

[4]Although "write" is often an activity, I consider this example the equivalent of "write a letter," an accomplishment.

```
7 Brett says, "shit"
8 Brett spews cherry coke
```

The next example is of an achievement in the MUD world. A blink is a Type 1 emote action, usually signaling that a character is "awake" and attentive to conversation after a period of idleness. Again, we interpret this as a just-completed event (or two).

(60) Ivan blinks, ughs.

Blob diagrams representing telic events are shown in Figure 15. In the MUD world, the moment of speech coincides with the utterance of the event, and the entire event is viewed as punctual. I represent this as I did for activities in the MUD world: with the moment of speech at the very end of the event blob. Events in the real world, on the other hand, occur before the speech point. I represent this by showing the tick mark further along the time line, with the event blob in the past.

MUD world

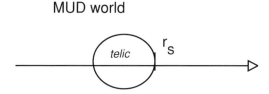

Real world

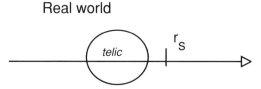

FIGURE 15   Telic events in MUD and real worlds

5.4.2   Contrast with Reportive Present Tense

Binnick (1991, p. 248) says that "the reportative use is essentially one involving telic, that is performance, predicates, ones with definite ends. If an observer reports of a man under observation, 'He runs,' the sense is implicitly an accomplishment—he runs a bit—and the addressee is entitled to infer that he has stopped running. If he fails to stop running, the accomplishment sense is inappropriate; from the point of view of the observer, it is an activity, and a report in the progressive is more proper: *He is running.*" If this situation is true of reportive speech, then the MUD register differs in that the simple present tense is equally appropriate for ongoing activities in the real-world frame. My sense is that the present tense activities within the MUD frame are in fact accomplishment-like, while activities in the real-world frame are potentially ongoing, although the judgments are fragile and depend both on how granular an activity is and on common-sense knowledge about the usual length of the activity.

In Cooper's (1986) discussion of reportive present tense, he claims that accomplishments are "odd" in present tense. In a look at the reportive sports commentary register, Ferguson (1983) in fact mentions two examples of accomplishments, both reported after the events occurred:

(61) a. The seal leaps 6 feet in the air, to get the fish.
      b. It bounces into the seats.

Cooper's analysis and his prediction of oddness do not seem in line with the facts.

Cooper does not discuss achievement sentences at all. Vendler (1967) suggests that achievement sentences cannot be used in the simple present (except for historical uses or immediate future readings), because of the short duration of the achievement action itself. Vendler argues that *Now he wins the match* is not found, but instead occurs in present perfect, as *Now he has won the match.* Verkuyl (1989) points out that in fact achievements do occur in simple present in sports commentary, citing such examples as "catch the ball," "hit the ground," and "score" (p. 55).

TABLE 7 MUD register and reportive speech, simple present

Aspect	MUD Register		Reportive Speech
	Real World	MUD World	
State	holds at r_s	holds at r_s	holds at r_s
Activity	May be ongoing	punctual at r_s	punctual before r_s
Accomplishment	punctual before r_s	punctual at r_s	punctual before r_s
Achievement	punctual before r_s	punctual at r_s	punctual before r_s

Table 7 summarizes the phenomena observed. ("Holds at r_s" means that the state holds at an instant, the instant of speech, as in ordinary registers.) It is important to remember that in reportive speech (and MUD register real-world reference) telic events are described after they have occurred, while in the MUD world the imaginary events occur at the moment of utterance. Speakers may be borrowing from their understanding of present tense use in reportive speech when they describe real-world telic events. The semantics of MUD world events may also be modeled after reportive speech semantics, with the exception that there is no real event being described, and so the MUD discourse evokes imaginary events.

5.4.3 Why Are Activities Odd?

Table 7 shows that activities pattern strangely, behaving differently in the MUD and real worlds. As a class, activities share properties of statives and of telic events. They are like statives in that they are homogeneous (down to a certain granularity). They also do not have clearly specified termination points. However, if a termination is provided, they can become telic. These examples are from Dowty 1986, p. 39:

(62) a. John walked. (activity)
      b. John walked a mile. (accomplishment)

Bare plurals can transform accomplishments or achievements into activities:

(63) a. John noticed the rare seashell on the beach. (achievement)
      b. John noticed rare seashells on the beach. (activity)
      c. John walked to train stations for two hours, delivering flyers. (activity)

For Dowty (1986), the relationships between events in discourses are largely pragmatic. Activities, like states, are determined to overlap preceding or following sentences' events according to real-world knowledge. In my discussion of MUD register activities, I suggested that pragmatics plays a large role in the interpretation of real-world activities: they seem completive if they describe short-term events, inceptive if they describe activities it is difficult to MUD during (e.g., "lynn brushes her teeth"), ongoing if they describe activities one can MUD during (e.g., "Shelley talks to Scott"). In the MUD world, an activity is usually understood as punctual or completive unless it is explicitly continued soon after its first mention: "Largo continues to eye Bryan warily." Their patterning with telic events as punctual, in the Kamp (1979) sense—no event of importance overlaps them—may be due to properties of the irrealis MUD world, or the nature of play in it. Another reason for the lack of ongoing activities in the MUD world may be that there is simply no evidence of their ongoing nature unless they are specifically described as continuing actions. With no evidence to the contrary, they are heard as completive, possibly because the progressive is available to unambiguously signal ongoing activity. Here is an irrealis MUD-world progressive:

(64) Tom is pawing at you, Ray, and the System Object.

This is the argument that Binnick (1991) seems to make for activities in reportive speech: the progressive is more appropriate for ongoing action, so activities in the simple present are heard as completive. Why then aren't progressives used solely for describing ongoing real-world activity in the MUD register? There is apparently some subtly different meaning attached to the simple present; the event is more completely captured in simple present tense, with just a suggestion that it may be ongoing. This distinction cannot be captured well in our semantics, and the intuitions are vague. One informant suggests that he would be more likely to use a simple present tense for an activity if he is introducing it as a new possible topic, and he would use a progressive if it were already established that there were something going on, for example, in response to the question "what are you doing now?" which presupposes that something is going on in the real world. Given the importance of pragmatics in the interpretation of activities, I am unsure to what degree I ought to make a distinction in the semantics between their interpretations in the MUD and real world. If no real distinction is needed, but pragmatics does the work (as in Dowty 1986), then the difference between the MUD world and the real world may be lessened, and the semantics of the MUD register may look more like that of reportive speech, which would be desirable.

5.4.4 Future

Simple present tense emotes can be used for future intentions or planned actions, as well as for current or just-completed ones.

In Example 65, Tom leaves for a meeting. He reports his intention to "really disconnect this time" in simple present tense, before doing it. He even says goodbye and leaves the room before disconnecting. Disconnection represents an achievement, aspectually.

Example (65):
Tom says, "time to go back to dealer"
Tom really disconnects this time.
Tom says, "bye"
Tom heads for the eastern end of the patio.
< disconnected: Tom (#73) on Wed at 16:51. On-line: 21. >

A similar case is below, in which the intention of the activity "taking a nap" is announced in present tense, probably because it is a relatively firm intention (evidenced by Bonny's quick departure from the MUD).

Example (66):
Bonny takes a nap.

```
Bonny waves.
lynn waves.
Bonny has disconnected.
```

In the next case (which represents an activity or an accomplishment), note the similarity to the stylized use of the first person present tense in the formulaic spoken "And I quote," which indicates immediately upcoming quoted material. (The "|" indicates a quotation pasted from another source.)

Example (67):
```
Tom quotes the rest of the paragraph about Robin
   (whose name rings a bell, but he doesn't think
   he knew her):
Tom | Robin Weiland continues to work on her writing in
   Minneapolis.  In the midst of a financial scandal,
   half of the Paydirt staff was laid off, giving her
   time for writing and career planning.
```

The following is an extreme example, sent to me by a participant who found it odd herself. (Verb formation from nonverbal material is a fairly productive phenomenon in the register, illustrating the interplay between "speech" and "action" in the MUD. See chapter 3. "Actuallies" is an unusual formation, understandable as "Pete says, 'Actually...' ") This example is a future accomplishment.

```
(68)  Pete actuallies, calls NES once he gets contact info
      from johnf
```

The oddity of the utterance is that the event intended (the calling) is nowhere near about to happen. I suggest that it is in simple present tense to communicate Pete's strength of intention. He indicates that he really will do it, so it can almost be considered an accomplished fact. This example is unusual, however, since most cases of futurate present in the MUD register are about the very near future. Additionally, in almost all cases I have seen, they refer to events in the real world (or intentions to perform real events, rather than intentions to perform imaginary MUD-world events).

Sometimes other events appear to be allowed between the utterance and the event's occurrence, for instance the exchange of waves before Bonny leaves in Example 66. It may be that leavetaking is effectively a part of the departure (which is preceded by an announcement that departure is imminent), and hence the intervening wave events can be considered just part of a larger event of leaving.

Any non-stative verb seems to be acceptable in the simple futurate.

Here is a case of the simple futurate ("goes shopping") contrasting with the ordinary future for a stative ("will be back").

(69) `Jim goes shopping, will be back later.`

Crucially, Jim does not say "`Jim goes shopping, is back later.`" I cannot find any clear cases of simple future statives in my logs, and sample examples sound strange to my informants.

(70) a. ? Jay is back in tinyfugue in a minute.
      b. ? Jim is in hot water tomorrow afternoon.

Dowty (1979) discusses the simple futurate as another meaning for the present tense in ordinary registers. Although planning or intention are a good indicator of when this is possible, they are not necessary.

(71) The sun sets tomorrow at 6:57 PM. (Dowty 1979, p. 156)

A better notion might be that the simple futurate is predetermined on the basis of past events (Goodman 1973; Leech 1971). The futurate progressive does not involve the same degree of certainty. Dowty gives these contrasts to establish the degree of certainty involved in the simple futurate.

(72) a. The Rosenbergs die tomorrow.
      b. The Rosenbergs are dying tomorrow.
      c. *The Rosenbergs die tomorrow, although the President may grant them a pardon.
      d. The Rosenbergs are dying tomorrow, although the President may grant them a pardon.
      e. The sun sets tomorrow at 6:57 PM.
      f. *The sun is setting tomorrow at 6:57 PM.

Goodman (1973) suggests something that initially appears different in MUD register: that the speaker can have no control over the planned event that is represented in the simple futurate. He presents these examples to support his argument (p. 78):

(73) a. Kurt has a date with Wanda June tomorrow.
      b. I have a date with Wanda June tomorrow.
      c. Kurt dates Wanda June tomorrow.
      d. ?* I date Wanda June tomorrow.

Use of the simple futurate in the MUD register clearly requires speaker intention, since simple present tense utterances are from a speaker's perspective about a speaker's actions. But, in fact, if Goodman's last case in Example 73d is changed to "I go out with Wanda June tomorrow," I believe it is fine. (See also Example 28, "I start at Oracle on Monday," and similarly sentences like "I leave on Tuesday.")

However, despite the disappearance of this difference, there is still something unusual in MUD-register future. Where MUD simple futures occur, they would be peculiar in normal speech. An announcement of intention to leave that appears in the MUD as "lynn goes now" (or "lynn disconnects now"), if reported face-to-face, would be more appropriately put in the progressive: "I am going now."

There are in fact examples of the futurate progressive in the MUD register. (Example 74b represents an irrealis MUD-world case; anne is not referring to a real situation.)

(74) a. Daffi is going home tomorrow!
      b. anne is going to fiji with damon, yeah.

With regard to the lack of irrealis MUD-world simple futurates, a possibility to consider is that there is no future in the irrealis MUD world—that there is only a present and a past. However, there do appear to be non-present-tense references to future events in irrealis MUD mode, as shown in line 2. (Type 5 emotes are in other tenses.)

Example (75):
1 Skot gets Sarcasm Points! Whee!
2 Skot will be Sarcasm_Point_King!

(Skot is not referring to any real status or position; he is making a spontaneous joke.)

One possible explanation for the behavior of the simple futurate in the MUD is that some of the progressive meaning has been transferred to the simple present tense. They remain distinct, however. The fact that the progressive does get used for some future events, and the fact that the simple futurate is ordinarily reserved for events that are just about to occur, seems to represent real differences between the two. Additionally, the fact that progressive futures allow irrealis event reference, but simple futurates don't appear to, suggests that they differ semantically.

5.4.5 Irrealis and Real Worlds

Although I do not intend to give a complete formal semantic analysis of tense and aspect in the MUD register here (see Cherny 1995d), I am going to invoke a little formalism to discuss the irrealis and real worlds I've been assuming above. Still, the intuitions here are more important than the formalism.

I borrow a modal version of Discourse Representation Theory (DRT) from Farkas 1993 (and Roberts 1989). In DRT, the truth of a discourse representation structure (DRS) for a discourse is determined by the embeddability of a DRS in a model. Farkas relativizes the model to worlds: "A stretch of discourse S is true in a world W if the DRS associated to

S is embeddable into W" (Farkas 1993, p. 12). The model M is defined as $M = \langle W, w_r, U, V, R \rangle$, where W is a set of worlds with a distinguished real world w_r, U is a function from worlds to the entities in those worlds (including events, in our analysis), V is a valuation function from $\langle w, C \rangle$ to $U(w)$ where C is a constant, and R is a set of accessibility relations among worlds. Individuals may exist in multiple worlds (Kripke 1971).[5]

A simple DRS is embeddable in the real world w_r iff (if and only if) it is possible to find for each discourse referent in the DRS an individual in w_r who satisfies the conditions in the DRS. Farkas (1993, p. 13) gives a simple modal case that generalizes this notion:

(76)   A man may be here.

Example (77):

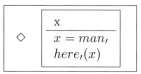

The outer DRS in Example 77 is embeddable into w_r iff there is a world w accessible to w_r such that the subordinate DRS box is embeddable into it. Take an accessibility relation R'. W' is the set of worlds R'-accessible to w_r. The main DRS is embeddable into w_r iff the subordinate box is embeddable into some subset of W' (as opposed to *all* worlds in W', as would be required if the ◇ had been □). Farkas calls the world or worlds that a box must be embedded in the *modal anchor*. The modal anchor of a matrix DRS is always w_r.

In Example 78, the modal anchor for the second sentence is the world of the dream (W_d) from the first sentence (Farkas 1993, p. 16):

Example (78):

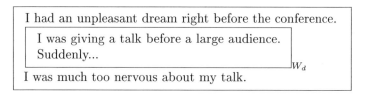

Modal anchors are notated as subscripts on embedded DRSes. Available modal anchors are introduced by the discourse, either by lexical items or by preceding modal context.

---

[5]Another option, if it seems philosophically wrong to treat MUD characters as identical to the users, is to define counterpart relations linking individuals in one world with those in other worlds (Lewis 1968).

We may borrow this notion of modal anchors for MUD discourse. An utterance is embedded either in a W_{mud} world or in the real world. Since Type 4 narration emotes, which refer to the real world, are much less common than the other types, which refer to the irrealis MUD context, we shall by default assume that events are embedded in the irrealis MUD world. Only if there is evidence that an event occurs in the real world is it not embedded in the MUD world. Utterances in the MUD world are trivially true: a statement that "Tom laughs" in the MUD introduces worlds in which it is true that Tom laughs, all of which are accessible to the real world, so the utterance is true.

Here is a sample embedded DRS for the MUD world (with the outer box representing the real world).

Example (79):

```
┌─────────────────────────────────────────┐
│  ┌───────────────────────────────────┐  │
│  │ Ava walks in from the sunroom.    │  │
│  │ Ava waves.                        │  │
│  │ Colm says, "aVa!"                 │  │
│  │ Ava is here.                      │  │
│  └───────────────────────────────────┘  │
│                                  W_mud   │
└─────────────────────────────────────────┘
```

Farkas states that if the real world is returned to after a modally subordinate stretch of discourse, an explicit indication of a change in modal anchoring is needed to return to a modal interpretation again (see also Polanyi 1996). This does not seem to be how the MUD register works; the real world is inferred at some points, but to return to the MUD world no explicit switch is needed. No explicit trigger is required for the real world to be inferred, either. In Example 59 (repeated here as Example 80), we infer that Brett spewed cherry coke in the real world when he laughed. Before we see line 8, we aren't sure the laughter is a real-world event. We must re-interpret the laughter to allow it to be a real-world event when we see line 8.

Example (80):
1 Tom says, "and have the say command always just
  print 'A cockroach click-clicks.'"
2 Bonny giggles.
3 Egypt [to lynn]: I was doing Rikki Tikki Tavi and
  Watership Down...
4 Phred thinks another FurryMUCK based in MOO would be
  neato.
5 Brett LAUGHS
6 Bonny says, "DISNEYMOO"

```
7 Brett says, "shit"
8 Brett spews cherry coke
```

Often it does not seem right to say that affect responses like the laughter above are confined either to the MUD world or to the real world. They may be true in both worlds: as instantaneous responses to conversation in the MUD, and yet also as documentation of real laughter. I propose that some events are interpreted relative to both worlds. The DRS below shows the updated interpretation of Brett's laughter in both worlds, with W_r representing the real world (as the external box does).

Example (81):

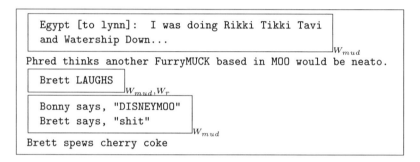

In order to interpret the utterance "Brett LAUGHS," we look for an individual in the MUD world who is identified with Brett and who laughs in the MUD world, and also for an individual in the real world who is also identified with Brett and who laughs in the real world.

We might ask whether it does any harm to initially interpret all utterances as occurring in both worlds. Is "Brett spews cherry coke" plausibly a MUD-world event as well as a real-world event? Since he reports it in MUD conversation, he presumably intends it to be relevant, and he uses the simple present tense. I don't have a good answer to this question, but my suspicion is that yes, he intends it to be a MUD event in some way. I feel fairly certain that Brett's spewing cherry coke is not intended to be a new topic per se, but is intended to communicate some information about his affect response that even the capitalized "LAUGHS" did not convey.[6] Another question we might ask is whether the MUD world, rather than the real world, should be the default anchor for the external DRS, since in a MUD the MUD world is primary. For

---

[6]This may be related to the practice of the informant mentioned earlier who uses activities in the present tense, rather than the progressive, to introduce a new topic.

now, at least, I prefer to be conservative and maintain the real world as anchor. Although people seem to be good at identifying whether an event has a real-world referent or not (or at least good at living with occasional ambiguity), I do not mean to imply that they are never concerned about frame reference; it's not uncommon for people to be confused about whether events are happening in real life ("irl") or online. The activity of talking may occur in a real-life frame, or in a MUD somewhere (multi-MUDding is common, so that users can be talking to someone on another MUD while they are in ElseMOO reporting the event).

Example (82):
```
Kelly talks for awhile with soime guy who talks
   baout sex with no introduction. Or rather,
   safe sex.
Ava peers at Kelly suspiciously.
lynn eyes Kelly askance.
Kelly [to Ava]: At MIT. I don't even know his name.
lynn [to Kelly]: irl?
```

Example (83):
```
Tom actually should probably just leave her out
   of the "people" section; she doesn't seem to
   mud anymore since the breakup.
lynn says, "breakup?"
Tom says, "with Willem"
lynn says, "oh."
Karen tries to remember waht the relationship was
Tom [to Karen]: capital r
Tom eyes himself warily.
Karen says, "irl?"
Tom nods.
```

Most requests for clarification about whether something happened in real life or on a MUD ("in vr") usually happen in the context of discussion about conversations or relationships, either of which could be occurring online or in real life. The semantics I have sketched out for irrealis events versus reports of real-life events does not distinguish between real events online and offline.[7]

MUD discourse is clearly very complex, as a result of the reflection of the real world in the irrealis context. Affect responses from real life

---

[7] Furthermore, I think it's difficult and problematic to make an a priori distinction between irrealis and realis events in a MUD-world context.

are often appropriated as MUD actions: the acronym "LOL" means "laughs out loud" and is regularly used by the community (e.g., "Brett LOL"). For at least one speaker, "LOL" does not require that he be really laughing out loud at his keyboard. It has become a purely MUD-world response, although it implies real-world behavior; he presumably uses that implication to communicate affect as a means of animating his textual persona.[8] As Goffman (1974) points out (and Danet, Ruedenberg, and Rosenbaum-Tamari 1998 and Ruedenberg, Danet, and Rosenbaum-Tamari 1995 describe for IRC), in fanciful activities like games, the frame of the play activity contains by necessity some reference anchoring it to the real world.

> The understanding that players and nonplayers have of where the claims of the ongoing world leave off and where the claims of play take over is part of what the players bring to their playing from the outside world, and yet is a necessary constituent of play. The very points at which the internal activity leaves off and the external activity takes over—the rim of the frame itself—become generalized by the individual and taken into his frame of interpretation, thus becoming, recursively, an additional part of the frame. In general, then, the assumptions that cut an activity off from the external surround also mark the ways in which this activity is inevitably bound to the surrounding world. (Goffman 1974, p. 249)

Just so are the worlds created by the MOO conversation a part of the real world, and vice versa, facts which the members of the community fully appreciate and plan for in their conversation.

5.4.6 Remaining Implications and Issues

In the examples above, I assume that the timeline increments with each utterance, in a particular world (this is an approximation; for more formal analysis, see Cherny 1995d). I predict that if an embedded DRS represents a sequence of events, the external DRS will not be affected by them (cf. Roberts 1989; Farkas 1993), since embedded entities are not accessible in the main DRS. In DRS Example 81, we see that, correctly, the timing of the spewing-cherry-coke event, in the real world, is not affected by the embedded spoken utterances in the irrealis MUD world DRS; we can maintain the sense that the "Shit" occurs after the spewing event, since they are not in the same DRS (if they were, the event time of the spewing would have to be after the "Shit"). There are two timelines

---

[8]This is considered odd by some MUDders who know how he uses it, though.

in effect, more or less.[9] But is this prediction right for all cases? What if an embedded MUD world DRS contained both emoted and "said" events? If the "said" events move the timeline along, emoted events can become out of synch with the imagined world, by appearing to occur too late. Example 13, repeated below as Example 84, illustrates this.

Example (84):

```
1  The Canadian guest lights smoke:
2  Tom eyes the Canadian guest warily.
3  lynn backs away from smoking.
4  Karen too!
5  Karen is allergic
6  The Canadian guest removes whisky bottle
   from pocket and takes a long hit:
7  The Canadian guest throws smoke out window
   and returns bottle to pocket:
8  Robin says, "hey how was the brunch thingy?"
9  Tom [to Robin]: ask bean
10 The Canadian guest runs hands threw greay hair:
11 Robin [to Tom]: okay.
12 Karen whispers to lynn, "what a dea guest"
13 Robin [to lynn]: fil is pretty normal...
14 Karen whispers to lynn, "what a dear
   guest, that is"
15 The Canadian guest removes biker jacket:
16 Tom [to the Canadian guest]: out of
   curiosity, why are you using : to end
   sentences?
17 Karen too Tom!
18 Karen was just typing it
19 lynn grins.
20 The Canadian guest drops jacket on floor
21 Robin hehs.
22 Tom says, "what floor?"
23 Karen [to Canadian guest]: did you notice
   we're in a ditch?
24 The Canadian guest bottle in jacket breaks
25 Karen says, "there's no floor or window"
26 Tom eyes the Canadian guest warily.
27 lynn eyes the Canadian guest warily.
```

---

[9]At least two; a new timeline may be created every time an embedded DRS is created.

```
28 Robin peers at the Canadian guest
   suspiciously.
29 The Canadian guest says, "when you drink
   and smoke as much as me, you loose track
   of things""
30 Tom feels like he's witnessing a really
   clumsy strip tease.
```

In line 20, the bottle is dropped when the guest's jacket drops. Various responses to this occur, and then in line 24 we see what should be the immediate effect of the dropping: the breakage. But intuitively our timeline has moved on. In fact, this discourse is deviant, according to the ElseMOO users. As I discussed earlier, it is unusual for a character to perform such extended role play without it being a group participation event. The Canadian guest may be said to occupy a non-propositional floor, as discussed in chapter 4; he does not acknowledge the others' contributions until line 29. The theory may help predict the deviance we see here.

The problem is probably a more general one, however. Kolko (1995) discusses similar problems, cases in which MUD users fail to mesh their storytelling because of the lag between the time an utterance is typed and the time it appears on the screens of other users. For instance, in play sequences, two players may contradict one another without intending to, each being unaware of what the other is typing.

Creating and narrating at cross-purposes is an all-too-often occurrence. One participant may narrate, 'John goes over and sits directly in the middle of the couch, his feet propped up on the coffee table,' and another simultaneously write, 'Katie stretches out on the couch, thoughtlessly taking up all the space, but too darn comfortable to care.' If both John and Katie have agreed to create belief together through their MOOtalk, one might say 'oops,' or another might say 'ouch.' But the reality of their virtual bodies colliding will be evident to all in the room, and it is highly likely that one of them will narrate a movement of his or her virtual body. (Kolko 1995, p. 114)

The urge to "fix" such mistakes is felt strongly. We might think of this in terms of two worlds being created, which deviate, and the speakers attempting to re-integrate them as quickly as possible.

In an alternative formulation for the semantics that takes into account multiple viewpoints on events, as well as multiple actors contributing and overwriting each other occasionally, we might treat the embedded DRSes as related to the notion of conversational floor.[10] A floor is an embedded DRS in which all participants are on the same topic, attempting to collaboratively describe events. The Canadian guest occupies a floor of his own, since he is not collaborating.

The notion of floor must be technically broadened to allow divergent floors to be created when cross-narration occurs with contradictory event sequences, however. There are other formal difficulties, as well: in Example 84, when does it become clear that the guest occupies his own floor? Perhaps when he doesn't answer Tom's query in line 16, but how long does one wait before deeming a question unanswered? Does his comment in line 29 constitute a revision of the floor, and if so, how far back? Does the floor suddenly get expanded backward to include Karen's query in line 23, which is plausibly what he responds to?

It seems likely that every participant models the floor structure for herself, dynamically changing the representations as she parses new information. The mechanics of handling this question properly are beyond the scope of this book.

5.5 Conclusion

In this chapter, I discussed the use of simple present tense in the MUD register, with which users not only simulate communicative "gestures," but also narrate their real-life actions while they are MUDding (e.g., "Marie packs for her trip"), in a manner reminiscent of that found in sports commentary register (Ferguson 1983). Linguists often dismiss non-habitual uses of the simple present tense as a random collection of odd data. The similarity of the MUD register to other uses of simple present tense that variously attempt to create spontaneous events or narrate actions occurring near the discourse location suggests that users in the MUD may be calling upon linguistic knowledge they do not realize they have about the present tense.

Actions within the MUD are always reported in the third person simple present tense, suggesting a similarity with speech acts like first person performatives (Searle 1969, 1989), which become true as they are uttered. However, actions that narrate real-life events, or meta-discourse behaviors, are not standard performatives. Actions that are part of byplay during conversation, back channels, or greeting rituals in the MUD may have no real-world referent, and they are interpreted as punctual, started and completed at the time of utterance. Actions that describe events happening outside the MUD show complexity, however; for instance, they may report either future intention to

---

[10]Thanks to Livia Polanyi for suggesting this modification.

do something ("Tom `really disconnects this time`") or actions already taken ("`Marie sends mail to the dispute list`"). I suggest that the aspectual class of the verb partly determines which interpretation is valid, along with reference to a world, either the irrealis MUD world or the real world. Activities are generally interpreted as ongoing events in the real world, but as punctual in the MUD world; and achievements and accomplishments are assumed to have just occurred in both worlds unless a simple futurate is invoked.

6

MUD Community

The popular press and media have frothed with enthusiasm about "virtual communities." "One revolutionary concept already obscured by bad software and outrageous hype is the notion of building 'community' on the Web," said the *New York Times* online in July 1997 (Tacy 1997). Esther Dyson's newsletter *Release 1.0* expresses skepticism about the overuse of "the C word" (Dyson 1997, p. 53), and notes that "everyone in the market is using [it]" and "they're using it in completely different ways."

In this chapter I will review some definitions of "the C word" proposed by sociologists and anthropologists. In chapter 1 I described some approaches to community that focus on discourse. A speech community, for instance, may be characterized as a community sharing rules of speaking and interpretations of speech performance (Hymes 1972) whose members frequently interact (Gumperz and Hymes 1964). The members must see language as playing a significant role in marking the community's boundary (Saville-Troike 1982, p. 20). Language helps to unify the members and exclude outsiders. Related to the notion of a speech community are discourse communities (Swales 1990; Gurak 1997) and communities of practice (Lave and Wenger 1991).

I've already described specific features of language use that define the speech community on ElseMOO, that reflect its history and relationship to other MUD communities, and that reflect internal relationships, power structures, and norms. In this chapter, I will discuss the community's history and characteristics in more detail, focusing on incidents that illustrate how other definitions of community may also be applicable.

6.1   Overview of Community Studies

The word "community" is used in a number of ways in the popular press, drawing on and contributing to folk understandings of the word.

It's used to refer to geographically bounded social groups—from local neighborhoods to nations—as well as to describe communities of shared values or interests. Some of its uses, particularly in advertisements, seem to be little more than attempts to conjure fellow-feeling. Journalists writing about online communities and business opportunities online are particularly likely to invoke the word, making it difficult to sort out the hype from the facts. Wellman et al. (1996) note that public discourse about the Internet tends to describe it as if it had been invented yesterday, as being either thoroughly good or evil, as if life online had no connection to life offline, and as if the past century's research on the nature of community were irrelevant.

There has been an astounding lack of consensus in the social science literature about just what is meant by the word "community." Stacey (1974, p. 13) concludes, "It is doubtful whether the concept 'community' refers to a useful abstraction." She suggests that institutions and local social systems are the objects worthy of study, preferring to avoid the term itself while still focusing on units of study that are frequently called evidence of "community."

Still, some particulars in definitions of community are often repeated. Hillery (1955, p. 118) compared 94 definitions from the literature and found that "69 are in accord that social interaction, area, and a common tie or ties are commonly found in community life." If area is omitted from consideration, 73 of the 94 agree that a community "is considered a group of people in social interaction having some ties or bonds in common. Finally, all but three of the definitions stress social interaction as a necessary element of community life." A more recent researcher, Smith (1992), offers a broad definition based on social interaction: "a set of ongoing social relations bound together by a common interest or shared circumstance."

If social interaction is a requirement for the existence of community, then the less interactive aspects of Internet use, for instance Web browsing and Web site building, probably don't support community on their own (unless "social interaction" is defined extremely loosely). Interest-based groups online who interact regularly in newsgroups, mailing lists, or chat conform to the requirements for social interaction and common ties, if not for shared geographical area.

Smith (1992) points out that communities may be intentional or unintentional; community participants may join together purposefully or be joined by circumstance. Intentional communities are more interesting because the motives of participants are more relevant than the external forces (political, economic, or social) that influence unintentional communities. Unintentional communities generally have externally enforced boundaries, allowing membership to be active or passive. Geographically-centered definitions of community generally describe unintentional communities (if we factor out the intentionality behind choice of geography; see Bellah et al. 1985 on "lifestyle enclaves"). Interest-based groups are generally intentional communities. Smith also notes that although the word "community" is often taken to denote cooperative, positive functions, in fact communities may be marked by conflict and divisiveness. The narratives I present in this chapter illustrate conflicts within the ElseMOO community, generally resulting in changes for the good of the community as a whole.

I group community research approaches into five categories: tradition and practice definitions, social network studies, cooperative action and collective goods definitions, boundary theories, and study of utopian representations. I will not dwell on specifically geographically-based definitions, although several of the definitions below (especially the collective goods ones) were inspired by study of geographical groups. My classification is somewhat ad hoc, and several of the definitions properly belong in multiple categories.

Tradition and Practice

The first set of definitions of community can be broadly characterized by a focus on the culture, tradition, or practices shared by a group of people. Of course, many definitions that I have categorized elsewhere also acknowledge tradition, culture, and practices in some form, but I group the following ones here because they seem to focus on these aspects of community most strongly.

Csikszentimihalyi and Rochberg-Halton (1981), in a study of domestic objects as symbols, cite Arendt's (1958) definition of community: the sum of the people, transactions, habitats, traditions, and institutions that form a vital aspect of everyday life. They expand this as the ensemble of relationships, experiences, values, and norms that serve to orient our actions and ultimate goals. Community, for them, is normative and purposive, suggesting norms of behavior for members and goals for the group as a whole. The purposive component to their definition aligns them with the collective action definitions, as well as with the discourse community definitions I discuss in chapter 1 and again below.

Bellah et al. (1985) suggest that tradition and commitment are features of community, especially of "communities of memory." A community of memory remembers its past and retells its "constitutive narrative," which features exemplary individuals and origin stories. Members are "socially interdependent" and participate in decision making. Bellah et al. describe communities as having practices that "both define the community and nurture it" (p. 333).

The "community of memory" concept resonates with that of "community of practice" (Lave and Wenger 1991, p. 98), in which knowledge resides and which provides "the interpretive support necessary for making sense of its heritage." Another closely related definition of community is in Bilson's performance-centered definition: "situations in which the participants (1) share a focused common interest, (2) get to know each other through attending multiple performances, and (3) have the option to participate more fully in the performance over time" (Bilson 1995, p. 18). One component of Lave and Wenger's "community of practice" is learning, particularly learning through participation. Lave and Wenger's "legitimate peripheral participation" is an important process through which community participants learn practices through peripheral participation and increase their involvement gradually; this concept might correspond to Bilson's third criterion.

I reviewed some concepts of community grounded in communication in chapter 1. The "discourse community" as defined by Swales (1990) was characterized as having (1) a broadly agreed-upon set of common public goals, (2) mechanisms for communication among the community members, (3) participatory mechanisms used primarily for information and feedback, (4) one or more genres, (5) a specific vocabulary of communication, and (6) a threshold level of members with a suitable degree of relevant content and discourse experience (pp. 24–27). Swales (1990) and Gurak (1997) have fairly specific and constrained notions of discourse community; a less constrained but related notion is Anderson's (1991) "imagined community." Anderson credits media and cultural media artifacts like newspapers and novels with spreading a sense of shared culture and community among consumers who will never meet, but who share cultural communion through these documents. Brown and Duguid (1995) expand further on "the social life of documents," illuminating how communities negotiate the meaning of documents. Community members share general strategies of interpretation for documents, although they may not share the same interpretations of meaning. Recall that one definition of "speech community" is a group that shares rules for speaking and interpretations of speech performance (Hymes 1972), which might be further refined as shared strategies for interpretations.

Social Network Studies

A significant part of modern work on community focuses on social network analysis (see, e.g., Scott 1991). Sociologist Barry Wellman has contributed a number of articles on network analysis of community in both geographical areas and cyberspace (Wellman et al. 1996; Wellman and Berkowitz 1988; Wellman and Gulia 1998; Wellman 1988a, 1988b).

He concludes, like other urban sociologists, that Western postindustrial people are not involved in the densely knit, tightly bounded networks that characterize the traditional notion of (rural) community; now most middle-class people participate in sparsely knit, loosely bounded, frequently changing networks. Membership in networks is increasingly limited, specialized, and interest-based. Such networks may not offer much generalized reciprocity, the informal mechanism by which members expect payment for favors done or infractions against them, even if not of the same type. Generalized reciprocity is based on trust and an expectation of long-term relationships offering many opportunities for redress or return favors among the network members (see, e.g., Smith 1992 and Coleman's 1990 discussion of the related notion of social capital). In a sparse network with little expectation of generalized reciprocity, collective action is hard to initiate. Under definitions of community that require a group to be able to take collective action should the need arise, community may indeed have declined in the Western urban world.

Social capital is embodied in the relations among persons in networks; it diminishes if it is not exercised and increases as it is called upon. Networks with a lot of social capital are networks with a lot of outstanding social obligations that haven't been "paid off" yet (Coleman 1990). There is a lot of trust among members in such networks, trust that the obligations will be met eventually. Information is an important form of social capital in networks: knowledge is a resource that can benefit both the individual and the network. Gossip is a mechanism of information exchange with associated value judgments about behavior, which also functions as a form of social control or as a norm enforcer (Merry 1984, Coleman 1990). Elias (1974) suggests that gossip is a criterion for community, and that the researcher can examine the extent to which people are involved in the gossip circuit and the extent to which they are susceptible to pressure for conformity from gossip. "A locality ceases to have the character of a community if the interdependence of the people who live there is so slight, if their relative independence is so great that they are no longer involved in the local gossip flow and remain indifferent to any gossip control or, for that matter, to any other form of communal control" (Elias 1974, p. xxviii). In my discussion at the end of this chapter, I will discuss how gossip exchange relationships illuminate ElseMOO social networks.

If social relationships between people constitute links in a network, then computer-mediated relationships constitute social networks as well. Like offline networks, online communities are increasingly specialized, with members participating in multiple communities or networks (Wellman et al. 1996) that only satisfy some dimensions of social support (e.g., emotional but not financial needs; see Wellman 1994). The network ties between people online may be strong or weak, and relationships may be broadly based or specialized depending on the forum and on the length of time the members have participated in it. As with the ElseMOO and LambdaMOO communities, interaction between members may occur both online and offline.

Milroy's (1987) seminal linguistic work studied the interaction between social networks and linguistic variation, showing that the greater the social network strength, the greater the incidence of vernacular forms in Belfast communities. "Vernacular norms" are norms perceived as symbolizing values of solidarity and reciprocity rather than status, norms not publicly codified or recognized (Milroy 1980). Such norms were found in working-class social networks, which are generally denser and more multiplex than middle-class networks. A close-knit network functions as a norm enforcer.

Cooperative Action and the Collective Good

For Smith (1992), as for Swales (1990) and Gurak (1997), cooperative action is a defining feature of community. In particular, community members must be committed to participating in the maintenance of the common good and to monitoring their own behavior and punishing wrongs committed by members against the group.

In a follow-up to Hillery's (1955) survey, Jonassen (1959) suggests that definitions of community often agree in requiring certain elements: population, a territorial base, the interdependency of specialized parts and a division of labor, a common culture and social system that integrate activity, a consciousness of unity or belonging among the inhabitants, and an ability to act in a corporate fashion to solve problems. He himself defines a community as "a group integrated through a system of spatially contingent, interdependent [biological], cultural, and social relations and structures which have evolved in the process of usual adjustment to environmental situations. It is a spatial group wherein the effects of interdependence and integration are made evident by the community's consciousness of unity and its ability to exercise adequate control over social, cultural, and [biological] processes within its boundaries" (pp. 20–21). The focus on community control and adjustment to environmental situations makes this definition a cooperative action/collective goods definition of community.

Kollock and Smith (1996) apply an economist's observations on face-to-face community workings to Usenet. They examine Ostrom's (1990) study of communities working with "the commons," the public resources available to all in a specific community. The dilemma posed by the commons (often known as "the tragedy of the commons") is the dilemma of individual benefit versus group benefit: the collective good will be at risk if individuals try to "free-ride" on the efforts of others. Protecting the common good is a function of a working community. Kollock and Smith list characteristics of face-to-face communities that function effectively (p. 117):

- Group boundaries are clearly defined.
- Rules governing the use of collective goods are well matched to local needs and conditions.
- Most individuals affected by these rules can participate in modifying the rules.
- The right of community members to devise their own rules is respected by external authorities.
- A system for monitoring members' behavior exists; this monitoring is undertaken by the community members themselves.
- A graduated system of sanctions is used.
- Community members have access to low-cost conflict resolution mechanisms.

The public "goods" or resources in an online situation are communicative resources like bandwidth, rather than physical resources such as Ostrom discussed.[1]

In a work loosely related to the more theoretical work on community resources, Hagel and Armstrong (1997) speculate about commercial opportunities on the Internet. They claim to "focus on basic principles of successful community development that will help unleash the creativity and innovation required to explore and to exploit the enormous potential embedded in the virtual community concept" (p. xi). Since their focus is business, it is not surprising that they want to create new forms of online community with a strong commercial element, which they believe will "enhance and expand the basic requirements of community." In their analysis, these requirements are trust and commitment, and

---

[1]See also Douglas and Isherwood 1996. The authors, an anthropologist and an economist, study consumption rituals and the role of goods as individual and community markers of identity. Communities that involve members in many social commitments have more consumption rituals (like holidays and birthdays, at which gifts are given). Consumption rituals are reciprocal and mark special occasions within communities. The value of objects is symbolic (see my discussion of utopian definitions, below) and is conferred within the cultural context. A theory of consumption requires a theory of culture and community, or at least an understanding of group social life. Douglas and Isherwood's work is a valuable resource for online commerce efforts focused on community building.

the desire for virtual communities grows from the need to meet these requirements. Virtual communities therefore arise, providing opportunities for interest-based groups, personal relationships, fantasy play (e.g., games and online role-playing), and transactional relationships (in which information is initially traded, followed by goods) (chapter 2).

They offer five defining elements of a business model of virtual community:

- a distinctive focus for communities
- the capacity to integrate content and communication, where by "content" they mean published content (generated by, e.g., the hosting vendor, rather than by members)
- an appreciation of member-generated content (they acknowledge that this is probably the single most "empowering" element of a virtual community)
- access to competing publishers and vendors (because members want access to the best products and prices for their needs)
- a commercial orientation

In one of their more daring rhetorical moves, they go from capitalizing on the popular use (and folk understanding) of the term "virtual community" to redefining it to match their own criteria above. They note that the word is used everywhere and that even a Web site can be called a virtual community; but "if we apply the five defining characteristics of virtual community outlined earlier, this abundance of so-called communities dissolves. In fact, we cannot yet point to a single example of a virtual community that robustly incorporates all 5 of the defining characteristics" (p. 37). They acknowledge that many early examples of so-called online communities are anti-commercial.

Boundaries

Although also classifiable within the traditions and practices category described above, Cohen's (1985) anthropological work specifically considers boundaries significant to a symbolic definition of community. Boundaries indicate who is inside and who is outside a community; they distinguish the members from those they differ from or wish to be seen as different from. These boundaries are usually in the minds of the members and those excluded from the group, and perceptions of the boundaries may differ among individuals, even those on the same side of a boundary. Boundaries are often symbolic, dependent on abstractions like friendship, rivalry, jealousy, similarity. As such they are often not clearly defined, contrary to Ostrom's first principle cited in Kollock and Smith 1996. This does not lessen their importance, however. "Community" is also a symbolic concept, and people invoke it and respond to it as they learn to be social and to interpret the symbols that compose their culture. This interest in the symbolic nature of community is also a characteristic of several of the study methods described in the next section, on utopian and symbolic definitions.

Suttles (1972) argues that communities are units that come into being through their recognition by a wider society, and community is a form of social differentiation within society. Local communities defend their status—and implicitly, their boundaries—by the ways they make their necessities into virtues, by their choice and articulation of perceived threats, by their opposition to competing residential areas, and by articulation of their historic grounds for claiming special status among residential areas. One might study the conflict between the larger society (the state, usually) and the local community as the local community attempts to defend its identity (both symbolically and politically, in terms of power it retains over self-government). This conflict is often articulated through boundary defenses like those listed above.

Utopian and Symbolic Definitions

In both the academic literature and more popular media reports, the word "community" is often invoked in a symbolic way, with a utopian subtext. Suttles (1972) notes the recurrent mingling of utopianism with other more descriptive aspects of community study. He describes the community of sentiment, in which "the utopian images evoked tend to make insignificant any actual communities that have existed. The community, then, is defended according to what it might become rather than for what it is or has been. Such utopias are a powerful lure tempting us to reconstruct history and dismiss the present" (p. 267).

Rather than dismiss such uses of the word as unscientific or vague, it's valuable to examine why the word is so overloaded with meaning. Some of the confusion surrounding the concept of community probably stems from the earliest work by Tönnies (1887). In *Community and Society*, Tönnies introduced the contrast between *gemeinschaft* (community) and *gesellschaft* (society). Tönnies incorporates idealism and utopian sentiment into his notion of community, as well as reliance on geographic locale, all of which have persisted within the community studies literature, arguably causing confusion between the study of community as it *is* (empirical description) and as it *should be* (normative prescription) (Bell and Newby 1974).

Working from an understanding of this dichotomy, Hummon (1990) offers some modern methods for examining and interpreting rhetoric about community. Among other focuses, he suggests we might study

- members' satisfaction with and attachment to the community
- community as text
- community imagery
- community ideology

Community satisfaction can be assessed from people's perceptions and judgments (invariably influenced by their expectations, values, and personalities) about the communities they live in. The older literature of urban sociology often attempted to document the "decline of community," or the loss of attachment to place. Louis Wirth's classic 1938 article "Urbanism as a Way of Life" typifies this attempt. His basic argument is that the scale and complexity of urban life weaken the primary ties and local sentiments of the urbanite, creating a person more blasé, cosmopolitan, rational, and disengaged. This literature's arguments have been attacked by both theorists and empiricists in the last two decades: attachment to place is still strong, and social ties to place are variable, depending on the characteristics of the place and on a person's stage of life. People may evaluate places in unfavorable terms but still have sentimental attachment to them. People in smaller places are slightly more likely to feel a sense of belonging but not more likely to say they are unwilling to move. Long-term residence increases attachment because people are more likely to have social ties in an area they have lived in for a while (Hummon 1990).

Another approach Hummon describes is the study of community as text: seeing icons, symbols, and slogans as extrinsic sources of meaning that influence how people conceive of and interpret their community. Residents "read" the landscape, for instance, when they read local journalists manipulating community imagery. Cities accumulate rich local lore in the shape of landmarks, slogans, bumper stickers, myths about founders. These usually advance the economic and political interests of a city, promoting tourism or consumption, for instance.

Related to this is the study of community imagery; responses to and invocations of the concept of community are often linked to systems of images (Meinig 1979). The image of the New England village, for example, is constituted of iconography: the Congregational church spire, white houses with metal roofs, and autumn leaves, suggesting intimacy, tradition, stability, prosperity, family life, and cohesion. Warner (1984) discusses antiurban slum imagery of the 19th and early 20th centuries: the image of the slum was part of a new way of conceiving of cities and poverty, created by middle-class residents who used it to secularize discussion of poverty into a reaction to a community form, rather than a discussion of religion or political economy.

"Ideology" refers to a way of thinking that is public and political (Geertz 1973). Hummon (1990, pp. 37–38), citing Keesing 1981, says, "Culture, through language, ideology, and other ideational systems, provides the symbolic resources [. . .] through which individuals and groups make sense of reality." Community ideology is the "system of belief that uses conceptions of community to describe, evaluate, and explain social reality, and that does so in such a manner [. . .] as to motivate commitment to community."

Community ideology allows people to define what places exist at all: for instance, suburbs don't even exist as a category, to some small-town enthusiasts. Ideology also helps people navigate the symbolic landscape, allowing them to contrast different imagery and choose between different stories about what communities "ought to be like." Beliefs about desired forms of community constitute the moral landscape of the ideology. Study of community accounts, like popular explanations of differences among communities, is one way of examining ideology. For example, folk explanations for why cities have more crime than rural towns illustrate ideological judgments. The ElseMOO narratives presented in the next section illustrate a number of examples of ideological conflicts within the community.

6.2   ElseMOO Narratives

Early definitions of community often require a shared geographical locale (Hillery 1955; Jonassen 1959). Clearly, ElseMOO users are not based within the same geographical area, and therefore definitions of community that rely on locale will not apply. However, it's interesting that there are several geographical concentrations of users, the largest being in Newark, and that some ElseMOO users have moved in real life to be near other ElseMOO users. There has always been a significant offline component to ElseMOO community (see also Wellman et al. 1996, which describes offline aspects of online relationships). With these geographical moves, the relationships between ElseMOO users have become more broadly based and less specialized. Real-life intimate relationships have also evolved out of online relationships (the ElseMOO population includes at least half a dozen couples who met in MUDs). Dismissing offline geography as irrelevant to online communities may be overly hasty. In fact, offline geography—and some users' physical proximity to each other—was a factor in some of the online tensions in ElseMOO that I describe below in my discussion of the Mouldy Couch Club.

Just as speech communities may be considered communities under sociological definitions as well, ElseMOO is similar to communities defined by criteria other than discourse. In the following sections, I will discuss some ways in which the ElseMOO community defined itself and was defined by others through symbolic and political means, including the use of metaphors and analogies to real-life organizations, ideological negotiation, community texts and labels, symbolic artifacts, and boundary disputes. I am not interested in testing ElseMOO against definitions in an attempt to determine whether it passes sociological tests for community, because definitions of community are so varied. Instead, I will apply aspects of different definitions and research traditions to ElseMOO while illustrating community crises and collective action.

6.2.1 Culture Shock

The social group loosely constituted by the power elite and their friends on LambdaMOO moved their public gatherings off LambdaMOO to ElseMOO after EM's founding. One regular on EM told me he got an EM character when all the people he talked to on LambdaMOO weren't in the Makeshift Cafe on LambdaMOO anymore. Not all the settlers on ElseMOO were programmers. For many of them (the group in late 1992–early 1993 probably numbered twenty at most), the move to ElseMOO was motivated by social connections rather than technical interests. Although Tom and Ray and the online information texts as of October 1993 ("help purpose" and the connection screen) defined the MOO as a place intended for programming projects, the social aspect of ElseMOO was most apparent and important to some early users, like Kurt and Ellen. Given this multiplicity of interests motivating use of the MOO, it's difficult to describe ElseMOO as a simplistically "purposive" community of interest. Existing social network links complicated the early attempts to define a purpose for the community, and also complicate the origin narratives told about the place now. The online texts and artifacts like the virtual geography (especially Ray's house and Tom's hometown) symbolically centralized power with a small group of the founders; attempts to control the distribution of programming bits further centralized power by restricting other users' ability to modify that very symbolic geography.

In 1993, more LambdaMOO people came to EM to stay, in what one LambdaMOO player called "urban flight syndrome." LambdaMOO was becoming crowded, suffering from more lag as system processes grew larger and more tasks were queued; the public areas were filling up with newbies and a class hierarchy based on age of character was settling into place. Older characters were fleeing LambdaMOO for lesser-known sites with fewer newbies.[2]

LambdaMOO was like a complex urban society with a formal political process, in contrast to the informally organized suburban Else-MOO. In 1993, LambdaMOO was in the throes of its attempt at effective democracy: the wizards had stepped aside and been replaced by the petition and ballot process. Anyone who wanted to could influence politics by drafting petitions or voting, and could influence the geography by building rooms or programming interactive objects. EM, on the other hand, was run "like a Random and Moira TinyMUD," i.e., "run by benevolent dictators," as Ray said. Tom and Ray and a few other EM founders remembered older MUDs before LambdaMOO, enabling them to make this comparison, but many of the people coming to EM from LambdaMOO had never experienced other MUDs and their expectations were based on LambdaMOO. Many of the things permitted on LambdaMOO were not permitted on EM, and culture shock was the inevitable result.

In describing the origins of the MOO, Tom and Ray spoke as representative founders, invoking imagery and ideology for the community.

```
Ray says, "EM was a big really long house party"
Tom says, "ray drew an analogy to a party on several
    occasions"
Tom says, "this doesn't mean it was one, it meant it
    shared characteristics"
Dorian [to Tom]: Characteristics such as?
Ray says, "mind you, we had disagreements on what this
    meant and whether it was valid"
Tom [to Dorian]: characteristics such as "if
    somebody's obnoxious, you make them leave".
Ray says, "people you know show up, hang out at your
    place"
```

The analogy to a private party of close friends, with the hosts empowered to throw disruptive elements out, contrasts with the way LambdaMOO

---

[2]EM was linked to LambdaMOO by a special network link that made it visible in the list of connected players shown by the "@who" command, as though "ElseMOO" were a player on LambdaMOO. The connected MOOs were fancifully thought of as orbiting MOOns by some. "ElseMOOn," visible on LambdaMOO via link and talked about in the LambdaMOO Living Room, drew LambdaMOO users.

evolved, with every wizardly action being questioned.[3] Note that they are careful to point out that not everyone agreed on the appropriateness of the house-party image. But clearly the ideologies of LambdaMOO and ElseMOO differed, even if there was debate on ElseMOO about ElseMOO's ideology.

The house-party analogy had a few other unfortunate connotations on EM. Since Ray's house featured prominently in the virtual geography, a clear artifact carrying some symbolic meaning for the group, visitors assumed, wrongly, that Ray was the primary dictator of EM social policies. This assumption appears in the Usenet post describing EM to the biology community in January 1993, which again uses the house analogy, generalized to the MOO as a whole:

The MOO we are using, [ElseMOO], belongs to [Ray]. We are guests in his "house" and we should act like guests. This means being very sensitive to any requests the primary users and developers of this MOO make of us.

One source of conflict on ElseMOO was ElseMOO's policy on building. The tightly realistic geographical theme was felt to be restrictive, and the fact that few people were allowed to do any building offended some newcomers. The restrictions on building were partly for security reasons; malicious programmers were not a problem the EM programmers and wizards wanted to be thinking about, so security wasn't a top priority in the coding they had already done. Nor did they want to have to police the programming of every new programmer on EM, so they were reluctant to give out programmer bits. Since on many social MUDs building is a big part of the fun, EM's policy was felt by many newcomers to be too restrictive.

The online "help programmer-policy" text says, "We understand that people from other MUDs are used to being able to create their own rooms, and might like to do so here as well. This kind of building is not consistent with the goals of EM." In fact, the geography shows that this policy has been applied inconsistently. Mike, a wizard, has his own house on E. Some Tree Street; Jeani, a friend of Mike's to whom he gave a programmer bit, has her own house; Ray has a room in the main

---

[3]Ironically, the house party analogy also appeared on LambdaMOO mailing lists before the wizards' abdication, although clearly this metaphor didn't ultimately work for LambdaMOO:

This is [the Archwizard]'s virtual "house" and we're all really just guests here, so he (or those he deputizes) has a perfect right to throw us out - this doesn't excuse them for bad manners, but there is no question of right/wrong here. (Message 331 on *life-issues)

house; Rick built himself a "dead room" as an alternative to the Living Room; and George has a sand-castle home. It wasn't clear to many people who saw themselves as regulars on EM why and how anyone got permission to build; they felt programmer bits were being handed out to pals of some wizards through acts of favoritism. In an interview, Kurt, one of EM's earliest users, told me he tried to get a bit for months, but his mail was ignored or overlooked. "The MOO had wizards coming out the wazoo, and it seemed like the only qualification for being a wizard was to be a chum of another wizard," Kurt told me. "Meanwhile, you couldn't get a programmer's bit without a handwritten note from God." Even when Kurt finally got a bit, he felt as if he were "eyed warily" for getting one by a couple of wizards (i.e., he felt they thought he shouldn't have one). Programming bits were a resource jealously guarded by the wizards responsible for distributing them, because it was felt that free distribution of bits would result in a poorly built landscape, threatening the collective good: a usable, attractive geographical design.

Ellen told me she also felt alienated at the time. She had been invited to "Ray's MOO" by Mike, a friend on LambdaMOO. "And I was never given the impression, in the very beginning, that I, as a non-programmer, was not welcome." But the sense of being unwelcome did grow. "Since I wasn't a programmer, I supposedly had nothing to contribute to EM." She had been an early recipient of a programmer's bit herself, because of her status as one of the first characters on the MOO, but she was not a programmer by education. "I know it made some people upset that they were, for example, fairly accomplished programmers at LambdaMOO, but couldn't get an EM prog bit, whereas there I was, an admitted non-programmer, with one." She intended to learn to program, as many people on MOOs do, but she remembers wizards saying (as was often said to newbies on EM), "EM isn't a learning MOO; go to LambdaMOO if you want to learn to program." As was common, ElseMOO was being defined in contrast to LambdaMOO.

ElseMOO was changing, policies and ideology were being determined by a subset of the population, and some others felt excluded from the ill-defined process. Kurt and Ellen both felt that EM had started as a social place, and only later became a hacking place. Initially, Kurt said, "it was so... social. Little technobabble, little politics. Mostly a bunch of people who didn't want to be on LambdaMOO either because of lag or idiot to clueful person ratio. If you were clueful enough to carry on a conversation and do so intelligently, you'd be accepted [on EM]."[4]

---

[4]LambdaMOO's process size and busyness have resulted in significant lag time between command transmission and execution. Lag is a serious inhibitor of real-time

6.2.2   The Mouldy Couch Club

Against the backdrop of disagreements over the community's purpose and attempts to differentiate it from LambdaMOO, the Mouldy Couch Club incident occurred. Although it was rarely discussed by the time I arrived on the MOO, it poignantly illustrates the tensions within the community over allocation of resources, location of power, and community ideology that EM has suffered from since 1993. The class distinction between programmers and non-programmers on the MOO was far from the only contributing factor.

Ellen remembers having gotten fed up about the problems developing on EM and feeling that no one shared her alienation. "Finally one night it kind of came to a head and I was (fairly loudly, probably) threatening MOOicide[5] and *anyway* saying that I was going to leave EM, probably for good. It just so happened that Fred and Sleep were on at that time, and just as I was saying some 'final' good-byes to some people, one of them paged me and told me to meet them in Fred's room. It was at this time that they told me they had been feeling much the same way I was, which completely surprised me (since Sleep and Fred were supposedly in the 'in' crowd)." Sleep and Fred were wizards on EM. Fred, a high school student in New England, and Sleep, a computer scientist in Australia, were both technically savvy power elite under many people's definitions of the PE. Fred was a member of the LambdaMOO Architecture Review Board, author of a player class on LambdaMOO, and friend of many members of the LambdaMOO power elite. Sleep had built important infrastructure (a popular bar) on LambdaMOO and had turned down the offer of LambdaMOO wizard status several times.

It wasn't the prevalence of technobabble on EM that alienated Sleep. Because of real-life commitments, he never had time to focus on EM's

---

conversation on LambdaMOO and is an eternal topic of complaint; in early 1994 there was even a lag-o-meter that displayed current lag-time in seconds on LambdaMOO's connection screen, where only the most important information about the MOO is posted. Complaining about lag time is the MUD version of complaining about the weather: it affects everyone, and everyone has something to say about it. EM users suffer from occasional Net lag, when the network between the MOO and users is busy (like the day the new version of X11, the Unix windowing environment, was released), but the MOO itself is almost never "lagged."

[5] Self-destruction of one's character is known as "MOOicide" and is an extreme means of registering unhappiness with a MOO. In 1994, there were several well-advertised MOOicides on LambdaMOO, due to personal problems as well as irritation with the political fighting and backbiting. There was one MOOicide that I know of on EM in 1994, and the perpetrator asked for his character to be reinstated afterward. I believe he MOOicided to broadcast his real-life unhappiness, not because he was upset with the community per se, although one may wonder why he chose such an extreme form of communication.

projects. "As a lot of the convo [conversation] at the time was discussing the cool projects in some depth, and no one seemed to have time to fill me in on any details, so a lot of the time I just sat there listening to people talk about things I didn't understand." As a result, he felt "unnecessary." However, the feeling that he was being ignored by people he'd considered friends was more painful. His friends would be talking about some project in the Living Room and he'd get no response, not even a hello, to anything he said.

Both Fred and Sleep felt that the real-life friendships among the southern Minnesota crowd had taken precedence over the online ones. A lot of technical discussion among Tom, Ray, and Pete seemed to happen in real life, particularly at a diner called Perkins. Their physical, geographical proximity threatened the online friendships by appearing to be more important. Fred and Sleep both cursed Perkins. Sleep said he'd be "sitting at work, feeling shitty, being ignored by all in the LR [Living Room], then suddenly someone says 'PERKINS' and you're no longer being ignored because you're alone." It was frustrating and depressing to feel left out of the real-life discussions about EM's directions of development. Perkins, a key piece of personal history for the Minnesotans who founded EM, is immortalized in a command on the MOO (one of the "Antisocial" commands, discussed in chapter 3): if a user, e.g., lynn, types "invite Tom," everyone in the room with lynn sees

    lynn [to Tom]: Come to Perkins!

Perkins was intended to be part of the EM geography, but Tanya, who had started building it, recycled it in anger during the period of social upset on EM in mid-1993. Recycling objects, particularly useful objects or parts of public geography, is extremely common on MUDs as a way of expressing anger, frustration, or dissatisfaction with events on the MUD. It's a local expression of power, a symbolic act affecting the public space, stressing the importance of the individual to the public good.[6] Interestingly, the **invite** command's output has evolved to mean a more general "join us in real life" rather than specifically "come to Perkins." People in Newark who have never been to Perkins invoke it as well.

Although in fact many of the most central programmers on EM were not in Minnesota (Penfold and Rick were in Seattle, Marie in Newark, Mike in California), the Minnesota real-life meetings particularly rankled. Ironically, in 1994 Kurt and Ellen moved to Minnesota together,[7]

---

[6]Like MOOicide, recycling one's work expresses unhappiness, but MOOicide is more extreme.

[7]In a discussion on *chitchat in summer 1995 about whether to create a special

but the Minnesota MUDders had by then moved on to Newark. By 1995 there were a dozen EM regulars gathered in Newark for work and school, Fred among them. The "real-life," geographically based extension of EM community has only grown more complex.[8]

In the summer of 1993, however, the unhappiness of Kurt, Sleep, Ellen, and Fred led to the formation of the Mouldy Couch Club, which met in a secret clubhouse called the Dark Hole with special locked doors that only the four club members could get through. The mouldy couch object in the Dark Hole was conceived as the evil twin of the couch in the Living Room, the main social hangout on the MOO. The club was a symbolic artifact drawing on imagery from alienated childhoods. The club's existence was kept hidden by a programming hack that made characters in the Dark Hole appear to be in a public room whenever anyone listed player locations on the MOO.

For Sleep, making the Dark Hole brought the four of them back to what he remembered as the early fun days on LambdaMOO. "It was what MOOing to me has always been about. Talking about any old crap, and playing with gadgets, like Fred's door into the Mouldy Couch Club." Building things together was particularly fun; on EM, Sleep had felt excluded from a lot of that process.

For Fred, building the tunnels and the locks on the Dark Hole's door was liberating; he had always thought that building on EM was subject to excessive scrutiny and criticism. He was tired of hearing how "less-than-perfect" everything was; "good lord, we're building a MUD, not writing a space shuttle launch program." He explained to me, "EM and the people that founded it have always had a tendency to want to make things just perfect. Alone this isn't a fault, it's striving for perfection. However, the tendency was to not build anything (or build something substandard and label it a 'hack'; or even build something serviceable and label it an 'awful gross hack' thereby discouraging its use) until the design was perfect. But nobody has enough time to design the perfect gizmo, so progress was slow."

There have been other complaints about the critical atmosphere on EM. Karen felt discouraged from learning to program in the MOO by the experience of having a line of her code pasted into a public conversation

Newark mailing list for people in Newark to use to organize social outings, Kurt posted, "I used to get depressed reading about the Minnesota announcements back when I was in British Columbia, but now I'm in Minnesota and none of you are so bite me anyway."

[8]However, not all EMers in Newark socialize together on a regular basis; and the real-life involvements among many of them do not generally deter them from MUD-ding on EM anyway.

and laughed at. Another person felt he was made to feel stupid for asking questions. (The atmosphere has since changed a lot, I believe, because people have been sensitized to the problem; but effects of the syndrome linger, partly because of the tension between protecting the collective resource of a well-designed world and allowing creative play with that world.)

Criticism (or comments perceived as critical) has rankled with others on EM, creating bad feelings that persist and inhibiting some people from building. As some EM regulars have noted, the insistence on quality programming has made EM a place where users can count on finding working code, unlike some MUDs where broken or half-finished objects litter the landscape. But EM remains a hobby for a group of friends, not a work environment where a supervisor can dictate standards; when one friend criticizes another's job, even if he's right, the experience isn't pleasant. There has been significant tension on EM about who works on what project, who has final say on decisions, and whether enough work is being done. Real-life jobs and schoolwork have significantly interfered with much EM development, as well. Tom spent much of 1994 frustrated at Ray for ignoring EM bug reports, while Ray worked on school and on MUD projects for companies in Newark and Texas. For some users, the environment was of less importance than the social relationships on the MOO, but for others, the environment—geography, projects, interactive objects—symbolically represented the purpose of the MOO, a place for programming and hopefully advancing the state of the art for MOO building. I think it likely that the well-designed environment was of less importance as a collective good than it was as a symbolic representation of the goals of the founders, a symbol that reminded and motivated.

The Mouldy Couch Club provided an alternative, focused sense of community for its members; its social goals were set down in the Club Oath text posted on the wall of the Dark Hole, and included directives to "Support those members in need," and "Visit with and otherwise hang around with other members." Originally the club members tried to avoid "Living Room people." Kurt said the club "was a friendly place [they] could hang out at and know [they] were welcome." A sign on the wall in the Dark Hole warned:

```
SIGN
====
```

This is NOT the living room.

And this is NOT LambdaMOO.

> This room is to be devoid of discussion of anything
> club members don't want to discuss. If you start
> discussing something they don't want discussed, you'll
> be pointed to this sign. Do it again, and you'll
> be summarily forced to leave.

Here the Living Room seems to be symbolically standing in for the rest of ElseMOO, at least ElseMOO-as-community-hangout. Suttles (1972) suggested that local communities defend themselves against larger societies by making their necessities virtues and by their choice of enemies. The secretive, exclusive nature of the club was both a necessity and a virtue, offering explicit but limited group membership (an "in-group") and rules of behavior defined in contrast to the larger Else-MOO society. But the club was most explicitly defined in opposition to LambdaMOO (or discourse about LambdaMOO), implying that Else-MOO's attempts to differentiate itself from LambdaMOO hadn't been as successful as some of the club members wanted. Certainly LambdaMOO politics were a recurrent topic during my research period, as I will illustrate later.

Inevitably the club was noticed, when the four of them stopped showing up in the Living Room. A wizard teleported in to join them and discovered the secret room they were sitting in. Kurt remembers people calling them exclusionary. Ellen remembers a lot of denial, with other people saying, in response to their complaints, "What problem? *I* don't see a problem." Sleep remembers being asked, "Why did you feel this was necessary?" "Some people were hurt for us," he said, "others with us, most [were] just surprised and/or shocked." Ellen had the feeling that people wanted the club removed, but Sleep felt they wanted the problem resolved so there wouldn't be a need for it. Tom remembers talking to them at length, trying to understand, but the problem was deep and he was apparently a part of it. Sleep felt the discovery of the club was important because it drew attention to the fact that EM was not the "MOOtopia" many of its users felt it to be. Lack of a coherent policy on the distribution of programmer bits, lack of people clearly responsible for decision making, an excess of wizards making what appeared to be arbitrary decisions about resource use, social and technical goals for the MOO that seemed to conflict—all this made it an unhappy place. Continuing political storms on LambdaMOO over the "power elite" tainted the air on EM as well, particularly when friends on EM behaved in the sorts of high-handed ways the PE were accused of acting on LambdaMOO.

Many people on EM have complained about the general policy preventing players from building private rooms and the lack of lockable rooms on the MOO. Although the Mouldy Couch Club appears a rebellious reaction to alienation and feelings of disempowerment, the artifacts that supported the club's formation—the secret room, the signs, the locked doors—and the disguise that prevented the room from appearing when players listed other players' locations could only have been created by programmers and wizards on the MOO. Disgruntled nonprogrammers on EM had (and have) no means of making a real impact on the face of the MOO, no means of gathering and protesting other than in the midst of other public conversation or in private page conversations with fellow malcontents, if such could be found.

And some players apparently felt locked out of even the Mouldy Couch Club, which appeared another in-group in itself. Egypt said, "I felt particular empathy with the Mouldy Couch Club, but even more alienated because ??I always felt locked out by them too...."[9] He later said, "The [Mouldy Couch Club] just appeared in the blink of an eye, no one was talking about it, I couldn't get added to the list—I had no idea it was a reaction to the same feelings I was experiencing—it just felt like something I was actively shut out of, instead of something I was merely shut out of in spirit."

The Mouldy Couch Club was a reaction to the conflict over resource distribution, alienation from the social scene that included real-life proximity for some people, and feelings of social disempowerment, despite the fact that several club members were wizards or programmers and therefore technically empowered. Community ideology came into question after the club's discovery. Shortly thereafter, a revised political structure was instituted in an attempt to address some of those problems; specifically, the Community Group was created to handle difficult social issues, which I'll discuss in the next section.

6.2.3 The Reorganization

Rather than just ignore the Mouldy Couch Club, the wizards on EM instigated a political reorganization, taking limited collective action to address the social problems revealed by the club. I say "limited" because the political reorganization was executed by a small subset of the population. However, they were attempting to redistribute power among more than just the wizards.

The social tensions online came to a head one night in October 1993, when Tom remembers anne calling wizards Tom and Pete "puffed-up and

---

[9]The "??" was in his MUD page to me; I interpret it as meaning that he isn't sure how to express this feeling or whether he is accurate in his portrayal of the club.

self-important" during a discussion of a new policy on programmer bits. During the ensuing fight, Ray shut the MOO down, graphically illustrating that ultimate power does rest with the person who has his finger on the button (or who owns the process). It remained officially down for a month and a half, although during the Shutdown it was in fact up and accessible to the wizards. During this period the wizards discussed policies for giving out programmer bits, whether everyone with a wizard bit needed one, how to handle social problems, and what administrative structure was needed. They also built EM Corporate Headquarters (in self-parody, Tom says, of the bureaucracy that was settling into place). During this period of secret meetings, Tom remembers Lenny telling them, "If you don't want to be thought of as a cabal then don't act like one," a sentiment that would be remembered during the conflicts over LambdaMOO politics several months later.

During the Shutdown, the Mouldy Couch Club moved to a MOO Kurt ran on his British Columbian school account. Sleep, however, had lost Net access, and he disappeared from sight for a long time. The club dissolved somewhat, although the Dark Hole remained a useful refuge for Kurt and Ellen from time to time. Kurt and Ellen were married in 1995, after becoming close friends during the club incident.

When EM came back on the Net in mid-November 1993, online "news" announced the political reorganization.

THE REORGANIZATION
    by ls on Sunday, November 14, 1993

Sorry about the recent downtime, folks. The MOO and
various people on it needed to sit around and
introspect for a while. A lot of changes have happened
during the time it was down. Some things to notice:

No more wizards. (!?) See 'help admin' for details.

[. . .]
So why'd this all happen? Well. The tale varies.
Ask around. Or don't. But here are a few important
points of it all:
- Programming bits and administrative bits are NOT a
  status symbol. They're a responsibility.
- The MOO is here mostly to make progress on various
  projects. If you want to help out, cool. If not,
  cool.

Wizards weren't eliminated entirely, but they weren't supposed to have the authority to make arbitrary decisions about MOO policy anymore. The MOO's project orientation was stated to be paramount; but, of course, the programmer wizards who set it up were the ones who decided its goals. As Ito (1997, 1994) points out, virtual worlds are grounded in physical resources and accountable people, who are empowered to direct those worlds.

The administrative reorganization resulted in three groups: the Steering Committee, responsible for "defining and maintaining the MOO's goals and objectives"; the Community Group (CG), responsible for "handling social problems and promoting a sense of community"; and the Tech Group, responsible for "technical development and maintenance of the MOO." The Steering Committee is responsible for granting programmer bits, approving programming projects, and approving new members for all groups. As of August 1995 it was made up of six wizards. Also as of that date, the Technical Group included the five wizards who have access to the Unix system administration of the MOO and do backups, restart the MOO server, etc.; the people with access to the MOO database core, i.e., all seventeen current wizards; and the thirty-seven programmers. The initial members of the Community Group, in December 1993, were Karen, ls, Pete, Kurt, Tanya, and anne. The latter three were not wizards, but an EM regular told me recently that she thought CG members were given wizard bits automatically in order to perform their functions. Wizard status is still commonly conflated with social policing.

Although the wizards were not officially in control of social policy after the reorganization, most of the decision-making is still done by characters with wizard bits. Not everyone heard or understood the announcement that there were "no more wizards on EM" after the shutdown; certainly wizard bits still exist and give users that possess them the ability to change more of the database than programmers can. One small but enormously visible power they hold is the ability to change the text of the "Welcome Message" on the MOO connection screen. This connection screen message is an important community text, advertising the MOO to visitors (or disguising it from them). Only wizards have access to the text, and in fact only a small subset of them (Tom, Ray, Pete, and Penfold) change it regularly. The text of the Welcome Message varies from cryptic quotes from street signs, dialog from movies, and lines from songs to humorous quotes from guests or regulars on the MOO. Quotes that deride the EM community are particularly favored: the urge to appropriate criticism for self-parody is strong on EM, though it is probably not recognized by outsiders. I've collected some of my favorite Welcome Messages in Appendix C.

The Community Group

The Community Group is supposed to "handle any social problems that may arise, mediate disputes, assist new players in becoming acclimated to EM, and promote community harmony" (from "help community-group"). CG members can boot (disconnect) obnoxious players, check connection site information, block sites (i.e., prevent users from connecting from certain Net sites), newt, and toad. The idea of a group that handles social problems without needing wizard bits is similar to the "sub-wizards" proposed on LambdaMOO in the fall of 1992; the idea of sub-wizards was rejected there because it appeared too likely that the power elite would become sub-wizards and oppress the population even more than they were already perceived as doing. It's possible that the Community Group was partially inspired by LambdaMOO's more inclusive politics. The CG was a concession to the non-technical, purely social side of the MOO's community, since the CG explicitly allowed non-wizard members and was chartered to "promote community harmony."

The CG has predictably become the focus of some dissatisfaction on EM. In 1994, there were three toadings, two of which were fairly controversial. The toadings have been the most public, visible actions of the CG, making a clear difference in the composition of the community because the toaded characters were either regulars or, in one case I'll detail below, politically visible on LambdaMOO. The more subtle efforts of the CG—improving how guests are treated, helping new users—are less noticeable.

Public perception of the CG varies widely. One user told me that she had no idea what the CG does or doesn't do, since the mailing list associated with the CG can be read only by members of the CG. (In fact, an attempt was made to set up a publicly readable CG-list in mid-1994, but it was removed when a user posted inflammatory personal and political attacks on it. That user was later toaded for various antisocial behavior. Interestingly, he did not target the most widely read list on EM, *chitchat, preferring instead the explicitly political forum.)

The toadings were particularly controversial actions. One user told me, "I dunno who's on [the CG], and as a result, I question its potency as a real social mover. I can't think of anything positive that the CG has done, and I don't consider newtings and toadings very positive no matter who the culprit is. So, I don't have any horrible feelings towards the CG, I just sorta look at them as a non-entity which has yet to prove itself as a positive social force." Two other users suggested they also disagreed with the toadings, and one reported of the toaded characters that "although they were jerks, hell I'm used to jerks... Some on here do consider them friends still." Another regular said publicly on *chitchat, "I don't like the exclusion of Dawn and Gremlin [two toaded characters]. I don't understand people's aversion to them and I don't believe the arguments against them [. . .]. Both individuals are intelligent, creative people whom I would be happy to share the MOO with."

According to one regular, the CG isn't needed as a separate entity, because the social interventions its members perform would be performed by those individuals anyway; helpful people are helpful regardless of committee structures. "Official," formal actions like toadings could be passed to another group, and in fact, many members of the CG are in other administrative groups anyway, she pointed out. Another regular approved of the CG: "I think the CG is great, because it allows action to be taken when necessary without a bunch of shenanigans (unlike LambdaMOO). I think that is because it is 'Ray and his friends,' or at least close enough to that to let everyone know that it isn't about being necessarily always impartial. I don't really know everyone who's on it. A benevolent dictatorship or oligarchy is always the best form of government."

One regular, who has been vocal about her dislike of the CG, said, "CG=Community Gesture." She sees the CG as "ill-defined," and suggests that "it's divisive, because it makes people think their opinions are valued when really they're not even being heard." She cites one toading, which she disagreed with, as an example of not being heard. She believes "there would be less friction if it were just openly understood that we [EM] toad at will. What it ends up being is a group of the power elite trying to look like they care about the peons while ridding the population of whatever they don't like." Interestingly, while several regulars apparently consider EM policy to be explicitly undemocratic, they disagree on whether or not this is a good thing. While the user quoted above considered it "the best form of government," Marie told one reporter matter-of-factly that EM is "a fascist environment—you suck up to the wizards or you're out of there."

Kollock and Smith's (1996) list of characteristics of communities that successfully defend the common good includes these principles:

1. Most individuals affected by these rules can participate in modifying the rules.
2. The right of community members to devise their own rules is respected by external authorities.

3. A system for monitoring members' behavior exists; this monitoring is undertaken by the community members themselves.

4. Community members have access to low-cost conflict resolution mechanisms.

The Community Group was an attempt to include more community members in the activity of monitoring other members' behavior (3), and to involve more people in setting and reinforcing standards of behavior on the MOO (1). The CG attempts to make decisions based on some input from regulars, but there is certainly no formal mechanism for registering opinions on EM, no process by which to modify the largely unwritten rules of good behavior. I'm not sure that a system like LambdaMOO's would be appropriate on ElseMOO, however; the LambdaMOO political process requires a huge coded infrastructure and is probably better suited to the larger population of LambdaMOO than the smaller ElseMOO group. But the CG, for all its good intentions, is vulnerable to the same criticisms that wizards face when they determine social policy on an ad hoc basis. The accusation that the CG acts to protect its own members and their friends may even be true, since they are the community members whose experiences and voices are most readily available, in the absence of any formal system for registering opinion. Toward the end of this chapter I expand on the role of gossip in this decision-making process.

Since there are not many explicit rules on the MOO (except the injunctions against harassing or overly familiar behavior in the "help manners" guidelines), execution of the Community Group charter is a difficult one. I saw a good deal of subjective interpretation of just what CG members should be "policing" and what form their policing should take. CG members who try to intercede in heated arguments have repeatedly ended up getting criticized for their involvement, and the angst has rarely been worth the intercession. Two members of the CG have resigned after such conflicts. Karen, a CG member who has frequently been the one to boot obnoxious guests or ask them to stop being abusive, reports that she is sick of being seen as "the bad cop" on the MOO. There is no "low-cost" conflict resolution mechanism, just argument and the often resulting acrimony. (Kolko and Reid 1998 describe some similar dysfunctional debates on other MOOs.)

Finally, there has always been an uneasy tension between the need to protect the community members and the need to protect visitors and guests. The porousness of the boundary between ElseMOO and the outside (represented by other MOO communities and by visitors who may or may not eventually become ElseMOO regulars) has been the chief site of conflict. Who do the community rules apply to, how are community standards interpreted when outsiders are involved, what is the collective good in such cases? It is not in the community's best interest to keep the door closed and prevent visitors. As in other communities of practice (Lave and Wenger 1991), newcomers regularly join the community and keep it energized. And finally, if it's ultimately the community itself that deserves protection, it is never clear just who the community *is*, because there is no explicit sign of community membership. Simply having a character is not a sufficient indicator.[10] Boundaries are continually being negotiated, expressed in dynamic symbolic language and evolving community policies.

6.2.4 Return of the Power Elite

The "power elite" was a symbolic category that centralized much debate about community ideology and the location of power on ElseMOO. I'll diverge from narrative to explore this symbolic category some more before continuing with the story of Dawn, who took on the power elite on their own ground.

Despite ElseMOO's constant attempts to differentiate itself from LambdaMOO, this category was inherited from LambdaMOO and took on new life on ElseMOO. The evolution of the meaning of "power elite" since 1992 has been just like the evolution of many a derogatory label. As Mouse, an insightful visitor from LambdaMOO, said, "It's run its course as a proper legend, with a completely plausible origination, loss of signal during the retelling, and a new meaning having arisen in its place to suit modern needs." Social types, like "redneck" and "greenhorn," often imply associated evaluations of the behavior of individuals so classified (Merry 1984); the "power elite" type carried associated positive and negative connotations, since the elite were seen as powerful, knowledgeable, and conversationally skilled, but also as arrogant, patronizing, and unfriendly.

By 1994, the term was being used to describe regular posters on *life-issues (Message 2104 on *life-issues),[11] the ARB ("I hear the ARB being collectively called a bunch of power-crazed power elite so much by people with one grudge or another that it really makes me want to just give my position up sometimes," says Message 2213 on *life-

---

[10]However, *not* having a character is an explicit indication of nonmembership. In the case of several ElseMOO visitors, explicit banishment in the form of toading did occur, despite lack of consensus from the community (in fact, there was no attempt to reach consensus). I will describe one case, the Dawn incident, in detail below.

[11]Despite the fact that the high-volume posters, at least at the end of 1994, were Dawn and assorted others not in the PE by most reckonings.

issues; also 4065 on *life-issues), and long-term users with low object numbers for their characters.[12] It was even being claimed satirically, when a candidate for the ARB referred to "white male trash Power Elite" (Message 2525 on *life-issues). A character called Upchuck proposed an amusing description of the social stratification of newbies and older users, based on the length of time they'd had a character on the MOO. Although it does not directly refer to the power elite, its terminology is similar.

for the sake of my argument, i'll provide the following breakdowns and terms, which many of you won't like. this message is very elitist and clique-ish, but is intended to make a small point. if you disagree with my classifications, feel free to calculate and adjust the numbers and percentages to your own liking.

then-elite = approx 800 players who have been on > 2 years
then-newbies = approx 650 players who have been on 1..2 years
now-newbies = approx 54000[13] players who have been on < 1 year

now-elite = then-elite + then-newbies = 1450

as then-newbies, many of the now-elite felt that the then-elite were asocial, and rude, etc, while the then-elite felt that the then-newbies were clueless, obnoxious, etc.

i'm tempted to think that the same holds true today (now-newbies think the now-elite are asocial, while the now-elite think the now-newbies are obnoxious, etc). however, because of the larger numbers (esp the greater newbie:elite ratio), the clique-ishness is much more apparent.

i think part of our problem is that the now-elite are trying to "fix" lambda, while they comprise only about 20% of the population. how can 20% of the population say that 80% are not acting within the accepted social norms? (Message 2654 on *life-issues)

---

[12]The approximate age of a character is indicated by how high its object number is. The object numbers of characters are often used as a social stratification mechanism: e.g., LambdaMOO users might refer to "players below 50K," or players with character numbers lower than #50000. Many LambdaMOOers know roughly when the 50K characters were created, so this dates the characters below #50000.
[13]This is probably a typo for 5400.

Here the elite are all the older characters, rather than just the small group of power elite who were arguably friends of the wizards on LambdaMOO. A difference in behavior norms between these older characters and newbies—another important social type—was described by the posters on *life-issues. It was seen as a difficulty that older characters no longer hang out in public rooms and therefore can't socialize the newbies. The conversational abilities of the newbies, who seemed to interact primarily with programmed toys such as bonkers, was frequently derided, suggesting that older characters were seen as conversationally skilled in comparison.

At least the "then-newbies" could spell, and didn't conduct conversation with bonkers. (Ray, in Message 2655 on *life-issues)

Maybe the living room denizens get a real kick out of having *their* bonker messages be the ones that get displayed. It's too noisy in there for real communication—there are too many of them to become Lambda Famous—everything you can imagine has been *done* already (or if it hasn't, it's only because the ARB looked askance at the holodeck and said "take that to TrekMOO, moron!"). There isn't any way to make a statement. So they bonk. And they fart. And they get people riled up because it's the only way they can even be *noticed*. (Marie, Message 2659 on *life-issues)

Since the "elite" aren't hanging around, newbies develop the impression that the typical Living Room immaturity personifies all moo interaction. Face it, when the upper class shuns an area, it turns into a slum. This is what the LR has become. (Message 2686 on *life-issues)

In the last post above, the poster offers a folk analysis juxtaposing class, maturity, and the slum (an undesirable community), reflecting the poster's own ideological stance toward community.

Some people pointed out that the newbies had come largely for tinysex. Brine, the creator of the Schmoo character class I discussed in chapter 2, seems to be pointing out the importance of history to the existing community on LambdaMOO (see Bellah et al. 1984 and "communities of memory"), a history the new players don't share and apparently don't care about:

I have a very definite sense of MOO history, and a reverence for it. There's an entire museum, and hundreds of objects at the disposal of anyone who wishes to find out more about our virtual home. The point, which you all seem to be missing, is that the annoying newbies don't give a fuck about history, or being snuggle-cuddled in your all-encompassing social hugs. They're here to get laid, to whine about not getting laid, to accuse women who don't lay them of being sluts, and to massacre the english language. (Brine, Message 2658 on *life-issues)

Brine and others relate their concern for the appropriate use of language to the character of the community they share. Clearly, just as it is on Usenet, the caliber of discourse is one public good worth defending (Kollock and Smith 1996). How to absorb new members and teach them history, norms of behavior, and appropriate discourse ethics was an enormous problem for LambdaMOO (as it has been for other fast-growing online communities; Smith 1992). Offline studies of language use in communities show similar resistance to newcomers on the part of established locals, often manifesting as a strengthening of linguistic difference that shows group affiliation. Labov (1972) describes how centralized vowels on Martha's Vineyard indicate local loyalty and solidarity. Martha's Vineyard, an island with a small permanent population, is regularly inundated by summer visitors, a situation not entirely unlike that on LambdaMOO.[14]

Ideological debates about the character of LambdaMOO raged through the LambdaMOO mailing lists. These mailing lists may have created Anderson's (1991) "imagined community" on LambdaMOO, by making audible the voices speaking for and to the diverse community (or communities); but they also broadcasted and perhaps amplified struggles over norms, ideology, and terminology. Such struggles are also obvious in other media forms offline. LambdaMOO, with over 8900 characters, faced the problems of many communities that retain some sense of global identity and character (well defined by the MOO space and the registered characters) while also hosting many diverse social networks. Character age, one's LambdaMOO circle of friends, and membership in other MUD communities are perhaps determinants of one's strongest community affiliations on LambdaMOO.

ElseMOO inherited and reacted against much LambdaMOO ideology. The LambdaMOO term "power elite" has been adopted by a few of the very people it was used to describe in 1992, but in a partly ironic,

---

[14]However, the parallel isn't that close, because the established locals on LambdaMOO see themselves as proponents of elite standards, as Brine's comment about massacring the English language illustrates. Usually established locals' linguistic variation differs from elite norms in nonstandard ways. This situation shows a different social stratification, seniority (and perhaps, in part, technical sophistication) being seen as elite.

self-censuring manner. For instance, in a discussion on EM of the petition to stop population growth on LambdaMOO, Pete made an ironic comment and eyed himself warily in the standard EM manner to indicate that his comment should not be understood as entirely serious:

```
Pete oks.  "from a power elite standpoint, obviously,
*p:zpg has its advantages.  it'll keep the
people we like there, while tending to lock
out alot of the newbies we don't.  but this
isn't necessarily a Good Thing.  what's a
power elite without a proletariat?
Pete eyes himself warily.
Tom says, "uh, i think LambdaMOO has enough proles to
last it for a while"
Tom eyes himself warily.
Tom also thinks the pe argument is pretty much outmoded,
seeing as how most of it doesn't even DO much there.
```

The PE could be joked about, as well. In the excerpt below, people joke about their own connections to it. "Orbital PE" probably refers to the occasionally expressed belief that EM "rules" LambdaMOO from orbit around it.

```
Ellen <- not really PE
George <- not really PE either
Ellen <- simply annoying PE satellite
Kelly <- hanger-on
Ellen <- Official Irritant to the PE
George . o O ( Orbital PE )
George eyes himself warily.
Phig <- Official Irritant to the PE (retired)
Kelly <- official irritant to Ellen
Marie is *above* being PE
```

One joke definition of the PE was remembered by Mike: "Tom was the one who described the power elite as 'a bunch of people who like to sit around and say non sequiturs a lot, and we like pizza too.'" Such jokes defuse the impact of the category, suggesting that there is no special group with special powers, or if there is, they are nonetheless fairly ordinary people.

According to Tom and Ray, one can become PE by association with the PE, suggesting that the PE are a visible social network. Karen, who is not known on LambdaMOO as PE, and is not thought of primarily as a programmer, is considered by many to be PE on EM. After I'd been around EM for a while, Tom tried to convinced me I was PE "by the age-old definition of power elite, people who hang out with the wizards." Karen said she had also been called PE long before she believed it. Tom emoted, "Tom loves watching people deny their power elite status, it's like Luke Skywalker and his dark side." However, when asked who the PE are now, most people on EM don't report sharing Tom's feeling that it is possible to become PE just by association.

There's an unsavory side to power elitism for women in particular. Perhaps because women don't usually maintain profiles as hackers on MUDs (with the exception of Marie), few women are considered PE. I've heard a couple of women called "token female members of the PE." At another point I witnessed two women discussing their status as "power elite groupies," including how many PE they had slept with (the public conversation did not get more detailed than "all of them, I think"). Ray supposedly posted on rec.games.mud a few years ago the theory that all well-known MOOers were part of one connected graph, based on who had slept with whom; "well-known" MOOers meant wizards or "power elite." This irritated Tom and Karen, who certainly disagreed.[15] (For discussion of the status of women and gender in another MUD community, see Kendall 1998.)

To the extent that the term is still recognized on EM by anyone other than the founders of EM, there are interesting differences of opinion over its meaning. For some people, visible exercise of power in a social context—perhaps censuring others for inappropriate behavior, or speaking "officially" for the MOO (as ls does when he posts "news" about the machine the server runs on)—is a determinant in being classified as PE. For another user, the PE are just the people on EM who act like insiders. The PE have "an air of 'I belong here, you don't.'" The names my informants listed as being PE varied a lot; in fact there was little agreement among them. Two people explicitly noted that Mike (who was voted PE on LambdaMOO in the 1992 survey) did not seem to count; "he's never wielded his 'power,'" one said, perhaps acknowledging that he does have it, but has withdrawn from any visible committee role on EM.

Another regular suggested that PE still connotes involvement on LambdaMOO for her. "I think you have to be active—meddling— in order to be PE." For her, the PE really was "the people who first started lambdamoo," the Archwizard's friends, specifically Marie, Honda, Lenny, and Ray (interestingly, Ray is not a wizard on Lamb-

---

[15]There are rumored to be similar graphs in the MUD dino community and in the linguistics community.

daMOO, and Tom, who is, was not mentioned). She noted that it means different things to different people; "I'm ambiguous about whether ARB members should automatically be PE, because they have power. Well, no, it's not just an LMOO thing, but I think you probably can't be PE unless you were There in the Early Days. The PE here is like george, ray, ls, karen, etc. I bet a lot of MOOers in general would think of them as PE but I think the only people who care about PE or not are ones who've done LMOO. And they'll tend to think that the PE are the oldbies (or if you're dawn, the EMers)."

Dawn, a character on LambdaMOO, believed that the EM players voted as a bloc on LambdaMOO, and that to avoid splitting the votes of other LambdaMOOers they cannily chose and promoted single candidates they believed they could control (Message 2910 on *life-issues). Her belief is reminiscent of the joke on EM and LambdaMOO, sometimes taken seriously, that EM "rules LambdaMOO from orbit."[16] The joke has occasionally bothered Tom and others on EM; Tom in particular has argued that posts from EM regulars on certain LambdaMOO disputes make it appear as if EM has a united voice and interest, which is certainly not true. As Penfold says, the idea that EM can agree on anything, let alone act in concert, is ludicrous. Yet the power elite remains an important symbolic category, suggesting similar interests shared by powerful individuals.

6.2.5   The Dawn Conflict

A collision of cultures, politics, and personalities occurred in early 1994 between several people from EM and one character from LambdaMOO, Dawn. The conflict illustrates aspects of the potential relationships and contrasts between MUD communities, the nature of privacy in the medium, the treatment of anonymous outsiders (guests) on MUDs, and the relationships between characters on different MUDs that are known to belong to the same user. Furthermore, as an example of an outsider confronting the boundaries of the EM group, it reveals aspects of the community that become apparent when its borders are threatened (Cohen 1985): access to EM is seen not as a "right" but as dependent on an agreement, whose type or manner is not specified, among the existing EM population (whereas some people appear to see LambdaMOO as generally open and inclusive). This incident also reveals attitudes, some of them emerging only during the conflict, about the status of community discourse as public or private. Just as LambdaMOO eventually voted to inform journalists and researchers that the discourse of the par-

---

[16]Some ElseMOOers think this idea originated with Brine.

ticipants could not be quoted without permission, ElseMOO evolved a policy that MOO conversation is private.

Dawn was never a regular visitor on EM, but only came to EM to confront people about political actions occurring on LambdaMOO. Ultimately she was among the few characters toaded on EM in 1994, because of her disagreements with EM regulars; along with the facets of MUD culture I list above, this incident serves as an example of how the EM community reaches a decision to toad, the ultimate exclusion from community membership. For ethical reasons, my discussion of Dawn's activities on LambdaMOO and EM comes from public mailing list records of events, rather than from personal observations or recorded conversation.

The Disputes

In January 1994 on LambdaMOO, Dawn called a dispute with Berry-Bush, the representative of the Architecture Review Board who had told her that the ARB had denied her request for extra building quota. Her dispute was more clearly with the ARB than with BerryBush per se; she hoped (as far as I can tell) to focus some attention on the ARB's functioning, which she saw as inconsistent and cloaked in secrecy, like some "old boys' network" (Message 46 on the dispute list *d:dawn.vs.BerryBush).[17]

Ray drafted a petition concurrent with the dispute that may have started as a joke but became more serious: Replace the ARB with Dawn. Very soon after, George drafted a sister petition: Toad Dawn, if Ray's petition succeeds. Their combined effect, as Ray pointed out, would be to abolish the ARB, as well as Dawn.

Although Ray's petition may have begun as a joke, there was a vein of seriousness in his posts on the matter: "Nothing in this petition says that Dawn has to do this by herself. She can organize a group of people, a board if you will, to advise her, so that she only has to do the final command, much like the current wizards do. Even from a strict conservative view, this petition does something that the so-called serious ones haven't done yet: make clear what the quota-distributing process is. The existing ARB has no mandate, and isn't elected, and has vast public opposition" (Message 29 on *p:Dawn). Other sentiments posted on the petition ranged from "shut the fuck up" to "why is it necessary

---

[17]Ultimately, the mediator in the dispute between Dawn and BerryBush found Berry-Bush not guilty of personal wrong against Dawn, but called on "the masses" to "clean the place up": "Throw them all out and start over. Make a new ARB with a CLEAR purpose. They can even write their own purpose, but hold them to it" (Message 238 on *d:dawn.vs.BB). The ARB has since become an elected body.

to 1) insult an individual player and 2) propose a quota distribution which is unlikely to earn popular support, in order to promote discussion about quota-distribution?" (Message 31 on *p:Dawn). As Ray noted, the petition was in fact the third highest signature getter, showing it to be quite popular (people were signing either because it was deemed humorous, because they thought it would be a good idea to replace the ARB with almost anything, or in protest against her dispute with BerryBush). Ray received a lot of hostility ("God your an ass Ray. Your an elitist son of a bitch wanabe prick") and Billock told him that Dawn wished he would "burn" (i.e., destroy) the petition. Ray, not having heard from her directly, kept it alive.

The LambdaMOO public seemed very interested in Ray's motive for writing the petition. His sarcasm was well-known ("Has Ray no rhetorical repetoire beyond demeaning sarcasm?"; "*p:Dawn is insulting to Dawn *to the extent* that people are presumed to think Ray does not really believe she would herself be an improvement over the ARB" [Message 54 on *p:Dawn]), but some suspected that his stubborn defense of his petition meant he was entirely serious, even if his methods for bringing about political reform were unorthodox.

Apparently unhappy with the discussion on LambdaMOO, Tom stepped in and posted:

This petition was my idea.

I thought, "wow, that would be a really silly petition". I did not consider it an insult to Dawn in any way, any more than I would consider an equivalent petition elevating Ray to the position of quota arbiter. It just struck me as amusing, the completely overkill idea of solving this group-dispute problem by removing quota authority to one person. [. . .]

However, at this point I believe that Ray, its nominal author, is sincere in his support. Message 29 struck me as particularly convincing; I nearly signed the petition after I read it. In addition, Ray has stated in private conversation and more recently on mailing lists his interest in disbanding the ARB. This petition would bring this about, without leaving us in a vacuum. (Note, please, that just because I think Ray is sincere doesn't mean I agree with him.) (Messages 49 and 50 on *p:Dawn)

And in response, Tom's status as a wizard on LambdaMOO was raised critically by Billock: "I have to say that I'm quite surprised that a wizard would suggest a petition to a player without thinking through the potential consequences. Wizards have a special duty to LambdaMOO, similar to a physician's: 'first, do no harm.' This is not to say that wizards should not author or propose petitions, just that they should do so in a responsible and ethical way. Proposing a petition as a joke which is likely to hurt a player is neither responsible nor ethical" (Message 57 on *p:Dawn).

Although the wizards had withdrawn from making social policy without community consent (by vote), some people equated their being involved in political processes (i.e., drafting petitions or suggesting them) with active social policy-making. The power that wizards have to enforce programmatic decisions gives them a status in the culture that apparently makes some people wary of their activity in the political arena. Billock went one step beyond wariness: he expressed the feeling that wizards, by virtue of their power, need to be particularly virtuous in their political actions, presumably because they are seen to set standards of behavior or be otherwise influential over other players.

The scrutiny that wizardly actions of any type are subjected to adds a degree of stress to the job. Wizard players often try to distinguish between their actions in an official capacity and their actions as "private citizens," by using two different characters as a means of distinguishing the two roles they play: the character with the wizard bit versus the ordinary player character. However, public knowledge that the same user controls both characters leads to a conflation of the two characters' actions in many people's eyes. Supporting a split identity online is not simple, once a typist is identified across characters.

Marie, a LambdaMOO wizard who is often vocal in her support or disapproval of petitions, said, "I am dismayed that Billock would like to take away from the wizards freedom of casual speech. I think it is clear that I am responsible for statements I make in an official forum (and especially statements that I make using the [wizard-character] persona), and on serious mailing lists such as this one and *life-issues. But if I want to post garbage to *bah! or make some outrageous statements in the ElseMOO living room, I should be at complete freedom to do so" (Message 59 on *p:Dawn).

Espionage

Outrageous comments made by wizards were the next focus of attack, when Dawn posted a log of conversation she had recorded in the EM Living Room while disguised as an anonymous guest. In the log, Rick, Marie, and Tom, who are all wizards on LambdaMOO as well as ElseMOO, discuss with Ray and George the wording of the controversial petitions. During this discussion, I asked what Dawn had done that was a toadable offense, and they responded that she'd done nothing but was a pain in the ass—which would only be a toadable offense if the first petition passed. I won't reproduce the posted dialogue because, although it was rendered public by her posting of it, most people concluded that her posting the log was egregious and that the conversation had not been intended for public display outside ElseMOO. Dawn concluded the posting by claiming that she had other transcripts from ElseMOO of conversations about recent LambdaMOO events and would display them upon request to show what "a bunch of lying weasels" the EM people were. (It's still not clear to me what ElseMOOers were supposed to be lying about.)

Although the conversation (which had not been intended for public display) was sarcastic and rather harsh, there was no acknowledgment from the quoted participants that they had done anything wrong. In response, Marie posted furiously (and copied the message to Dawn): "You, of course, are incapable of understanding this, but I made no statements in there that were 'against' you. George has a petition against you. I corrected TECHNICAL MISSTATEMENTS in that petition, making no comment on the social value of that petition. I *was* planning on voting *against* both petitions that are against you. Do you see my signature on them?" (Message 71 on *p:Dawn).

Shortly thereafter, Ray was convinced to destroy the petition by being directed to read Dawn's character description, which contained not just descriptive content but also a sort of letter to the masses, informing them that she was aware of the two petitions and did not support them. She considered them hurtful and suggested that she would handle Johnson and his friends IRL (in real life) after the petitions were dealt with.[18]

The reference to Ray's real name (Johnson) and to dealing with him "IRL" did not go over well with Ray, and logging conversations as an anonymous guest on ElseMOO, as Dawn had apparently done, made hostilities plain. Dawn came to EM as Dawn (i.e., using a character called "Dawn" instead of using a guest) and argued fruitlessly with Ray and Marie about whether she was owed an apology or they were owed one. Ray saved a log of the conversation on a public ftp site (as documentary evidence, perhaps) along with the text of the recycled petition and its associated mailing list.

When Ray mentioned that he had saved this log, Via, who had been

---

[18]Dawn's threats to take the disagreement with Ray "et al." into real life did not go far, perhaps because she realized that the system administrator she would have to appeal to if she wanted their MOO access revoked was ls, a regular on ElseMOO who provides the MOO with a site.

part of the conversation, commented sarcastically, "Cool. My total over-tired null content silliness immortalized in ASCII." In fact, Tom suggested after he read it that EM regulars didn't behave any better than Dawn did—the log contained private whispers from one person to Ray about intent to "bait" Dawn, and another person told Dawn "FUCK YOU" twenty-seven times (using a programmed macro, presumably).

Guests

Paranoia about guests after Dawn's visits reached an all-time high. A new guest character was created called "Dawn guest," allocated to guest connections from her site. Any guest using her Internet service provider ended up being called "Dawn guest." Inevitably, the "Dawn guest" character was subject to random hostility and wariness. Dawn claimed on LambdaMOO that guests were being booted off ElseMOO for connecting from her site (Message 2903 on *life-issues). Concern for legitimate guests using her connection site finally prompted the removal of the "Dawn guest" character.

As far as I know, there were no overt showdowns between ElseMOO users and Dawn connected as a guest, although Tom considered confronting her. Ray briefly considered "ElseMOO.vs.Dawn" as a potential dispute on LambdaMOO, but there was no precedent for a class action suit on behalf of an entire MUD community. And there was no way the EM community could be represented as monolithic.[19]

Soon after the guest espionage period, Dawn's supposed email address was posted to a mailing list on LambdaMOO by a guest. She immediately suspected that the culprit was an ElseMOO regular disguised as a guest, since her site had been a matter of some discussion. She claimed publicly that the posted address was not her main Internet account but was an account she sometimes used (Message 2887 on *life-issues).

On EM, it is generally understood that users give correct email addresses when they register for a character. This creates a link between a real user and a character, important for establishing accountability for the character's actions. Dawn was toaded on EM after she refused

---

[19]Dawn herself had disputed an individual as a representative of the ARB, not the ARB itself. Only a few months later, another player on LambdaMOO would call a dispute against EM as a whole, cunningly using the non-player network character called "ElseMOO" that linked the two MOOs across the Net as his disputant. Treating the link character as an ambassador from EM, he asked that it be toaded, because the inter-MOO connection was undesirable while EM practiced the sorts of "fascist" state policies that had gotten him toaded on EM. The dispute was entertaining (to me, anyway, though not to many EM regulars) but deemed spurious, since the inanimate link character had done nothing to wrong him.

to provide a correct email address. Although her refusal was the official reason, the toading was almost certainly also due to her hostility toward the EM community. As Penfold tried to make clear, EM did not consider access a "right" she was guaranteed, especially since she was clearly hostile to the community and seemed to visit only to spy or argue about LambdaMOO events. Penfold told her, "You have no *right* to be here, none of us does." The relative speed and ease with which the Community Group expelled Dawn for her violation of a privacy norm (and violation of the email address rule) contrasts with the Well case reported in Smith 1992 in which a user made public the contents of a private forum. The Well has few formal rules or sanctions and operates under a largely libertarian philosophy; this philosophy of tolerance and lack of formal sanctions lead to unresolvable community conflicts. ElseMOO's far more restrictive philosophy and explicitly undemocratic politics make collective action (on the part of those empowered to act) far simpler, but community conflicts still occur over the location of power and the nature of the actions taken.

In the end, Dawn's logging of conversation was deemed a violation of cultural norms and resulted in the addition of a clause to the "help manners" document on EM stating that logging and posting the log without permission from all participants is unethical.[20] In part because of Dawn's use of the guest character and other abuses of the guest character by others, site information for guests became publicly available on EM as a means of reducing the anonymity guest characters have and the license this gives them to ignore the community's norms of behavior. More generally, Dawn's involvement with the EM community drew attention to potential problematic relations between MUD communities when users of one MUD are known to use another one and standards of behavior are not necessarily the same on both. Dawn's assumption that she had a right to be on EM, listening to the community discuss LambdaMOO politics, was contested by the EM community.

6.3 Gossip

One of the risks inherent in discussing community as an abstraction is that the motives and roles of individuals can be so easily overlooked. I've tried to capture individual voices in these narratives, perhaps at the expense of more high-level abstraction and analysis. Nevertheless, when I showed an early draft of parts of this chapter to ElseMOO in 1995, one

---

[20]The "help manners" document on EM says, "Making logs of EM conversation for the purpose of public posting is considered unethical unless each participant in the discussion expressly agrees to allow the conversation to be posted." See Appendix B.

user was very depressed that he didn't appear more often in the narratives. He said he wished he were "more important." When I asked him how "importance" is manifested in EM, he suggested that he would like to be better informed about events: "Knowledge is power—especially in an environment *literally* built of knowledge." This observation suggested to me that serious thought needed to be given to gossip and its function in this type of community, with some concern for individuals in the transmission of information. A look at some of the literature on gossip shows that it has immediate bearing on the study of community.

Merry 1984 is an excellent anthropological study of gossip (and see also the interesting eclectic collection, Goodman and Ben-Ze'ev 1994). Merry defines gossip as "informal private communication between an individual and a small selected audience concerning the conduct of absent persons or events. Gossip thrives when the facts are uncertain, neither publicly known nor easily discovered. Gossip generally contains some element of evaluation or interpretation of the event or person, but it may be implicit or unstated" (p. 275). She points out that, although anthropologists have assumed that gossip and scandal serve as effective modes of informal social control, gossip actually plays different roles in different types of societies. In close-knit societies that are stable, well bounded, and morally homogenous, gossip can have much more impact than in fluid, open, morally heterogeneous societies. This fact is related to the expectation that informal social controls are replaced by formal controls as small-scale societies grow into complex urban ones (Black 1976).

In the MOO arena, we can contrast ElseMOO and LambdaMOO in terms of scale and complexity: ElseMOO is a smaller community with a far less formal infrastructure than LambdaMOO, which has a complex and formalized system for disputes and voting. ElseMOO is the community in which decisions are made on an apparently subjective, ad hoc basis by members of the community who attempt to informally gauge public opinion. ElseMOO is a community run largely by gossip. Merry notes that gossip is usually part of other social processes, which often lead to social and political sanctions. It is the people most vulnerable to the social processes who are most vulnerable to gossip. Elites with power and control of resources are often immune. The power elite on ElseMOO (and LambdaMOO) are such a group to the extent that they actually hold power through wizard or programmer status, or can influence people with such status through social network ties. Arguably, expelled characters like Dawn were vulnerable, marginal figures seen as disruptive influences on the existing social networks.

Gossip reinforces community norms and checks infringements of them. Since much gossip is about moral behavior, individuals gossip to check their understandings of the moral climate with other individuals who are expected to share the same understandings of correct behavior. The very act of gossiping reinforces ties between people. Because gossip is often about the morality of others, it is also about reputations. Reputation depends on persistent, known identities. Online communities without persistent identities (or in which it is difficult to establish known identities that have reputations) will have less gossip, and probably no moral climate for discussion. Although most MUDs have persistent identities through registered characters, anonymous guests often pose problems. Dawn deliberately used a guest character to eavesdrop on ElseMOO regulars, rather than using a character that people would recognize and remember from visit to visit. The guest character allowed her to temporarily become anonymous and avoid accountability for her actions.

Understanding gossip in a community means being able to understand the underlying rules, values, and expectations of the culture and knowing large amounts about individuals and their relationships, reputations, and idiosyncrasies. Understanding gossip in a new environment therefore requires serious ethnographic commitment. In ElseMOO, much gossip is transmitted through the private page mode. It took me at least two months to realize how much paging was going on and to form close enough relationships to participate in page conversations. Paging someone you're not on close terms with is seen as an imposition; many guests or newcomers who try to initiate page conversations on ElseMOO are asked to speak "out loud." Toward the end of my research, I asked regulars to volunteer the names of people with whom they had regular page conversations. These relationships are shown in Figure 16. (The nodes are disguised for obvious reasons of privacy.)

Gossip flows best in highly connected social networks, networks in which two parties know a third person about whom they are gossiping. The more people they know in common, the more people they can discuss (Merry 1984). Although only fifteen people responded to my request (the nodes in boxes), there is a fair amount of interconnectivity in the graph. These self-reported relationships probably reflect friendship (or close acquaintanceship) ties rather than actual exchanges, and there are obvious asymmetries.[21] A number of people reported regularly paging people who did not mention them in return. In only two cases did a pair

---

[21]Wellman (1988b) notes that network ties are usually asymmetric in the amounts and kinds of resources that flow from one to another. Asymmetric ties are nevertheless crucial in connecting individuals and connecting networks of individuals to larger social networks.

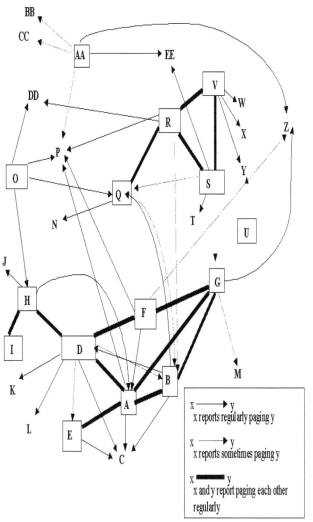

FIGURE 16 Graph of (self-reported) page relationships in ElseMOO

report page relationships that differed in terms of perceived frequency: D said that he sometimes paged B while B reported regularly paging D, and similarly for B and Q.[22] If the B-Q relationship were symmetric, it would more closely tie the top nodes to the bottom nodes—although clearly if P had responded and reported symmetrical relationships with F and A, the graph would also be more densely connected.

There are a few interesting observations to make about relationships revealed in this graph.

- The nodes F, A, B, and C are individuals often cited as power elite, and D and E are arguably power elite on ElseMOO if not LambdaMOO. G is generally *not* considered power elite, despite close ties to the others here, although G eventually became a member of the Community Group.

- Q, R, B, and N all maintained characters on Seashore as well as ElseMOO (and LambdaMOO to different degrees). (G began hanging out on Seashore after this survey, I believe.)

- AA, whom no one mentioned as a page partner, has long been a troubled and alienated member of the community. He has since left the community.

- Despite stereotypes of gossip as a women's behavior (but see critical arguments in Goodman and Ben Ze'ev 1994), there is no clear gender bias among individuals frequently listed as page partners. Some of the more frequently mentioned page partners by gender: A (male, 6 in-links), B (male, 5 in-links), P (female, 5 in-links), C (male, 4 in-links), D (female, 4 in-links), G (female, 4 in-links).

- The individual who told me he wished he were "more important," or more knowledgeable about events on ElseMOO, is a member of the Q-R-V-S sub-network; these nodes, and in fact most of the nodes in the top half of the graph (with the exception of Z), are more recent members of the community than the nodes in the bottom half. His primary social affiliations probably account for his ignorance of some of the MOO history involving more senior users.

Although Figure 16 is not intended to suffice as a social network graph of the community, the paging relationships clearly have some relevance to general social network ties. These links were self-reported, and there is a good deal of asymmetry (e.g., F reports paging A, but A does not list F). Many of these cases are probably oversights. Such oversights are interesting in themselves, suggesting that people were reporting their

---

[22]Note that B did not report any occasional paging links for himself, however.

most memorable or important private communication relationships, not simple facts.

Logs and "Evidence"

Scandal is gossip elevated into the public arena, when "everyone knows that everyone knows." LambdaMOO mailing lists, especially the list I call *life-issues, which had a very broad readership, became forums for scandal. When Dawn posted her log of ElseMOO conversation, she attempted to elevate the conversational activities of ElseMOO into scandal; arguably, her action partly backfired on her, because it was the act of posting (and logging), as much as the contents of the post, that caused public comment. An important facet of information exchange on MUDs (and in other textual online communities) is the relative persistence of that information in the form of texts. A key difference between face-to-face gossip and online gossip is the fact that documentary "evidence" can sometimes be produced in online forums: logs, or quoted posts. Despite the violation of trust or politeness norms inherent in the action, I've witnessed private conversation being pasted to third parties on several occasions, as evidence about behavior under discussion—behavior of the quoted person, or behavior of someone discussed in the quoted text. Quoting amusing or off-color remarks produced by guests or newbies is absolutely commonplace, reinforcing a sense of "us" versus "them" (as well as being amusing for its own sake).

I have been the recipient and the victim of such quotation of (and by) other community members; for instance, during a discussion about the (in)appropriateness of a character's description, someone pasted to that character a critical comment I had made privately about the description. His behavior was probably in part meant to signify a rejection of the norms I felt the description violated. Since we obviously didn't share those norms, and he aligned himself with a stranger rather than with me (a regular), I stopped gossiping with him. Gossip generally only occurs between individuals sharing similar perspectives on the moral climate of the community.

Gossip thrives when the facts are uncertain. But logs and quotations of individual lines apparently make the "facts" less uncertain than facts discussed in face-to-face gossip. They also help people share contexts for events. The greater the shared context, the closer the community members are to one another.

Nevertheless, posters of logs of MUD conversation are condemned for this action in general. But the contents of the logs, even when they might easily have been tampered with or entirely fabricated, may still affect public opinion toward the players appearing in the logs. Public opinion is important when reputations affect social processes, access to resources, or relationships. LambdaMOO's democratic process can be influenced, as Dawn hoped to do when she posted evidence that ElseMOO regulars used ElseMOO to discuss LambdaMOO politics.

Dawn's posted log may indeed have affected public opinion about ElseMOO, or at least bolstered a generally shared view about Else-MOO. A reporter came to EM one day in late 1994 to interview Ray about the history of EM. A huge crowd gathered to listen and kibitz.[23] The reporter brought with him expectations based on LambdaMOO's public perception of EM as a place where conspiracies are concocted and cabals meet to discuss how to "rule LambdaMOO from orbit." There were differences of opinion among the regulars present about how to portray their political activities, sometimes even semantic ones. Ray suggested that it was easy to believe, as some on LambdaMOO do, that the wizardly response to one uproar on LambdaMOO (the Mr. Bungle "netrape" case, Dibbell 1993) was "planned in a smoke-filled back room," i.e., on EM by some secret group, while Karen and others argued with that image because it suggested conspiracy plots that they didn't want associated with EM. Ray countered by saying that in fact a bunch of friends on EM discussing "how to deal with something" occurring on LambdaMOO is not so different from the popular image of a "power elite" cabal working on EM. (After some argument over semantics, Ray concluded, "Nobody speaks for this place. As you can tell, we can't agree."[24]) In part, this was an argument over community ideology and associated imagery (Hummon 1990) regarding the framing of conversation.

What is the status of a log? Certainly Dawn and Ray were treating logs as evidence of some kind, attaching significance to off-the-cuff unedited spontaneous remarks, posting them and preserving them. Similar transcripts have shown up on other LambdaMOO lists from other players, and there is a general MUD tradition of posting secretly recorded logs of tinysex encounters to Usenet newsgroups about MUDs. The response is usually hostile—logs are spammy (containing much irrelevant conversation) and easily edited, making their status as "proof" uncertain. They also threaten the collective understanding of MUDs as

---

[23] Much of my analysis of the events leading to the Shutdown was inspired by Ray's version of events, particularly the culture clash between LambdaMOO-style government and building policies and the more old-fashioned ("like a Random and Moira MUD") centralized wizardocracy on EM in the early days.

[24] However, it's still significant—and a source of tension on EM—that Ray is frequently the one asked to speak for EM history.

"off-the-record" escapes from real life, Oldenburg's "third places" away from home and work (Oldenburg 1997) where people go to hang out. In reality, logging is not uncommon on MUDs. Special "on-the-record" meetings, like the Tuesday Night Cafe series of meetings that formerly met on MediaMOO, are logged and made available for people who couldn't be there. Some people save logs of interesting conversation— Tom saved a log of his first conversation with ls about running EM on a machine at RNU, for instance. On Seashore MUSH, isolated quotes (taken out of context) are regularly saved by people in quote files, for later pasting into MUD "quotefests" for their humor value. On LambdaMOO and EM, players send quotes to the mailing list *qooc (short for "quote out of context")—usually comments that can be read as sexual innuendo, which irritates or bores some EM regulars.[25]

Because most MUDders use a client to MUD with, and clients often come with logging facilities, saving text is easy. Many regulars on EM use an Emacs client, allowing the buffer to grow huge before the process must be restarted, which provides a temporary record for reference. The MOO habit of pasting past quotes as a way to bring into focus comments that were overlooked or ignored depends on the existence of this record of recent history (see chapter 4). A frequent visitor to ElseMOO once commented, "The scariest thing about you guys is the way you manipulate long-past scrollback with speed and ease."

Zuboff's (1988) panoptic text is only a step away, given all this persistent text. Zuboff detailed how at "DrugCorp" the company culture was changed by the use of electronic mail and mailing lists; the casual joke became immortalized and carried a significance in text that it wouldn't have if it were spoken and ephemeral. People posting felt watched over by administrators. The Community Group watched over community and visitor behavior during times of tension on ElseMOO, sometimes idling in the Living Room in order to collect scrollback for later reading.[26]

If gossip acts as a dynamic repository of community memory (Merry 1984), the sometimes transitory, sometimes persistent MUD conversation forms another repository of community memory. And past MUD conversation is sometimes used in current conversation as documentation of events. Despite the ease with which MUD logs can be tampered

---

[25] Possibly because they're preserved on a mailing list, the ritual of an interactive quotefest doesn't occur on EM. Shelley, however, does occasionally save amusing quotes from people to paste later.

[26] However, the use of idle characters as recorders irritates some people. Not everyone wants to tailor their conversation for the audience of idle overhearers as well as the active participants.

with, logs are seen as powerful and potentially threatening texts.[27] Fully understanding MUD culture requires understanding the ambivalence of MUDders toward their texts, which remain poised between the transience of speech and the persistence of documents.

6.4 Conclusion

ElseMOO community members not only have special speech characteristics that define them as a speech community (as described in chapter 3), they show characteristics of other types of community as well. They may be considered a "community of memory" (Bellah et al. 1985), in that they remember and tell their origin stories.

The MUDders who frequent ElseMOO feel a strong sense of community identity, both as EMers and as members of other MUD groups. EM subgroups include the wizards, the programmers, and the "power elite," all groups that have high social status because of their programming abilities or technical powers in the MOO; another subgroup, the Mouldy Couch Club, was made up of both technical and less technical individuals who felt alienated from the community for various reasons, including their lack of access to face-to-face meetings among other Else-MOOers. Online community has resulted in offline relationships for many ElseMOOers—romantic relationships as well as job opportunities.

ElseMOO community members display consciousness of common goods, like the value of certain styles of conversation, as complaints about newbies' discourse practices illustrate. As Kollock and Smith (1996) point out, the conversational floor also constitutes a common good, which must be defended by all participants or coherent conversation cannot occur. As I described in chapter 4, the floor is often collaborative, and speakers must provide feedback in the form of back channels to signal understanding and attention. Conversation requires turn-level coordination as well as an understanding of acceptable discourse forms, such as those described in chapter 3. Language attitudes on ElseMOO (and LambdaMOO) are based on social network ties, status, and character age (all of which are interrelated).

Another common good is an understanding of audience, based on the known identities of regular characters and on awareness of who is in the room. This good may be threatened by malicious use of anonymous guest characters, as it was when Dawn used an ElseMOO guest to spy

---

[27]After I concluded my research, one person on ElseMOO expressed some concern about the logs I had recorded. He was not so much concerned with my future use of them as with their accessibility to anyone with malicious intent toward the community. (I consider the logs to be private, and they are no longer on a machine accessible over the Internet.)

on ElseMOO conversations about LambdaMOO. Understandings about audience (and related understandings about privacy) were threatened by Dawn's posting of ElseMOO conversation on LambdaMOO. Dawn's expulsion from ElseMOO (the ultimate social sanction on a MUD) can be considered a defense of ElseMOO's boundary against an outsider who threatened the common good of the MOO's conversation space.

Collective action by the community as a whole is difficult when power is unevenly distributed among wizards, programmers, and non-programmers. However, responding to the unhappiness signaled by the Mouldy Couch Club, a handful of wizards refined the political structure of the MOO. They created the Community Group, which included non-wizard members and was explicitly chartered with overseeing the happiness of the community. Despite the more-inclusive Community Group, some regulars still see the place as "run by wizards," by "Ray and his friends," or by the power elite (a concept inherited from LambdaMOO). The wizards involved in the reorganization also defined the community as primarily a place for technical projects rather than a social hangout.

Imagery and texts play an important role in defining the community, by specifying both what it is and what it would like to be. Some of these images, like that of Ray's house, are embodied in the artifacts that are the central geography of the MOO, and they send confusing messages about the location of power on the MOO. The text of "help manners" represents codified norms of behavior, the violation of which can result in temporary or permanent expulsion from the community. The text of "help purpose" defines the community as a place for technical projects, acting as a reminder to the founders of their early ideals and motivating current regulars to maintain them. The image of a house party was an important ideological motivator in the early days of the MOO, and is still reported in narratives about the founding of the community. The MOO is explicitly undemocratic and is ideologically defined in contrast to LambdaMOO.

Gossip can be considered a defining criterion for community, in that it indicates resource flow through a social network and reflects and reinforces established norms of behavior. Gossip is not trivial and malicious communication, but informal private communication concerning the conduct of absent persons and events. Such communication may be malicious and divisive, if that is the intent of the communicator, but it may also serve to strengthen social ties and influence social processes. Gossip in a virtual community requires mechanisms for private communication, persistent identities, and long-term relationships. Persistent identities and long-term relationships result in reputations associated with identities, reputations that are sensitive to gossip if they are associated with people well connected in the social network.

On ElseMOO, one conduit for gossip is the page command. A fairly dense social network is reflected in the diagram of page relationships, through which community members keep one another informed about events on the MUD as well as about personal information. The gossip network shows sub-networks corresponding to the "power elite" and newer members of the community, as well as relationships between people who frequent Seashore MUSH.

Just as language used in computer-mediated communication shows characteristics of both oral speech and written language (as reviewed in chapter 1), gossip in a MUD differs from face-to-face gossip because of the medium used. Documentary evidence, in the form of logs, is available to support reports of behavior, although direct quotation is understood as at least a minor breach of etiquette. Nevertheless, direct quotation does occur, particularly in one-on-one page conversations, where the behavior has a semi-licit flavor.[28] Mailing lists, the most persistent form of text in the MOO environment, are the MOO counterpart of the mass media, providing an "on-the-record" forum for public discussion; quotation of MOO conversation in these forums is seen as entirely inappropriate (with the exception of LambdaMOO dispute mailing lists, where recorded logs may be posted as evidence in a dispute). Interestingly, the ElseMOO social mailing lists were never forums for conflict and controversy the way the LambdaMOO mailing lists were, probably because most substantive social interaction on ElseMOO occurred in conversation (or on private committee mailing lists that were unreadable by the general population). The more centralized government on ElseMOO probably encouraged more informal forms of resistance through gossip, which is a classic form of resistance to hierarchy (Goodman and Ben-Ze'ev 1994).

---

[28]Quotation behavior, in my estimation, is more acceptable between individuals on very intimate terms, particularly when the impact of the quoted material is judged greater than the breach of etiquette involved in reporting it.

7

Postscript: Method and Ethics

In writing about cyberspace communities, the ethnographer must also grapple with data significantly different from that gathered in many other ethnographic sites, and with the often thorny problem of obtaining informed consent from research subjects. In most virtual communities, even establishing who the population is can be difficult, given the possibility of lurking, transient visitors and the communities' shifting, disputed boundaries, which are rarely reified in anything other than words.[1] MUDs as sites for ethnographic research offer further, specific challenges, because many MUDders are wary of being "studied" by researchers. In the next sections, I will discuss my own decisions with respect to MUDs as sites, my data collection methods, general issues about ethics in research on computer-mediated communication, and the impact of my final writeup on my informants.

Skeggs (1995) argues that ethnography is not itself a method, but rather a combination of different methods. It may be considered a theory of the research process, producing an account of context, usually based on fieldwork conducted over a prolonged period of time within the settings of the participants. Ethnography usually involves study of the "other"; it involves the researcher in both observation and participation, and includes an account of the development of relationships between the researcher and the researched. It focuses on experience and practice, frequently with culture as its central focus, and it treats participants as microcosms of wider structural processes. Other methods that expand the context, such as historical documentation and statistical analysis, are certainly compatible with ethnographic methods (Skeggs, p. 192).

---

[1] Certainly some of these problems hold for the study of physical communities as well, but it bears stressing that they are complexities that the online researcher must face immediately.

297

Although ethnography is largely method for Skeggs, she argues that all ethnography is informed by theory even if theory is not acknowledged. Theory informs crucial methodological decisions, such as reasons for choosing ethnography, which methods are used, who the researcher(s) and informants are, what relationship exists between them, what writing strategies are used, and how the informants are represented (p. 193). During my fieldwork, I progressed from an interest in abstract linguistic phenomena to a more general fascination with the social and discourse complexities of the socio-technical system I was studying; I wrestled with ethical issues involving online data collection and got repeatedly lost in a sea of ethnographic data I wasn't prepared to sort out properly. Despite the remembered chaos of my research period, I appreciate Skeggs's acknowledgment that theory informs method, and I hope to give some sense of the depth of my concern for appropriate ethics and methods in this chapter. As Skeggs says, "Sensitivity to, and responsibility for, power relations, representation, and dissemination are, I would argue, far more important than issues of which method to use. And attention to the processes by which we produce our research and theories is far more important than the concern with 'getting it right'" (p. 203). This sentiment is particularly appropriate where online research is concerned.

Incorporating the first person viewpoint in the ethnographic text is crucial for conveying the researcher's thought processes and assumptions and their basis in experience. However, first person accounts are often seen as "unscientific" by audiences not versed in the latest reflexive anthropology methods. In Cherny 1995d I was extremely restrained in my use of first person pronouns. I hope this chapter, reflecting on my methodological choices after three years have passed, can partly correct that omission.

7.1   Context for MUD Research

In 1995, MUDs had had two years of active press and a growing amount of research attention, and writing anything about MUDs had become a delicate business. MUDders in some MUDs are sensitive to the impact of attention from naive outsiders investigating on behalf of the popular press, and some MUDders are alienated by research interests.

Reporters are viewed with suspicion because they can't necessarily be trusted to have MUDders' interests at heart in their stories, or to understand the communities as well as insiders do. It was common in some CMC forums for news articles on MUDs to be typed in for discussion. After discussion of the *Atlantic* article on MUDs (Leslie 1993), a poster on rec.games.mud.misc criticized the reporter for "that damnably annoying media trend to blatantly pigeon-hole *anyone* with some degree of competency in handling a computer as a 'hacker'" (rec.games.mud.misc, August 19, 1993). MUDders are a broader section of the public than the term "hackers" ordinarily refers to. The focus on "netsex" (or interactive textual expressions of sexual actions) in several articles in the popular press was particularly alienating to many (e.g., Quittner 1994). One MUDder on LambdaMOO asked, "Why is it that articles about LambdaMOO are always about either cybersex or [the Archwizard]'s other project (the graphicy, windowy one he mentioned in the Wired interview)? How come nobody ever writes an article about the chaotic social structure of LambdaMOO or our incredible diversity?"[2] (Message 2678 on *life-issues).

Paranoia about reporters is most extreme on Seashore, a MUD populated by long-time MUDders ("dinos"), because of a bad experience with a journalist. One MUDder told me that every time she visited Seashore she was asked if she was a reporter by one paranoid old-timer who forgot who she was between her visits. The same old-timer told me that he dislikes anyone profiting off MUDs. Benefits to one's research career are a form of profit, certainly, a conundrum I have no good answer to.

That reporters will publish the site addresses of MUDs (usually without permission from the communities) is a serious worry, because large numbers of tourists coming online to see the sights can be exasperating and destructive. Newbies often don't understand that there are local standards of behavior, a fact usually not conveyed by articles celebrating the Net's potential for freeing people from their everyday constraints. (See Marvin and Schultze 1977 on the destruction of CB communities by incoming newbies after mass media attention.) According to LambdaMOOers, LambdaMOO's enormous population growth in 1994 was a direct result of media coverage, including the publishing of its address. The drain on resources resulted in a community decision in the summer of 1994 to limit population growth by restricting the creation of new characters.

Researchers can inadvertently cause population growth, even after their best efforts to protect the communities in their publications. Reid (1996) describes how her early MUD research (Reid 1994a, 1994b) on a community eager to participate affected that community after her work was made available on the Internet. On a MUD intended for survivors of sexual abuse, subjects were eager to be quoted and gave far more intimate detail than she felt comfortable reporting. Readers of her

---

[2]Articles on such topics are subject to other criticism, of course.

work (some of them other social scientists wanting to study the same community) asked her for referrals to the administrator of the MUD, and the number of users on the MUD increased, threatening its existing social networks. She concludes that although "adverse consequences can result despite even the best and most well-meaning of efforts, we must not allow this to excuse us from the obligation to make these efforts" (p. 173).

Research, whether conducted by insiders or outsiders, is subject to critical examination by MUDder informants. The MUDder who manages to convince her English teacher or sociology professor to accept a paper on MUDs may be seen as acceptable—even subversive, for managing to dress up a hobby as respectable work. But the researcher or academic who builds a reputation on them is another matter. Xerox PARC scientist Pavel Curtis is regarded with some wariness by many MUDders because he has been credited in the media with inventing MOOs (Bennahum 1994) (despite his own attempts to communicate that he did not, I gather) or popularizing MUDs; in fact MUDs existed well before Curtis began LambdaMOO in 1990, and a MUD hacker named Stephen White created the first MOO server and the first version of the programming language. Appropriation of MUDs by industry for computer-supported cooperative work (CSCW) is another topic evoking ambivalence in MUDders. Curtis and Nichols' 1993 paper "MUDs Grow Up" describes Jupiter, a MUD augmented with video and audio for collaborative work. Many MUDders would argue that this type of MUD misses the point: MUDs are recreational, and they are fun because of the textual play in them.[3] Even the title of this paper seems to denigrate the rich tradition of MUDding in text, the communities of users who built worlds and interactive art purely for fun (see Marvin 1983 on the significance of play with communications media). According to MUDders, the researchers who speak for them by virtue of having the attention of the press or being funded by prestigious labs don't necessarily "get it" and often appear to be colonizing land already well populated by MUDders who do understand what's "cool" about MUDs.

Paccagnella (1997) points out that "many of the most interesting virtual communities are also very proud of their exclusive culture. A stranger wanting to do academic research is sometimes seen as an unwelcome arbitrary intrusion" (p. 5). He doesn't explore the ethical relationship between the researcher and the informants who resist being

---

[3]On the other hand, many MUDders, particularly from the community I participated in, are themselves seeking and sometimes getting jobs working on CSCW MUD projects or industrial MUD development.

researched. Seldom is an entire group (or "community") united in its opinion of academic research either in general or in specific cases. Researchers must navigate individuals' needs and the group needs. These may be in conflict, requiring complex judgment calls.

Nevertheless, academics are wandering into existing MUDs in growing numbers, often unaware of community mores about recording ("logging," in text forums) without permission or of the academic debates about online research ethics. The "natives" in MUDs are increasingly cognizant and wary of outsiders' research agendas. As Rosaldo (1989) reports, "Such terms as *objectivity, neutrality,* and *impartiality* refer to subject positions once endowed with great institutional authority, but they are arguably neither more nor less valid than those of more engaged, yet equally perceptive, knowledgeable social actors. Social analysis must now grapple with the realization that its objects of analysis are also analyzing subjects who critically interrogate ethnographers—their writings, their ethics, and their politics" (p. 21). The researcher entering a cyberspace community must grapple with community members who are often aware of and interested in what is being written about them and capable of putting up barriers to protect themselves from such attention. Any writeup of work involving such interested actors that doesn't address these problems is incomplete.

7.2 Entrance Conditions and Disclosure

Like many students who become interested in CMC, I was a participant in ElseMOO before I formed a research plan centering on that community. Being a participant first, and sharing the community's response to much media coverage of MUDs, I no doubt had an easier entree as a researcher. Also, my stated focus on language study and my early papers probably made my work more acceptable. However, my increasing interest in ethnographic writing and community history caused complications.

My research interests evolved over time, from an initial study of gendered language and behavior patterns (Cherny 1995a) into a dissertation. The community was informed of my research, and read my intermediate papers and one dissertation chapter draft (the chapter on ethnographic background, parts of which are included in chapters 2 and 6 of this book). I discussed my work with them, posted on an internal mailing list notifying them, and changed my character description to indicate my research intentions:

A short woman in a black dress who wishes she were reading something trashy everytime she opens an academic journal. Her shadow is in the shape of an unfinished dissertation on MOO conversation structure, so she may be logging conversation around here, just so you know...

I don't feel that simply putting a statement of research interests in one's character description is sufficient to inform subjects of ongoing research; not everyone passing through the MUD reads the character descriptions.[4] However, other methods are problematic as well: people may miss mail postings or not be present for discussions. Multiple methods have the best chance of reaching everyone it is most important to reach. For one paper, I obtained consent by email to quote certain speakers. This is another potential method for obtaining informed consent, but it depends on a closed, predetermined set of informants being known in advance and on the informants' willingness to reveal their "true" identities and email addresses to the researcher (not a given in most MUDs, where the users' real-life identities are hidden). It's also difficult in most online communities to identify exactly who to obtain informed consent from, given the different commitments of different individuals to the group and the sometimes high percentage of transient users. In the early stages of research, it's extremely difficult to know who needs to be informed and how best to inform them of the research process. An initial period of exploratory participation may make this easier.

Certainly asking the administrator of a particular MUD for permission to study it—and its resident community—does not seem a sufficiently nuanced approach to obtaining informed consent. (Reid [1996] reports that she did this originally, assuming the administrator was in a position to speak for the community as a whole. This assumption was apparently shared by the administrator and users, but she has subsequently questioned it. Allen [1996b] also reports meeting with the administrator of LambdaMOO and informing him of her research intent, presumably because she also thought this was appropriate.) Although most of cyberspace is at the whim of the technical elite (the people with their fingers on the machine buttons), it is certainly incumbent upon ethnographers to question that location of power and to refrain from reifying it further by granting the system administrator decision-making power on such an issue for the entire resident community of

---

[4]On the other hand, it's perhaps reasonable to assume that the regulars will all eventually read each other's descriptions at some point. At one point, a visitor who apparently had just read my description pasted it to the occupants of the room, perhaps indicating that he was interested in discussing the fact that I was doing research, but no one took up the topic. I took this to suggest that the others there were all quite familiar with my research agenda.

users. One of the uncomfortable implications of having an administrator's permission to study a MUD is that the researcher has potential access to programmatic tools with which she can observe, collect statistics, and otherwise obtain data that an ordinary participant would not have access to (Allen reports using such data, although of an unspecified nature; see also Schiano 1997). I am exceedingly uncomfortable with such administrator-sanctioned and -enabled data collection methods, and never pursued the possibility of wizardly statistics gathering myself. Obviously this severely limited the conclusions I could draw about the frequency of use of various speech commands on ElseMOO.[5] Every researcher must make trade-offs between generality and specificity according to her ethical concerns, and every researcher's work must be assessed in light of these trade-offs. I failed to be a fully "scientific" linguist and rise beyond the specifics of my logs because of my anthropological scruples, and on some days this decision seems strange to me now.

ElseMOOers have begun referring to "drive-by researchers," researchers who pop in briefly to ask a few questions. One self-proclaimed "traveling anthropologist" came to the MOO and said, "Tell me what's deviant here." Tom responded, "Surely that's for you to determine." The "drive-by researcher," often a student working on a short-term paper, has become increasingly common on MUDs and also, I believe, in other CMC forums. Lurking without participating is noticeable and ultimately difficult on MUDs; on the other hand, because MUDs are highly interactive, a researcher may develop a lasting relationship with the community and engage in a dialogue with informants about ethics, research methods, and representations of the community in her writings (see Allen 1996a). I believe researchers who put in sufficient effort, who develop a presence and show some commitment to the community, will have an easier time gaining informed consent for their research. However, as my own experience showed, commitment to the community may leave one's research hostage to the community's approval. In the current climate of methodological uncertainty in anthropology, compounded with the uncertainties of online data collection, trying to navigate conflicting needs and establish where one's ultimate loyalties lie can be stressful and traumatic. Since I finished my research, I've read work from other disciplinary backgrounds discussing ethnographic work of various types on MUDs, including some that referred to ElseMOO (under different

---

[5] The counter that was created to track uses of Antisocial commands was fortuitously implemented by a curious ElseMOO wizard without any suggestion from me, and he made the data available to anyone interested.

names); other researchers were often less concerned than I was about community acceptance of their writing or about disguise of the community and its members. Most of these researchers weren't as accessible to the community as I made myself, or as vulnerable to the community's reaction to their work. In some cases, their work feels richer (and, occasionally, more lurid).

7.3   Data in Computer-Mediated Communication

Research on CMC, particularly research on Internet communities, offers a new set of challenges: new types of data, new kinds of reference materials, new forms of publishing. Anyone (with appropriate access, of course) may publish on the World Wide Web. Increasing numbers of papers are being written by MUDders about their experiences (e.g., Carlstrom 1992; McRae 1996; Rosenburg 1992). Ordinarily, academic writing is at least superficially in debate form: previous literature is reviewed and dismissed for whatever inadequacies or errors it contains, and a "better" theory or story is offered instead. What is the appropriate ethnographic approach to previous work by the MUD community, which is articulate, educated, and speaking for itself, but speaking to audiences and with intents that are often not easily discerned by the reader?

Many documents, like Wetmore 1993, have the character of casual texts intended for friends and are filled with in-jokes and asides rather than exhaustive historical research for outsiders' consumption. There are ever-growing archives of MUD references on the Web for diverse audiences, MUD logs, papers by MUDders or by students or by other researchers. There are newsgroups dedicated to MUD discussion; there are mailing lists (run by MUDders for MUDders and run by academics about MUDders). Some refereed journals do publish on the Web (the Journal of Computer-Mediated Communication, for one), and certainly there are copies of refereed papers available on researchers' home pages; but a large percentage of documents on the Web are informal, unreviewed papers, intended for a variety of different audiences. Documents posted on Web pages may change or disappear at any time, making them unstable reference materials at best. CMC texts are malleable, editable, destroyable with a minor sequence of keystrokes. The interactivity of much CMC gives less credibility to the texts produced; although hypothetically permanent, their significance often lasts only days (Aycock and Buchignani 1995).

However, despite the difficulty of using Internet documents (Web pages and newsgroup postings), I believe the researcher studying Internet community must carefully review these potential sources. The half-life of Internet communities is short, the Internet changes character quickly, and there's a large time lag in print publishing—the researcher who limits herself to refereed journal articles because Web documents are unstable and difficult to evaluate is doomed to miss an enormous lode of reference material.

In researching this book, I have used MUDder online documents and papers about MUDs in MUD archives (referee-reviewed or not), and followed some discussion on mailing lists and newsgroups about MUDs. Because of the transience of Web documents, references cannot be guaranteed.

Logs

Most of my data has come from normal MUD conversation; my logs constitute a year's worth of participant-observation on ElseMOO (and occasionally LambdaMOO), about twenty-five megabytes worth. Like many MUDders on EM, I was usually connected to the MUD while working during the day, so each day's log consists of about eight hours of intermittent activity and idleness on the MUD.

Fieldnotes, the chief working tool of the ethnographer, are texts, subject to multiple interpretations (Sanjek 1990); even the ethnographer must interpret them as a reader after the fact, a process that may be influenced by experiences since they were recorded. At first look, a textually mediated interaction like MUD dialog provides a good opportunity for recording interactions. Initially I thought my logs of MUD conversation were the perfect fieldnotes; but months into my research, after my newbie bafflement had abated, I realized I had little record of my experiences of confusion and alienation except for the text record of what I said on the MUD and how MUDders reacted to me. As an experienced member trying to interpret those logs, I must reconstruct my own initiation into the speech community.[6]

The conventional ethnographer's authority comes from "being there" and being able to convey that experience successfully; but since there is no "there" in a CMC forum, what are the requirements for fieldwork? Even in a synchronous forum like a MUD, the text can be saved and read later; does the rereading constitute being there? I would argue that it does not, since the experience of timing and the feel of the text flow importantly influence the perception of the event (which is another

---

[6]I have some handwritten notes on early logs, and email to a friend who MUDded at the time, as well. I made notes selectively about my responses to events on LambdaMOO mailing lists, but they were lost during a move to another machine caused by quota problems.

reason that logs fail to capture the precise event). Furthermore, participation in the real exchange is important in understanding how it compels and affects the real lives of the community members (Quittner 1994). I have therefore been present and active during all of my research, rather than using "listening devices" to record conversation, or leaving my connection open but idle and saving my "scrollback" as data.[7]

In retrospect, I believe that my reluctance to fall "idle" in public rooms and save the data limited me both as a researcher and as a participant. I do not have many daily logs that I can extract good statistical data from for certain analyses, e.g., a profile of activity in one MUD room over a long period of time. Moreover, many MUDders fall idle during conversations, and they may remain idle for hours; on becoming active again, they may read recent conversational context and comment on it, becoming almost retroactive participants in the events they missed. Although idling does cause critical comment when too many people idle for too long in the main conversation rooms on EM, in practice it is tolerated up to a point. The option of intermittently taking part in the conversation and intermittently idling allows one to take part in the ebb and flow of conversation more fluidly than if one leaves the room entirely to idle somewhere private. My scruples about logging when I wasn't able to fully participate prevented me from moving in and out of conversation easily; instead I had to explicitly rejoin the group when I felt I had time to commit (and I was usually ignorant of the current topic of conversation, unless someone had paged me with a teaser precis). When my workload was bad, I spent entire days idling somewhere, with only an occasional page conversation breaking up my idleness. Toward the end of my research I developed a very bad typing injury, which made it still more difficult for me to participate fully, and I became almost permanently idle on the MUD, a regular non-participant. (Interestingly, it was still extremely difficult to stop connecting entirely—the occasional page conversation, combined with listing player locations and groups on the MUD, made me feel that I was still in contact with the community in some important way—important to *me*, at any rate.)

In addition to the logs, I have conducted a few surveys via MOO mail, asking both focused questions on specific topics and more general questions inviting broader answers: for instance, investigating users' demographic background and polling opinions. I also read mailing lists on LambdaMOO and ElseMOO regularly, and some of those more public, seemingly on-the-record lists formed the basis for much of the history

---

[7]For interesting community response to being "recorded" for research purposes by an automatic device, the reader is pointed to the mailing list *research on LambdaMOO.

and one of the conflicts I discussed in chapter 6. I will discuss the relative notions of public and private data further in the next section.

After some time doing participant-observation, when I was closer to a conception of what topics would be addressed in my writeup, I conducted some informal online private and public "interviews" addressing issues like the history of the Mouldy Couch Club and the origins of many speech routines on the MUD. (Many of the comments on the Antisocial commands in chapter 3 came from the group discussion generated when I went through the commands and asked for origin and usage stories.)

Although I socialized with a handful of MUDders "in real life" and talked to several more on the telephone, my only recording was done in the MUD context. I did not have the resources to fund systematic face-to-face interviews, given the geographical dispersion of the ElseMOOers, but ideally such interviews would be a part of any ethnography of an online community, particularly of a community like ElseMOO in which many participants have met each other and socialize face-to-face as well (see Kendall 1998).

The researcher working on CMC, using logs or posts to mailing lists and newsgroups, is always at risk of drowning in data. Data management is a serious issue that shouldn't be underestimated. As I said above, I took far too few notes as I went along, and when it came time to look for a particular linguistic phenomenon or find a particular type of interaction, I faced an enormous number of dated but unindexed computer files. (I did, however, take notes on the contents of mailing lists as I read through them; this proved invaluable.) My programming skills were sufficient to enable me to write Perl scripts to search my logs for occurrences of phenomena, to do rudimentary statistical analysis on features of the conversation, and to search for information like room locations, my movements on the MUD, the number of participants in conversations, etc. As Paccagnella (1997) says, one of the great opportunities of CMC data is the possibility of combining quantitative analysis with qualitative analysis. Doing both well is a true challenge. I'm afraid my lack of proper data management at the start meant that I relied too heavily on statistical and programmatic data analysis later; and my limited programming and statistical skills constrained my quantitative analysis as well.

7.4 Privacy and Ethics Issues

7.4.1 Public vs. Private

Many of the issues that concern social scientists in studying CMC are also matters of concern and debate in the daily lives of CMC users. Are

CMC forums public or private spaces? Usenet, with its high percentage of non-posting "lurkers" (McLaughlin, Osborne, and Smith 1995), might seem like a public forum, but the posters on alt.sexual.abuse.recovery may not feel that way. Rightly or wrongly, the posters and readers on a newsgroup or in a chat room may have expectations about the group's members and their agendas for reading or participating. Understanding what those expectations are is a crucial part of the research process. Unfortunately, this presents the researcher with a chicken-and-egg problem in deciding how to approach an online group advertising a research intent. Ethics for research as well as for participation are still evolving.

Most researchers concerned about informants' privacy and the ethics of data collection are often uncertain about what stance to take toward data collected online. "The ease of covert observation, the occasional blurry distinction between public and private venues, and the difficulty of obtaining the informed consent of subjects make cyberresearch particularly vulnerable to ethical breaches by even the most scrupulous scholars" (Thomas 1996, p. 108). The 1996 issue of *The Information Society* devoted to this topic illustrated contrasting perspectives, from the position that maximal effort should be made to protect subjects, since even "public" arenas online (like Usenet) are often host to postings more appropriate for private consumption (King 1996), to a relativist position that the type of research done may not be potentially damaging and therefore privacy concerns are not so critical (e.g., in linguistic work on discourse structure, Herring 1996b), to the postmodern position that ethics are locally determined in conjunction with subjects involved (Allen 1996a). Paccagnella 1997 reports the conclusion reached by the "project H. research group," a team of researchers who collaborated in 1993–94 on a quantitative study of electronic discussion: they concluded that they would not seek permission for recording and analysis of publicly posted messages (although individual, institution, and list identities would be shielded). Paccagnella classes "publicly accessible IRC channels" with messages posted on newsgroups as examples of public discourse.

The most extreme position on group protection is represented by King (1996) and Waskul and Douglass (1996). They argue that participants in online communities sometimes act according to a perception of privacy even in apparently highly public settings (like newsgroups). The very accessibility of many online groups makes distinctions between public and private that are based on cultural constructs of the physical world (space, walls, doors, for example) inapplicable. King argues for initially treating all electronic communications as "private," in order to protect informants from unforeseen harm, especially due to their potential perception of privacy. However, he recognizes a continuum and suggests that "the lower the level of group accessibility and the higher the degree of perceived privacy, the more care must be taken to avoid harming group members" (p. 126).

Herring (1996b) counters this position with the argument that we should instead recognize the de facto public nature of most CMC and declare such varieties public by default, citing mailing lists, newsgroups, chat channels, and MUDs as examples that are all generally public. She states that since private varieties of most of these communications forums are possible (lists requiring a list owner's approval to join, private chat channels and MUD rooms), the onus is on the administrators of the systems to make them private—and she discounts simple statements that a group is private as ineffectual without the technical means to protect it. She feels that users need to be educated about the default "public" nature of their communication in the absence of such technical protections, and about the risks this public nature presents for them; meanwhile, considerate researchers must shield participants who discuss sensitive topics in public, unprotected forums.

She acknowledges that this position assumes that participants in online forums are primarily responsible for protecting their own privacy. I find this position troubling, at least at this point in Internet development; users of the Internet vary in their understanding of the technology they use, not to mention their understanding of the implications of a large lurking audience, and of the technical options available to protect them from perhaps unimaginable situations (e.g., publication of their words in an academic forum). Further, in this scenario responsibility really lies with the list owner or administrator of an online forum, since she is the one who implements technological privacy protection for the group. I can imagine situations in which the group is divided about what efforts to make to protect privacy, particularly since the technical implementation of privacy usually severely restricts access even to legitimate new members who are not a threat to the group's privacy. As a researcher sensitive to the conversation and to the group as a whole, I would be uncomfortable deciding that a mailing list was public—for the purposes of recording and reproducing its contents in research—solely because the list owner didn't screen all applicants. (Note the relevance of this concern to the issue of who owns "informed consent" for a group—the list owner or administrator, or members of the group themselves.)

The case of MUDs is even more complicated. Most MUDs are not simplistically classifiable as public space; MUDs often have some rooms that are clearly private (for instance, lockable or with access restrictions). And just as different rooms on MUDs may have different informal or formal access policies, MUDs as a whole may have different policies about access. If there is a continuum of public and private spaces on the Net, different MUDs fall all along it. Some MUD administrators make efforts to limit incoming population by preventing the address of the MUD from appearing in widely distributed MUD listings, such as the recurrent posting on rec.games.muds.misc, or on Web pages. This was the policy on ElseMOO, because large numbers of newbies were viewed as disruptive to the existing community. However, newcomers were welcome in small numbers, especially if they had gotten the address from someone familiar with the MUD, in an informal referral process. Often MUDs have guest characters with limited functionality that allow access to some rooms on the MUD, but in order to get full access a user must go through a registration process. This registration process may involve screening by a human or may be automated, but it is still intended to limit registered numbers in some way.

I found a great deal of evidence that MUD users indeed operate with a perception of privacy, or at least a preconception of what audience they expect in certain rooms on the MUD. The Dawn incident is an example of a challenge to those assumptions, when an outsider from another MUD recorded conversation in what might be considered a public room (the main gathering spot). Chapter 6 shows how MUDders themselves continually debate the public/private status of conversation in MUD rooms. Users who confess that they maintain archives of log files are viewed with suspicion because of past misuse of such logs. MUDders themselves debate whether MUD logs are "evidence" of anything, whether their conversation is private, whether it ought to be "published" on mailing lists, on Usenet, or in print. In one verdict on this matter, LambdaMOO users voted to add a notice to the connection screen of LambdaMOO asking that researchers and journalists obtain permission to quote conversations before publishing them, despite the apparently rather public nature of the MOO (with its enormous population and traffic). (Smith 1992 discusses the Well's policy that posters own their own words: posters make their own decisions about use of their contributions outside of Well forums. This policy has protected contributors and encourages use of the system, particularly the private forums.)

Notions of "public" and "private" are relative to local cultures and expectations about audiences and uses of data (primarily by the ordinary audience of local participants, and secondarily by researchers, a significant minority). Analogies between public behavior in Western urban settings—e.g., behavior appropriate to a sidewalk cafe as opposed to a bedroom—and behavior on mailing lists or newsgroups are strained at best. Until the posting population understands what public and private mean for postings, readers, and potential audiences, researchers can't hope to find the basis for a consistent ethics, and an ethical policy that piggybacks on offline cultural understandings will never take into account the growing multicultural Internet population.

7.4.2 Protecting Identities

The researcher may protect the privacy of individuals and the community by a number of different mechanisms. She may disguise individuals' identities and the name of the community, and remove or disguise possibly compromising details from her discussion and from the content of example discourses. She may pursue a number of ethnographic techniques, like creating composite characters out of individuals in the community, fictionalizing certain details, and breaking identifiable individuals into multiple identities in the writeup. The extent to which she works to protect the group depends on what she perceives the risk to be and what her research field dictates she should do. There is an essential conflict between protecting identities and giving credit for authorship (e.g., under the assumption that CMC is subject to copyright; see Herring 1996b on this conflict). Ethnographers have traditionally chosen protecting identities over providing full citation.

Most MUDs make a practice of allowing pseudonymous "character" names instead of real names, which might seem to be sufficient in itself to protect MUD players from invasion of privacy. This simple, first-pass analysis is a naive one, however. I saw the effects of the much-discussed *Village Voice* article, in which real character names were used (Dibbell 1993), when guests on LambdaMOO asked questions of one of the "netrape" victims. Use of real character names can affect the MUDders' experiences in their community, e.g., if the researcher reveals information that they would not want their fellows to know. In this book, the names of MUD characters in the ElseMOO community have all been changed, and when I discuss articles posted on the World Wide Web and Usenet I reference pseudonyms instead of the real character names used in those posts and articles.[8]

I also disguised the names of active MUDs, with the exception of LambdaMOO, which, on account of its size—about 8900 registered characters as of August 1995—and the publicity it has already received, seems more plausibly a "public" place now. This reasoning matches that in Allen 1996a and 1996b. Because the LambdaMOO mailing lists I used were available for ftp outside the MOO on a Xerox ftp site, and

---

[8]Mnookin (1996), in contrast, discusses postings on mailing lists on LambdaMOO with full citations to original articles and authors. However, she does not provide an ethnographic discussion, which for me complicated the author citation problem.

because the reading public on LambdaMOO itself is so large, I decided to treat the list posts as quotable without the authors' explicit permission, but I have disguised the authors' identities. I have also selectively disguised the names of some of the mailing lists, since as Allen (1996a) points out, it is easy for a determined reader to do a text search on a list archive and find out which disguise corresponds to which character identity.

Of course, my decision to quote but disguise authors, and my use of partially disguised citation information, may be a useless middle road between privacy protection and research rigor. Research rigor usually demands that the researcher provide a trail of supporting evidence sufficient for another researcher to duplicate her efforts and reach similar conclusions from the data. This is Herring's (1996b) justification for naming the academic mailing lists on which she did her gender research. Privacy protection, on the other hand, means thwarting just such a research duplication. However, the ethnographer must be pragmatic about how much protection is needed and how much effort anyone is likely to take to uncover identities and locations. In my case, it was necessary to avoid references to papers, Web pages, and postings that would reveal the identities of my informants.

Although I didn't create composite characters or other such fictional devices to protect individuals further, in retrospect I should have done so; this mechanism would have protected the individuals from their fellows better than the use of new pseudonyms alone, since most EM community members (and people close to the community) were able to guess identities in my dissertation. I released a draft of my chapter on ethnographic background prematurely, because I yielded to pressure from one concerned individual who wanted it made available sooner rather than later; I was still conducting discussions with several of the key informants about their portrayal in it, and hadn't adequately understood some of their privacy concerns by the time I released it for general discussion. After release of that draft chapter and ensuing heated discussions about its contents (see below), I broke one identity up into two for the final writeup and for this book.

Despite my decision to err on the side of identity protection, I spent some time concerned about whether I ought to be giving citation credit to the authors of the often wonderful posts I was quoting.[9] On LambdaMOO there is a well-developed tradition of impassioned (and often tiring) debate about virtual government and standards of behavior (e.g., the debate about "netrape" and how to define it on the peti-

---

[9]I'm indebted to Mimi Ito for first raising this concern to me in 1994.

tion *p:antirape; see Mnookin 1996 for an excellent discussion). The participants, many of them among the original LambdaMOO settlers, are usually articulate and intelligent, and they speak from convictions both political and personal. It seems presumptuous to speak for them by paraphrasing all their contributions, and changing their character names removes any connection they have as authors to their words. Some MUDders have even attached copyright notices to poetry they've written in MUDs or to text generated from interactive object manipulation. For one early paper, I obtained permission to use real character names to credit authors of interactive text objects, but ended up changing those same characters' names when quoting MUD dialogue, which felt "different" to me (less edited, perhaps). But the decision was not a comfortable one, and I've since decided to change all names for consistency's sake. Some MUDders did express the desire to be credited for their words, but since others were unsure about wanting their names associated with certain quotes I used, it seemed safer to change all names rather than deal with each person on a quote-by-quote basis. Using a mix of real character names and pseudonyms would be more confusing to the reader, and would also make it appear that there were twice as many characters involved as there are.

7.5 Reading the Writing, "Informed" Consent, and After

The subject of informed consent is a vexing one in multiple dimensions. Just what does a community (or an individual) believe it has consented to, and what information does the researcher provide about the research process? How much negotiation between informants and researchers can there be or should there be during the research and then during the writeup? When the researcher's conclusions differ from what the community considers acceptable (because of politics or their differently positioned views of events), what are the researcher's responsibilities— to appease the community, or to satisfy more vague academic or professional requirements?

Reid (1996) reports that the MUD users she approached about her study were extremely eager to participate, and even "manufactured" quotable quotes for her. After her research publicized one MUD (despite her care not to identify it) and threatened the MUD's development with population growth, she decided that her informants' enthusiasm for her study could not be assumed to indicate knowledge and acceptance of the risks participation might entail. "No matter what measures we may take to protect our subjects from the onslaught of outside interest, the experience of scrutiny inherent in being involved in a research project may itself be damaging." However, she concludes that in choosing to conduct social science research "we have all presumably decided that the value of knowledge is at least sometimes greater than the value of personal safety" (p. 173).

Skeggs (1995) describes her research with a group of working-class women, and her evolution in thought as she was exposed to different academic writings. The women in her study rejected very basic categorizations, including that of "working-class," an identity they spent their lives fighting against. Answerable to academic demands, her writeup had to reflect her theoretical positioning and experiences, as well as her career's needs. She was concerned about alienating them with her representation of them, as well as potential risk to them from her revelations about their dealings with social services bureaus. Throughout the writing and research phases, she engaged them in dialogue, but there were unresolvable conflicts.

Allen (1996a) argues that we cannot know the perceptions of the participants in online forums with respect to the public or private nature of their interactions without engaging in a dialogue with informants. Even within a particular group, individual perceptions differ. Her own research, which consisted primarily of case studies of particular LambdaMOO users, involved ongoing dialogue with them about their representation in her work, which she facilitated by making drafts available during the process. Making drafts available to the population studied is one way of attempting to deal with "informing" the informants about research results—albeit after much of the research has been done already. I chose this route myself.

The benefits of a small study focusing on selected individuals, like Allen's, is obvious: the possibility for dialogue between researcher and informants about ethics and analysis is optimal, and concerns about obtaining informed consent from large, possibly transient populations largely disappear. However, even a study of an individual's experiences in a community can affect other members of the community, and the difficulty of obtaining informed consent from individuals who might be affected by the stories told still remains. Likewise, there remains the difficulty of obtaining informed consent for an unwritten, unforseeable analysis, which may also be uninterpretable by the informants because of the academic language it must appear in.

Rosaldo (1989) warns that our subjects' criticism may be "insightful, sociologically correct, axe-grinding, self-interested, or mistaken" (p. 50), just as criticism from colleagues may be. Processing and interpreting informants' criticism is a difficult feat in itself, quite apart from the possibility that they are axe-grinding or mistaken, since they are re-sponding to a text not intended for them as primary audience, and a text potentially confusing in its rhetorical style or political slant.

Skeggs (1995) notes that theory requires different language, drawing on concepts not used on a daily basis, and perhaps confusing or incomprehensible to informants. Brettel (1996) reports that in her history she drew comparisons that her informants found opaque or irrelevant, and that they considered these comparisons to be her most egregious error. The very act of doing research on a population positions the researcher differently from the population, gives her access to knowledge she wouldn't have as an ordinary participant, and requires a different rhetorical position because her audience is generally different from the population studied (although she may attempt to also speak to that population in some way). Brettel ends wondering if a single ethnographic text can ever successfully satisfy the diverse readership it receives.

Skeggs (p. 201) asks mournfully, "If the theorist can't theorize, why bother doing research?" Herring (1996b) argues that critical work cannot be done when the population being studied has final veto power over the researcher's analysis. There is a middle ground between discussing research writeup with informants and allowing them final veto power. The researcher who makes drafts available to the community for comment must make a judgment call about whose criticisms are valid (especially when reactions differ, as they inevitably will), keeping in mind both Rosaldo's warning and what release of the drafts may do to her position in and access to the community, especially if her analysis isn't favored. Such disagreements can be dangerous, particularly when her political positioning and those of her informants differ.

The Response to My Work

Although I had always intended to provide ethnographic background on the speech community, I informed my friends on ElseMOO when I began my research that my interest was largely linguistic. Certainly the word "linguistic" can mean many things, even to a linguist, a fact I didn't take into account when I began my research. My early papers used quotations of exchanges exemplifying the use of particular emotes or phrases, mostly de-contextualized, and mostly unthreatening to the community in their content. The more time I spent participating, however, the more importance I saw in the community context that helped define some of these linguistic practices. And language, of course, significantly defined the community as similar to and different from other communities on related MUDs.

When I wrote the ethnographic background chapter, I decided that it would not be fair to the community to report on many of the incidents that had occurred while I was a participant, because my linguistic agenda in their eyes did not give me permission to use my logs to report stories of political intrigue and personal conflict among community members. I therefore decided to tell a historical account of ElseMOO's development out of LambdaMOO, including one extended incident that occurred during my ethnography (the Dawn conflict), which involved the complicated relationship between the two MOOs and was made very public on LambdaMOO mailing lists. My quotations in the ethnographic chapter were taken from mailing lists and direct interviews.

My decision to tell the story of the Mouldy Couch Club, although it was only a rarely discussed historical incident when I arrived on ElseMOO, was not as innocuous as I expected. Histories are problematic in ways that I hadn't fully appreciated when I opted for this approach. The past is a cultural possession (Brettel 1996) which it can be dangerous to interpret or juxtapose with the present, particularly as an outsider. As Brettel (1996) notes in her reflection on her history's reception, "If selective memory reshapes history, selective reporting can reshape a text, and often does so for readership appeal" (p. 102). Selective reporting may also reshape history, I fear, and affect the present.

Making the story of the Mouldy Couch Club current again, making it public and a matter of discussion, and particularly making the social problems that led to the club's creation a matter of discussion, had ramifications. One person confessed publicly after reading the draft that he had had no idea such events were happening; I had the strong impression that at least one of the people in the room would have been happier if he hadn't found out. After the informant discussion of the chapter, discussion that largely centered on the Mouldy Couch Club (the most meaningful for the community, for various reasons), I noticed that a bunch of people were hanging out in the Dark Hole again. Its popularity lasted no more than a few weeks, but it felt significant. I had made an almost forgotten place and associated events significant, by selecting them for inclusion in my writeup. Hanging out there was an act of protest in itself (although of what exactly, I wasn't sure). I suppose I could read this as a sign that I touched a nerve, because some of the issues that caused the club's founding were still felt occasionally. Indeed, I thought the story was important because it illustrated some of the serious internal conflicts the community still wrestled with even two years later, when the club itself was almost never talked about. Utopian sentiment—what everyone wanted ElseMOO to be—may have been responsible for the fact that the Mouldy Couch Club was not publicly remembered; as Suttles (1972) says, "utopias are a powerful lure tempting us to reconstruct history" (p. 267).

But because the club represented painful alienation to some people, for them it was better forgotten, because to forget it meant to go on, get past it, heal the alienation. Some people believed the MOO had moved past that phase, and making it salient again perhaps made them question the degree to which things had changed. Some people achieved status through the report I wrote, became central in the only published history there is of the MOO, and other people received unwanted attention.

Certainly, release of my paper drafts and release of the ethnographic background chapter of my dissertation had an impact both on community behavior and on how I was regarded as a participant. After Cherny 1995a, which analyzed gender distributions of certain MUD emotes, my informants deliberately used those emotes in ways different from my analysis (often for humorous effect, and usually drawing my attention to them). I was relieved that I hadn't informed the community of my particular linguistic focus in that study. Similarly, after discussion of the tallies in the automatic counter that recorded usage of the Antisocial commands (after several months of its operation), some people tried to skew the frequencies of their favorite commands by automatically producing them in large numbers. (I didn't report numbers past that period, which is why my statistics cover such a short period of time.) Selective "informing" about linguistic research, in order to ensure cleaner data, seems inevitably necessary.

Months after I was finished with my dissertation work and had ceased saving logs, I found out that one member of the community had been doing some data analysis of his own, using logs of conversation. He had produced a graph of who had spoken to whom over a lengthy period of time in the Living Room. Because this was something I had been thinking about doing at one point, I had a page conversation with him about how he had generated it. I was then, as usual, idling somewhere away from the main party in the Living Room. I received a page or two from other people in the Living Room after my chat with him, and I realized that the group was discussing my interest in his graph. I joined the party and discovered significant concern about my interest and about data analysis in general. They were having a heated discussion about the use of such graphic illustrations and about what might be inferred from them, even speciously. His graph, which was labeled with real character names, showed a strong link between two characters who had had a long argument the night he was logging. Someone suggested that it was dangerous to reveal such a relationship in the graph, especially with identities visible. Someone might conclude, for instance, that two people were particularly good friends because they spoke to each other a lot (despite the fact that a protracted argument resulted in the same graphical relationship). Their anxiety seemed to focus on how relationships—the social networks—could be inferred from these statistical illustrations, perhaps erroneously. Of course, I was interested in exactly this myself.

Some of the extreme concern about my interest was probably because identities in my dissertation were not sufficiently disguised and my informants could figure out who was who. Saying that such a graph should have coded identities was insufficient to remove the risk they perceived. Arguing that graphical representations may be read incorrectly, or incorrect conclusions could be drawn from them, only added to their anxiety. And finally, there was another concern: did everyone have to be on guard against future disruptions from my publishing interests forever, or was I done? I decided that night that I was done, within certain bounds. Shortly after that, I stopped connecting, in an effort to make a cleaner break.

What bounds? I had already signed a book contract, but I decided that the book would not include significant new writing that dealt with details about the community's social nature, participants, or history.[10] Any new linguistic analysis I have performed was minimally invasive, using old logs, with maximal care in disguising identities and content of a revealing nature. My concern over content has prevented me from pursuing some new analyses. I haven't pursued my interest in patterns of directed speech use and how those might illuminate the social networks on the MUD, because of that last night's conversation.

7.6   Representational Challenges for the Ethnographer

Although many forms of presentation of ethnographic work are both valid and problematic on various fronts (see, e.g., Van Maanen 1988), in this book I took a roughly historical narrative approach to presenting issues that illustrate important elements of the community I participated in: the evolution of one MUD community out of another MUD community, boundary challenges from outsiders, norms of behavior emerging with respect to the public or private nature of text conversations in various contexts, identities and anonymity in dispute in the medium. The narrative approach allows the interactions between specific agents in the community and the social structures to be viewed in a temporal context, with the drama and disarray of real events visible (Rosaldo 1989).

---

[10]The discussion of gossip is new, but is based on a survey I did during my original research.

The decision to write something largely historical, as I said, was due to my concerns about what the community believed I was planning to write about, and my own evolution of interests as I participated over two years. My belief that this would be more acceptable than writing about recent events was certainly naive.

An ethnography is usually an account reflecting fieldwork done to give the researcher insight into the community's interpretive system. The "participant-observer" role adopted by most ethnographers is full of tensions, implying a "continuous tacking between the 'inside' and 'outside' of events: on the one hand grasping the sense of specific occurrences [. . .] empathically, on the other stepping back to situate these meanings in wider contexts" (Clifford 1983, p. 127). The conflict and contradictions in the role, and the multiple types of positionings by the researcher that are possible with respect to the community, are represented in the debates about textual authority by reflexive ethnographers (e.g., Marcus and Cushman 1982; Clifford 1983; Clifford and Marcus 1986; Rosaldo 1989). The ethnographer communicates authority in a text by giving evidence of significant fieldwork, choosing details to provide a sense of concrete reality experienced first-hand (Marcus and Cushman 1982). The ethnographer's attempt to speak for a culture is problematic; among other worries, she runs the risk of writing either an overly closed, neat account (as expected by most readers outside ethnography's theoretical debates) that represents only her own experiences and interpretations, or an account that is open-ended, ambiguous, and possibly confusing to the reader.

Describing a culture today no longer means representing a homogeneous, self-contained, static entity. Rosaldo (1989) argues that time, individuals, and awareness of multiple community memberships are components of modern analysis. Class, for instance, is the result of an "active process rather than a static product; it becomes evident only over the course of extended struggle, and it cannot be frozen for analytic inspection. When preserved as a static object within a slice in time, the phenomenon of class crumbles into so many discrete individuals" (p. 106). Bourdieu (1977) suggests that cultural practices need to be seen as constituted by the tempo of daily lives, with individuals midstream in events, planning their strategies to cope with uncertain futures. "A renewed concept of culture thus refers less to a unified entity (a 'culture') than to the mundane practices of everyday life" (Rosaldo, p. 217). Individuals share memberships in multiple communities, and the boundaries between those communities are porous. There are no self-contained cultures with perfect specimens of cultural purity. Members of a "culture" and the ethnographers who write about them have multiple positionings and perspectives on the various communities they belong to, based, for instance, on age, ethnicity, politics, education, interests, and friendships. Presenting narratives, as I did to represent the community history and events I experienced, gives a sense of the interplay among events, individual agency, and social structures (Rosaldo 1989). Time is a crucial element, and social structures can be seen to be emergent or contested in narratives of revolution or reform. My historical narrative of the creation of EM by people from LambdaMOO, and of the culture clash that led in part to the Mouldy Couch Club and to the Shutdown, illustrates how multiple community memberships can be problematic for individuals as well as how expectations about resources, freedoms, and friendships can be the source of social upheaval, even in a text-based environment. Presenting narratives, however, requires making sense of multiple individual views of events, imposing causal relations between actions and events that not all analysts or participants might agree with. A narrative is an analytic tool in itself, as well as a method of presentation, but the analyst risks leaving out conflicting voices and versions of events in the attempt to find coherence.

Individual views of a community or of multiple communities are contingent on individuals' positionings in them, and on how empowered or disempowered they feel. The choice of which narrative to tell, and how to incorporate multiple views of the events but still maintain a coherent story, is a political decision in itself. My focus on the power elite as a narrative thread to link the communities on LambdaMOO and EM and as a source of conflict between those communities may do the regulars on EM who are not involved in LambdaMOO a disservice. In fact, many regulars on EM were not named in my account but are still important to the community.

Not all EM MUDding is political action; indeed, to an outsider, all the social behavior on any MUD is just conversation in a text window. A large part of the community identity of a MUD group is linguistic, as I show in chapter 3; many text routines and rituals on EM signal its non-political relationships to other MUDs, such as Seashore MUSH. Many of the linguistic routines and conventions were born in playful moments of ordinary conversation, rather than moments of political intrigue or upheaval. The mundane activities of everyday life are far harder to describe than narratives of high-profile events, however. Even ordinary conversation can become a point of conflict, though, as the posts about newbies and their spammy style of interaction versus older players' preferences illustrated.

Just as narratives may present problematically neat accounts of events, labels for people are always problematic. I discussed wizards, programmers, Community Group members, guests, power elites, regulars, randoms, newbies. Definitions of each of these groups are shifting, relative, contingent on who defines them and when, as the participants in the EM community are well aware. People may be in multiple groups and on multiple MUDs; wizards on LambdaMOO may be non-wizards on EM, but their conversation on EM about politics on LambdaMOO may be held against them on LambdaMOO. Wizards may or may not "wield" their power. Guests may be regulars "in disguise" in order to achieve extra anonymity. Newbies are "new" in relation to an older player's perception of their awareness of commands and cultural norms on a MUD. Programmers may have a bit or may not, on EM; the bit may or may not coincide with knowledge of MOO programming.

Just as these labels and categories are problematic, but useful in the presentation of research, the myth of the perfect member of a community is called into question by the shifting memberships and labels that apply to any one person. The myth of the objective ethnographer is similarly called into question by the myriad possible positionings. Rosaldo (1989) discusses how every speaker's life experiences and relative empowerment and identity affect her social knowledge, making detached observation impossible. In my participation in the EM community, I have gone from MUD newbie to regular and friend of many regulars, particularly several people who might be considered "power elite." I've made an attempt to represent the voices of people who were not particular friends of mine, of course, but the bias of my network of friends is obvious (see Rabinow 1977 for a discussion of friendships with informants). Although I was ultimately given a programmer's bit because I intended to work on some geography, I do not come from a largely computer science background, and I rarely participated in programming conversations on EM, which are common. Of course, not all EM regulars participate, either. I MUDded on LambdaMOO after I realized it was historically important to EM, but I rarely did more than read mailing lists, like older users of LambdaMOO who avoid public conversation spots in favor of following the mailing list discussions. I never MUDded on Seashore MUSH, despite the influence Seashore has had on EM discourse habits (see chapter 3) and the fact that several regulars on EM are Seashore regulars too. One trait I shared with many EM regulars (possibly the trait that most affected who I became friends with) was my ability to MUD from work during the day, as many EM regulars do. This style of MUDding meant I was most in touch with the day crowd; some folks who MUD from home late at night are only occasionally on in the day, making them less available for conversation. In sum, my membership in and understanding of EM's many subcommunities and related communities is partial, just as many regulars' membership is partial.

Ultimately, culture is composed of individuals in multiple communities that may overlap or come into conflict; the interplay among individual agency, social structures, and events is the source of narratives that illustrate cultural processes occurring in time. The choice of narratives, like the choice of which voices to represent, is inherently political, and their presentation is analytic, imposing causal links on events and individual actions. The positions I occupied as a member of the Else-MOO community and as a participant in its subcommunities give me authority—and bias me—when I tell the story of ElseMOO in this book. But no member of the community is necessarily more privileged than any other, since all positionings are relatively powerful or weak with respect to different analyses. The narratives in this book would have been different but no less interesting if they had been told by Shelley, Egypt, Fred, or any other ElseMOO regular.

Appendix A: LambdaMOO's "Help Manners" File

(This version dates from 1995.)

LambdaMOO, like other MUDs, is a social community; it is populated by real people interacting through the computer network. Like members of other communities, the inhabitants of LambdaMOO have certain expectations about the behavior of members and visitors. This article lays out a system of rules of courteous behavior, or "manners", which has been agreed upon by popular vote.

First of all, any action that threatens the functional integrity of the MOO, or might cause legal trouble for the MOO's supporters, will get the player responsible thrown off by the wizards. If you find a loophole or bug in the core, report it to a wizard without attempting to take advantage of it. Cracking falls outside the realm of manners. Read 'help cracking' for more information.

Additionally, other loopholes should also not be exploited. This rule was established by *B:Patch-Arbitration-Loopholes (#4223):

If you find a loophole in the social system, make an Arbitration Proposal or petition to fix it. If you find a place where the documentation does not match the standing law on the subject, report it to a wizard without attempting to take advantage of it.

Taking personal advantage of loopholes and bugs to personal ends will be regarded as an antisocial act by arbitrators (see Self Defense below). The purpose of the social system here is to allow us to work together, not to allow us opportunities to revel in how we can beat the system.

Beyond that, there are two basic principles of friendly MOOing: let the MOO function and don't abuse other players.

LET THE MOO FUNCTION

Besides not trying to hack or break things, this means not hogging resources by taking up more memory or processing time than necessary.

To help keep database bloat down, please @create thoughtfully, @recycle unused objects, @rmmail when done with it, use feature objects instead of copying lots of verbs, and don't recycle and recreate objects seeking "interesting" numbers (this inflates all the object #'s, which are long enough already).

The MOO server is carefully shared among all the connected players so that everyone gets a chance to execute their commands. The more demanding players' commands are, the more of a load there is on the server, and thus the more lag there is.

If you are writing a program that will run for a long time, please make it wait at least five seconds between iterations (use 'fork (n)' or 'suspend(n)' where 'n' is at least 5). This will give others a chance to get their commands in between yours.

DON'T ABUSE OTHER PLAYERS

The MOO is a fun place to socialize, program, and play as long as people are polite to each other. Rudeness and harassment make LambdaMOO less pleasant for everyone. Do not harass or abuse other players, using any tactic including:

- Spamming (filling their screen with unwanted text)
- Teleporting them or their objects without consent
- Emoted violence or obscenities
- Shouting (sending a message to all connected players)
  Don't shout unless you have something everyone needs to hear. This basically means emergency system messages from wizards.
- Spoofing (causing messages to appear that are not attributed to your character)
  Spoofs can be funny and expressive when used with forethought. If you spoof, use a polite version than announces itself as a spoof promptly, and use it sparingly. See 'help spoofing' for more information.
- Spying
  Don't create or use spying devices. If you reset your teleport message, make sure it is set to something, so that you don't teleport silently. Besides having a disorienting effect on people, silent teleportation is a form of spying.
- Sexual harassment (particularly involving unsolicited acts which simulate rape against unwilling participants) Such behavior is not

tolerated by the LambdaMOO community. A single incidence of such an act may, as a consequence of due process, result in permanent explusion from LambdaMOO.

- Hate speech in the public areas. This is generally frowned upon though not forbidden (see the paragraph headed "General"). LambdaMOOers are generally very tolerant of all races, religions, sexual orientations, and just about whatever else you can think of. They do not tend to tolerate hatred based on such distinctions.

- Try to respect other players' privacy and their right to control their own objects, including the right to decide who may enter or remain in their rooms.

- Respect other players' sensibilities. MOO inhabitants and visitors come from a wide range of cultural backgrounds both in the U.S. and abroad, and have varying ideas of what constitutes offensive speech or descriptions. Please keep text that other players can casually run across as free of potentially-offensive material as you can. If you want to build objects or areas that are likely to offend some segment of the community, please give sufficient warning to casual explorers so that they can choose to avoid those objects or areas.

- General:
  Although it is not technically against MOO law to harass people, it is suggested that you do not. The advice here is intended to make the MOO a better place for everyone, not to limit freedom of expression. However, the legal system on the MOO is evolving at this time, and it is not well understood just how some laws from the real world might apply. As things stand within the MOO, the arbitrators have broad powers to decide how disputes should be settled. If you are disputed by someone it is possible you will be punished by anything up to and including permanent banishment from LambdaMOO. There is some disagreement in the LambdaMOO community about how much protection for free speech rights should be provided. This document, while not favoring censorship, encourages you to think about what you say and do. This is not only for the good of the community, but also to minimize your chances of having someone file a dispute against you, resulting in possible censure. Type 'help arbitration' for more information on the dispute process.

SELF-DEFENSE

Avoid revenge!

If someone is bothering you, you have several options. The appropriate first step is usually to ask them to stop.

If this fails, and avoiding the person is insufficient, useful verbs include @gag, @refuse, and @eject. Help is available on all of these.

Note these following rules established by the passage of *B:Patch-Arbitration-Loopholes (#4223):

- All characters are bound by some system of justice which has been voted by the people.

  Characters are free to suggest that this is not so, but such suggestions will regarded as "mere speech" and will carry no force of law. In particular, Arbitrators will not consider such claims of exemption to be material. Characters who wish not to be subject to the lawfully created rules of this MOO are, like anyone else, free to request that their accounts be turned off.

- No character may in any way exploit the use of multiple characters to beat the system.

  For example, if a character is newted for punitive reasons, all characters controlled by that typist will be newted AND if that typist shows up controlling a guest during that period, he is still not welcome.

If you have a serious problem with another player, you may want to consider invoking arbitration, in which another player decides the dispute. Since arbitration is some trouble and is binding on both parties, make sure you really want it before invoking it. See 'help arbitration' for details.

PROBLEMS WITH GUESTS

If you are having a problem with someone logged in as a Guest, you have another recourse: you may @boot them. Type @boot ¡guest-name¿

This will ask you for a reason. Enter the reason on multiple lines, followed by a '.' on a separate line. Please note that abuse of guest-booting is quite serious, and are subject to the arbitration process. All guest-bootings are logged.

This text may be changed by later petitions. In addition, wizards may add mention of new self-defense, mediation, help, or related techniques or verbs without the need for separate public approval of the added text.

If you have a question about something in this text, or about anything else on the MOO, type 'help' to see a listing of available help texts. If you don't see what you're looking for, page Help or use the Helpful

Person Finder in the Living Room to find someone who can answer your questions.

If you couldn't read the above text because it scrolled off your screen and you don't have any text capture mechanism available on your host, type 'help @pagelength' and 'help @linelength' to learn how MOO can help you read this and other lengthy text.

Appendix B: ElseMOO Online Documents

help manners
(As of 21 Nov 95)

EM, like other MUDs, is a social community; it is populated by real people interacting via a computer network. Like members of other communities, the inhabitants of EM have certain expectations about the behavior of its members and visitors. Thus, the Community Group (CG) provides this general outline for social conduct here; please familiarize yourself with and observe these guidelines when you log into EM.

In general:

Behavior that would be considered rude in 'face-to-face' interaction is rude here, too.

Some ways to interpret that:

Be nice. Don't be rude or annoy other people. If someone requests that you stop a particular behavior or action, please respect eir wishes.

Avoid interrupting other people who are working or conversing with their friends. You're welcome to explore the public places and ask for advice if you're stuck, but please try to read the online documentation and help yourself, first.

In addition, please realize that many players who log in here are busy with other things, both virtually and in real life, and therefore may not always be able respond to you immediately.

Harrassment of other players will not be tolerated. Emoted violence and obscenities are considered inappropriate in the social context of EM.

It isn't reasonable to ':kiss' or ':hug' folks you don't know. Also, speak out loud to people you don't know, rather than paging or whispering.

Respect other player's sensibilities. MOO inhabitants and visitors come from a diverse range of cultural backgrounds, both in the U.S. and abroad, and have varying ideas of what constitutes offensive expression. Please keep text as free of potentially-offensive language and material as you can.

Making logs of EM conversation for the purpose of public posting is considered unethical unless each participant in the discussion expressly agrees to allow the conversation to be posted.

Try to avoid arguing or debating with another player in a crowded public room; such interactions interrupt the other players in the room. Instead, consider paging or moving your conversation to one of the many empty public rooms.

Although visitors to EM are asked to use one of the guest characters for initial explorations, we encourage character creation if you become a frequent visitor. That way, you become a fuller part of the EM community.

Rude or offensive behavior can result, unfortunately, in your removal, either temporarily or permanently, from EM.

If you are uncertain about the meaning of any part of this document and would like clarification, please consult a Community Group member (type 'help cg' for a listing of players involved in the group or mail to *cg, the mailing list associated with the Community Group).

Documentation on ElseMOO Admin
(As of 3 Aug 95)

ElseMOO relies on three separate (but not necessarily disjoint) groups of administrators, with different roles and responsibilities. You can get help about each of the following groups, listed here with a brief explanation of what it is they're responsible for.

- steering-committee
  defining and maintaining the MOO's goals and objectives
- tech-group
  technical development and maintenance of the MOO
- community-group
  handling social problems and promoting a sense of community

By defining the responsibilities of the various types of administrators, we hope to clear up any confusion about what a person 'in charge' is supposed to be doing, and what authority that person has.

The Community Group

(As of 3 Aug 95)

Members of the community group handle any social problems that may arise, mediate disputes, assist new players in becoming acclimated to EM, and promote community harmony.

They have the ability to boot characters from the MOO, limit access from remote sites, check network connections, and use related commands that may be useful when dealing with problematic situations.

They can also help if you forget your password, need to change your email address, or have a problem using the MOO.

@911 (also called @helpme) pages members of the CG who are on-line. Please use this when problems occur. (There is help on this command.) If you have a complaint about a member of the CG and don't feel comfortable bringing it directly to that person or to the group as a whole yourself, please talk to another member of the CG. If even that would be uncomfortable, speak to one of the steering committee members.

If there are no members of the CG on-line, you can send mail to the *Community-Group mailing list (*cg).

Current members: [6 characters, including 4 wizards, 3 male, 3 female]

The Steering Committee

(As of 3 Aug 95)

This document details the role of the ElseMOO Steering Committee (or SC). The SC defines the goals and objectives of EM, and makes decisions related to the accomplishment of those goals.

ORGANIZATION

The Steering Committee members may be reached via the *sc mailing list. All of the requests below should be mailed to this list.

The Steering Committee meets at least once a month to discuss any issues from the mailing list that could not (or should not) be resolved in email, and to deal with any other issues related to EM that should be discussed interactively.

The leader of the Steering Committee plans the agenda for the SC meetings, resolves disputes between members of the SC, and makes any 'hard' decisions that can not be reached by consensus.

DECISIONS

The following decisions must be made by the Steering Committee. Others should be added to this list as necessary.

Approve new programmers

A request to make someone a programmer should be be submitted to the SC by a metaproject leader. (The prospective programmer must be planning to work on a project within that leader's metaproject.) The leader must get verbal or email approval of all active SC members. Once this has happened, the leader may make the person a programmer, and the fact shall be recorded in the programmer-log.

Approve new metaprojects and metaproject leaders

A metaproject (or area of interest) should be submitted to the SC, which should discuss it at an SC meeting. It must be approved by a full consensus of SC members, either at the meeting, or via mail if any member of the SC was not present at the meeting. If the person who has submitted the metaproject is not already a metaproject leader, e must also be approved to become a metaproject leader.

Discontinue metaprojects

A metaproject may be discontinued simply by the choice of the metaproject leader, or by full consensus of the SC.

Approve new members of the Steering Committee

A request should be submitted to the SC. All active members of the SC and the potential new member must approve the request. MOOmail is sufficient.

Approve new members of the DB group

A request should be submitted to the SC. All active members of the SC and the potential new member must approve the request. MOOmail is sufficient.

Approve new members of the Unix group

A request should be submitted to the SC. All active members of the SC must approve the request. The Unix systems administrator of the computer that EM is running on must also approve the addition.

Approve new members of the Community group

A request should be submitted to the SC. All active members of the SC and the potential new member must approve the request. MOOmail is sufficient.

Dismissals

All dismissals from the above posts are approved by consensus of the members of the SC, minus the person in question. Requests to resign should be handled in the best and most polite manner.

THEORY OF OPERATION

Many details in the above decisions have not been explicitly stated, and it is assumed they will simply be handled reasonably. If this turns out not to be the case, or if some method of decision-making is ambiguous, this document should be modified by the leader of the steering committee.

Current members: [6 characters, all wizards, 1 female, 5 male]

The Tech Group

(As of 3 Aug 95)

The ElseMOO 'Tech' Group are people who deal with the technical operation of the MOO. This consists of three types of jobs:

THE DB GROUP

People who have superuser (wheel) access to the MOO database for maintenance purposes. This is to be used for hacking on core objects, fixing bugs, or making global changes related to programming projects, and should not be used for non-technical purposes.

If you have questions, comments, or suggestions about the core database, send mail to the *DB-Issues mailing list. If you think you've found a bug in the core database, send mail to the *Bug-Reports mailing list. If you think you've found a security hole, send mail to the *Security mailing list, which is only readable to members of the DB group.

Current members: [17 characters, all wizards, 2 female, 15 male]

THE UNIX GROUP

The set of people who deal with unix-level administration of the MOO. They deal with startup, shutdowns, backups, memory usage, and management of auxiliary processes.

Current members: [5 characters, all wizards, all male]

THE PROGRAMMING GROUP

People who program verbs. See 'help programmer-policy' for what it takes to become a programmer.

Current members: [37 characters, 17 wizards, 6 female, 31 male]

The ElseMOO Programmer Policy

(As of 22 Nov 95)

ElseMOO's objective is to perform research and development of topics that further EM's purpose (see 'help purpose'). In order to be effective in accomplishing this goal, we need to be able to put a great deal of trust in our builders and programmers. And in order to maintain focus, we limit the work being done to a set of well-defined projects. Unfortunately, this is quite different from the policies on some other MOOs, and there is a bit of a culture shock for people who log in here and expect to be made programmers immediately. This document is about how we decide who is to be on our programming team. If you don't care about that, you may still want to skip ahead to the section on 'Other Options'.

Becoming a Programmer

Potential programmers need to be registered characters and have a project as well as certain other qualities.

Project

Programmers need to have an interest in working on one or more of the projects being worked on here. (See 'help projects' for more information about them.)

In particular, every programmer needs a project leader's support. If you've been here a while and would like to contribute to one of our projects, talk to its leader about what you'd like to do. If the leader wants you to work on the project, and the steering committee approves, you'll be given a programmer bit for the project.

Programmers who are not actively working on projects will not have the responsibilities nor the privileges of having a programmer bit. (If you need to go on vacation for a while, that's okay; when you have time to work on EM projects again, let the project leader know. This just helps us keep track of things like who's working on projects and which projects are actively being pursued.)

Qualifications

These are some of the specific things we look for:

- Experience. Programming ability is a plus. Knowing MOO-code is a help, but having spent a lot of time dealing with the programming environment of LambdaMOO may not. Experience with programming in general, and particularly object-oriented programming, is valued.

- Ideas. We need people who are creative and have good suggestions. In particular we want ideas that are good for *here*, that are related to our ongoing projects. We'd love to hear about your general ideas, but if they'll diffuse EM's energies, we'd probably suggest they be implemented somewhere else.

- Familiarity. Once you've been here for a while, you'll understand the goals of the MOO and various projects better, and perhaps even some of the personalities. Being familiar with the way this MOO works is important.

- Trust. Malicious programmers are a problem we don't want to deal with.

The main point to take from this can be summed up as follows: if you're interested in working with us, hang around for a while first. That way, project leaders can get a good impression of your skills and ideas, instead of just relying on first impressions or an impressive resume. Sorry, but we have to have time to make good decisions.

Other Options

If you don't know MOO-code yet, and are seriously interested in learning it, we recommend the following:

LambdaMOO—The original—more code than the human mind can comprehend.
The Sprawl—Free progbits, lotsa space, no restrictions.
MuMOO—Fairly small, goofy but in a nice way.

If you know MOO-code and are just interested in looking around, you can type '@programmer me'; this won't actually give you a programmer bit, but it will make you a child of the generic programmer. @list and @d will work for you; other things, like eval and any attempt to program, will not, and may crash in unfriendly ways.

One final note: we understand that people from other MUDs are used to being able to create their own rooms, and might like to do so here as well. This kind of building is not consistent with the goals of EM.

Appendix C: Some Welcome Messages on ElseMOO

8 Dec 93

```
+--------------------+
| Welcome to ElseMOO |
+--------------------+
```

This isn't a game. It's a place where friends hang out and people work on various projects. For more information, type 'help purpose' once you've connected.

A few useful commands:
```
'connect Guest'                  to connect to a guest character.
'@quit'                          to disconnect, either now or
                                 later.
'connect <character-name> <password>' if you have a
                                 character.
```

George . o O (Reports of our death have been greatly
  exaggerated.)

24 Mar 94
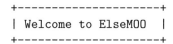
```
>restart
Your score is 15 (total of 350 points), in 23 moves.
This gives you the rank of Beginner.
Do you wish to restart? (Y is affirmative): >Y
Restarting.
```

ELSEMOO: The Great Minnesotan Empire

This isn't a game. It's a place where friends hang out
and people work on various projects. For more
information, type 'help purpose' once you've connected.

A few useful commands:
'connect Guest'   to connect to a guest character.
'@quit'   to disconnect, either now or
                                   later.
'connect <character-name> <password>' if you have a
                                   character.

---
20 June 94

Ray dit, "so it est politics, plain et simple"
Ray dit, "nous avons good net, good machine, et il
wants to sponge off nous"
Ray dit, "et le price est, il must use mon software"

Welcome to EM.

This isn't a game. It's a place where friends hang out
and people work on various projects. For more
information, type 'help purpose' once you've connected.

A few useful commands:
'connect Guest'   to connect to a guest character.
'@quit'   to disconnect, either now or
                                   later.
'connect <character-name> <password>' if you have a
                                   character.

(Tom dit, "ca ete incredible, vous were un perfect
sinister francais villain")
The average idle time is 5 hours, 35 minutes, and 1 second;
there are 26 connected.

---
1 July 94

Welcome to EM -- Maybe you can get some respect here.

This isn't a game. It's a place where friends hang out

and people work on various projects. For more
information, type 'help purpose' once you've connected.

A few useful commands:
'connect Guest'   to connect to a guest character.
'@quit'   to disconnect, either now or
                             later.
'connect <character-name> <password>' if you have a
                             character.
'idle'   to see roughly how idle EM is.

(I doubt it, though.)

22 July 94

The guest says, "this has got to be THE MOST BORING MOO
I have ever seen!"

This isn't a game. It's a place where friends hang out
and people work on various projects. For more
information, type 'help purpose' once you've connected.

A few useful commands:
'connect Guest'   to connect to a guest character.
'@quit'   to disconnect, either now or
                             later.
'connect <character-name> <password>' if you have a
                             character.
'idle'   to see roughly how idle EM is.

(Shelley [to Tom]: put the guest line in teh connection
message...maybe everyone will stay away and we can be
alone on our little boring fascist moo)

14 Oct 94

Welcome to EM--coming from Pete, that's entirely phatic.

This isn't a game. It's a place where friends hang out
and people work on various projects. For more
information, type 'help purpose' once you've connected.

A few useful commands:
'connect Guest'   to connect to a guest character.

```
'@quit'                    to disconnect, either now or
                           later.
'connect <character-name> <password>' if you have a
                           character.
'idle'                     to see roughly how idle EM is.
```

(phat.ic \'fat-ik\ \-i-k(*-)le-\ aj [Gk phatos, verbal
of phanai to speak] : revealing or sharing feelings
or establishing an atmosphere of sociability rather
than communicating ideas {~ communion} -
phat.i.cal.ly av)

| 24 Mar 95 |

Welcome to EM--Someone says, "It's a moo"

This isn't a game. It's a place where friends hang out
and people work on various projects. For more
information, type 'help purpose' once you've connected.

A few useful commands:
```
'connect Guest'            to connect to a guest character.
'@quit'                    to disconnect, either now or
                           later.
'connect <character-name> <password>' if you have a
                           character.
'idle'                     to see roughly how idle EM is.
```

(Someone says, "Is it like aol?"")

| 8 Aug 95 |

Welcome to EM--"this is just like IRC <g>.. with fun
things to do"

This isn't a game. It's a place where friends hang out
and people work on various projects. For more
information, type 'help purpose' once you've connected.

A few useful commands:
```
'connect Guest'            to connect to a guest character.
'@quit'                    to disconnect, either now or
                           later.
'connect <character-name> <password>' if you have a
```

	character.
'idle'	to see roughly how idle EM is.

(Bonny [to the Canadian guest]: except we don't say <g> here.)

References

Abrahams, R. D. (1992) Insult. In R. Bauman, ed., *Folklore, cultural performances, and popular entertainments*, pp. 145–149. New York: Oxford University Press.

Ackerman, M. and J. Muramatsu. (1998) Computing, social activity, and entertainment: A field study of a game MUD. *Computer-Supported Cooperative Work* 7.

Allen, C. (1996a) What's wrong with the "golden rule?" Conundrums of conducting ethical research in cyberspace. *The Information Society* 12, pp. 175–187.

Allen, C. (1996b) *Virtual identities: The social construction of cybered selves.* Dissertation, Northwestern University.

Amende, K. (1993) Manuscript on the Schmoo Wars. Bryn Mawr College.

Anderson, B. (1991) *Imagined communities: Reflections on the origin and spread of nationalism.* (Revised edition.) London: Verso.

Anderson, J. (1996) Not for the faint of heart: Contemplations on Usenet. In L. Cherny and B. Weise, eds., *Wired women: Gender and new realities in cyberspace.* Seattle: Seal Press.

Arendt, H. (1958) *The human condition.* Chicago: University Of Chicago Press.

Arnaut, G. (1998) Internet chat rooms becoming a popular forum for business. *New York Times Cyber Times*, January 26. http://www.nytimes.com/library/cyber/week/012698chat.html.

Aronoff, M. (1985) Orthography and linguistic theory. *Language* 61, pp. 68–72.

Austin, J. (1962) *How to do things with words.* Cowford: Cowford University Press.

Aycock, A. and N. Buchignani. (1995) The e-mail murders: Reflections on "dead" letters. In S. Jones, ed., *Cybersociety: Computer-mediated communication and community*, pp. 184–231. Thousand Oaks, CA: Sage.

Bach, E. (1981) On time, tense, and aspect: An essay in English metaphysics. In P. Cole, ed., *Radical pragmatics*, pp. 63–82. New York: Academic Press.

Baecker, R., ed. (1993) *Readings in groupware and computer-supported cooperative work*. San Mateo, CA: Morgan Kaufmann.

Bales, R. F. (1950) A set of categories for the analysis of small group interaction. *American Sociological Review* 15, pp. 257–263.

Baron, N. S. (1984) Computer mediated communication as a force in language change. *Visible Language* 18(2), pp. 118–141.

Bartle, R. (1990) Interactive multi-user computer games. Available at ftp: //ftp.lambda.moo.mud.org/pub/MOO/papers/mudreport.txt.

Basso, K. (1989) The ethnography of writing. In R. Bauman and J. Sherzer, eds., *Explorations in the ethnography of speaking*. (Second edition.) Cambridge: Cambridge University Press.

Bateson, G. (1972) A theory of play and fantasy. In G. Bateson, *Steps to An Ecology of Mind*, pp. 177–193. New York: Ballantine.

Bauerle, R., U. Egli, and A. von Stechow, eds. (1979) *Semantics from different points of view*, pp. 376–471. Berlin: Springer Verlag.

Bauman, R. (1975) Verbal art as performance. *American Anthropologist* 77, pp. 290–311.

Baym, N. (1993) Interpreting soap operas and creating community: Inside a computer-mediated fan culture. *Journal of Folklore Research* 30(2/3), pp. 143–176.

Baym, N. (1995) The emergence of community in computer-mediated communication. In S. Jones, ed., *Cybersociety: Computer-mediated Communication and Community*, pp. 138–163. Thousand Oaks, CA: Sage.

Beaudouin-Lafon, M. and A. Karsenty. (1992) Transparency and awareness in a real-time groupware system. Proceedings of UIST '92.

Bell, C. and H. Newby, eds. (1974) *The sociology of community: A selection of readings*. London: Cass.

Bellah, R., R. Madsen, W. Sullivan, A. Swidler, and S. Tipton. (1984) *Habits of the heart: Individualism and commitment in American life*. Berkeley: University of California Press.

Bender, T. (1978) *Community and social change in America*. New Brunswick, NJ: Rutgers University Press.

Benedikt, M., ed. (1991) *Cyberspace: First steps*. Cambridge: MIT Press.

Beniger, J. R. (1987) Personalization of the mass media and the growth of the pseudo-community. *Communication Research* 14, pp. 352–370.

Bennahum, D. (1994) Fly me to the MOO. *Lingua Franca*, June.

Berlo, D. (1969) *The process of communication.* New York: Holt, Rinehart & Winston.

Biber, D. (1986) Spoken and written textual dimensions in English: Resolving the contradictory findings. *Language* 62(2), pp. 384–414.

Biber, D. (1988) *Variation across speech and writing.* Cambridge: Cambridge University Press.

Biber, D. (1994) An analytical framework for register studies. In D. Biber and E. Finegan, eds., *Sociolinguistic perspectives on register*, pp. 31–58. New York: Oxford University Press.

Biber, D. and E. Finegan. (1994) Introduction: Situating register in sociolinguistics. In D. Biber and E. Finegan, eds., *Sociolinguistic perspectives on register*, pp. 3–14. New York: Oxford University Press.

Bilson, A. J. (1995) Get into the groove: Designing for participation. *Interactions* 2(2), pp. 17–22.

Binnick, R. (1991) *Time and the verb.* Oxford: Oxford University Press.

Biocca, F., ed. (1992) Virtual Reality: A Communication Perspective. Special issue of *Journal of Communication* 42(4).

Birdwhistell, R. (1970) *Kinesics and context: Essays on body motion communication.* Philadelphia: University of Pennsylvania Press.

Black, D. (1976) *The behavior of law.* New York: Academic Press.

Black, S., J. Levin, H. Mehan, and C. Quinn. (1983) Real and non-real time interaction: Unraveling multiple threads of discourse. *Discourse Processes* 6, pp. 59–75.

Bourdieu, P. (1977) *Outline of a theory of practice.* New York: Cambridge University Press.

Bransten, L. (1997) New uses for chat software could improve its reputation. *The Wall Street Journal*, interactive edition, December 15. Available at http://interactive.wsj.com/public/current/articles/SB881769705975878000.htm

Brenneis, D. (1986) Shared territory: Audience, indirection, and meaning. *Text* 6(3), pp. 339–347.

Brettel, C. (1996) Whose history is it? Selection and representation in the creation of a text. In C. Brettel, ed., *When they read what we write: The politics of ethnography*, pp. 93–106. Westport, CT: Bergin and Garvey.

Bretz, R. (1983) *Media for interactive communication.* Beverly Hills, CA: Sage.

Brown, J. S. and P. Duguid. (1995) The social life of documents. In E. Dyson, ed., *Release 1.0*, October 11. Also published May 1996 in *First Monday* 1(1), available at http://www.firstmonday.dk/issues/issue1/index.html.

Brown, P. and S. Levinson. (1987) *Politeness: Some universals in language usage.* Cambridge: Cambridge University Press.

Bruckman, A. (1992) Identity workshop: Emergent social and psychological phenomena in text-based virtual reality. Available from http://www.cc.gatech. edu/fac/Amy.Bruckman/papers/index.html.

Bruckman, A. (1993) Gender swapping on the Internet. Proceedings of INET '93. Available from http://www.cc.gatech.edu/fac/Amy.Bruckman/papers/ index.html.

Bruckman, A. (1994) Programming for fun: MUDs as a context for collaborative learning. Paper presented at the National Educational Computing Conference in Boston, MA. Available from http://www.cc.gatech.edu /fac/Amy.Bruckman/papers/index.html.

Bruckman, A. (1997) MOOSE crossing: Construction, community, and learning in a networked virtual world for kids. Ph.D. dissertation, Massachusetts Institute of Technology.

Bruckman, A. and M. Resnick. (1995) The MediaMOO project: Constructionism and professional community. *Convergence* 1(1), pp. 94–109. Available from http://www.cc.gatech.edu/fac/Amy.Bruckman/papers/index.html.

Brundage, M. (1998) Network Places. Available from http://spider.ipac.caltech.edu/staff/brundage/np/index.html.

Burka, L. (1993) A hypertext history of multi-user dimensions. Available at http://www.apocalypse.org/pub/u/lpb/muddex/essay/.

Burka, L. (1995) The mudline. Available at http://www.apocalypse.org/pub/ u/lpb/muddex/mudline.html.

Burgoon, J. K., D. B. Buller, J. L. Hale, and M. A. deTurck. (1984) Relational messages associated with nonverbal behaviors. *Human Communication Research* 10, pp. 351–378.

Burgoon, J. K., D. B. Buller, and W. G. Woodall. (1989) *Nonverbal communication: The unspoken dialogue.* New York: Harper and Row.

Cappel, J. (1993) Closing the e-mail privacy gap: Employer monitoring of employee e-mail. *Journal of Systems Management* 44(12), pp. 6–11.

Carey, J. (1980) Paralanguage in computer-mediated communication. In N. K. Sondheimer, ed., *The 18th annual meeting of the Association for Computational Linguistics and parasession on topics in interactive discourse: Proceedings of the conference*, p. 67–69. Philadelphia: University of Pennsylvania.

Carlstrom, E. (1992) Better living through language: The communicative implications of a text-only virtual environment. ftp://ftp.lambda.moo.mud.org /pub/MOO/papers/communicative.txt.

Carnevale, P. J. D., D. G. Pruitt, and S. D. Selheimer. (1981) Looking and competing: Accountability and visual access in integrative bargaining. *Journal of Personality and Social Psychology* 40, pp. 111–120.

Carter, R. (1988) Front pages: lexis, style, and newspaper reports. In M. Ghadessy, ed., *Registers of written English*, pp. 8–16. London: Pinter.

Chafe, W. (1982) Integration in involvement in speaking, writing, and oral literature. In D. Tannen, ed., *Spoken and written language: Exploring orality and literacy*, pp. 35–53. Norwood, NJ: Ablex.

Chaika, E. (1980) Jargons and language change. *Anthropological Linguistics* 22(2), pp. 77–96.

Chayko, M. (1993) What is real in the age of virtual reality? "Reframing" frame analysis for a technological world. *Symbolic Interaction* 16(2), pp. 171–181.

Cherny, L. (1995a) Gender differences in text-based virtual reality. In M. Bucholtz, A. Liang, L. Sutton, and C. Hines, eds., *Communicating in, through, and across cultures: Proceedings of the third Berkeley Women and Language Conference.* Berkeley: Berkeley Women and Language Group. Available at ftp://ftp.lambda.moo.mud.org/pub/MOO/papers/GenderMOO.ps.

Cherny, L. (1995b) 'Objectifying' the Body in the Discourse of an Object-Oriented MUD. In C. Stivale, ed., *Cyberspaces: Pedagogy and performance on the electronic frontier.* Special issue of *Works and Days*, 26. Available from http://acorn.grove.iup.edu/en/workdays/toc.html.

Cherny, L. (1995c) The modal complexity of speech events in a social MUD. *Electronic Journal of Communication* 5(4).

Cherny, L. (1995d) *The MUD register: Conversational modes of action in a text-based virtual reality.* Dissertation, Stanford University.

Clark, H. H. and S. E. Brennan. (1991) Grounding in communication. In L. B. Resnick, J. H. Levine, and S. D. Teasley, eds., *Perspectives on socially shared cognition*, pp. 127–149. Washington: American Psychological Association.

Clark, H. H. and E. F. Schaefer. (1989) Contributing to discourse. *Cognitive Science* 13, pp. 259–294.

Clerc, S. (1996) Estrogen brigades and "big tits" threads: Media fandom on- and off-line. In L. Cherny and B. Weise, eds., *Wired women: Gender and new realities in cyberspace.* Seattle: Seal Press.

Clifford, J. (1983) On ethnographic authority. *Representations* 12, pp. 118–146.

Clifford, J. and G. Marcus. (1986) *Writing culture: The poetics and politics of ethnography.* Berkeley: University of California Press.

Clodius, J. (1994) Ethnographic fieldwork on the internet. *Anthropology Newsletter* 35(9), p. 12. Available at http://dragonmud.org/people/jen/afa.html.

Cohen, A. (1985) *The symbolic construction of community.* New York: Routledge.

Cohen, P. (1984) The pragmatics of referring and the modality of communication. *Computational Linguistics* 10(2), pp. 97–146.

Coleman, J. (1990) *Foundations of social theory.* Cambridge: Harvard University Press.

Collot, M. and N. Belmore. (1992) Electronic language: A new variety of English. In J. Aarts, P. de Haan, and N. Oostdijk, eds., *Papers from the Thirteenth International Conference on English Language Research on Computerized Corpora.*

Condon, S. and C. Cech. (1996) Functional comparisons of face-to-face and computer-mediated decision making interactions. In S. Herring, ed., *Computer-mediated communication: Linguistic, social and cross-cultural perspectives,* pp. 65–80. Philadelphia: John Benjamins.

Cooper, R. (1986) Tense and discourse location in situation semantics. *Linguistics and Philosophy* 9, pp. 17–36.

Coulmas, F., ed. (1981) *Conversational routine: Explorations in standardized communication situations and prepatterned speech.* The Hague: Mouton Publishers.

Coulthard, M. (1977) *An introduction to discourse analysis.* Harlow, U.K.: Longman.

Cowan, A. (1997) History of MUDs. Available at http://www.mudconnect.com/mud_intro.html.

Crane, G. (1991) Composing culture: The authority of an electronic text. *Current Anthropology* 32(3), pp. 293–311.

Csikszentimihalyi, M. and E. Rochberg-Halton. (1981) *The meaning of things: Domestic symbols and the self.* Cambridge: Cambridge University Press.

Culnan, M. and M. L. Markus. (1987) Information technologies. In F. M. Jablin, L. L. Putnam, K. H. Roberts, and L. W. Porter, eds., *Handbook of organizational communication: An interdisciplinary perspective,* pp. 420–443. Newbury Park, CA: Sage.

Curtis, P. (1992) Mudding: Social phenomena in text-based virtual realities. Intertrek 3(3), pp. 26–34. Available at ftp://ftp.lambda.moo.mud.org /pub/MOO/papers/DIAC92.{txt, ps}.

Curtis, P. and D. Nichols. (1993) MUDs grow up: Social virtual reality in the real world. Paper presented at the Third International Conference on Cyberspace in Austin, Texas, May. ftp://ftp.lambda.moo.mud.org /pub/MOO/papers/MUDsGrowUp.{ps, txt}.

Daft, R. L. and R. H. Lengel. (1984) Information richness: A new approach to managerial behavior and organization design. In B. M. Staw and L. L. Cummings, eds., *Research in Organizational Behavior* 6, pp. 191–233. Greenwich, CT: JAI Press.

Daft, R. L. and R. H. Lengel. (1986) Organizational information requirements, media richness, structural determinants. *Management Science* 32, pp. 554–571.

Danet, B., L. Ruedenberg, and Y. Rosenbaum-Tamari. (1998) Smoking dope at a virtual party: Writing, play and performance on Internet Relay Chat. In F. Sudweeks, M. McLaughlin, and S. Rafaeli, eds., *Network and netplay: Virtual groups on the Internet*. Cambridge: AAAI/MIT Press.

Dannefer, W. and N. Poushinsky. (1977) Language and community. *Journal of Communication* 27, pp. 122–126.

Davis, E. (1994) It's a MUD, MUD, MUD, MUD world. *Village Voice*, February 22, pp. 42–44.

December, J. (1993) Characteristics of oral culture in discourse on the net. Paper presented at the Twelfth Annual Penn State Conference on Rhetoric and Composition, July.

Dibbell, J. (1993) Rape in cyberspace, or how an evil clown, a haitian trickster spirit, two wizards, and a cast of dozens turned a database into a society. *Village Voice*, December 21, pp. 36–42.

Diversity University. (1998) Home page at http://www.du.org/.

Dixon, R. (1971) A method of semantic description. In D. Steinberg and L. Jakobovits, eds., *Semantics: An interdisciplinary reader in philosophy, linguistics, and psychology*. Cambridge: Cambridge University Press.

Doheny-Farina, S. (1995) Representation(s) and a sense of self: The subtle abstractions of MOO talk. *Computer-Mediated Communication Magazine* 2(5), p. 15.

Douglas, M. and B. Isherwood. (1996 [1979]) *The world of goods: Towards an anthropology of consumption*. New York: Routledge.

Dourish, P. (1995) Developing a reflective model of collaborative systems. *ACM Transations on Computer-Human Interaction* 2(1), pp. 40–63.

Dourish, P. and S. Bly. (1992) Portholes: Supporting awareness in distributed work groups. Proceedings of CHI '92, Human Factors in Computer Systems, Monterey, CA.

Dowty, D. (1979) *Word meaning and Montague grammar*. Dordrecht: Reidel.

Dowty, D. (1986) The effects of aspectual class on the temporal structure of discourse: semantics or pragmatics? *Linguistics and Philosophy* 9, pp. 37–61.

Duncan, S. (1973) Towards a grammar for dyadic conversation. *Semiotica* 9(1), pp. 29–46.

Duncan, S. and D. Fiske. (1977) *Face-to-face interaction: Research, methods, and theory*. New Jersey: Lawrence Erlbaum Associates.

Duncan, S. and G. Niederehe. (1974) On signalling that it is your turn to speak. *Journal of Experimental Psychology* 10, pp. 234–247.

Duranti, A. (1988) Ethnography of speaking: Towards a linguistics of the praxis. In F. Newmeyer, ed., *Language: the socio-cultural context*, pp. 210–228. New York: Cambridge University Press.

Durlak, J. T. (1987) A typology for interactive media. *Communication Yearbook* 10, pp. 743–757.

Dyson, E. (1997) *Release 1.0*. March.

Eckert, P. and S. McConnell-Ginet. (1992) Think practically and look locally: Language and gender as community-based practice. *Annual Review of Anthropology* 21, pp. 461–490.

Edelsky, C. (1993) Who's got the floor? In D. Tannen, ed., *Gender and conversational interaction*, pp. 189–230. New York: Oxford University Press.

Egido, C. (1988) Videoconferencing as a technology to support group work: A review of its failures. Proceedings of CSCW '88. ACM Press.

Eisenberg, E. (1984) Ambiguity as strategy in organizational communication. *Communication Monographs* 51, pp. 227–242.

Elias, N. (1974) Foreword. In C. Bell and H. Newby, eds., *The sociology of community: A selection of readings*. London: Cass.

Ellis, C. A., S. J. Gibbs, and G. L. Rein. (1991) Groupware: Some issues and experiences. *Communications of the ACM* 34(1), pp. 39–58.

Emmett, R. (1981) Vnet or gripenet? *Datamation* 27(11), pp. 48–58.

Erickson, F. (1982) Money tree, lasagna bush, salt and pepper: social construction of topical cohesion in a conversation among Italian-Americans. In D. Tannen, ed., *Analyzing discourse: Text and talk*. Washington, DC: Georgetown University Press.

Erickson, T. (1997) Social interaction on the net: Virtual community as participatory genre. Proceedings of the 30th Hawaii International Conference on System Sciences, January.

Erikson, E. (1985) *Childhood and society*. New York: W. W. Norton and Company.

Etzioni, A. (1991) *The responsive society*. San Francisco: Jossey-Bass.

Evard, R. (1993) Collaborative networked communication: MUDs as systems tools. Paper given at LISA, Monterey, CA.

Fanderclai, T. L. (1996) Like magic, only real. In L. Cherny and B. Weise, eds., *Wired women: Gender and new realities in cyberspace*. Seattle: Seal Press.

Farkas, D. (1993) Modal anchoring and NP scope. Technical report LRC-93-08, Linguistics Research Center, Cowell College, UC Santa Cruz.

Ferguson, C. (1964) Baby talk in six languages. In J. Gumperz and D. Hymes, eds., *The ethnography of communication*, pp. 103–114. Washington, DC: American Anthropological Association.

Ferguson, C. (1975) Toward a characterization of English foreigner talk. *Anthropological Linguistics* 17(1), pp. 1–14.

Ferguson, C. (1977) Sociolinguistic settings of language planning. In J. Rubin, B. Jernudd, J. Das Gupta, J. Fishman, and C. Ferguson, eds., *Language planning processes*, pp. 9–30. The Hague: Mouton.

Ferguson, C. (1983) Sports announcer talk: Syntactic aspects of register variation. *Language in Society* 12, pp. 153–172.

Ferguson, C. (1985) Editor's introduction. Special issue of *Discourse Processes* 8, pp. 391–394.

Ferguson, C. (1994) Dialect, register, and genre: Working assumptions about conventionalization. In D. Biber and E. Finegan, eds., *Sociolinguistic perspectives on register*, pp. 15–30. New York: Oxford University Press.

Ferrara, K., H. Brunner, and G. Whittemore. (1991) Interactive written discourse as an emergent register. *Written Communication* 8(1), pp. 8–33.

Firth, R. (1972) Verbal and bodily rituals of greeting and parting. In J. S. La Fontaine, ed., *The interpretation of ritual*, pp. 1–38. London: Tavistock Publications.

Fischer, C. (1992) *America calling: A social history of the telephone to 1940*. Berkeley: University of California Press.

Flynn, L. (1997) Companies try to refashion the world of chat. *New York Times Cyber Times*, June 13. Available at http://www.nytimes.com/library/cyber/week/061397talkcity.html.

Fries, C. (1952) *The structure of English*. New York: Harcourt Brace.

Geertz, C. (1973) *The interpretation of cultures: Selected essays*. New York: Basic Books.

Georgedon, A. (1967) Some functions of gaze direction in social interaction. *Acta Psychologica* 26, pp. 22–63.

Germain, E. (1993) In the jungle of MUD. *Time*, September 13, p. 49.

Gibbon, D. (1981) Idiomaticity and functional variation: A case study of international amateur radio talk. *Language in Society* 10, pp. 21–42.

Gibbon, D. (1985) Context and variation in two-way radio discourse. *Discourse Processes* 8, pp. 395–419.

Gilboa, N. (1996) Elites, lamers, narcs, and whores: Exploring the computer underground. In L. Cherny and B. Weise, eds., *Wired women: Gender and new realities in cyberspace*. Seattle: Seal Press.

Glusman, G. (1997) BioMOO homepage at http://bioinformatics.weizmann. ac.il/BioMOO/.

Goffman, E. (1953) Communication conduct in an island community. Ph.D. dissertation, University of Chicago.

Goffman, E. (1957) Alienation from interaction. *Human Relations* 10, pp. 47–59.

Goffman, E. (1963) *Behavior in public places: Notes on the social organization of gatherings*. New York: The Free Press.

Goffman, E. (1967) *Interaction ritual: Essays on face-to-face behavior*. Chicago: Aldine.

Goffman, E. (1974) *Frame analysis: An essay on the organization of experience*. New York: Harper & Row.

Goodman, F. (1973) On the semantics of future sentences. *Ohio State Working Papers in Linguistics* 16, pp. 76–89.

Goodman, R. and A. Ben-Ze'ev, eds. (1994) *Good gossip*. University Press of Kansas.

Goodwin, C. (1981) *Conversational organization: Interaction between speakers and hearers*. New York: Academic Press.

Goodwin, C. (1986) Between and within: Alternative sequential treatments of continuers and assessments. *Human Studies* 9, pp. 205–217.

Grice, H. P. (1975) Logic and conversation. In P. Cole and J. Morgan, eds., *Syntax and semantics 3: Speech acts*, pp. 41–58. New York: Academic Press.

Grice, H. P. (1978) Further notes on logic and conversation. In P. Cole, ed., *Syntax and semantics 9: Pragmatics*, pp. 113–128. New York: Academic Press.

Grosz, B. and C. Sidner. (1986) Attentions, intentions, and the structure of discourse. *Computational Linguistics* 12(3), pp. 175–204.

Gumperz, J. (1972) Introduction. In J. Gumperz and D. Hymes, eds., *Directions in sociolinguistics*. Cowford: Blackwell.

Gumperz, J. (1982) *Discourse strategies*. Cambridge: Cambridge University Press.

Gumperz, J. and D. Hymes. (1964) *The ethnography of communication*. Washington: American Anthropological Association.

Gurak, L. (1997) *Persuasion and privacy in cyberspace: The online protests over Lotus Marketplace and the Clipper Chip*. New Haven: Yale University Press.

Hagel, J. and A. Armstrong. (1997) *Net gain: Expanding markets through virtual communities*. Boston: Harvard Business School Press.

Halliday, M. A. K. (1979) Differences between spoken and written language: Some implications for literacy teaching. In G. Page et al., eds., *Communication Through Reading: Proceedings of the 4th Australian Reading Conference* 2, pp. 37–52. Adelaide: Australian Reading Association.

Haraway, D. J. (1991) *Simians, cyborgs, and women: The reinvention of nature*. London: Free Association Books.

Harris, J. (1989) The idea of community in the study of writing. *College Composition and Communication* 40(1), pp. 11–22.

Harvey, D. (1989) *The condition of postmodernity*. Oxford: Blackwell.

Hayashi, R. (1991) Floor structure of English and Japanese conversation. *Journal of Pragmatics* 16, pp. 1–30.

Haynes, C. and J. R. Holmevik, eds. (1998) *High wired: On the design, use, and theory of educational MOOs*. University of Michigan Press.

Heath, C. and P. Luff. (1991a) Disembodied conduct: communication through video on a multi-media office environment. Proceedings of CHI 91, pp. 99–103.

Heath, C. and P. Luff. (1991b) Collaborative activity and technological design: Task coordination in London underground control rooms. Proceedings of the European Conference on Computer Supported Cooperative Work, pp. 65–80. Amsterdam: Kluwer.

Heeter, C. (1989) Classifying mediated communication systems. *Communication Yearbook* 12, pp. 477–489.

Heritage, J. (1984) A change-of-state token and aspects of its sequential placement. In J. Heritage and J. M. Atkinson, eds., *Structures of social action*, pp. 299–345. Cambridge: Cambridge University Press.

Herring, S. (1993) Gender and democracy in computer-mediated communication. *Electronic Journal of Communication* 3(2).

Herring, S. (1995) Politeness in computer culture: Why women thank and men flame. In M. Bucholtz, A. Liang, L. Sutton, and C. Hines, eds., *Communicating in, through, and across cultures: Proceedings of the Third Berkeley Women and Language Conference*. Berkeley: Berkeley Women and Language Group.

Herring, S., ed. (1996a) *Computer-mediated communication: Linguistic, social and cross-cultural perspectives*. Amsterdam: John Benjamins.

Herring, S. (1996b) Linguistic and critical analysis of computer-mediated communication: Some ethical and scholarly considerations. *The Information Society* 12, pp. 153–168.

Herring, S. (1996c) Posting in a different voice: Gender and ethics in computer-mediated communication. In C. Ess, ed., *Philosophical perspectives on computer-mediated communication*. Albany: SUNY Press.

Herring, S. (1996d) Two variants of an electronic message schema. In S. Herring, ed., *Computer-mediated communication: Linguistic, social and cross-cultural perspectives*, pp. 81–106. Philadelphia: John Benjamins.

Herring, S., D. Johnson, and T. DiBenedetto. (1995) "This discussion is going too far!" Male resistance to female participation on the Internet. In M. Bucholtz and K. Hall, eds., *Gender articulated: Language and the socially constructed Self*. New York: Routledge.

Hiemstra, G. (1982) Teleconferencing, concern for face, and organizational culture. In M. Burgoon, ed., *Communication Yearbook* 6, pp. 874–904. Beverly Hills, CA: Sage.

Hillery, G. A. (1955) Definitions of community: Areas of agreement. *Rural Sociology* 20, pp. 111–123.

Hiltz, S. R., K. Johnson, and G. Agle. (1978) Replicating Bales' problem solving experiments on a computerized conference: A pilot study (Research Report No. 8). Newark: New Jersey Institute of Technology, Computerized Conferencing and Communications Center.

Hiltz, S. R., K. Johnson, and A. M. Rabke. (1980) The process of communication in face to face vs. computerized conferences: A controlled experiment using Bales interaction process analysis. In N. K. Sondheimer, ed., *The 18th Annual Meeting of the Association for Computational Linguistics and Parasession on Topics in Interactive Discourse: Proceedings of the Conference*. Philadelphia: University of Pennsylvania.

Hiltz, S. R., K. Johnson, and M. Turoff. (1986) Experiments in group decision making: Communication process and outcome in face-to-face versus computerized conferences. *Human Communication Research* 13(2), pp. 225–252.

Hiltz, S. R. and M. Turoff. (1978) *The network nation: Human communication via computer*. Reading, MA: Addison-Wesley.

Hiltz, S. R. and M. Turoff. (1981) The evolution of user behavior in a computerized conference system. *Communications of the ACM* 24, pp. 739–751.

Hiltz, S. R., M. Turoff, and K. Johnson. (1989) Experiments in group decision making: Disinhibition, de-individuation, and group process in pen name and real name computer conferences. *Decision Support Systems* 5, pp. 217–232.

Hinrichs, E. (1986) Temporal anaphora in discourses of English. *Linguistics and Philosophy* 9, pp. 63–82.

Hirschman, J. (1997) Web servers - adding chat to your Web site. BUILDER. COM. Available off http://www.cnet.com/Content/Builder/Servers/Chat/index.html.

Hobbs, J. (1980) Interactive discourse: Influence of social context. In N. K. Sondheimer, ed., *The 18th Annual Meeting of the Association for Com-*

putational Linguistics and Parasession on Topics in Interactive Discourse: Proceedings of the Conference. Philadelphia: University of Pennsylvania.

Hof, R., S. Browder, and P. Elstrom. (1997) Internet communities. *Business Week*, May 5. pp. 66–84.

Holmes, M. and E. Dishman. (1994) Social action in synchronous computer-mediated communication: A comparison of two genres. Paper presented at Western States Communication Association, San Jose, CA.

Horn, S. (1998) *Cyberville: Clicks, culture, and the creation of an online town.* New York: Warner Books.

Houghton, D. (1988) Creationist writings. In M. Ghadessy, ed., *Registers of eritten English*, pp. 67–84. London: Pinter.

Hughes, B. and J. Walters. (1995) Children, MUDs, and learning. Paper presented at American Educational Research Association, April.

Huizinga, J. (1955) *Homo ludens: A study of the play-element in culture.* Boston: Beacon.

Hummon, D. (1990) *Commonplaces: Community ideology and identity in American culture.* New York: State University of New York Press.

Hymes, D. (1964) Introduction: Towards ethnographies of communication. In J. Gumperz and D. Hymes, eds., *The ethnography of communication*, pp. 1–34. Washington: American Anthropological Association.

Hymes, D. (1972) Models of the interaction of language and social life. In J. Gumperz and D. Hymes, eds., *Directions in sociolinguistics*, pp. 35–71. New York: Holt, Rinehart, and Winston.

Ito, M. (1994) Cybernetic fantasies: Extensions of selfhood in a multi-user dungeon. Paper presented at the annual meeting of the American Anthropological Association, Atlanta, Georgia.

Ito, M. (1997) Virtually embodied: The reality of fantasy in a multi-user dungeon. In D. Porter, ed., *Internet culture.* New York: Routledge.

Jacobson, D. (1997) On doing social research in cyberspace. Paper presented at the annual meeting of the American Anthropological Association, Washington, DC.

Jaffe, J. and S. Feldstein. (1970) *Rhythms of dialogue.* New York: Academic Press.

Janda, R. (1985) Note-taking English as a simplified register. *Discourse Processes* 8, pp. 437–454.

Jefferson, G. (1981) "Caveat speaker": A preliminary exploration of shift implicative reciency in the articulation of topic. End of grant report, Social Science Research Council, London.

Jefferson, G. and J. Schenkein. (1978) Some sequential negotiations in conversation. In J. Schenkein, ed., *Studies in the organization of conversational interaction*. New York: Academic Press.

Johansen, R., J. Vallee, and K. Spangler, eds. (1979) *Electronic meetings: Technical alternatives and social choices*. Reading, MA: Addison-Wesley.

Jonassen, C. (1959) Community typology. In M. Sussman, ed., *Community structure and analysis*, pp. 15–36. Westport, CT: Greenwood Press.

Jones, S. (1995) Understanding community in the information age. In S. Jones, ed., *Cybersociety: Computer-mediated communication and community*, pp. 10–35. Thousand Oaks, CA: Sage.

Jones, S. (1997) *Virtual culture: Identity and communication in cybersociety*. Thousand Oaks, CA: Sage.

Jones, S. (1998) *Cybersociety 2.0: Revisiting computer-mediated communication and community (New Media Cultures, V. 2)*. Thousand Oaks, CA: Sage.

Kalcik, S. (1985) Women's handles and the performance of identity in the CB community. In R. Jordan and S. Kalcik, eds., *Women's folklore, women's culture*. Philadelphia: University of Pennsylvania Press.

Kamp, H. (1979) Events, instants, and temporal reference. In R. Baüerle, U. Egli, and A. von Stechow, eds., *Semantics from different points of view*, pp. 376–417. Berlin: Springer-Verlag.

Kamp, H. (1984) A theory of truth and semantic representation. In J. Groenendijk, T. Janssen, and M. Stokhof, eds., *Truth, interpretation, and information*, pp. 1–41. Dordrecht: Foris.

Kamp, H. and U. Reyle. (1993) *From discourse to logic: Introduction to modeltheoretic semantics of natural language, formal logic and discourse representation theory*. Boston: Kluwer.

Kay, P. (1977) Language evolution and speech style. In B. G. Blount and M. Sanches, eds., *Sociocultural dimensions of language change*, pp. 21–33. New York: Academic Press.

Keegan, M. (1997) MUD tree. Available at http://camelot.cyburbia.net.au/~martin/cgi-bin/mud-tree.cgi.

Keesing, R. (1981). Theories of culture. In R. Casson, ed., *Language, culture, and cognition*. New York: MacMillan.

Kelly, K. and H. Rheingold. (1994) The dragon ate my homework. *Wired* 1.3.

Kendall, L. (1996) MUDder? I hardly know 'er! Adventures of a feminist MUDder. In L. Cherny and B. Weise, eds., *Wired women: Gender and new realities in cyberspace*. Seattle: Seal Press.

Kendall, L. (1998) Hanging out in the virtual pub: Identity, masculinities, and relationships online. Ph.D. dissertation, University of California at Davis.

Kiesler, S., J. Siegel, and T. W. McGuire. (1984) Social psychological aspects of computer-mediated communication. *American Psychologist* 39(10), pp. 1123–1134.

Kiesler, S. and L. Sproull. (1986) Reducing social context cues: Electronic mail in organizational communication. *Management Science* 32(11), pp. 1492–1512.

Kiesler, S., D. Zubrow, A. M. Moses, and V. Geller. (1985) Affect in computer-mediated communication: An experiment in synchronous terminal-to-terminal discussion. *Human-Computer Interaction* 1, pp. 77–104.

King, S. (1996) Researching Internet communities: Proposed ethical guidelines for the reporting of results. *The Information Society* 12, pp. 119–128.

Kling, R. (1996) Social relationships in electronic forums: hangouts, salons, workplaces, and communities. In R. Kling, ed., *Computerization and controversy*. San Diego: Academic Press.

Kochman, T., ed. (1972) Rappin' and stylin' out: Communication in urban black America. Urbana: University of Illinois Press.

Kolko, E. (1995) Building a world with words: The narrative reality of virtual communities. In C. Stivale, ed., *CyberSpaces: Pedagogy and performance on the electronic frontier.* Special issue of *Works and Days*, 26. Available from http://acorn.grove.iup.edu/en/workdays/toc.html.

Kolko, B. and E. Reid. (1998) Dissolution and fragmentation: Problems in online communities. In S. Jones, ed., *Cybersociety 2.0: Revisiting Computer Mediated Communication and Community*, pp. 212–229. Thousand Oaks, CA: Sage Publications.

Kollock, P. and M. Smith. (1996) Managing the virtual commons: Cooperation and conflict in computer communities: In S. Herring, ed., *Computer-mediated communication: Linguistic, social and cross-cultural perspectives*, pp. 109–128. Philadelphia: John Benjamins.

Kripke, S. (1971) Identity and necessity. In M. Munitz, ed., *Identity and individuation*, pp. 135–164. New York: New York University Press.

Kuhn, T. (1989) Tense and time. In D. Gabbay and F. Guenthner, eds., *Handbook of philosophical logic*, vol. IV, pp. 513–552. Dordrecht: Reidel.

Kuiper, K. (1996) *Smooth talkers: The linguistic performance of auctioneers and sportscasters.* Mahwah, NJ: Lawrence Erlbaum Associates.

Labov, W. (1972) *Sociolinguistic patterns.* Philadelphia: University of Pennsylvania Press.

Lakoff, R. (1992) The silencing of women. In *Locating Power: Proceedings of the 1992 Berkeley Women and Language Conference.* Berkeley: Berkeley Linguistics Society.

Laurel, B. (1992) *Computers as theater.* Reading, MA: Addison-Wesley.

Lave, J. and E. Wenger. (1991) *Situated learning: Legitimate peripheral participation.* Cambridge: Cambridge University Press.

Laver, J. (1974) *Semiotic aspects of spoken communication.* London: Edward Arnold.

Lea, M., T. O'Shea, P. Fung, and R. Spears. (1992) "Flaming" in computer-mediated communication. In M. Lea, ed., *Contexts of computer-mediated communication*, pp. 89–112. New York: Harvester Wheatsheaf.

Lea, M. and R. Spears. (1991) Computer-mediated communication, de-individuation, and group decision-making. *International Journal of Man-Machine Studies* 39, pp. 283–301.

Leech, G. (1971) *Meaning and the English verb.* Harlow: Longman.

Leong, L. (1998) MUD Resource Collection. Available at http://www.godlike.com/muds/.

Leslie, J. (1993) Technology: MUDroom. *Atlantic Monthly* 272, September, 1993, pp. 28–34. Also available as an electronic ms. from Leslie at jacques@well.sf.ca.us.

Levinson, S. (1983) *Pragmatics.* Cambridge: Cambridge University Press.

Lewis, D. (1968) Counterpart theory and quantified modal logic. *Journal of Philosophy* 65, pp. 113–126.

Licklider, J. and R. Taylor. (1968) The computer as communication device. *Science and Technology*, April, pp. 21–31.

MacKinnon, R. C. (1995) Searching for the Leviathan in Usenet. In S. Jones, ed., *Cybersociety: Computer-mediated communication and community*, pp. 112–137. Thousand Oaks, CA: Sage.

Mantovani, G. (1994) Is computer-mediated communication intrinsically apt to enhance democracy in organizations? *Human Relations* 47(1), pp. 45–62.

Marcus, G. E. and D. Cushman. (1982) Ethnographies as texts. *Annual Review of Anthropology* 11, pp. 25–69.

Markus, M. L. (1994) Finding a happy medium: Explaining the negative effects of electronic communication on social life at work. *ACM Transactions on Information Systems* 12(2), pp. 119–149.

Marvin, C. (1983) Telecommunications policy and the pleasure principle. *Telecommunications Policy*, March 1983.

Marvin, C. (1988) *When old technologies were new.* New York: Oxford University Press.

Marvin, C. and Q. J. Schultze. (1977) CB: The first thirty years. *Journal of Communication* 27, pp. 104–117.

Marvin, L. (1995) Spoof, spam, lurk and lag: The aesthetics of text-based virtual realities. *Journal of Computer-Mediated Communication* 1(2). Available at http://shum.huji.ac.il/jcmc/vol1/issue2/marvin.html.

Mason, B. L. (1990) "Smileys" and "sad faces:" A little bit of Net lore. Paper presented at the the annual meeting of the American Folklore Society, Oakland, California, October.

Masterson, J. (1996) Nonverbal communication in text-based virtual realities. M.A. Thesis, University of Montana.

Maynor, N. (1994) The language of electronic mail: Written speech? In M. Montgomery and G. Little, eds., *Centennial usage studies*. Publications of the American Dialect Society Series. University of Alabama Press.

McCarthy, J. C., V. C. Miles, A. F. Monk, M. D. Harrison, A. J. Dix, and P. C. Wright. (1993) Text-based on-line conferencing: A conceptual and empirical analysis using a minimal prototype. *Human-Computer Interaction* 8, pp. 147–183.

McKinlay, A., R. Procter, O. Masting, R. Woodburn, and J. Arnott. (1994) Studies of turn-taking in computer-mediated communications. *Interacting with Computers* 6(2), pp. 151–171.

McLaughlin, M. L., K. K. Osborne, and C. B. Smith. (1995) Standards of conduct on Usenet. In S. Jones, ed., *Cybersociety: Computer-mediated communication and community*, pp. 90–111. Thousand Oaks, CA: Sage.

McLuhan, M. (1967) *The medium is the massage*. New York: Random House.

McRae, S. (1996) Coming apart at the seams: The erotics of virtual embodiment. In L. Cherny and B. Weise, eds., *Wired women: Gender and new realities in cyberspace*. Seattle: Seal Press.

Meinig, D. (1979) Symbolic landscapes: Some idealizations of american communities. In D. Meinig, ed., *The interpretation of ordinary landscapes: Geographical essays*, pp. 135–145. New York: Oxford University Press..

Merry, S. E. (1984) Rethinking gossip and scandal. In D. Black, ed., *Toward a general theory of social control: Fundamentals*, pp. 271–301. New York: Academic Press.

Meyer, G. and J. Thomas. (1990) The baudy world of the byte bandit: A postmodernist interpretation of the computer underground. In F. Schmalleger, ed., *Computers in criminal justice*. Bristol, IN: Wyndham Hall.

Meyrowitz, J. (1985) *No sense of place*. New York: Oxford University Press.

Millard, W. (1995) 'A great flame follows a little spark': Metaflaming, functions of the 'dis,' and conditions of closure in the rhetoric of a discussion list. In C. Stivale, ed., *CyberSpaces: Pedagogy and performance on the electronic frontier*. Special issue of *Works and Days*, 26. Available from http://acorn.grove.iup.edu/cn/workdays/toc.html.

Milroy, L. (1980) Social network and language maintenance. In A. Pugh, V.

Lee, and J. Swann, eds., *Language and language use: A reader*. London: Heinemann.

Milroy, L. (1987) *Language and social networks*. (Second edition.) Oxford: Blackwell.

Mnookin, J. (1996) Virtual(ly) law: The emergence of law in LambdaMOO. *Journal of Computer-Mediated Communication* 2(1). Available at http://jcmc.huji.ac.il/vol2/issue1/lambda.html.

Morgenthaler, L. (1990) A study of group process: Who's got what floor? *Journal of Pragmatics* 14, pp. 537–557.

Morley, I. E. and G. M. Stephenson. (1969) Interpersonal and interparty exchange: A laboratory simulation of an industrial negotiation at the plant level. *British Journal of Psychology* 60, pp. 543–545.

Morley, I. E. and G. M. Stephenson. (1970) Formality in experimental negotiations: A validation study. *British Journal of Psychology* 61, p. 383.

Morningstar, C. and R. Farmer. (1991) The lessons of Lucasfilm's Habitat. In M. Benedikt, ed., *Cyberspace: First steps*. Cambridge: MIT Press.

Morris, M. (1992) The man in the mirror: David Harvey's "condition" of postmodernity. *Theory, Culture, and Society* 9, pp. 253–279.

Murray, D. E. (1985) Conversation for action: The computer terminal as medium of communication. Ph.D. dissertation, Stanford University.

Murray, D. E. (1989) When the medium determines turns: Turn-taking in computer conversation. In H. Coleman, ed., *Working with language*, pp. 319–338. New York: Mouton de Gruyter.

Murray, D. E. (1991) The composing process for computer conversation. *Written Communication* 8(1), pp. 35–55.

Myers, D. (1987a) "Anonymity is part of the magic": Individual manipulation of computer-mediated communication contexts. *Qualitative Sociology* 10(3), pp. 251–266.

Myers, D. (1987b) A new environment for communication play: On-line play. In G.A. Fine, ed., *Meaningful play, playful meaning*, pp. 231–245. Champaign, IL: Human Kinetics.

Novick, D. and J. Walpole. (1990) Enhancing the efficiency of multiparty interaction through computer mediation. *Interacting with Computers* 2(2), pp. 229–245.

O'Conaill, B., S. Whittaker, and S. Wilbur. (1993) Conversations over video conferences: An evaluation of the spoken aspects of video-mediated communication. *Human-Computer Interaction* 8, pp. 389–428.

O'Day, V. L., D. G. Bobrow, and M. Shirley. (1996) The social-technical design circle. Proceedings of the Conference on Computer Supported Cooperative Work, Boston.

O'Day, V. L., D. G. Bobrow, B. Hughes, K. Bobrow, V. Saraswat, J. Talazus, J. Walters, and C. Welbes. (1996) Community designers. Proceedings of the Participatory Design Conference, Boston.

O'Donnell, R. C. (1974) Syntactic differences between speech and writing. *American Speech* 49, pp. 102–110.

Oldenburg, R. (1997) *The great good place.* (Second edition.) New York: Marlowe and Company.

Ong, W. J. (1982) *Orality and literacy: The technologizing of the word.* London: Methuen.

Örestrom, B. (1983) *Turn-taking in English conversation.* Lund Studies in English. Lund: CWK Gleerup.

Ostrom, E. (1990) *Governing the commons: The evolution of institutions for collective action.* New York: Cambridge University Press.

Oviatt, S. and P. Cohen. (1988) Discourse structure and performance efficiency in interactive and noninteractive spoken modalities. Technical Report 454. Menlo Park, CA: SRI International.

Oviatt, S. and P. Cohen. (1991a) The contributing influence of speech and interaction on human discourse patterns. In J. Sullivan and S. Tyler, eds., *Intelligent user interfaces.* New York: ACM Press.

Oviatt, S. and P. Cohen. (1991b) Discourse structure and performance efficiency in interactive and noninteractive spoken modalities. *Computer Speech and Language* 5, pp. 297–326.

Paccagnella, L. (1997) Getting the seats of your pants dirty: Strategies for ethnographic research on virtual communities. *Journal of Computer-Mediated Communication* 3(1), June.

Paisley, W. and M. Chen. (1982) *Children and electronic text: Challenges and opportunities of the new literacy.* Stanford, CA: Stanford University Institute for Communication Research.

Papert, S. (1991). Situating constructionism. In I. Harel and S. Papert, eds., *Constructionism.* Norwood, NJ: Ablex Publishing.

Partee, B. (1973) Some structural analogies between tenses and pronouns in English. *Journal of Philosophy* 70, pp. 601–609.

Partee, B. (1984) Nominal and temporal anaphora. *Linguistics and Philosophy* 7, pp. 243–286.

Philips, S. (1972) Participant structure and communicative competence. In C.B. Cazden, V. John, and D. Hymes, eds., *Functions of language in the classroom*, pp. 370–394. New York: Teachers College Press.

Polanyi, L. (1996) The linguistic structure of discourse. Technical Report CSLI-96-200, CSLI (Center for the Study of Language and Information), Stanford University, Palo Alto, CA.

Pool, I. (1978) *The social impact of the telephone*. Cambridge: MIT Press.

Poole, M. E. and T. W. Field. (1976) A comparison of oral and written code elaboration. *Language and Speech* 19, pp. 305–311.

Poster, M. (1990) *The mode of information*. Cambridge, UK: Polity.

Powell, J. (1983) CB: An inquiry into a novel state of communication. In D. L. Lewis and L. Goldstein, eds., *The automobile and American culture*, pp. 257–261. Ann Arbor: University of Michigan Press.

Powell, J. and D. Ary. (1977) Communication without commitment. *Journal of Communication* 27, pp. 118–121.

Quittner, J. (1993) Far out: Welcome to their world built of MUD. *Newsday*, November 7.

Quittner, J. (1994) Johnny Manhattan meets the furrymuckers. *Wired*, March 1994, pp. 92–97.

Rabinow, P. (1977) *Reflections on fieldwork in Morocco*. Berkeley: University of California Press.

Rafaeli, S. (1988) Interactivity: From new media to communication. In R.B. Pawkins, J.M. Wiemann, and S. Pingree, eds., *Advancing communication science: Merging mass and interpersonal processes*, vol. 16, pp. 110–133. Sage Annual Reviews of Communication Research. Beverly Hills, CA: Sage.

Rakow, L. (1988) Women and the telephone: The gendering of a communications technology. In C. Kramarae, ed., *Technology and women's voices*. New York: Routledge and Kegan Paul.

Raymond, E., ed. (1991) *The new hacker's dictionary*. Cambridge: MIT Press.

Reichard, K. (1997) Hosting your own chat. *Internet World*, October, pp. 100– 102.

Reid, E. (1991) Electropolis: Communication and community on Internet Relay Chat. Adapted from a B.A. Honors thesis, University of Melbourne, Australia. Available at http://www.eff.org/pub/Publications/CuD/Papers/electropolis.txt.gz.

Reid, E. (1994a) Virtual worlds: Culture and imagination. In S. Jones, ed., *Cybersociety: Computer-mediated communication and community*, pp. 164–183. Thousand Oaks, CA: Sage Publications.

Reid, E. (1994b) Cultural formations in text-based virtual reality. Master's thesis, University of Melbourne, Australia. Available at ftp://ftp.lambda.moo.mud.org/pub/MOO/papers/CulturalFormations.txt.

Reid, E. (1996) Informed consent in the study of online communities: a reflection on the effects of computer-mediated social research. *The Information Society* 12, pp. 169–174.

Reinman, S. (1995) Electronic mail: Where does it fall in the oral/literate continuum? Unpublished paper.

Rheingold, H. (1993a) *The virtual community*. Reading, MA: Addison-Wesley.

Rheingold, H. (1993b) A slice of life in my virtual community. In L. Harasim, ed., *Global networks*, pp. 57–80. Cambridge: MIT Press. Electronic ms. available from Rheingold at hlr@well.sf.ca.us.

Rice, R. E. (1980) The impacts of computer-mediated organizational and interpersonal communication. In M. E. Williams, ed., *Annual review of information science and technology*, vol. 15, pp. 221–249. White Plains, NY: Knowledge Industry Publications.

Rice, R. E. (1984) Mediated group communication. In R. E. Rice and Associates, eds., *The new media: Communication, research and technology*, pp. 925–944. Beverly Hills, CA: Sage.

Rice, R. E. (1989) Issues and concepts in research on computer-mediated communication systems. *Communication Yearbook* 12, pp. 436–476.

Rice, R. E. (1993) Media appropriateness: Using social presence theory to compare traditional and new organizational media. *Human Communication Research* 19(4), pp. 451–484.

Rice, R. E. and Associates. (1984) *The new media: Communication, research and technology*. Beverly Hills, CA: Sage.

Rice, R. E. and G. Love. (1987) Electronic emotion: Socioemotional content in a computer-mediated communication network. *Communication Research* 14(1), pp. 85–108.

Rice, R. E. and F. Williams. (1984) Theories old and new: The study of new media. In R. E. Rice and Associates, eds., *The new media: Communication, research and technology*. Beverly Hills, CA: Sage.

Rigdon, J. (1995) Playing in the MUD. *Wall Street Journal*, September.

Roberts, C. (1989) Modal subordination and pronominal anaphora in discourse. *Language and Philosophy* 12(6), pp. 683–722.

Rosaldo, R. (1989) *Culture and truth*. Boston: Beacon Press.

Rosenburg, M. S. (1992) Virtual reality: Reflections of life, dreams, and technology: An ethnography of a computer society. Available at http://lucien. berkeley.edu/MOO/ethnography.txt.

Royce, A. P. (1992) Mime. In R. Bauman, ed., *Folklore, cultural performances, and popular entertainments*, pp. 191–195. New York: Oxford University Press.

Ruedenberg, L., B. Danet, and Y. Rosenbaum-Tamari. (1995) Virtual virtuosos: Play and performance at the computer keyboard. *Electronic Journal of Communication* 5(4).

Rutter, D. (1984) *Looking and seeing: The role of visual communication in social interaction.* Chichester: John Wiley.

Rutter, D. (1987) *Communicating by telephone.* Oxford: Pergamon Press.

Ryan, S. (1997) Building online communities. BUILDER.COM. Available at http://www.cnet.com/Content/Builder/Business/Community/index.html?st.cn.fd.

Sacks, H., E. Schegloff, and G. Jefferson. (1974) A simplest systematics for the organization of turn-taking for conversation. *Language* 50, pp. 696–735.

Sadock, J. (1988) Speech act distinctions in grammar. In F. Newmeyer, ed., *Linguistics: The Cambridge survey,* vol. 2, pp. 183–197. Cambridge: Cambridge University Press.

Sanjek, R., ed. (1990) *Fieldnotes: The makings of anthropology.* Ithaca: Cornell University Press.

Saville-Troike, M. (1982) *The ethnography of communication: An introduction.* Oxford: Basil Blackwell.

Schegloff, E. (1972) Sequencing in conversational openings. In J. Gumperz and D. Hymes, eds., *Directions in sociolinguistics,* pp. 346–380. Cowford: Blackwell.

Schegloff, E. (1977) Identification and recognition in interactional openings. In I. Pool, ed., *The social impact of the telephone,* pp. 415–450. Cambridge: MIT Press.

Schegloff, E. (1982) Discourse as an interactional achievement: Some uses of 'uh huh' and other things that come between sentences. In D. Tannen, ed., *Analyzing discourse: Text and talk,* pp. 71–93. Washington, DC: Georgetown University Press.

Schegloff, E. and H. Sacks. (1974) Opening up closings. In R. Turner, ed., *Ethnomethodology: Selected readings.* Baltimore: Penguin.

Schiano, D. (1997) Convergent methodologies in cyber-psychology: A case study. *Behavior Research Instruments, Methods and Computers,* 29(2).

Schiffrin, D. (1981) Tense variation in narrative. *Language* 57(1), pp. 45–62.

Schneider, D. (1976) Notes towards a theory of culture. In K. R. Basso and H. A. Selby, eds., *Meaning in anthropology,* pp. 197–220. Albuquerque: University of New Mexico Press.

Schutz, A. (1970) *On phenomenology and social relations.* Chicago: Chicago University Press.

Schwartz, J. (1994) A terminal obsession. *Washington Post,* March 27.

Scott, J. (1991) *Social network analysis: A handbook.* Thousand Oaks, CA: Sage Publications.

Searle, J. (1969) *Speech acts.* Cambridge: Cambridge University Press.

Searle, J. (1989) How performatives work. *Linguistics and Philosophy* 12, pp. 535–558.

Selfe, C. and P. Meyer. (1991) Testing claims for on-line conferences. *Written Communication* 8(2), pp. 163–192.

Serpentelli, J. (1993) Conversational structure and personality correlates of electronic communication. Available at ftp://ftp.lambda.moo.mud.org/pub/ MOO/papers/conv-structure.txt.

Short, J., E. Williams, and B. Christie. (1976) *The social psychology of telecommunications*. New York: Wiley.

Shultz, J. J., S. Florio, and F. Erickson. (1982) Where's the floor? Aspects of the cultural organization of social relationships in communication at home and in school. In P. Gilmore and A. A. Glatthorn, eds., *Children in and out of school*, pp. 88–123. Washington, DC: Center for Applied Linguistics.

Siegel, J., V. Dubrovsky, S. Kiesler, and T. McGuire. (1986) Group processes in computer-mediated communication. *Organizational Behavior and Human Decision Processes* 37, pp. 157–187.

Skeggs, B. (1995) Theorizing, ethics and representation in feminist ethnography. In B. Skeggs, ed., *Feminist cultural theory*, pp. 190–206. Manchester University Press.

Smith, C. (1986) A speaker-based approach to aspect. *Linguistics and Philosophy* 9, pp. 97–115.

Smith, C. (1991) *The parameter of aspect*. Dordrecht: Reidel.

Smith, J. (1995) Frequently asked questions: Basic information about MUDs and MUDding. Posted on rec.games.mud and available at ftp://muds.okstate. edu/pub/jds/misc/mud-faq/.

Smith, J. J. (1979) Male and female ways of speaking: Elaborately restricted codes in a CB speech community. *Papers in Linguistics* 12(1-2), pp. 163–184.

Smith, M. (1992) Voices from the WELL: The logic of the virtual commons. Master's thesis, UCLA. Available at http://www.sscnet.ucla.edu/soc/csoc/ papers/voices/.

Soja, E. (1989) *Postmodern geographies: The reassertion of space in critical social theory*. London: Verso.

Spears, R. and M. Lea. (1992) Social influence and the influence of the "social" in computer-mediated communication. In M. Lea, ed., *Contexts of computer-mediated communication*, pp. 30–65. New York: Harvester Wheatsheaf.

Sproull, L. and S. Kiesler. (1986) Reducing social context cues: Electronic mail in organizational communication. *Management Science* 32, pp. 1492–1512.

Sproull, L. and S. Kiesler. (1991) *Connections: New ways of working in the networked organization*. Cambridge: MIT Press.

Stacey, M. (1974) The myth of community studies. In C. Bell and H. Newby, eds., *The sociology of community*, pp. 13–26. London: Frank Cass & Co., Ltd.

Steinfield, C. W. (1986) Computer-mediated communication in an organizational setting: Explaining task-related and socioemotional uses. In M. McLaughlin, ed., *Communication Yearbook 9*, pp. 777–804. Newbury Park: Sage.

Steuer, J. (1992) Defining virtual reality: Dimensions determining telepresence. *Journal of Communication* 42(4), pp. 73–93.

Stivale, C. (1995) Response to Cherny (1995b). In C. Stivale, ed., *CyberSpaces: pedagogy and performance on the electronic frontier*. Special issue of *Works and Days*, 26. Available from http://acorn.grove.iup.edu/en/workdays/toc.html.

Stone, A. R. (1991) Will the real body please stand up?: Boundary stories about virtual cultures. In M. Benedikt, ed., *Cyberspace: First steps*. Cambridge: MIT Press.

Stone, A. R. (1995) *The war of desire and technology at the close of the mechanical age*. Cambridge: MIT Press.

Straumann, H. (1935) *Newspaper headlines: A study in linguistic method*. London: Allen and Unwin.

Suchman, L. (1987) *Plans and situated actions*. Cambridge: Cambridge University Press.

Suttles, G. (1972) *The social construction of communities*. Chicago: University of Chicago Press.

Sutton, L. (1994) Using USENET: Gender, power, and silence in electronic discourse. *Proceedings of the twentieth annual meeting of the Berkeley Linguistics Society*. Berkeley: Berkeley Linguistics Society, 506–20.

Sutton, L. (1996) Cocktails and thumbtacks: What would Emily Post say? In L. Cherny and B. Weise, eds., *Wired women: Gender and new realities in cyberspace*. Seattle: Seal Press.

Swales, J. (1990) *Genre analysis: English in academic and research settings*. Cambridge: Cambridge University Press.

Tacy, C. (1997) For now, 'community' is just a Web buzzword. *New York Times*, July 2. Available at http://www.nytimes.com/library/cyber/under/070297under.html.

Tang, J., E. Isaacs, and M. Rua. (1994) Supporting distributed groups with a montage of lightweight interactions. Unpublished manuscript, Sunsoft, Mountain View, CA.

Tannen, D. (1982a) The myth of orality and literacy. In W. Frawley, ed., *Linguistics and literacy*, pp. 37–50. New York: Plenum.

Tannen, D. (1982b) The oral/literate continuum in discourse. In D. Tannen, ed., *Spoken and written language*, pp. 1–16. Norwood, NJ: Ablex.

Tatar, D., G. Foster, and D. Bobrow. (1991) Design for conversation: Lessons from Cognoter. *International Journal of Man-Machine Studies* 34(2), pp. 185–210.

Tepper, M. (1997) Usenet communities and the cultural politics of information. In D. Porter, ed., *Internet culture*. New York: Routledge.

Thomas, J. (1996) Introduction: A debate about the ethics of fair practices for collecting social science data in cyberspace. *The Information Society* 12, pp. 107–118.

Thorne, J. (1988) The language of synopses. In M. Ghadessy, ed., *Registers of written English*, pp. 137–144. London: Pinter.

Tönnies, F. (1887) *Gemeinschaft und Gesellschaft*. Berlin.

Trevino, L. K., R. L. Daft, and R. H. Lengel. (1990) Understanding managers' media choices: A symbolic interactionist perspective. In J. Fulk and C. Steinfield, eds., *Organizations and communication technology*, pp. 71–94. Newbury Park, CA: Sage.

Trevino, L. K., R. H. Lengel, and R. L. Daft. (1987) Media symbolism, media richness, and media choice in organizations. *Communication Research* 14, pp. 553–574.

Turkle, S. (1984) *The second self: Computers and the human spirit*. New York: Simon & Schuster.

Turkle, S. (1996) *Life on the screen: Identity in the age of the Internet*. New York: Simon & Schuster.

Ure, J. (1982) Introduction: Approaches to the study of register range. *International Journal of the Sociology of Language* 35, pp. 5–23.

Vallee, J. (1984) *Computer message systems*. New York: McGraw Hill.

Van Buren, D., P. Curtis, D. Nichols, and M. Brundage. (1994) The AstroVR Collaboratory, an on-line multi-user environment for research in astrophysics. Proceedings of the 1994 ADASS Conference, Baltimore.

Van Maanen, J. (1988) *Tales of the field*. Chicago: University of Chicago Press.

Van Maanen, J. and S. Barley. (1984) Occupational communities: Culture and control in organizations. In B. M. Staw and L. L. Cummings, eds., *Research in organizational behavior*, vol. 6. Greenwich, CT: JAI Press.

Van Maanen, J. and S. Barley. (1985) Cultural organization: Fragments of a theory. In P. J. Frost et al., eds., *Organizational culture*, pp. 31–53. Beverly Hills, CA: Sage, 1985. 31–53.

Vendler, Z. (1967) *Linguistics in philosophy*. Ithaca: Cornell University Press.

Verkuyl, H. (1989) Aspectual classes and aspectual composition. *Linguistics and Philosophy* 12, pp. 39–94.

Verschueren, J. (1994) The conceptual basis of performativity. Unpublished manuscript.

Walls, J. (1993) Global networking for local development: Task focus and relationship focus in cross-cultural communication. In L. Harasim, ed., *Global networks: Computers and international communication*, pp. 153–166. Cambridge: MIT Press.

Walther, J. B. (1992) Interpersonal effects in computer-mediated interaction: A relational perspective. *Communication Research* 19, pp. 52–90.

Walther, J. B. and J. K. Burgoon. (1992) Relational communication in computer-mediated interaction. *Human Communication Research* 19(1), pp. 50–88.

Warner, S. (1984) Slums and skyscrapers: Urban images, symbols, and ideology. In L. Rodwin and R. Hollister, eds., *Cities of the mind*, pp. 181–196. Hollister, NY: Plenum Press.

Waskul, D. and M. Douglass. (1996) Considering the electronic participant: Some polemical observations on the ethics of online research. *The Information Society* 12, pp. 129–140.

Watabe, K., et al. (1990) A distributed multiparty desktop conferencing system and its architecture. Proceedings of the IEEE Phoenix Conference on Computers and Communications, pp. 386–393. New York: IEEE.

Watson, N. (1997) Why we argue about virtual community: A case study of the Phish.net fan community. In S. Jones, ed., *Virtual culture: Identity and communication in cybersociety*. Thousand Oaks, CA: Sage.

Wellman, B. (1988a) The community question re-evaluated. In M. P. Smith, ed., *Power, community, and the city*. New Brunswick, NJ: Transaction.

Wellman, B. (1988b) Structural analysis: From method and metaphor to theory and substance. In B. Wellman and S.D. Berkowitz, eds., *Social structures: A network approach*, pp. 19–61. Cambridge: Cambridge University Press.

Wellman, B. (1994) Personal communities: Some basic characteristics. In J. Cecora, ed., *Changing values and attitudes in family households with rural peer groups, social networks, and action spaces*, pp. 75–85. Bonn: Society for Agricultural Policy Research and Rural Sociology.

Wellman, B. and S. D. Berkowitz. (1988) *Social structures: A network approach*. Cambridge: Cambridge University Press.

Wellman, B. and M. Gulia. (1998) Net surfers don't ride alone: Virtual communities as communities. In P. Kollock and M. Smith, eds., *Communities in cyberspace*. Berkeley: University of California Press.

Wellman, B., J. Salaff, D. Dimitrova, L. Garton, M. Gulia, and C. Haythornthwaite. (1996) Computer networks as social networks: Collaborative work, telework, and virtual community. *Annual Review of Sociology* 22, pp. 213–238.

Werry, C. (1996) Linguistic and interactional features of Internet Relay Chat. In S. Herring, ed., *Computer-mediated communication: Linguistic, social and cross-cultural perspectives*, pp. 47–64. Philadelphia: John Benjamins.

Wetmore, P. (1993) Hurin's history of TinyMUDs. Posted to rec.games.mud. misc and available at http://www.apocalypse.org/pub/u/lpb/muddex/hurin-history.txt.

White, S. (1989) Backchannels across cultures: A study of Americans and Japanese. *Language in Society* 18, pp. 59–76.

Whittaker, S. (1994) A communication framework for mediated interaction. Unpublished draft, Lotus Development Corporation.

Whittaker, S., S. E. Brennan, and H. H. Clark. (1991) Coordinating activity: An analysis of interaction in computer-supported cooperative work. Proceedings of CHI 91, pp. 361–367.

Whittaker, S., D. Frohlich, and O. Daly-Jones. (1994) Informal workplace communication: What is it like and how might we support it? Proceedings of CHI 94, pp. 131–137.

Wilkins, H. (1991) Computer talk. *Written Communication* 8(1), pp. 56–78.

Williams, E. (1977) Experimental comparisons of face-to-face and mediated communication: A review. *Psychological Bulletin* 84, pp. 963–976.

Winner, L. (1986) Do artifacts have politics? In L. Winner, *The whale and the reactor*. Chicago: University of Chicago Press.

Wirth, L. (1938) Urbanism as a way of life. *American Journal of Sociology* 44 (July), pp. 1–24.

Wolfson, N. (1982) *CHP: The conversational historical present in American English narrative*. Dordrecht: Foris.

Woodburn, R., R. Procter, J. Arnott, and A. Newell. (1991) A study of conversational turn-taking in a communication aid for the disabled. Proceedings of HCI 91: People and Computers VI, pp. 359–371. Cambridge: Cambridge University Press.

Yates, S. (1996) Oral and written linguistic aspects of computer conferencing. In S. Herring, ed., *Computer-mediated communication: Linguistic, social and cross-cultural perspectives*, pp. 29–46. Philadelphia: John Benjamins.

Yngve, V. (1970) On getting a word in edgewise. Papers from the Sixth Regional Meeting, Chicago Linguistic Society, pp. 567–577. Chicago: Chicago Linguistic Society.

Zuboff, S. (1988) *In the age of the smart machine*. New York: Basic Books.